Principles of Sustainable Project Management

Mohamed Salama

(G) Goodfellow Publishers Ltd

Published by Goodfellow Publishers Limited,
Woodeaton, Oxford, OX3 9TJ
http://www.goodfellowpublishers.com

British Library Cataloguing in Publication Data: a catalogue record for this title is available from the British Library.

Library of Congress Catalog Card Number: on file.

ISBN: 978-1-911396-85-7

 Design and typesetting by P.K. McBride, www.macbride.org.uk

Cover design by Cylinder

Printed by Baker & Taylor, www.baker-taylor.com

Contents

Case studies related to the material in Chapter 1, 11 and 12 can be downloaded from this book's page at the publisher's website:
http://www.goodfellowpublishers.com/sustprojman

Dedications

To my Mum & Dad, my lovely wife Zaza and our boys Omar and Ally. You are the most precious!

Preface

In the era of digital transformation, sharing economy, smart cities and disruptive innovation, change is imperative. The evolution of disruptive innovation in the context of sustainability is not limited to the emerging new products and services but extends to impact business models and the subsequent systems and processes. Project management practice has been historically guided by the relevant knowledge areas and a set of allied processes. Certainly, the existing knowledge areas and processes need a critical review in order to cope with the prevalent change. It is oblivious to believe that future projects can still be managed by implementing concepts, processes and methods from the past. And more importantly, while doing so, project managers still embrace a mindset from the past and acquire a set of skills that are at best, suboptimal, not to mention obsolete, in some aspects.

The wind of change is blowing through the project management practice and whether we like it or not, theory must embrace this change and hopefully can take the lead soon, as should be case. In the early 2000s, a similar situation, perhaps not as intensive, occurred when project management practice decided that the prevalent methodologies are suboptimal, in the case of software development projects. Agile project management evolved, set by practitioners, primarily to change the practice, and it did. This was then followed by academic research to explicate and endorse this change. This seemed like a reverse engineering approach. Ideally, it should be the other way round.

In this textbook, the authors are seeking to improvise suitable approaches to cope with the blowing wind of change, utilizing the emerging theories, frameworks and models in the allied areas within the business management discipline. The focus of its 12 chapters is to provide project managers with the knowledge and the skills they need to improve the current practice, in line with the pressing requirements of the evolving technology-driven transformation towards sustainable business environment.

It was decided to present this book in three parts. Part One covers Chapters 1- 5, and presents the new thoughts, emerging theoretical frameworks and models the authors are putting forward to project management academics and practitioners, based on the authors' research outcome, in pursuit of developing the existing theory and guiding the practice towards sustainable processes that produce sustainable products and services.

Part Two, Chapters 6-8, is titled 'The Guiding Hand of Technology' as it provides project managers with the basic, yet essential information about the emerging advanced technology and how it can be utilized in managing projects.

Part Three recognizes and further appreciates that project management is a very practical domain, led by experienced and smart practitioners who like to see that the suggested theory can work in a practical context, in their own sector.

For example, the construction project management theory is swamped with cost models that have been resting on the shelves for decades. The sophisticated black-box of advanced math and statistics used to build those models was mostly not well comprehended by practitioners. Consequently, project managers did not use such models to make investment or financial decisions. Hence, in Part Three the presented theory is endorsed by real life case studies in four selected sectors due to their impact on the economy in most countries: construction, energy, tourism and logistics and supply chain..

In Chapter 1, the editor produces the Sustainable Project Management Model (SPMM) which is the cornerstone of this book. The underpinning theory is explicated following the critical review of a wide range of literature coupled by the examination of the existing methodologies such the PMBoK, (Traditional Project Management Methodology) and the Agile methodologies. The SPMM aims to address the existing gap featured in the absence or negligence of the explicit consideration of the impact of the digital transformation which is guiding the path towards sustainable products and services, as well as redefining the associated processes, in the context of a sustainable project management practice. The dimensions and associated factors of the SPMM are discussed, illustrating the rationale and justifying the need for such a forward-looking, sustainability orientated model amid the existing models. In addition, an Appendix, by the co-author of this chapter, provide a set of case studies that can be a very useful learning tool towards understanding the application of suitability in project management context. This section reflects on the theory and concepts discussed in the previous sections of the chapter on sustainability and sustainable development and resonates well with the first dimension of the SPMM.

The following chapters will elucidate further on the key building blocks of the SPMM, explicating the relevant theory, and illustrating the application in practice through real life examples and case studies. The main emphasis is on two dimensions; 1) the soft skills for both team members and the project manager; and 2) the emergent areas of knowledge, and the allied competencies. The soft skills include teamwork as well as leadership skills. The emergent knowledge areas include: fundamentals of sustainability, sustainable development, adaptive leadership, eco-innovation management, sustainable business modelling, sustainable change management and ICT for managers. The latter opens doors for further sub-level of knowledge areas, mainly those related with the application of the relevant technologies such as Block Chain Technology (BCT) in project management; e.g. smart contracts. The following chapters in Part One will discuss the required soft skills and emerging knowledge areas in further depth.

Chapter 2 examines the essential soft skills that both team members and the project manager should acquire and relate to team work, communication, emotional intelligence, trust and dealing with different cultures. Examining two types of project teams; virtual teams in a multicultural context and self-organising team under Scrum, the chapter provides a comparative discussion that is very practical oriented, in an academic disguise.

Chapter 3 introduces the work of the authors on the area of adaptive leadership, an emerging new school of thought that claims can provide better outcomes in the context of project management. Two practical case studies are portrayed, to demonstrate how project managers can apply the presented new concepts in real life situation. Chapter 4 introduces the work of the authors in the area on eco-innovation utilizing the Lean startup (LS) approach. The chapter explicates the theory and illustrates how this knowledge can be utilized towards building a sustainable business model. Perhaps this can be perceived as a strategic level that is beyond the scope of projects and the knowledge areas that should be acquired by project managers. If you think so, then this book might not be suitable for you. In this book we advocate that modern project managers should learn how to think and act strategically and innovatively, at corporate and business level. Meanwhile, they know and certainly can manage, operate and deliver at operational level. The segregation of project managers versus programme managers is a notion from the past and should stay there.

Chapter 5 starts with an introduction to the concept and details of Agile project management with emphasis on Scrum, by the editor, to set the scene for the following ride. Then Ed Capaldi, the main author, takes the reader on a roller coaster: describing, explaining and discussing how to manage change using a case study that is fictitious yet most of the details match real-life cases that he has guided in practice with the same tools. The case is a very practical application of the presented 12 traits of sustainable change management and goes beyond the software development application of scrum to the wider business domain. This is a typical illustration of our claim at the start that by introducing a new model we do not aim to scrap the previous tools but rather build on it and utilizes it where appropriate.

Chapters 6, 7 and 8 aim to provide the reader with what can be called a short course in *"Advanced Technology for Managers"* Indeed, this is essential that every manger must know at present and more so for the future. The chapters are together as a block that should be read in sequence particularly Chapters 6 and 7 where the former provides the basic concepts about and the latter delves into realms of Artificial Intelligence (AI) with emphasis on Block chain Technology BCT. Chapter 7 provides a very comprehensive content that takes the reader from scratch (101 level – no pre-requisites) about BCT to a very reasonable stance whereby an illustration of how to use BCT in smart contracts as well as the practical applications of BCT in the built environment. Chapter 8 is about New Product Development, an integral part of the project management practice with emphasis on the use of virtual reality technology in producing new products and services. Dr. Wallace Wisthance- Smith in this chapter reflects on his own work as an entrepreneur, business developer and an academic who teaches both alongside operations and project management.

Chapters 9, 10, 11 and 12 form Part Three of this book, and aim to provide sectorial application of the new mindset that is advocated throughout this book starting by the SPMM. Chapter 9 covers the construction with emphasis on the green buildings as an example of sustainable construction. It introduces a strategic model for implementing green buildings that was developed by the two authors of the chapter. This is an example of a strategic model that is typically interesting for project managers working for local authorities' level and the associated parties. In addition, the chapter introduces a comprehensive list of challenges and enablers for a case study of implementing green buildings in Dubai that can be useful for practitioners in general, especially as Dubai is a mix of different trends, cultures, practices. Chapter 10 cintroduces the basic concepts of sustainable logistics and supply chain management, with emphasis on port and maritime logistics. The importance of this chapter is due to the fact that every project, in pursuit of a sustainable project management practice, will have to embrace a sustainable logistics system. In general, logistics and supply chain management is a key area of knowledge that dose not get adequate attention in the project management literature despite the imperative need to understand and even master some of the basic concepts that fall beyond the procurement context.

Chapter 11 addresses another quite a different sector, that is the tourism sector. Tourism contributes to circa 10% of the global GPD and it is a major contributor in many economies. An examining eye will realise that the emerging sustainable tourism will need to utilize project management tools and techniques since to manage the change and to develop new products and services. The relationship between tourism and the hospitality sectors, and project management has been an old one but usually disguised under *Event Management*" yet applying the same set of tools and techniques mostly those from the traditional project management school of thought such as the PMBoK and the like.

Chapter 12 examine the Energy sector with case studies on renewable energy and on sustainable waste management. The chapter starts by comparing the different types of Renewable Energy Technologies (RETs) and discusses the importance of RETs for sustainable development. The first case study looks at the potential for biofuels in the UAE, the second related case presents the key features of a Biofuel Refinery Plant Project as an example of sustainable development projects in the Energy Sector. This is the only project of its kind in the Middle East and particularly the Gulf region and it was based on primary data collected by Adel Haloub, for a research project conducted by the authors. The third case study provides a very useful example on how to conduct a feasibility study to build a Waste-To-Energy (WTE) Incineration Plant as an example of sustainable recycling project. Similarly, the case study was based on primary data collected by Yara Al Jundy as part of a research project conducted by the authors.

Finally, the SPMM aims primarily to change the mindset, not only the tools and techniques! Once the mindset changes, the need for new set of tool and techniques (alongside some of the existing ones) as those introduced in the SPMM will be realized. As a matter of fact, the existing literature tend to agree with these statements in part; that is the impact of innovation on projects as well as the need to lay more emphasis and give more attention to the project managers' skills (we prefer to use competences, but both will be used interchangeably in this book). However, the literature does not seem to have translated those findings into useful practical tools that can guide project managers, in practice on how to do so. When we started this book, we were tasked to address this gap. We aimed to balance the theory and practice as much as we can, so most chapters were supported with good examples and some cases to illustrate the theory. We tried to steer clear from the traditional style of providing templates, registers and the like, because we believe these hinder innovation and limits creativity. We still advocate the use of the existing tools and techniques as appropriate and when deemed useful or can serve the purpose, such as most of the core processes typically needed in project planning; those discussed in our textbook *"Project Management"* by Haniff and Salama, (2016)[1]. Attention should be given though to the inputs and the context; as discussed in the sixth dimension of the SPMM.

Mohamed Salama & the Team

Acknowledgments

The editor is grateful to the wonderful team of authors who have put significant time and effort, illustrating an exemplary collaboration, despite the distance and all other commitments. We are also grateful to the very professional team at Goodfellow Publishers who were instrumental in the production of this book. It was a pleasure to work with you.

---

1 Haniff, A. and Salama, M. (2016) Project Management. Goodfellow, Oxford, UK

About the authors

Dr. Mohamed Salama is academic head of Strategy, Operations and Projects, and Director of Corporate Executive relations at School of Social Sciences at Heriot Watt University, Dubai Campus. Mohamed has circa 20 years of academic experience with focus on project management and strategic management, and over 30 years of work experience as a practitioner in the areas of project management, strategic management and mergers and acquisitions. His research interests and main publications are in the area construction project management and sustainable project management. His book on Project management is the teaching textbook at Heriot Watt University, He is currently the academic chair of 'Lean and Agile Middle East Summit' an annual conference that takes place in Dubai.

Dr.Ahmad Muhamad Salih, architect by origin, GIS and IT by experience and project manager/Strategist by profession, is also a certified Project Management Professional. He has lead many cultural change programs and established the project management office within Khatib and Alami, a multi-national AEC consultancy, in UAE in 2006. His research interests are in leadership studies, culture, Douglasian Cultural Framework and Cultural Intelligence, and qualitative research methods.

Dr. Hind Zantout is the Director of the MSc Data Science Programme in the School of Mathematical & Computer Sciences at Heriot-Watt Dubai. Her academic and research interests include interdisciplinary topics that link computing and informatics with business and society. under this umbrella, big data, innovation, data mining, knowledge management and green it are all employed to support work on business analytics, smart digital communities and the knowledge economy.

Prof. Norbert Seyff is a professor at the University of Applied Sciences and Arts Northwestern Switzerland and a senior research associate at the University of Zurich. His current research focus on requirements engineering, software modeling and sustainability design. He has a particular interest in empowering and supporting end-users participation in system development.

Dr. Shereen Nassar is an Assistant Professor in Operations, Supply Chain and Logistics Management at Heriot-Watt University. Prior to her appointment at Heriot-Watt University, she taught in one of the UAE Academic institutions and a number of well-regarded Egyptian academic institutions. Dr. Nassar's main research interest is Supply Chain visibility driven by the advancement of tracking and tracing technology.

Alberto Peralta is currently a lecturer of Strategy and Business Innovation at EAE Business School (Madrid, Spain), while researching on business innovation and new business strategies. Recent publications relate Business Model Innovation to European and Spanish investors, and the impact of Business Model Innovation in the Circular Economy. He translates the work of Steve Blank, and collaborates with relevant academics and practitioners from USA, Latin-America and Europe, to build a network that helps improve the chances of success of new businesses.

Jorge Castellote is co-founding partner of Innoway. Before that he spent more than seven years in Palladium, a consulting firm specializing in Strategy Execution. Jorge is a dynamic and independent business management consultant with more than 16 years of international experience with a proven track record of delivering world-class strategy and innovation related solutions in Europe, Africa and the Middle East. He is currently focusing on providing guidance in strategy and innovation to empower companies in the Middle East and Africa region, including volunteer work with entrepreneurs in Africa.

Jelena Janjusevic is Assistant Professor at Heriot Watt University, Dubai Campus. Mrs. Janjusevic has strong managerial and research experience. Along with managing the Centre for Sustainable Development, with amission to support sustainable development policy implementation, she was engaged on many different projects dealing with macroeconomic, sustainable development, and public administration capacity building. In over 16 years of experience, she worked with many people and organisations at national and international level, including the government of Montenegro, the World Bank, IFC, EBRD, USAID, UNDP, CHF, EC, and domestic and foreign private companies). She is author and co-author of more than 30 papers and reports published in national and international publications and journals.

Ljubomir Janjusevic comes from the business sector as an experienced, senior-level professional with a strong history of driving dynamic product sales, managing client relationships, and substantially increasing revenues. He has more than 16 years of professional experience, mainly in senior management positions. He has worked in different sectors, both in retail and wholesale from FMCG, tourism, advertising. Currently he works as Marketing and External Relation Associate at Heriot Watt University, Dubai Campus. He is owner and CEO of JSM Company, with operations in wholesale and tourism sector in Montenegro and Europe.

Ashraf Raouf Hana has 29 years of experience in corporate life with emphasis on design, contracting, construction & project management, sales management and business development management. In 2011, he joined Heriot-Watt University, School of Management and Languages, Dubai Campus as adjunct faculty. His research is focused on green buildings and sustainable construction in the United Arab Emirates and he produced the UAE green building strategic model (UAE GBSM) that was published and presented to the 29th annual ARCOM conference .

Dr. Mutasim Nour is the Director of MSc Energy and Renewable Energy programs at Heriot-Watt University, Dubai Campus. He had previously worked at the University of Nottingham Malaysia Campus, where he initiated and led the Power Electronics, Control and Renewable Energy Research Group. Dr. Nour has served as a consultant in the areas of energy storage, efficiency control of AC machines and energy saving solutions. He is currently involved in research projects in the fields of PV inverter system and solar tracker, energy demand management, Energy Efficiency, renewable energy storage systems and applications of artificial intelligence in power systems.

Maria Mataj has an international background with work experience in London, San Francisco and Dubai. Maria is currently working in MedNet, a Munich Re company based in Dubai, where she is deeply involved in transformation programs with the focus on digitalization, automation and innovation. She has also conducted research in virtual teams due to her on-going experience in a virtual ecosystem.

Dr. Yannis Karamitsos has over 25 years industry and research experience as an executive manager, working in the private and public sectors and in European, Middle East and Chinese companies. Since 2010, he has been a Digital Transformation Technologist at Orange Business Services, working with clients to develop and deliver their strategies and transform their organisations into Smart and Digital Cities. Yannis is member of Dubai Silicon Oasis Authority (DSOA)-Dubai Innovation Advisory Board. In 2016, he joined the Department of Electrical Engineering as an adjunct professor at Rochester Institute of Technology Dubai.

Dr. Wallace Whistance-Smith is Professor of Business Management, Ryerson University, Toronto, Canada. Wallace is an experienced executive, entrepreneur, keynote speaker, media personality, and business owner, and has a wide-ranging career portfolio including expertise in manufacturing, purchasing, operations & supply chain management, IT, engineering, finance, economics, marketing and communications. A multi award-winning lecturer, winner of numerous awards of distinction in manufacturing, Wallace holds four innovative product patents with current research interests in the design and development of new products and operational efficiency.

Mohamed El Gindy is a Project Manager at AECOM, a multinational engineering and management services firm. Mohammed served as a consultant to several clients on prominent construction projects in the UAE. He is an enthusiast of the application of disruptive technologies such as blockchain in the urban development and infrastructure industry. This was the main drive for his research during his study of MSc in Strategic Project Management at Heriot-Watt University.

Adel Haloub, since 2016, Adel has been Business Development Manager for Florexx international investment responsible for achieving the company's vision by investing in the renewable energy projects around the world. Prior to that, he worked as a senior consultant for Price Waterhouse Coopers for three years.

Yara Al Jundy has had over 10 years of professional experience in the fields of Environment and Sustainability, with a BSc in Environmental Engineering, MSc in Energy, and multiple certifications from local and international institutes. Her skills were developed by working closely on high profile projects in different project phases, such as construction (monitoring and due diligence), design (EIA, permitting and designing waste management plans) and operation & maintenance (sustainable facility management and operations).

1 The Sustainable Project Management Model

Mohamed Salama and Jelena Janjusevic

Learning outcomes

By completing this chapter, the reader will be able to:

- Compare the listed project management methodologies
- Understand the concept of sustainable development
- Appreciate the need to develop sustainable project management practice
- Discuss the literature review on sustainable project management
- Discuss the Strategic Project Management Model SPMM

Introduction

In the era of digital transformation, following the emergence of disruptive technologies that guided and facilitated the shift towards sharing economy, change is imperative. Imagine the very nice-looking carriages that you see in the royal weddings and compare them to the latest generation of Tesla cars. Or compare the set of skills required to fly Yakovlev Air-5 model 1931 vis-a-vis the Dassault Rafale or the F16 Fighting Falcon (Top 10 fighters, 2017). Before embarking on driving/flying the latter, regardless how competent with the former, the driver/pilot needs to acquire relevant knowledge and master a new set of skills and techniques, and learn different methods in order to be able to deal with the state-of-the-art technology.

The vibrant business environment that has become even turbulent amid the digital transformation is analogous to the rough sea with unfavourable conditions. Those who are not ahead of the game, vigilant, and aware of what they need to do in order to sail safe will have an unpleasant ending, regardless of how successful they are at present. The Titanic is just one example.

However, from a risk exploitation perspective, these conditions can be turned into competitive advantage, with the appropriate strategy, plans and actions. Scholars across the board have already started exploring how to utilize this unprecedented development in technology in reviewing and developing the current practices in almost every field. Management scholars are no different and indeed project management should top the list of areas that should be reviewed. Change is imperative.

Historically, project management methodologies have been selected as the most suitable for managing change. Construction projects introduce change to the building site as does upgrading an assembly line in a manufacturing plant. Projects can take different forms such as new product development (NPD) and new service development (NSD); developing new software, business restructuring and reengineering, mergers and acquisition, event management, etc.

Over the past decades, the traditional project management methodologies have been reviewed, criticized and challenged by professionals from sectors where these methodologies were not the best fit, such as the software development sector. New methodologies such as Agile project management emerged, mostly driven by the practice rather than academia, in response to the needs of the sector. Academic research then followed and this is now a well-researched area. It was quite unusual, given the hypothetical view within the academic world, to be leading the practice by providing knowledge and guidance. Yet necessity is the mother of inventions. So, when there is a need that is not fulfilled by academia, practitioners will act – and they did.

Interestingly, this seems to be reoccurring at present.

Sustainability is perhaps the most popular term in almost every aspect of the business environment, directly or indirectly, on daily basis. Direct examples include: sustainable development, sustainable products, sustainable construction; indirect examples include: smart cities, green logistics, renewable energy.

It imperative that this change towards sustainable practices across various sectors should be guided by project management methodologies. And it should be logical to realize that the requirements for managing this change will need a different approach, based on a different perspective and a different set of skills; someone who can fly the F16 Fighting Falcon!

In this chapter, and indeed throughout the rest of this book, a new model for sustainable project management is introduced and discussed to address this need. However, this does not mean scrapping the past, but rather building on it and developing it. Needless to say that the current project management metholodology recognized by professional bodies such as Project Management Institute (PMI) and known as the traditional methodology, has been popular for decades; delivering projects successfully. When the Agile methodology emerged as a better fit for managing software development projects, some key building blocks were imported from the traditional methodology, despite the claims otherwise.

Certainly, the Agile approach embraced a different mindset and introduced significant changes that yielded better results, in the context of software development projects in particular, as well as with other appropriate types of project. Hence, like driving a car, whilst the driver must keep an eye on the central and side mirrors to consider what is behind, the main focus should be on looking forward.

The suggested model presented in this chapter, while considering the appropriate building blocks of existing methodologies, introduces a different approach to managing projects that embraces the sustainability dimensions and the advances in technology. Consequently, changes in the key areas of knowledge included in the existing methodologies will be imperative due to the inclusion of these new dimensions. In addition, the inclusion of advanced technology in a sustainability context will require a change in mindset and different skills when managing projects; geared towards eco-innovation and sustainable change management.

Chapter structure

At the start, a critical review of the relevant literature supports the call for this change and justifies the claim of an existing gap that the model aims to address. Then a brief review of the exiting methodologies will be presented from a comparative perspective. The model will be introduced, explained and discussed. The chapter will wrap up with a section about the structure of the book and how the following chapters link to and reflect on the model. There are set of case studies online that can be a useful learning tool in context. These are available at:
www.goodfellowpublishers.com/sustprojman.

Development of the project management methodologies

Traditional project management

The traditional project management methodology, also known as the waterfall model, has been prevalent for decades and forms the basis of the PMBoK (PMI body of knowledge). The PMBoK offers guidance on how to effectively manage any project a set of processes required by the project manager to follow. The PMBoK method comprises 10 knowledge areas and 5 process groups; Planning, Initiation, Execution, Monitoring and Control, and Closing. These also refer to the project life cycle phases. The 10 knowledge areas include: Integration, Scope, Time, Quality, Cost, Human Resources, Communications, Procurement, Risk, Stakeholders. In the process groups, the process outputs become inputs to the subsequent process. Such activities overlap and take place at divergent degrees of intensity all through the project. The list of 10 knowledge areas, process groups and the subsequent processes are shown in Table 1.1. Clearly, there is an interaction between the different life cycle phases and the associated process as shown in Figure 1.1

Table 1.1: PMBoK Knowledge Areas and process groups source: PMBok 5th Edition

Knowledge Areas	Project Management Process Groups				
	Initiating Process Group	Planning Process Group	Executing Process Group	Monitoring and Controlling	Closing Process
4. Project Integration Management	4.1 Develop Project Charter	4.2 Develop Project Management Plan	4.3 Direct and Manage Project Work	4.4 Monitor and Control Project Work 4.5 Perform Integrated Change Control	4.6 Close Project or Phase
5. Project Scope Management		5.1 Plan Scope Management 5.2 Collect Requirements 5.3 Define Scope 5.4 Create WBS		5.5 Validate Scope 5.6 Control Scope	
6. Project Time Management		6.1 Plan Schedule Management 6.2 Define Activities 6.3 Sequence Activities 6.4 Estimate Activity Resources 6.5 Estimate Activity Durations 6.6 Develop Schedule		6.7 Control Schedule	
7. Project Cost Management		7.1 Plan Cost Management 7.2 Estimate Costs 7.3 Determine Budget		7.4 Control Costs	
8. Project Quality Management		8.1 Plan Quality Management	8.2 Perform Quality Assurance	8.3 Control Quality	
9. Project Human Resource Management		9.1 Plan Human Resource Management	9.2 Acquire Project Team 9.3 Develop Project Team 9.4 Manage Project Team		
10. Project Communications Management		10.1 Plan Communications Management	10.2 Manage Communications	10.3 Control Communications	
11. Project Risk Management		11.1 Plan Risk Management 11.2 Identify Risks 11.3 Perform Qualitative Risk Analysis 11.4 Perform Quantitative Risk Analysis 11.5 Plan Risk Responses		11.6 Control Risks	
12. Project Procurement Management		12.1 Plan Procurement Management	12.2 Conduct Procurements	12.3 Control Procurements	12.4 Close Procurements
13. Project Stakeholder Management	13.1 Identify Stakeholders	13.2 Plan Stakeholder Management	13.3 Manage Stakeholder Engagement	13.4 Control Stakeholder Engagement	

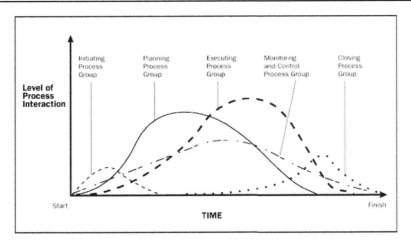

Figure 1.1: Level of interaction through the project life cycle.

Over the years, the waterfall has been commended for its advantages as well criticized for some shortfalls. A list of the main advantages and disadvantages of the traditional waterfall model is shown in Table 1.2.

Table 1.2: Advantages and disadvantages of waterfall model

Advantages	Disadvantages
Depends on following a series of sequential generic processes that can be applied to any type of project.	Depends on following a series of sequential processes. Hence, unanticipated revisions and changes can be challenging.
The framework tends to be simple as all projects follow the same set of processes. Each process has well defined inputs, tools and techniques and output feeding into the following process.	Is a static model with emphasis on the 'iron triangle' of Time, Cost and Quality. This can be a disadvantage amid the turbulent business (project) environment
The project teams have to complete each step prior to moving to the next. This reduces the probability of changes and re-work due to change in design in the case of fast-track or other methods.	The waterfall method tends to become an increasingly internal process that excludes the project sponsor and client, as well as the end users. The key purpose is to assist the internal teams in moving efficiently throughout the project phases.
Well defined scope from the outset enables the project team to gain awareness of the project's overall goal with less potential of getting lost in the project details as it moves ahead.	The use of waterfalls has a higher degree of uncertainty and risk; given that the testing and review occurs after completion.

Agile project management

The use of the waterfall model was mainly detrimental in the case of software development projects due to the specific nature of this type of projects, where it is quite challenging to have a well-defined scope at the outset. This gave rise to an alternative methodology that can better cater for the needs of these projects. The history of Agile project management is best phrased by David F. Rico:

> *"Agile methods were direct spinoffs of software methods from the 1980s, namely Joint Application Design (1986), Rapid Systems Development (1987), and Rapid Application Development (1991). However, they were rooted in earlier paradigms, such as Total Quality Management (1984), New Product Development Game (1986), Agile Leadership (1989), Agile Manufacturing (1994), and Agile Organizations (1996). The euphoria surrounding businesses as complex adaptive systems was also a major influence, namely Ecosystems (1995), Adaptive Learning (1996), Structured Chaos (1997), etc. Agile methods formally began in the 1990s with Crystal (1991), Scrum (1993), Dynamic Systems Development (1994), Synch-n-Stabilize (1995), Feature Driven Development (1996), Judo Strategy (1997), and Internet Time (1998). Other agile methods included New Development Rhythm (1989), Adaptive Software Development (1999), Open Source Software Development (1999), Lean Development (2003), and Agile Unified Process (2005)… Early agile methods had their own built-in agile or adaptive project management frameworks, namely Scrum and Extreme Programming (XP)."*

http://davidfrico.com/rico-apm-frame.pdf

In February 2001, the Manifesto for Agile Software Development was created by 17 people with the desire to find alternative approaches to software development based on four core values:

1 **Individuals and interactions** over processes and tools

2 **Working software** over comprehensive documentation

3 **Customer collaboration** over contract negotiation

4 **Responding to change** over following a plan

The Agile manifesto listed 12 principles as follows:

1 Our highest priority is to satisfy the customer through early and continuous delivery of valuable software.

2 Welcome changing requirements, even late in development. Agile processes harness change for the customer's competitive advantage.

3 Deliver working software frequently, from a couple of weeks to a couple of months, with a preference to the shorter timescale.

4 Business people and developers must work together daily throughout the project.

5 Build projects around motivated individuals. Give them the environment and support they need and trust them to get the job done.

6 The most efficient and effective method of conveying information to and within a development team is face-to-face conversation.

7 Working software is the primary measure of progress.

8 Agile processes promote sustainable development. The sponsors, developers, and users should be able to maintain a constant pace indefinitely.

9 Continuous attention to technical excellence and good design enhances agility.

10 Simplicity – the art of maximizing the amount of work not done – is essential.

11 The best architectures, requirements, and designs emerge from self-organizing teams.

12 At regular intervals, the team reflects on how to become more effective, then tunes and adjusts its behaviour accordingly. (http://agilemanifesto.org/)

The main Agile methodologies are listed in Table 1.3

Table 1.3: Main Agile project management methods, models and frameworks

2001	XP	Beck	Release planning (Stories, Scope, Velocity), Iteration Planning (Tasks, Schedule, Dev.).
2004	SCRUM	Schwaber	Sprint Planning, Sprint (Dev.), Daily Scrum, Sprint Review, Sprint Retrospective.
2004	FLEXIBLE	DeCarlo	Visionate (Vision), Speculate (Plan), Innovate (Dev.), Reevaluate (Rev.), Disseminate (Dep.).
2005	LEADERSHIP	Augustine	Alignment (Teams, Vision), Emergence (Rules, Collaborate, Coach), Learning (Adaptation).
2010	AGILE	Highsmith	Envision (Vision), Speculate (Release), Explore (Iterate), Launch (Deploy), Close (Doc.).
2010	ADAPTIVE	Wysocki	Version Scope, Cycle Plan, Client Checkpoint, Post-Version Review.
2011	SCALABLE	Leffingwell	Portfolio (Vision, Architecture), Program (Product, Release), Team (Spikes, Iterations).

Source: http://davidfrico.com/rico-apm-frame.pdf

Table 1.4 provides a self-explanatory comparison between the traditional Agile approaches.

Table 1.4: Traditional vs Agile approaches. Adapted from Shenhar and Dvir (2007)

	Waterfall	Spiral	Iterative	SCRUM
Defined process	Needed	Needed	Needed	Needed for planning and closure only
Final product	Decided during planning	Decided during planning	Established during project	Established during project
Cost of project	Decided during planning	Partially changeable	Established during project	Established during project
Date of completion	Decided during planning	Partially changeable	Established during project	Established during project
Responsiveness to environment	Only planning	Primary planning	End of each iteration	Throughout
Flexibility and creativity of team	Limited	Limited	Limited	Unlimited during iterations
Knowledge transfer	Training needed before project	Training needed before project	Training needed before project	Teamwork needed during project
Probability of success	Low	Medium low	Medium	High

Traditional and Agile models

Agile models are based on adaptable techniques, whereas the waterfall model focuses on analytical and predictable approaches. In the Agile model, a detailed plan does not exist, and future tasks are function of the deliverables. Traditional methods on the other hand, focus on documentation and project clarification for the development team, so that no concerns are raised about project details. A comparison between the models is shown in Table 1.5. Table 1.6 illustrates a comparison between the attributes of Agile and traditional approaches on the set dimensions (Stoica et al., 2013; Peterson and Wohlin, 2009)

Table 1.5: Comparison between Traditional and Agile development.

Approach	Traditional	Agile
Project objectives	Focus on completing the project on time, cost and quality requirements	Focus on business results, achieve multiple success criteria
Project plan	A collection of activities that are performed as planned to meet the triple constraint (time, cost and quality)	An organization and the process to achieve the expected goals and results for the business
Planning	Held once early in the project	Performed at the beginning and held whenever necessary
Managerial approach	Rigid, focusing on the initial plan	Flexible, adaptive variable
Work/execution	Predictable, measurable, linear, simple	Unpredictable and not measurable, non-linear, complex
Organizational influence	Minimum, impartial, from the project kick-off	Affect the project throughout its execution
Project control	Identify deviations from the original plan and correct the work to follow the plan	Identify changes in the environment and adjust the plan accordingly
Methodology application	Generic and equal application across all projects	Process adaptation depending on the project type
Management style	A model serves all project types	Adaptive approach, a single model does not attend all project types

Table1. 6: Comparison between Traditional and Agile attributes

	Traditional	Agile
Hypothesis (Fundamental)	Fully specified systems that are predictable and developed through thorough planning.	Adaptive software improved by smaller teams that constantly enhance design/ test according to feed-back and change.
Style of management	Control and command.	Team collaboration and leadership.
Knowledge management	Accurate	Unspoken
Communication style	Formal	Informal
Development model	Spiral, Waterfall and other models that have been modified.	Evolutionary distribution model
Structure of organization	Targets large organizations and is mechanical.	Targets small to medium organizations and is organic.
Control of quality	Planning is detailed and control is strict. Late testing and difficult.	Testing, control, requirements and design and solutions is permanent.
Requirements of the user	Requirements defined and detailed before coding and implementation.	The input is interactive.

	Traditional	Agile
Restart cost	High	Low
Direction of development	Fixed	Easily changeable
Testing	Completed after coding.	Completed during every iteration.
Client involvement	Low	High
Additional abilities needed from team	Nothing	Knowledge and interpersonal skills.
Scale of project	Large	Low to medium
Team members	Able and oriented on the plan.	Advanced knowledge and cooperative.
Clients	Right of entry to knowledge, empowered and accommodating.	Well-informed, committed, accommodating and empowered.
Requirements	Known in advance and is very stable.	Rapidly changing and developing.
Architecture	Designed for predictable conditions.	Designed for present conditions.
Remodeling	Expensive.	Inexpensive.
Objectives (Primary)	High safety	Fast value

Source: Collated from (Stoica et al., 2013; Peterson and Wohlin, 2009; Nerur et. al., 2005).

A detailed discussion of the application of the Agile methods, in the context of sustainable change management is presented with a case study in Chapter 5.

Strategic project management

Strategic project management evolution was driven by the organisational need to integrate related or unrelated projects used as a vehicle to deliver the set strategic objectives. Appropriate systems and processes were required: programmes and portfolios. A *programme* is typically a group of related projects, whereas a *portfolio* can comprise a group of unrelated projects. Individual projects are analogous to a static snapshot, whereas projects within programmes and portfolios are moving pictures that can change with the dynamic business environment. Programme managers can put some projects on hold, change their sequence or even pull the plug when needed. The array of projects that aim to deliver the strategic objectives of the organisation are now in harmony, playing the same tune led by one maestro – the programme manager. While the project management approach focuses on individual projects, this can easily be in disarray amid the turbulence of the business environment. The strategic project management approach provides better alignment, and when applied properly can provide organisations seeking to deliver their strategic objectives via projects, with a competitive edge.

The details of the processes included in the strategic project management approach is beyond the scope of this book. Briefly, it is an enterprise-wide system that starts with governance and appropriate structures, with emphasis on strategic alignment and benefit realisation management from the outset. Both guide the subsequent processes included in the planning and execution phases of the programme and the individual projects. Artto et al. (2009) list the distinctive characteristics that mark the difference between programme and project (Table 1.7).

Table 1.7: Distinctive characteristics programmes vs projects

Characteristic	Distinctiveness of programs	Distinctiveness of projects
Themes	Several topical and focused themes of management science: manufacturing, quality, work and organization change, product development	One dominant theme: product development
Evolutionary pattern of themes	Emphasis on different themes change. Major changes in industry & society introduce contemporary themes that programs are expected to address	Evolution within the same thematic line of literature, product development
Dominant theory bases	Organizational theories and strategy	Product development
Additional theory bases	Several additional theory bases: product development, manufacturing, quality, industrial, economic, institutional, work and organizational change	Organizational theories
Missing theory basis	Ignorance of original theoretical roots of program and project management	Similar ignorance of original theoretical roots
Evolutionary pattern of theory bases	Within organizational theories, evolution towards balance between alternatives. Between dominant and additional theory bases, from organization theory focus towards more balance among themes	Increasing focus in product development
Level of analysis	Organization and its major parts. However, no evident focus on multi-project organizing	Single project
Object	Change of permanent organization	Narrowly defined task or temporary organizational entity. Permanent organization serves as an influence factor of project success
System	Systems thinking	No systems thinking
Types of innovation	Various types that reflect an open system nature of organizations in their environments; e.g, process innovation, organizational innovation and change, infrastructure and systems innovation	Product innovation
Types of outcome	Wide set of impacts. Broader, fuzzier and more indirect and far-reaching effects with long-term implications in the future	Concrete business results that directly contribute in a foreseeable manner to business success. Focus on short-term outputs (project or product success)

A final word before concluding this section. The task of setting the project success criteria and the associated critical success factors will differ in strategic project management from the traditional project management approach. What if the project was completed on time, within budget and according to the set specifications, but did not contribute to the strategic objective as intended, for whatever reason? From an individual project management perception, the project is successful but from strategic perspective, there was no benefit released from such claimed success. This is analogous to a team of swimmers in a relay. If one swimmer has the world record in his style while the others hold below average records, then the overall performance of the team will still be below average. Indeed, in his stretch this distinguished swimmer will be a show, but this has limited impact on the overall rank of the team. It is the cumulative contribution of all swimmers that will determine the rank of the team. Similarly, in strategic project management individual project performance may not count. For more details on programme and portfolio management, see Morris and Pinto (2007); Reiss et. al. (2010).

In the following section, the relevant project management literature is discussed with emphasis on sustainable project management. It starts with a brief introduction to the concepts of sustainability and sustainable development from a project management perspective.

Sustainable development

"What is needed now is a new era of economic growth that is forceful and at the same time socially and environmentally sustainable." This call in the foreword of the 1987 Brundtland Report, *Our Common Future*, still rings true 30 years later. Sustainable development – defined by the Brundtland Commission as development that *"meets the needs of the present without compromising the ability of future generations to meet their own needs"* (WCED[1], 1987, p.41) – has been enshrined in documents approved at the highest political level.

Current consumption and production levels are 25% higher than the earth's sustainable carrying capacity, according to the Ecological Footprint Sustainability Measure, an independent measure based on United Nations statistics. If everyone in the world were to live like an average person in the high-income countries, we would need 2.6 additional planets to support us all.

WCED broad definition of sustainable development emphasises the aspect of future orientation as a basic element of sustainability. Sustainability relates primarily to environmental and demographic concerns but, in the light of the recent economic and fiscal crises across Europe and the USA, it increasingly includes social issues such as equality, social mobility, social renewal and financial sustainability. In addition to the growing political interest in sustainability, there are many studies on sustainability both as an academic field of research and as an area of practice. For example, the study conducted by McKinsey shows that energy efficiency can save the United States $1.2 trillion a year.

Majority of definitions and studies on sustainable development imply optimal use of natural resources, and decrease of our environmental footprint. For example, the OECD (1990) states that *"the sustainable development concept constitutes a further elaboration of the close links between economic activity and the conservation of environmental resources. It implies strong connection and 'joint venture' between the environment and the economy."* Other authors, like Barbier (1987), link sustainable development to *"increasing the material standard of living of the poor at the 'grassroots' level, which can be quantitatively measured in terms of increased food, real income, educational services, healthcare, sanitation and water supply, emergency stocks of food and cash, etc."* The link between the social and environmental dimensions of sustainability can be found in the earlier-mentioned report by the United Nations World

---

1   World Commission on Environment and Development

Commission on Environment and Development (1987). The report states that, *"in its broadest sense, sustainable development strategy aims at promoting harmony among human beings and between humanity and nature"*. John Elkington (1997), in his book *Cannibals with Forks: the Triple Bottom Line of 21st Century Business*, identified this as the 'triple bottom line' or 'Triple-P (People, Planet, Profit)' concept.

Sustainability is about the balance or harmony between economic sustainability, social sustainability and environmental sustainability.

Later, the International Institute for Sustainable Development (2010) emphasised the need for sustainable management of organisations:

"Adopting business strategies and activities that meet the needs of the enterprise and its stakeholders today while protecting, sustaining and enhancing the human and natural resources that will be needed in the future."

Important in this definition is the mentioning of the *"needs of the enterprise and its stakeholders today"*. This aspect recognises the required balance between the present and future.

Definitions of sustainability and sustainable development in the literature refer to three key elements of sustainability which can be identified (Dyllick and Hockerts, 2002).

1 integrating economic, environmental and social aspects;

2 integrating short-term and long-term aspects;

3 consuming the income and not the capital.

Incorporating sustainability into the scope and processes of the businesses has much wider effect. It influences the lives and functions of shareholders, employees, customers, and communities at large. A sustainable approach to business is more about the link between organisation and the wider society, including:

■ **Human rights:** discrimination of vulnerable groups, civil rights, and fundamental rights and principles at work;

■ **Labour practices:** conditions of work, health and safety, and development and training;

■ **The environment:** sustainable resource use, pollution prevention, and climate change mitigation;

■ **Fair operating practices:** anti-corruption, fair competition, and respect for property rights;

■ **Consumer issues:** fair contractual practices, dispute resolution, and fair marketing;

■ **Community involvement and engagement:** employee training and skills development, wealth and income creation, and community involvement.

Although presented at the organization level, these elements are applicable at the project level and should be incorporated within projects seeking sound and sustainable project management.

It is obvious that the nature, life support systems and community need to be sustained and people, economy and society need to be developed. Sustainability has been incorporated at multiple levels ranging from macro or global level to the micro or project level. From the global perspective, organisations brought attention to common issues such as:

- Continued support for human life on earth,
- Long-term maintenance of biological and agricultural resources,
- Stable human populations,
- Limited growth economies,
- Small scale,
- Self-reliance and quality

In New York, the Heads of State and Government and High Representatives during their meeting at the United Nations Headquarters from 25-27 September 2015, decided on new global Sustainable Development Goals and Agenda 2013: 17 Goals and 169 targets with emphasis on 5 P's: People, Planet, Prosperity, Peace and Partnership. Today, almost every government, globally, has incorporated all these endeavours into national policies; focused and adjusted to the country specific needs; within scope of the Sustainable Development Goals and Agenda 2030. The common goals are seen as:

- Social progress which encompasses community health, education and inclusion;
- Protection of the environment, species and their habitat; prudent environmental resource usage; and
- Maintenance of economic growth and employment.

Businesses are mandated to integrate the sustainable development principles at both strategic and operational levels. For example, companies like Unilever, General Electric and Walmart have shown integration at a strategic level by designating corporate sustainability officers, integrating sustainability in their corporate communication strategy and producing sustainability reports (Planko & Silvius, 2012). Integration at the operational level involves a change in production and procurement systems to incorporate environmental management systems. Additionally, it involves the adoption of reporting systems that assess, evaluate and monitor the business processes based on the triple bottom line criteria (Labuschagne & Brent, 2006).

Last but not least, sustainability has to be integrated at the project level since traditional project management techniques provide limited consideration for sustainable development (Labuschagne & Brent, 2005). If realised, it can improve the reputation of the project, reduce financial risks and potential litigations, as well as develop a competitive edge. At present, governments in many countries require environmental assessments prior to granting approvals for projects, for example the Canadian Environmental Assessment Act 2012.

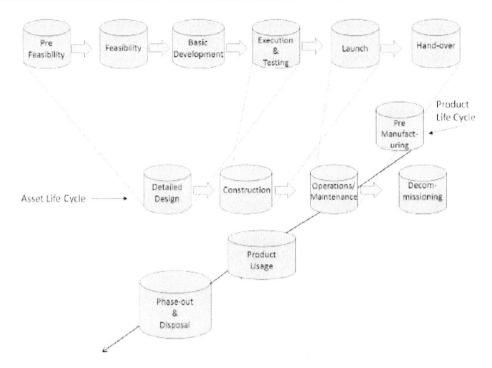

Figure 1.2: Interrelating life-cycles (based on Labuschagne & Brent 2006)

As project-based economic activities are on the rise, sustainable project management can provide the building blocks for a more sustainable economy and a better society at large. Sustainable project management is a field of study currently in its infancy, yet with great potential given the benefits projects offer as vehicles of change.

Sustainability and project management

Many research studies linked sustainability with the project management. Since project management entails the application of knowledge, skills, tools and techniques to achieve the project deliverables, within the set constraints (PMI, 2013), sustainability ought to be applied to all these components as shown in Table 1.8.

Academics and many practitioners are interested in finding and understanding the link between sustainable development and project management (Silvius, 2013). The Association for Project Management's (APM) and International Project Management Association's (IPMA), have both called for project and programme managers to take responsibility for and contribute towards sustainable management practices (Silvius, 2012). Increasing interest in this discipline and area of research can be emphasised in the need for shifting from Corporate Social Responsibility (CSR) to 'sustainability' as the focus has moved away from enterprise and supply chain to projects.

Authors	Concepts of sustainability			Implications for project management
	Triple-P approach	Integrating long and short term	Consuming income not capital	
Labuschagne and Brent (2006)	✓	✓		Project managers should take into account the Triple-P aspects in the interacting life cycles of the project, the asset and the product.
APM (2006)	✓			Project and program managers are well placed to make contributions to sustainable management practices at many levels on their projects
Russell (2008)		✓		Corporate social responsibility will become increasingly important
Taylor (2008)		✓		Sustainability checklist for project managers
Eid (2009)	✓	✓		Project management processes provide leverage points to introduce sustainable development to project management standards
Silvius et al. (2009)	✓	✓		Concepts and framework for sustainability indicators in projects
Gareis et al. (2009)	✓	✓	✓	Directions for further development in project management
Turner and Huemann (2010)	✓	✓	✓	A framework for considering sustainable development in project management
Silvius et al. (2010)	✓	✓	✓	An overview of concepts and frameworks for integrating sustainability in projects management

Table 1.8: Studies on sustainability in project management

Despite the rising interest among academics for defining the sustainable project management, a limited number of scholars provide definition of the term. Ning (2009) emphasise the need to undertake business activities without negatively impacting future generations through a diminishing use of finite resources, energy, pollution and waste. Deland (2009) calls for minimisation in use of both resources and labour throughout all phases of a project. Tam (2010) incorporates all three pillars of sustainability – social, environmental and economic – in the definition by urging for a promotion of positive and reduction of negative sustainability impacts over project phases.

Elkington (1997), the first to build a case for simultaneous and equal consideration of economic, environmental and social goals when delivering products and services, showed that business objectives are indivisible from the environment and society in which organisations operate. Thus, sustainable development needs to concurrently build on all three pillars. Elkington connected environmental sustainability with the necessity to *"keep the natural capital intact"*. The social dimension is emphasised through *"unity and continuity of the society with practices that allow people to work towards shared goals"*. Economic sustainability can be interpreted in terms of present generations performing economic activities without burdening future generations through the creation of liabilities (Schieg, 2009).

A literature review on sustainability in project management performed by Silvius & Schipper (2014) reported that 86% of 164 publications referred to the triple bottom line when conceptualising sustainability, but their consideration of the three pillars is different: 96% of the papers discuss the economic, 89% the social and 86% the environmental dimension. Previous findings further support the occasional omission of the social and environmental dimensions (Labuschagne & Brent, 2004; Silvius et al., 2013) which can be explained by organisational endeavour to primarily compensate and reward investors' capital (Martens & Carvalho, 2013). Additionally, the level of consideration of the three pillars differs in projects based on the macroeconomic climate of a country. For example, projects show a bigger emphasis on environmental concerns in Western Europe as compared to a prevalent social consideration in Africa (Silvius & Schipper, 2010).

Nevertheless, the economic, environmental and social dimensions of sustainability need to be seen as interrelated as they influence each other in different ways. The three dimensions can provide harmonized and balanced relation between them in creating good effects on sustainability from the start.

- **Economic sustainability** – achieving economic sustainability is much more than company performance indicators such ROI (return on investment) on specific project. It is more related to connecting the project and its goals and results with main economic drivers in the organization, how the project will support organization as whole, and how the project will ensure financial sustainability of the business.

- **Social sustainability** – social dimension in the projects is essential for the long-term growth and sustainability of a company. It is related to development of sustainable organizational culture, processes and procedures that take care of the culture, gender and other social aspects of employees, shareholders, partners and other stakeholders, both inside the firm and throughout the value chain.

- **Environmental sustainability** – to work in line with nature is one of the basic requirements and most recognisable elements of sustainable management. Environmental sustainability should be main principle of planning and doing business, and relates to the evaluation of capital equipment and facilities requirements, use of resources, purchasing practices, contract management, and industry standards.

Sustainability as integration of economic, environmental and social aspects

The scheme below presents the 'three-P concept' (Elkington, 1997) pointing to the 'three pillars' of sustainability: Social, Environmental and Economic. The concept suggests that three dimensions are inter-related and therefore may influence each other in multiple ways.

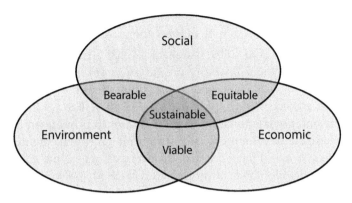

Figure 1.3: The triple-P concept of sustainability

Sustainability as integration of short-and long-term aspects

The time dimension is one more aspect that should be taken into consideration when speaking about sustainability. From economic point of view, because of discount rates, short term effects are more valuable compared to long term effects, whereas social impacts or environmental degradation may not occur before the long-term.

Following Sawaf et al. (2014), the authors of this book endorse and further emphasise the need to add a fourth dimension, that is 'Culture', which will be included in the discussion to follow throughout this book.

Sustainable project management

The main concerns about sustainable development are related to the current way of living, production and consumption, etc. Our current way of 'doing things' is not sustainable, therefore change is imperative. Bearing in mind that any launch, whether of a new production plant, product, business process or resource, is seen as a project (Silvius and Batenburg 2009), it can be concluded that a more sustainable society requires more sustainable projects.

What are the main elements of sustainability in the project management? This question can be challenging, as all the above-mentioned elements of sustainability are rather conceptual than practical (Moneva et al., 2006; Pope et al., 2004). The concept of sustainability is understood intuitively, but is not easily expressed in concrete operational terms (Briassoulis, 2001).

The relation between project management and sustainable management is still an emerging field of study. Only a few studies have been published recently. Labuschagne and Brent (2006), the Association for Project Management (2006) and Russell (2008) focus on the implications of sustainability for business strategy and policies, and thereby on the content of projects. More specifically, they focus on how sustainability dimensions should be considered in defining projects. These studies cover important aspects of sustainable project management, however they pay little attention to the implications of sustainability on project management processes and on the competencies of the project manager.

Other studies (Eid, 2009; Gareis et al., 2009; Turner & Huemann, 2010) focus on the impact of sustainability on the *process* of managing projects rather than on the end *product*. They tend to pay little attention to the contribution of projects and project management to sustainability. The triple bottom line element of sustainability has to be taken into account to provide an integrated approach to sustainable development and project management; the need for inclusion of both People and Planet performance indicators in the management systems, formats and governance of projects (Silvius et al., 2009). Current project management is focused on a different 'triple-constraint' – time, cost and quality (Project Management Institute, 2008), clearly putting emphasis on the profit 'P'. The social and environmental aspects may be included as part of the quality dimension, but they are bound to get less attention.

Given the future-orientation of sustainability, we should consider the full life-cycle of a project, from its conception to its disposal. This view is further developed by Labuschagne and Brent (2006) who argue that when assessing sustainability in project management, the total life cycle of the project (e.g. initiation-development-execution-testing-launch) should be considered. As the project aims to deliver a product or a service, the focus on the life cycle seems process-oriented, when in fact the sustainable project management approach should focus on both: the process and the product or service delivered.

Combining the triple-P element of sustainability and the life cycle views, the following definition of sustainable project management can be derived:

> *Sustainable project management is the sustainable management of change, utilising sustainable innovation approaches while considering the economic, social, cultural and environmental impact of the project, its deliverables and the consequent impact, for now and future generations.*

Sustainable project management is primarily about meeting the time, cost and quality targets for project outputs, and at the same time maximizing the project benefits to stakeholders and community. Aspects related to social, cultural, economic and environmental sustainability, such as community engagement, national capacity development and gender mainstreaming, to deliver added value to project beneficiaries, should be prioritized.

To conclude this section about the academic literature on sustainable project management, two interesting studies will be presented in some details.

Analysis of project management research by Kwak and Anbari (2009)

Kwak and Anbari (2009, presented a comprehensive analysis of project management research, covering more than 500 journal articles from the selected 18 top journals in the management and business fields published from the 1950s to the summer of 2007, excluding project management focused journals. The main objectives were to acquire better understanding of the evolution of project management as a field of practice and an academic discipline, and to provide suggestions for future PM research opportunities. They suggested eight categories to represent the disciplines that embrace PM research as follows:

1 "Operations Research/ Decision Sciences/ Operation Management/ Supply Chain Management (OR/DS/OM/ SCM) refers to the discipline associated with quantitative decision analysis and management principles, including various optimization tools and techniques, network analysis, resource leveling, simulation, etc.

2 Organizational Behavior/ Human Resources Management (OB/HR) refers to the discipline associated with organizational structure, organizational dynamics, motivation, leadership, conflict management, etc.

3 Information Technology/ Information Systems (IT/IS) refers to the discipline associated with the use of computers and computer systems to process, transmit, store, and retrieve information for better management decisions.

4 Technology Applications/ Innovation/ New Product Development/ Research and Development (TECH/INNOV/ NPD/R&D) refers to the discipline associated with the concepts of making innovative and technological improvements and the research and development of new products, services, and processes.

5 Engineering and Construction /Contracts/ Legal Aspects/ Expert Witness (EC/CONTRACT/LEGAL) refers to the discipline associated with the use of a broad range of professional expertise to resolve issues related to engineering and construction, contracts, expert witness, and their legal implications.

6 Strategy/ Integration/ Portfolio Management/ Value of Project Management/ Marketing (STRATEGY/PPM) refers to the concepts of organizing and managing resources to maximize profit, minimize cost, and support the overall strategy of the organization.

7 Performance Management/ Earned Value Management/ Project Finance and Accounting (PERFORMANCE/EVM) refers to the concepts and techniques that measure project progress objectively by combining measurements of technical performance, schedule performance, and cost performance.

8 Quality Management/ Six Sigma/ Process Improvement (QM/6SIGMA/PI) refers to the concepts of improving processes, minimizing defects, and reducing cost by implementing continual improvement principles and specific measures and metrics."

(Kwak and Anbari, 2009)

The main findings presented as shown in Table 1.8 indicated that STRATEGY/ PPM (30%) is the most important project management research subject and is showing an upward trend, followed by the traditional OR/DS/OM/SCM (23%) and OB/HRM (13%) categories that are showing downward trend. TECH/INNOV/ NPD/R&D (11%), IT/IS (11%) and PERFORMANCE/EVM (7%) are showing an upward trend whereas QM/ 6SIGMA/PI (2%) and EC/CONTRACT/LEGAL(3%) seem to attract much less attention. The following quotation eloquently summaries the findings of the study:

> *PM is one of the youngest, most vibrant, and dynamic fields among various management disciplines ... In recent years, research interests in cross-disciplinary studies between PM and allied disciplines have become more popular evidenced by increased publications on these integrated subjects in mainstream business and management journals.... It is important to note that PM is no longer merely a practice to plan, schedule, and execute projects effectively, but it is an academic field and one of the key management disciplines that consist of both practical/ empirical research and theoretical research-based on solid academic theories and foundations.* (Kwak and Anbari, 2009)

Table 1.9: Journal publications based on eight categories. Source: Kwak and Anbari, (2009)

Allied disciplines	50–59	60–69	70–79	80–89	90–99	00–07	Total	%
OR/DS/OM/SCM	3	20	37	49	65	54	228	23
OB/HRM	1	5	18	14	46	43	127	13
IT/IS	2	2	7	22	35	37	105	11
TECH/INNOV/NPD/R&D	0	1	12	13	39	46	111	11
EC/CONTRACT/LEGAL	1	4	2	4	10	7	28	3
STRATEGY/PPM	2	10	48	74	78	83	295	30
PERFORMANCE/EVM	1	6	10	11	12	28	68	7
QM/6SIGMA/PI	0	1	2	1	7	7	18	2
Total	10	49	136	188	292	305	980	100
Percentage	1%	5%	14%	19%	30%	31%	100%	

These findings are much in line with our call for a change in mindset in order to cope with the emerging and fast-growing digital transformation of business, while embracing the principles of sustainability.

Six cecades of PM research, analysed by Padalkar and Gopinath (2016)

Padalkar and Gopinath (2016) covered six decades of project management research, aiming to highlight thematic trends and future opportunities. It is worth noting that there are 7 years between the two studies; the former was submitted in June 2008 and the latter in September 2015. The authors criticised the first study for having excluded the project management focused journals and questioned how the findings can be significant for the project management research agenda. Perhaps they have a point! They used Effective Annualized Citation Rate (EACR) as a measure of influence for articles published in any given year to filter over 2500 papers down to 189 papers. The study reviewed three main journals *IJPM*, *PMJ*, and *International Journal of Managing Projects in Business* (IJMPB) as the sources over the period of 2000–2015. From 34 themes, the top 17 themes were selected based on their EACR values, and the period was divided into three sub-periods: 2000–2005, 2006–2010, 2011–2015 to form longitudinal view of thematic evolution as shown in **bold** in Table 1.10. Three perspectives were used: deterministic, explanatory and non-deterministic. The study suggested that the evolution from deterministic to explanatory is a shift in orientation from means to ends. Both assume traceability, unlike the non-deterministic research which relaxes the assumption of tractability. Furthermore, Padalkar and Gopinath (2016) concluded that the accord of the three eras from mid-'90s, coupled by the thematic diversity, indicated weak ontological, epistemological, or methodological convergence in project management research.

Table 1.10: Distribution of 17 themes (in bold) by perspectives and time periods

Period	Deterministic	Explanatory	Non-deterministic
2000–2005	Project methods Success factors **Risk management** **Public private partnership** **Knowledge management** **Project organization** **Program management** **Project environment** Stakeholder management	Project methods Success factors Performance management Resource management Risk management Partnering Project environment Knowledge management Project scope Public private partnership Team integration	Project environment Project methods Risk management

2006–2010	Project strategy
	Project culture
	Collaboration with
	  customers
	Project methods
	Research methods
	Public private partnership
	Human resource
	  management
	Program management office
	Project portfolio
	  management
	Risk management
	Project management
	  education
		Success factors
		Project strategy
		Governance & control
		Performance management
		Program management
		Project methods
		Project environment
		Project portfolio management
		Project resources
		Procurement
		Public private partnership
		Risk management
		Stakeholder management
		Team integration
		Change management
		Knowledge management
		Industry-related
		Regional themes
			Risk management
			Project complexity
			Project uncertainty
			Project strategy
			Project management
			education
			Project methods

2011–2015	Knowledge management Performance management Project strategy Governance & control **Procurement** **Communication** **Project methods** **Quality management**	Project management office Success factors Project methods Project team dynamics Project portfolio management Knowledge management Performance management Risk management	Risk management Project complexity Governance & control Project uncertainty

The study also collated the research questions in each article included in the considered papers under 11 themes:

1. Governance & control
2. Knowledge management
3. Performance management
4. Project complexity
5. Project methods

6. Project strategy
7. Project uncertainty
8. Public private partnership
9. Risk management
10. Stakeholder management
11. Success factors

Reviewing the listed research question, with emphasis on three terms key to our model: Sustainability; innovation, and technology. None of these terms were mentioned explicitly in the research questions of all the paper reviewed under the 11 themes. In addition, throughout the entire paper, the terms 'sustainability' and 'innovation' are mentioned only once, while citing the work of Artto et al., (2009) mentioned earlier in this chapter. This gives rise to question of the direction of current project management research and how it is linked or otherwise to the real world and the needs of the practice in this era of digital transformation, disruptive innovation and rapid changes in the technology.

Finally, the study presented a ranking of the knowledge areas based on count (frequency) and based on influence (EACR) as shown in Table 1.11.

Table 1.11: Ranking of knowledge areas by research quantum and influence. Source: Padalkar and Gopinath, (2016)

PMBOK® Knowledge area/other topic	Article counts	Rank by counts	Rank by influence	Trend
Risk	39	1	1	
Success *	23	2	2	↑
Knowledge *	17	3	3	↑
Time	17	3	4	↓
Portfolio *	14	5	6	↓
Performance *	12	6	5	↑
Human resources	12	6	7	↓
Stakeholder	11	8	8	
Relationship *	9	9	10	↓
Leadership *	8	10	9	↑
Organization *	7	11	11	
Cost	5	12	12	↑
PM maturity *	4	13	13	
External *	4	13	14	↓
Procurement	2	15	16	↓
PPP *	2	15	15	
Communication	1	17	17	
Quality	1	17	18	↓
PMO *	1	17	19	↓
Scope	0	20	20	
Integration	0	20	20	
Total	189			

*Areas other than the PMI BoK knowledge Areas - D: Deterministic; E: Explanatory; ND: Non-deterministic.

Both studies indicate that the project management research need a face lift and change in mindset. This supports our call for a new model that embraces the dimensions of sustainability and breeds innovation as one of the key skills to be acquired by project managers alongside a plethora of a other factors. These include other essential soft skills, knowledge areas, tools and techniques that seem unheeded by stream project management literature.

In the following section, the Sustainable Project Management Model that is produced by the first author of this chapter, the editor of this textbook, will be presented and explained in pursuit of addressing the gap identified through the review of the literature.

Sustainable Project Management Model (SPMM)

Rationale and context

The review of the literature and the existing project management methodologies, frameworks models, processes and tools and techniques, indicated that there is seldom mention of the sustainability dimensions, explicitly, with clear description as to how these can be embraced in the initiation, planning and execution of projects. At best, some of the previous research did call for the need for delivering sustainable projects, so as if stating the 'what' without providing the 'how'. Others have indicated the need to consider the environment and the social contexts, still in a subtle form without elucidating on how to pursue this in the practical world of projects to be delivered in a very dynamic business environment that can be heavily regulated and/or amid dire economic conditions.

In addition, the current project management education is still lingering in the realms of the traditional concepts of the iron triangle and Gantt charts. Indeed, the basics of project management time planning, cost budgeting, quality and risk management systems will remain building blocks that form the essential foundation for further theoretical and applied constructs. However, this is analogous to the claim that basic computer literacy is all what university graduates need to know in the context of ICT competences. Perhaps this was acceptable 20 years ago but not at present. Graduates across the board are expected to have developed some applied IT competences relevant to their disciplines such as Primavera or MS project (or the like) in the case of project management. While delivering a lecture on project management to third year students in the fall of 2017, I asked the class whether they heard of block chain technology and surprisingly out of the 200 plus students, only a few raised their hands. Out of those few only one or two had some basic knowledge of BC and the rest (of the few) heard only of it or mentioned something about Bitcoin. Imagine, those who did not raise their hands (roughly 90%), had not even heard of it! I deliberately verified this because some students are shy to raise their hands. In a year or two this group will be the project team members and a few years later they will become project managers.

We need to take a step back and consider the status quo before we dream about the future, if we want our dreams come true. Among the fundamentals of strategic management is the analysis of the current position. It is obvious that the current set of skills coupled with the existing models and the associated tools and techniques, at least in the context of project management, belong to the past. There has always a debate about the gap between academia and practice. I witnessed this since the early 2000s in the context of construction project management. This was even more obvious with the evolution of Agile project management. Compared to numerous options for studying an academic course in project management, even specialisation at both undergraduate and post graduate levels, a Google search could not identify universities offering academic courses in Agile project management with academic credits. All the existing courses fell under the category of executive education or training and developing skills.

This introduction, endorsed by the review of the literature discussed earlier in this chapter, justify the need for a new approach in managing projects that should have academic underpinning, while being applicable to the practical world; otherwise the gap will remain.

In the following section, the development of the Sustainable Project Management Model will be explained. Then, the following chapters of this textbook will reflect on the components of the model with examples and case studies, primarily to address the how having stated the why and the what in this chapter.

SPMM dimensions and subsequent factors

The Sustainable Project Management Model comprises six main dimensions; each dimension is further broken down into a set of factors that reflects on, informs and guides towards the achievement of the relevant dimension. The six dimensions complement one another and are neither exclusive nor exhaustive, but should be regarded as the jigsaws that when set in place appropriately complete the project canvas. This model targets the end-product or service, as well the process implemented to produce the desired product or service, since both are equally vital from sustainability perspective.

The six main components of the SPMM as shown in Table 1.12, are **S**ustainability; **A**daptive leadership; **L**ife cycle assessment; **A**dopting advanced technology; **M**anaging innovation and **A**ssurances and Control.

When combined, they make the acronym **SALAMA** which in Arabic means SAFETY and in Finish means FLASH or lightning, and in other languages such as Farsi and Pilipino Salamat is a greeting word for hello / thank you and good health. All seem very positive and quite indicative of purpose of this model!! Ostensibly, this resembles the name of the author of the model but can be regarded as an unanticipated by-product! An alternative elected acronym was **MASALA** but it has been resolved that this might be too spicy…hence we shall settle with SALAMA as a *safer* option.

The last row in the table is an anticipated end rather than an inherent dimension (mean) hence the difference in colour. However, the listing of Maturity aimed to identify the desired end, and its allied factors which are inherent factors in the six dimensions.

Table 1.12: Sustainable Project Management Model - SPMM (SALAMA)

	Dimensions	Factors
S	Sustainability Dimensions – (SECE)	Social Environmental Cultural Economic
A	Adaptive Leadership – AL (ASECC)	Adaptive leadership Soft skills for teams Emotional intelligence Cultural intelligence Corporate social responsibility

L	Life Cycle Assessment - LCA
	(BLAC)
		Assessment criteria – success criteria
		Economic assessment
		  • Environmental assessment
		  • Social
		  • Cultural
		Critical success factors (CSF)
		Life cycle costing
		Benefit realization management

A	Adopting Advanced Technology - AI (BAII)	ICT AI IOT BCT (DLT)
M	Managing Innovation (ELESA)	Eco-innovation Lean startups Exponential organisation Sustainable business modelling Agile management
A	Assurances and Control	Scope Management OBS – WBS – TRM (RAM) – Communication Plan Stakeholder management Schedule planning, monitoring and control Cost budgeting and control Risk management system Quality management system Configuration management system Project plan review and feedback
M	Maturity	Continuous improvement through agility, lean and sustainable innovation

In the following, each dimension will be discussed alongside the allied factors:

Sustainability

- **Social**. The social factor embraces the impact of the project on the society including the project team, the stakeholders and the wider community. For example, there is a growing interest in concept of the corporate social responsibility in the context of managing projects. In addition, some countries have started imposing regulations with minimum standards for labour accommodation in construction sites. Research indicated that contractors exceeded these requirements having realised the benefits manifested in higher productivity, less turnover and other intangible benefits. Project managers should acquire the relevant knowledge and skills to include this factor when planning projects, regardless of the discipline.

- **Environment**. Typically, projects have impact on the environment. Project managers have to consider such impact. Some counties mandate undertaking environmental assessment prior to granting permits or approvals for projects. The subsequent implications, in order to comply, affect the design and execution of project. This should be a common practice regardless whether it is mandated or otherwise. The required knowledge and relevant skills should be part of the project management practice.

- **Cultural**. The academic literature has abundance of research on the importance of culture in the context of managing projects. Still, reflecting on experience, having taught project managers for almost 20 years, the majority cannot provide a simple definition of the term 'culture', not to mention embrace it in the context of sustainability, in managing projects. Some do it intuitively after years of experience, but this is neither an excuse nor the way it should be. This is an area of knowledge that needs to be acquired, mastered and applied in context. Cultural intelligence is an emerging concept that will be discussed under adaptive leadership dimension.

- **Economic**. This is an imperative factor, yet the sustainability context implies the consideration of factors beyond the standard cost-benefit analysis typically conducted during the feasibility study. Environmental as well as social variables, both tangible and intangible, have to be quantified and considered where possible. In addition, the economic dimension implies conducting full life cycle costing – a well-established area of knowledge. This will be further discussed under the life cycle assessment dimension.

Adaptive Leadership

- **Adaptive leadership.** This is a new emergent approach that is discussed in detail in Chapter 3 and is considered one of contributions of this textbook alongside this model.

- **Soft skills for teams**. These include communication and negotiations skills, and the ability to integrate and deliver team goals in a complex, setting which is typically the case in projects. Chapter 2 discusses the soft skills, process and details of managing virtual teams, which are a growing trend in project teams amid the digital transformation and the globalisation of business.

■ **Emotional intelligence**. Chapter 2 discusses in depth EI and its impact on project teams and team performance

■ **Cultural intelligence**. Chapter 3 provides a detail discussion about CQ, the criticism it attracted in the literature and the emergence of the metacognitive dimension of CQ. The discussion will include the Douglasian Cultural Framework (DCF).

The four factors under the adaptive leadership form the content of Chapters 2 and 3, where the discussion will guide the reader to understand the concept as well as the application of the concept in the context of projects

Life Cycle Assessment

The term 'life cycle assessment' was created in 1990, during an international workshop (in Smugglers Notch, Vermont, USA) sponsored by the Society of Environmental Toxicology and Chemistry (SETAC). Also in the context of terminology, the term 'cradle-to-grave' is typically associated with LCA and means that all the important steps in the life cycle of a product are included in the analysis

■ **Assessment Criteria – Success Criteria**. At the start the project manager must distinguish between the success criteria and success factors. The former represents a set of benchmarks that will determine the successful delivery of the project or otherwise. Whereas the latter refers to the assurances and safeguards that should be embedded in the process to facilitate and enhance the successful delivery of the project. Both should be set for each project based on the sought output. Following a LCA approach, the success criteria have to include the full life cycle of the project including the operation (use) phase and the decommissioning phase. This is profoundly different from the traditional time, cost and quality trinity.

■ **Critical Success Factors (CSF)**. Similarly, the factors that will facilitate the achievement of the success criteria will consider the entire life cycle of the project. Sometimes this can be challenging since the project manager has limited control (if any) on the later phases of the projects following the commission and handover, i.e. the use and decommissioning phases. For example, in construction, the project managers complete the project (e.g. residential building) in say 2 years, then the building is in use for 100 years or more. However, the LCA implies the introduction of factors and inputs in the design phase that would have positive impact during the use phase. Consider water and energy consumption – both can be significantly optimised through appropriate measures introduced during the design phase. The green buildings that have now developed into SMART Buildings can be a good example of full life cycle management through the measures introduced during the design phase that optimise the use of water and energy, in addition to including a sustainable waste management system.

- **Life Cycle Costing**. Unlike the traditional methods that limit the project costing to the phases controlled by the project team, excluding the use phase and the decommissioning phase, the full life cycle costing includes all phases, thus selecting the most sustainably viable project.

- **Benefit Realization Management**. Although this is a concept usually associated with programme management, it should be considered in the context of managing projects, while considering the full life cycle, in pursuit of sustainable project management. Overlooking this factor can yield projects that are allegedly successful but delivering no benefit, which deviates from the concept of sustainability. The project manager should be aware of the tools and techniques used in managing benefits rather than just focusing on the process details. Typically, this is an integral role for programme managers and there is no reason why the same should not apply to project managers. They should learn these skills, stay vigilant and through effective communication with the programme managers, the sought benefits will more likely be realised.

Adopting advanced technology

This dimension refers to the essential skills that every project manager should acquire and master amid the digital transformation of the business management practice and the sharing economy that is driven by the advancement in the technology. Part two of this textbook, that includes Chapters 6, 7 and 8, has been dedicated to discussing the advanced technology; concept and applications in the context of projects. This include all the four listed factors: ICT, AI, IOT and BCT (DLT), with emphasis on Information and Communication Technology - ICT (Chapter 6) and blockchain Technology – BCT (Chapter7).

Managing innovation

The term innovation was mentioned as amongst the most cited in academic research in project management (Artto et. al., 2009). It seems to appear in the academic research cited in business management journal and not the project management journals as mentioned earlier in this chapter. However, it seems to be implicitly included in the practice. For example, the Agile model allegedly supports innovation, but looking at methods such as Scrum, it is merely an efficient communication and team management method, yet is highly adaptable and can facilitate managing innovation once the appropriate tools are in place. Hence, it was resolved that including these techniques will equip project managers with essential knowledge in an applied context that can facilitate the delivery of sustainable projects. This dimension unlike the other 5 dimensions offer the choice among the listed factors. Project managers can choose the most applicable approach that suits the project in hand.

- **Eco-innovation – Lean startups**. The concept of eco-innovation, with the emerging new trend of lean startups for managing business innovation, are discussed in Chapter 4. This is essential knowledge for managing business innovation, addressing both the process and the product. In pursuit of sustainable project management, the product should be sustainable as well as the means leading to the end – the process.

- **Exponential organisation**. The concept of exponential organisation was introduced by Salim Ismail who stated that

    The business world has learned over the last two decades how to scale technology, but now it's time to scale your organization. A new breed of Exponential Organizations - companies that grow at a minimum pace of 10x better than their peers - is delivering a new way of doing business.

    Source: http://www.salimismail.com/

By leveraging new advanced technologies and applying the EXO canvas, business can achieve exponential growth. The Exo canvas builds on the concept of MTP (Massive Transformative Purpose) and can make the acronym SCALE as shown in Figure1.4. An example of exponential organisations and how fast growing they are compared by traditional organisations is shown in Table 1.13.

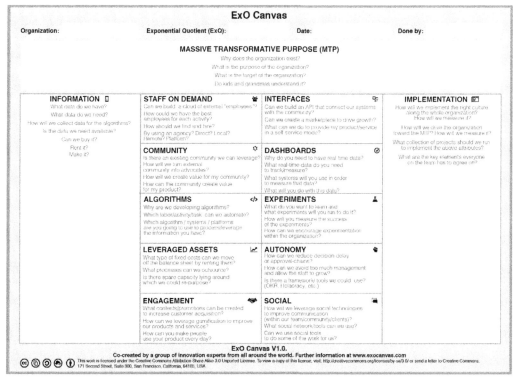

Figure 1.4: The ExO Canvas

- **Sustainable Business Modelling**. Chapter 4 has details of modelling using the business canvas. It delivers a critical review covering the concepts of sustainable business modelling, eco-innovation and Lean startups in a comparative approach.

- **Agile Management.** Chapter 5 has a detailed discussion on Agile method, followed by a case study that guides project managers on how to use the Agile method in the context of sustainable change management.

Company	Age (years)	2011 valuation	2014 valuation	Increase
Haier	30	$19 billion	$60 billion	3x
Valve	18	$1.5 billion	$4.5 billion	3x
Google	17	$150 billion	$400 billion	2.5x
Uber	7	$2 billion	$17 billion	8.5x
Airbnb	6	$2 billion	$10 billion	5x
Github	6	$500 million (est.)	$7 billion	14x
Waze	6	$25 million	$1 billion (in 2013)	50x
Quirky	5	$50 million	$2 billion	40x
Snapchat	3	0	$10 billion	10,000x +

Table 1.13: Examples of exponential organisations

Assurances and control

This last dimension sums up the core processes that are included in the traditional project management methodologies, such the PMBok. As previously mentioned, the call for a new model does not mean scrapping the existing ones but rather building on them and developing to suit the requirements of the new era, the digital transformation, the sharing economy, under the umbrella of sustainability.

Typically managing projects must have a set of assurances and control, as we call them under this model. The assurances are the processes included in the initiation and planning phases of the project in order to ensure its successful delivery. The control includes the processes that are most likely to occur in the execution phase. These include:

- **Scope management:** a clearly defined scope with well identified procedure for managing scope changes
- **Stakeholder management**: A clearly stated and well-defined stakeholder management plan
- **Communication plan – OBS – WBS – TRM:**
    1 A **communication plan** that links team members to the tasks to be delivered stating who communicates with who, why (purpose), how (medium/channel), how often (frequency) and what is the outcome of this communication (actions).
    2 **Organisation Breakdown Structure – OBS** with clear authority, contractual and communication links
    3 **Work Breakdown structure – WBS** as an analytical tool to breakdown the project into activities for more accurate time and cost estimates.
    4 **Task Responsibility Matrix – TRM or RAM** that links the OBS and the WBS thus indicating the responsibility of each member
- **Cost budgeting and control**: this include cost estimating and resource planning during the planning phase. During execution the actual expenditures will

be compared with the planned, applying methods such Earned Value Analysis to generate variances, analyse it and take corrective actions.

- **Schedule planning, monitoring and control**: time scheduling will include estimating activity duration, producing a project master schedule using methods such as CPM or PERT, during the planning phase. During the execution phase, progress will be monitored and corrective actions or catch up plans applied where needed. This can use trade-off analysis such as crashing.

- **Configuration management system**: the need to establish a system during the planning phase to facilitate the smooth management of change if it occurs during the execution phase. The configuration management system refers to the structure and relations within this structure that will manage the change. In brief, this is a simplified version of the OBS tasked with managing the change

- **Risk management system**: this identifies the risk events, and conducts analysis, leading to the appropriate risk responses and the associated risk reserves that should be reflected in the project budget if and when needed.

- **Quality management system**: setting quality objectives based on the set policy. The quality assurance measures are factored into the execution phase and the appropriate quality control measures are used for testing.

- **Project plan review and feedback**: the project plan will document all the above and include feedback to close the loop.

This seems as if we are replicating the traditional approach. The answer is yes, and no. Regardless how developed your IT skills are, you will always need to know now to type and how to use the functions of word processing, Excel sheets, etc. The difference is how you are going to use it and what you are going to do with it. For example, you can type a basic word document, or you can develop a webpage; both needs typing skills. Yet in order to produce a webpage you need additional knowledge and skills on top of the basics, that are indispensable. Similarly, the basic processes of time scheduling and cost budgeting will forever remain building blocks of any project management model. The difference is in the content and the approach: what is included in the budget and how you do the estimating; how the output of the life cycle assessment dimension will feed into the budget. It is the same for a scope management system. Defining the scope of the project will be influenced by the output of other dimensions including the sustainability dimension, the advanced technology and managing innovation.

Maturity

The last row in the model, Maturity, can be an imperative destination rather than a component, if the six components are managed properly, in context. Hence, this row was indicated in a different colour. The SPMM model claims to have embraced the safeguards and the assurances that should yield the desired maturity. This should eliminate the need to have another model, specifically for maturity. However, the need to assess the maturity against the criteria set in the six components will be part of this last row

This is not a rigid stance against maturity models, that are quite popular in the project management literature since the publishing of the Capability Maturity Model for Software (CMM-SW), developed by the Software Engineering Institute at Carnegie Mellon University, Pittsburgh, PA, which stressed that maturity can be expressed by identifying a hierarchy across several capability areas (Humphreys, 1992; Paulk et al., 1993). Other maturity models have since been developed for the assessment of organizations against a range of practices and topics, including strategic management, innovation, contract management, and leadership.

The Project management literature includes an array of maturity models. Many of these have adopted a similar framework to that of the Capability Maturity Model, with five assessed levels of maturity and capability areas across which the practices of each level are described (Mullaly and Thomas, 2010).

Maturity models have attracted criticism in the literature which endorses our stance to deviate from the concept and provide a sustainable alternative as above mentioned. So, we shall save the reader another round of comprehensive literature review stick to the key points in context. Briefly, Mullaly and Thomas (2010) stressed that while maturity models claims to associate improvements in process with the successful delivery of project based on the success criteria (Kwak & Ibbs, 2000), contingency theory suggests that it is necessary to understand both context and structure/process to establish a link with performance. The assessment models used in evaluating maturity yield a long list of strengths and weaknesses yet do not identify specific strategies towards competitive advantage. Add to this the challenge of identifying what implementations are appropriate for a specific context (Mullaly and Thomas, 2010), leaves researchers and practitioners puzzled either to predict or prescribe the factors that will enable the attainment of fit. Moreover, many maturity models are prescriptive and narrowly focussed in nature unlike employing contingency theory whereby organizations can be successful based upon different capabilities, provided that the strategy, structure, and process of that organization is internally and externally consistent. Mullaly and Thomas, (2010) stressed that maturity should ignore the external factors and contingent variables that different organizations encounter in different situations, economies, and environments, as they describe one specific way of managing and presume a universal set of practices that must be adopted by all organizations. Maturity models by their nature are abstractions, and describe a specific place or static representation, ignoring the dynamic nature of fit and the fact that *"sustained competitive advantage is a product of movement and an ability to change than it is of location or position"* (Duncan et al., 1998).

To conclude this section, it is worth noting that the introduced model was developed based on clear theoretical underpinning following the literature review whereby all the included dimensions were identified in the literature as influential, individually, yet were not integrated in a coherent construct to guide the delivery of sustainable projects despite the call for sustainable project management practices that yield sustainable products and services. In addition, the model answers the call by academics and practitioners to improve the practice by laying more emphasis on skills, innovation and sustainability. The following chapters will shed more light on how to apply this model with further elaboration on the knowledge areas and the application of the allied factors, using case studies, with Part Three covering four main sectors as examples of sustainable projects: the construction sector, the logistics and sustainable supply chain, the tourism sector and finally the renewable energy and waste management projects.

Summary

The chapter gave a brief review on the development of project management methodologies, that was followed by a critical review of the literature that covered the concept of sustainability, sustainable development, sustainable project management, and concluded with a detailed review of two studies of the project management research agenda over recent years. The review of the literature provided the underpinning theory that was used in building the SPMM model. The model has six dimensions that when combined make the acronym SALAMA. Each component is broken down into allied factors that guide the design and implementation of sustainable projects that yield sustainable products and services.

A set of case studies that can be a useful learning tool in context, are available at: www.goodfellowpublishers.com/sustprojman.

End of chapter exercises

Only one answer is correct.

1 Sustainable development is:
   a. Achieving as much profit as possible;
   b. Country having high GDP and income per capita;
   c. Development that "meets the needs of the present without compromising the ability of future generations to meet their own needs

2 The common goals of every government today is:
   a. social progress which encompasses community health,
   b. education and inclusion;
   c. protection of the environment, species and their habitat; prudent environmental resource usage and maintenance of economic growth and employment
   d. All of the above.

3 Integrating sustainable development at the operational level may not involve:
   a. production systems to incorporate environmental management systems;
   b. change of people's behaviour;
   c. investment of lot of funds;
   d. adoption of reporting systems that assess, evaluate and monitor the business processes based on the triple bottom line criteria.

4   Sustainability relates primarily to:

    a.   Investment of funds

    b.   Only to ecology

    c.   Only to social aspect of society

    d.   Environmental, social and demographic concerns.

5   A sustainable way of doing business is:

    a.   Having high ROI;

    b.   Owning lots of buildings and land;

    c.   Finding link between company and the wider society including human rights, labour policies, the environment, consumer issues, fair operating practices.

6   Sustainable Project Management is:

    a.   About having sustainable and long term investments,

    b.   Having high profit rates in long run

    c.   Simultaneous and equal consideration of economic, social and environmental goals when delivering products and services.

7   What is sustainable project management?

    a.   Sustainable Project Management is the management of project-organised change in policies, assets or organisations, with consideration of the economic, social and environmental impact of the project, its result and its effect, for now and future generations.

    b.   Sustainable project management is about meeting the time, cost and quality targets for project outputs, and in the same time on increasing the impact of the project to stakeholders and community.

    c.   Both a and b.

8   The evolution of sustainable development can be followed through three periods (i) the period before the International Conference on the Human Environment, (ii) the period from the above conference to the Report "Our Common future" and (iii) the period after the Report.

    a.   True

    b.   False

References

Artto, K., Martinsuo, M., Gemünden, H.G., Murtoaro, J., (2009). Foundations of program management: A bibliometric view. *International Journal of Project Management, 27* (1),

Association for Project Management. (2006). 'APM supports sustainability outlooks'. Available from: http://www.apm.org.uk/page.asp?categoryID=4.

Barbier, E. (1987). The concept of sustainable economic development. *Environmental Conservation* **14** (2), 101–110.

Briassoulis, H. (2001). Sustainable development and its indicators: Through a (planner's) glass darkly. *Journal of Environmental Planning and Management* **44** (3), 27–409

Dyllick, T; Hockerts, K. (2002). Beyond the business case for corporate sustainability'. *Business Strategy and the Environment* **11**, 130–141.

Elkington, J. (1997). *Cannibals with Forks: The Triple Bottom Line of 21st Century Business.* Oxford: Capstone Publishing Ltd.

Ferreira, D., Costa, F., Alonso, F., Alves, P. and Nunes, T. (2005). *SCRUM An Agile Model for Software Project Management.* https://paginas.fe.up.pt/~aaguiar/es/artigos%20finais/es_final_19.pdf

Gareis, R; Huemann, M; Martinuzzi, A. (2009). *Relating Sustainable Development and Project Management.* Berlin: IRNOP IX.

Holliday C. (2001). Sustainable growth, the DuPont way. *Harvard Business Review* September: 129–134.

International Institute for Sustainable Development (IISD). (2010). Accessed September 2010. Available from: http://www.iisd.org/sd/

International Project Management Association. (2006). *IPMA Competence Baseline version 3.0.* Nijkerk, the Netherlands: IPMA,

Kwak, Y. H., & Ibbs, C. W. (2000). Calculating project management's return on investment. *Project Management Journal,* **31**(2), 38.

Kwak, Y.H., Anbari, F.T., (2009). Analyzing project management research: perspectives from top management journals. *International Journal of Project Management, 27* (5), 435–446.

Labuschagne, C; Brent, A C. 2006. 'Social indicators for sustainable project and technology life cycle management in the process industry'. *International Journal of Life Cycle Assessment* **11** (1), 3–15.

Moneva, J M; Archel, P; Correa, C. 2006. GRI and the camouflaging of corporate sustainability. *Accounting Forum* **30**, 121–137.

Mullaly, M. E. & Thomas, J. (2010). Re-thinking project management maturity: perspectives gained from explorations of fit and value. Paper presented at PMI® Research Conference: Defining the Future of Project Management, Washington, DC. Newtown Square, PA: Project Management Institute.

Nerur, S., Mahapatra, R. and Mangalaraj, G. (2005) Challenges of migrating to agile methodologies, *Communications of the ACM* (May) 72–78.

OECD. 1990. *Issues papers: On Integrating Environment and Economics.* Paris: OECD.

Padalkar, M and Gopinath, S (2016). Six decades of project management research: Thematic trends and future opportunities. *International Journal of Project Management, 34* 1305–1321

Peterson, K. and Wohlin, C. (2009) *A Comparison of Issues and Advantages in Agile and Incremental Development between State of the Art and an Industrial Case.* Journal of System and Software.

Pope, J; Annandale, D; Morris-Saunders, A. (2004). Conceptualising sustainable assessment. *Environmental Impact Assessment Review, 24*: 595–616.

Project Management Institute. (2008). *A Guide to Project Management Body of Knowledge (PMBOK Guide)*. 4th edn. Newtown Square, PA USA: Project Management Institute.

Russell, J. (2008) Corporate social responsibility: What it means for the project manager. In *Proceedings of PMI Europe Congress*, Malta, Philadelphia, PA: Project Management Institute

Sawaf, A. and Gabrielle, R. (2014). *Sacred Commerce: A Blueprint for a New Humanity* (2nd Edition). EQ Enterprises. pp. 24–28.

Shenhar, A.J. and Dvir, D., (2007). Project management research-the challenge and opportunity. *Project Management Journal*, **38**(2), 93.

Silvius, A. J. G. and Batenburg, R. (2009). Future development of project management competences. Paper presented at the 42nd Hawaii International Conference on Systems Science (HICSS), Waikoloa HI, January.

Silvius, A. J. G., Brink, J. van der and Köhler, A. (2009). Views on sustainable project management. In *Human Side of Projects in Modern Business*, edited by Kähköhnen, K., Kazi, A. S. and Rekola, M. Helsinki, Finland: IPMA Scientific Research Paper Series.

Silvius, A. J. G., Brink, J. van der and Köhler, A. (2010). The concept of sustainability and its application to project management. Paper presented at IPMA Expert Seminar Survival and Sustainability as Challenges for Projects, Zurich.

Stoica, M., Mircea, M. and Ghilic-Micu, B. (2013). Software Development: Agile vs. Traditional. *Informatica Economică*. 17 (4), 64-74.

Taylor, T. (2008). *A Sustainability Checklist for Managers of Projects*. Available from: http://www.pmforum.org/library/papers/2008/PDFs/Taylor-1-08.pdf.

Top 10 fighters (2017) https://www.aviationcv.com/aviation-blog/2017/top-10-fighter-jets-world-2017

Turner, R. and Huemann, M. (2010). Responsibilities for sustainable development in project and program management. IPMA Expert Seminar Survival and Sustainability as Challenges for Projects, Zurich.

World Commission on Environment and Development. (1987). *Our Common Future*. Great Britain: Oxford University Press.

Answer to exercises

1 c

2 d

3 c

4 d

5 c

6 c

7d

8 a

Self-Organising and Virtual Teams:
Culture, Emotional Intelligence, Trust and Communication

Mohamed Salama and Maria Mataj

Learning Outcomes

Upon the completion of this chapter, the reader will be able to:

- Compare the different types of project teams.

- Discuss how self-organising teams operate within agile projects management methodologies.

- Discuss the factors that impact virtual teams in project context.

- Understand the relationship between culture, emotion intelligence and virtual teams' performance.

- Evaluate the impact of trust and communication on a virtual team's success.

Introduction

Amid the shift towards digital economies in the context of globalisation, project team members are required to work together remotely, utilising the current highly accessible technology (Han and Beyerlein, 2016). Virtual teams are growing rapidly in today's world as companies are being involved in a constant fight for existence, due to the very vibrant and continuous competition which makes organizations emerge in different countries. Being a global organisation involves synchronization among people situated in diverse geographical areas, thus there arises the necessity for managing global virtual teams, assigned to resolve issues at a global level (Paul et al., 2016).

The existence of a variety of technologies allows companies to have access to a large pool of talented people located all over the world, as it reduces costs and facilitates cooperation among different locations and time zones (Paul et al., 2016). According to Hertel et al. (2005), the allocation of work among employees has become more efficient due to the evolvement of technology.

Consequently, for international companies to collaborate with each other and to have high performing virtual teams, there has been a need to consider the impact of cultural diversity on virtual teams' practices and performance (Han and Beyerlein, 2016). This discussion should also include self-organising teams in the context of agile methodologies and beyond. In addition, studies have been focusing on how emotional intelligence impacts teams and groups (Wolff et al., 2001). However, limited research has been conducted on how culture and emotional intelligence impact virtual team performance in the context of project management.

This chapter aims to discuss the critical area of managing project teams with emphasis on the relationship between culture, communication, emotional intelligence and trust in self-organising and virtual teams, and how the interaction between these factors impact team performance. This attempts to answer the call by the sixth edition of the *PMI PMBOK* that emphasised the importance of developing the soft skills of project managers in the pursuit of enhancing project management practice amid the growing interest in sustainability in general. In addition, this endorses and further justifies the suggested paradigm shift that the authors advocate, in pursuit of sustainable project management.

Definition of a team

A 'team' can be defined as a group of people highly task oriented compared to other groups, which follow certain rules and rewards set at the very beginning. Over the years, both the terms 'group' and 'team' have been utilized to depict little collections of individuals working together. Even though these terms have been regularly utilized in traditional and virtual teams, recently there has been questioning whether it makes sense to interchange the terms (Powell et. al., 2004). Many authors recommend that the usage of the term 'team' be saved for those gatherings that show abnormal amounts of interdependency and coordination among individuals.

A generally acknowledged definition of a team is: "A team is a gathering of people who are associated in their undertakings, who share obligation regarding results, who see themselves and who are seen by others as a complete social substance installed in at least one bigger social frameworks, and who deal with their relationship crosswise over hierarchical limits" (Bailey and Cohen, 1997, p. 241, cited in Tirmizi, 2008).

This definition is sufficiently general to be applicable to both traditional and virtual teams while explicitly recognizing the characterizing components of a team: its solidarity of reason, its way of life as a social structure, and its individuals' shared duty regarding results.

Katzenbach and Smith (1993) make a distinction between teams and groups as shown in Table 2.1; looking at leadership, reliability, meeting procedures and productivity. Nonetheless, by observing these distinctions – for instance, the third point on 'a specific purpose' – it can easily be argued that any collective of people is considerate about the organization's goals and purpose. Having said that, since groups and team members are part of an organization they can't be isolated from the organizations' mission, hence why this point is applicable to both parties.

Table 2.1: Differences between teams and groups (Source: Katzenbach and Smith, 1993; adapted from Mataj, 2017)

Teams	Groups
Shared leadership	Strong, clearly focused leader
Individual and mutual accountability	Individual accountability
A specific purpose that the team itself delivers	Purpose is the same as the larger organizational mission
Collective work products	Individual work products
Open-ended discussion and active problem solving in meetings	Focus on efficiency in meetings

Types of teams

Teams can be categorized in six different types: formal teams, informal teams, task forces, committees, self-managed teams and virtual teams (Tirmizi, 2008). These types, despite their unique characteristics, share a few common attributes.

■ **Formal teams** are seen as the fundamental blocks of an organization. Their organizational structure is very firm as team members are assigned distinct roles which contribute to the fair allocation of workload amongst them. These kinds of teams might be set up to facilitate the completion of tasks that the company intends to accomplish within a particular timeframe. There is high dependency amongst the team members and it is their performance that determines the success of the team.

■ **Informal teams** are formed to resolve issues that the company is facing. Their roles are usually flexible and can change, based on the different tasks that are being presented to them. Informal team members, unlike formal teams, have a low dependency amongst them and the organizational structure is not as firm.

■ **Task forces** are usually created when there is a need for particular projects and the company itself tends to manage them. Team members have high dependency on each other, as there is pressure on their performance and sticking to the timelines set by the organization.

■ **A committee** is made of a group of people that are asked to execute a task that could be a strategy, finalizing a decision etc. This sort of team has resemblances with the task forces team as it focuses on project delivery within a definite timeframe. Committees' members can have a mixture of dependency degrees amongst themselves and also different levels of independency towards the organization's members.

- **Self-managed teams** have high level of independence from the company and are highly focused on performance. Self-managed teams have a mixture of characteristics from both informal and formal teams. In self-managed teams the majority of decisions are made by the whole group, keeping in mind the end goal that needs to be achieved.

- In the project management world, particularly in agile methodologies a new type, known as **Scrum teams** and **self-organised teams**, also known as **self-organising teams** have been frequently adopted in the last years.

Scrum teams

Scrum is the most common development framework that applies agile methodologies and helps to enhance efficiency, productivity and work quality of teams. It is a framework where people can concentrate on complicated and adaptive issues while focusing on delivering products creatively and productively. Scrum has established itself to be one of the more accepted process frameworks that are practical for agile principles, and development teams have discovered success in using agile even for hardware development. Collaborative projects are carried out by teams in the software development process and approaches that can balance flexibility and control, hence, agile approaches were created (Backblaze, 2015; Schwaber and Sutherland, 2014)

The Scrum team consists of a Product owner, a Scrum master and the Scrum team. These types of teams are usually self-organizing and they decide the best way to complete their work, rather than being directed by an external source, as they possess all the requirements and knowledge needed to complete the work without relying on anyone else. The Scrum team model is designed in such a way that it helps boost productivity, creativity and flexibility. Usually a Scrum team has five to seven members and when there are twelve or more, they are split into smaller Scrums, and in this way they communicate and work independently during the project duration (D'Souza, 2016)

The Scrum team members work together collaboratively. The team and their contributions are as follows: (Schwaber and Sutherland, 2014; Schwaber, 2009).

1 The **product owner** is the product champion. Their focus revolves around understanding the business and requirements of the market. The owners manage and build the product backlog and ensure that the team members understand the items on the log. They give the team guidance on what to deliver and when to ship the product towards fast delivery. However, the owners do not manage the status of the program and focus on making certain that the team delivers the best value.

2 **Scrum master** are accountable for ensuring that the team members comprehend the process of Scrum. They are referred to as the champions of the team and do their part to act as a coach to the team, the product owner and the business. The Scrum master should understand the team members; the work the team does and help in the optimization of delivery flow.

3 The **Scrum team** involves knowledgeable professionals who work to deliver a good product at the end of a sprint. They are composed of empowered individuals who self-organize and manage their own work. Scrum teams are most efficient when they have five to seven members. They estimate the work they think they can finish over iterations and they steer the plan for each sprint.

Self-organizing teams

Scrum teams are usually self-organizing and composed of people who can manage their own work, collaborate amongst each other and make decisions together (Chow and Cao, 2008; Schwaber, 2009). These teams tend to meet new tests and challenges and manage their work based on the task details given. They usually need to have a common goal, trust and respect amongst each other and high levels of collaboration to be effective. Self-management assists in increasing rapidity and problem-solving precision, because decision-making ability is brought to the operational level (Cockburn and Highsmith, 2001; Sharp and Robinson, 2008; Larsen, 2004). Table 2.2 illustrates the elements of self-organizing teams:

Table 2.2: Elements of self-organizing teams (Source: Chow and Cao, 2008; Schwaber, 2009; Cockburn, and Highsmith, 2001; Sharp and Robinson, 2008; Dirks and Ferrin, 2001; Larsen, 2004; adapted from D'Souza, 2016).

Element	Description
Competence	Competence is required of people in self-organising teams as the process is rather complex and rapidly changing.
Communication	If the team members are communicative then they could explain their concerns to each other and work accordingly which would pave the way to success.
Collaboration	A collaborative culture is a key to success as team work would be supported.
Motivation	Team members who are motivated will always work to the best of their abilities.
Respect and Trust	Fellow team members should be able to trust and respect each other in order to grow and help solve any issues that may arise.
Continuity/ Employee Engagement	Continuity is the key and team members need to work together for a good duration of time and be able to engage each other and encourage one another as well, which in turn builds a good working environment.

Challenges for self-organizing teams

Scholars who studied self organizing teams have identified a number of challenges that face these team. The main challenges have been collated from the literature and are presented in detail in Table 2.3.

Table 2.3: Challenges of self-organizing teams (Source: Schwaber and Sutherland, 2014; Cockburn and Highsmith, 2001; Sharp and Robinson, 2008; Larsen, 2004; collated by D'Souza, 2016).

Challenges	Description
Inertia in the team	As time goes by, challenges may start arising for the team to tackle, and this could result in the team falling back on old working methods, even if initially the teams are enthusiastic about the adoption of agile methodologies. This could result in situations worse than before if not tackled properly.
Clash of personalities	In a self-organizing team, the team needs to manage itself and since people have different personalities, sometimes they are incompatible. To be successful, team members need to work on being able to communicate and collaborate to deliver.
Stakeholders changing their minds.	In traditional methods, changes could be made but Scrum does not work this way, which can lead to disagreements unless proactive steps are taken. It can be hard for stakeholders to understand and put into practice this new method of working.
The shifting process	Scrum gives more free will to team members and since there is no such role in traditional methods, this can be a huge shift for the Scrum master and those involved as well. Any mistakes by this person can have grave outcomes so it is also important that others comprehend and regulate their communication with him/her.
Scattered team (geo-graphically)	Some teams work from different locations in the world and decreased contact and communication could be a problem. Though technology helps to a certain extent, it is not the same as face to face communication and this could become a hindrance.
Measurement and Status report reduc-tions	Usually status reports and measurements would help illuminate the team and were the source of information through which they could monitor progress and decide what actions to take next and. However, sometimes information can be received in an up-to-date method but old methods are used, and this can lead to frustration if information is not properly received.
Efficiency Drop	Scrum can be time consuming and since participation of the team is vital, this could lead to a decrease in the productivity of individuals and involvement.
Lack of indi-vidual answer-ability	The Scrum master's role is very restricted in terms of answerability. The team works together and they are usually the ones that can be held accountable but since there is no real way of having one person responsible, any mistakes could result into hindrances towards the entire success of the project.

Success factors and key performance indicators of self-organizing teams

It is imperative for the effective management of teams in general and self-organising teams in particular to identify the critical success factors as well as the key performance indicators (KPIs / success criteria). A list of the critical success factors with detailed description as well as the corresponding KPIs are collated from the literature and presented in Table 2.4.

Table 2.4: Success factors and Key Performance Indicators of self-organizing teams (Source: (Wageman, 2001; Chow and Cao, 2008; Schwaber, 2009; Cockburn, and Highsmith, 2001; Sharp and Robinson, 2008; Dirks and Ferrin, 2001; Larsen, 2004; collated by D'Souza 2016).

Success factors	Description	Key Performance Indicators (KPIs)
Clear, engaging direction	The most effective teams have clear direction of where they are going. This is the best way to increase motivation for the team that leads to higher productivity.	Clear direction Increase in revenue Improved cycle time Improved relationship with customers
A real team task	A self-organizing team needs teamwork and the time spent as a team aids in motivation, and collaboration leading to team efficiency.	Regular meetings Destruction conflict Happy team Higher team spirit Respect for fellow team members
Rewards for team excellence	When team rewards are given, it acts as an incentive and is linked to higher level team self-management.	Lower absenteeism Lower turnover
Basic material resources	The tools the team requires such as meeting space, computers and other resources so that the team can work in an valuable way. Teams that have all the resources they need are more operational that teams that do not.	Increase of individuals' input and contribution to team output.
Authority to manage work	Self-organizing teams by their name itself, are able to self-manage themselves and have the right to make decisions regarding strategy as well.	Respect for the coach/Scrum master Higher levels of collaboration with fellow members Greater ability to make decisions independently
Smart goals	This is important and the team should have goals that are linked to the objectives of the organization.	Clear quantifiable goals completed on time
Team norms that promote strategic thinking	Norms steer the behaviour of the team members. Self-managing teams need to be focused and aware of the environment and team effectiveness is associated with members that are encouraged to try new creative ways to work.	Reduced time needed to respond to change requests.

Team size

Usually a Scrum team has five to seven members, and when there are twelve or more, they are split into smaller Scrums and thus they communicate and work independently during the project duration. Team size is important in the context of self-organizing teams, because it is essential that the team is small enough to stay agile and large enough to complete the work required. Teams that are too small have decreased amounts of communication and interaction which result in less productivity and efficiency, and teams that are too large become too complex to handle and manage.

Agile methodologies are people-focused and there is a further obligation to understand how the size of the teams could affect the behavior of individuals, and affect efficiency and effectiveness. This brings about the question of what factors need consideration in order to manage self-organizing teams to make them effective and increase performance and productivity? (Schwaber and Sutherland, 2014; Bustamante and Sawhney, 2011). Research indicates that team size could have a direct impact on communication and performance, which are two very important factors. A lot of the time, more emphasis is given to the projects rather than people and they may not be working up to their optimum potential.

One of the main reasons projects can face problems is because of lack of communication and the larger the team, communication lines tend to slowly break down. Individuals also have different personalities and are just expected to work together a team. Emphasis should be put on collaboration and team members need to feel empowered and motivated by the leader, as team productivity and increased performance is dependent on the communication and collaboration between members (Abilla, 2006).

Application of Scrum to other teams

The Agile framework can be adopted by organizations that control complex process in order to make the process more flexible and quicker. Figures 2.1 and 2.2 illustrate the work process of virtual teams, event management teams and interior design and renovation teams:

Figure 2.1: Event management team process (Source: Cotter, 2014).

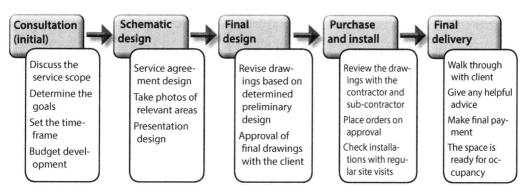

Figure 2.2: Interior design and renovation team process.

Leadership

In this section, the traditional schools of leadership will be presented and discussed. This will then be compared and contrasted with the new emerging adaptive leadership school of thought, towards sustainable project management, in the next chapter of this textbook.

Many academic studies have shown that good leadership is required to direct the team towards success. (Thite, 2000; Barber and Warn, 2005). Leaders that are able to motivate their teams have a higher tendency to be more successful and the same goes for leadership in self-organizing teams. Although the name suggests that these types of teams are without a leader and are uncontrolled, leadership is certainly required in any type of organization or team. (Cockburn and Highsmith, 2001). Table 2.5 illustrates the different styles of leadership:

Table 2.5: Different styles of leadership (collated from Cribari, 2013; Cockburn and Highsmith, 2001; Thite, 2000; Barber and Warn, 2005).

Style of leadership	Description
Directive style	These leaders are always in command and obvious about getting things done through their team members. Arguments or suggestions from the team upset them. New or inexperienced staff do not mind this style.
Coaching or Mentoring style	These leaders usually adopt a style that is more open as they request for suggestions and ideas but in the end decide with their own instincts while guiding staff under close supervision.
Supportive style	These leaders make it a routine for the team to make daily decisions supporting them for this kind of approach while monitoring them closely.
Delegating style	These leaders allow decisions from the team within boundaries set by them while supporting them with their availability and monitoring them.

The road to great leadership shares five common elements that are illustrated in Table 2.6:

Table 2.6: Common elements for great leadership (collated from ((Cribari, 2013; Cockburn and Highsmith, 2001; Thite, 2000; Barber and Warn, 2005).

Element	Description
Testing the process	The initial step would be to locate the process that needs to be improved.
Motivating the team to share a vision	Explaining the vision and making sure it is understood by followers.
Inspiring others to act	Allowing for problem solving through necessary tools and methods.
Leading the way	Leading the change the leader wishes to see.
Being an encouragement	Encouraging and motivating the followers by sharing the successes as well as failures.
Getting the work done	Through commitment, hard work, will power and flexibility.

Transformational leadership

Agile methods requires a leader who acts on building trust, is supportive of the team's decisions, and is facilitating and motivating, rather than just a leader who focuses on planning, control, direction and management. This allows for a more transformational type of leadership when leading agile software development projects, and can be rather appealing to describe, as this style of leadership is supposed to be adaptive and the leader needs to continuously provide feedback and sensitive direction. (Augustine et al., 2005; Anderson et al., 2003; Chau and Maurer, 2004).

A Scrum master is believed to be a transformational leader due to the skills of motivation, encouragement and coaching. Feedback from the Scrum master helps motivate and speed up high levels of performance and this approach is vital in creating a successful working environment (Cribari, 2013). Transformational leaders are usually given the managerial positions in companies that are in the process of adopting Scrum. This type of leader is captivating and a visionary who uses his/her knowledge and expertise to serve as a coach and mentor. The Scrum master plays an important role, which includes allowing the self-organizing team to take care of the tasks and perform themselves. (Hoda et al., 2010).

Transformational leadership consists of the following attributes which are:

■ Idealized influence
■ Inspirational motivation
■ Intellectual stimulation
■ Individualized consideration

Table 2.7 shows the similarities between a Scrum master and a transformational leader: (Schwaber and Sutherland, 2014; Larsen, 2004; White, 2002).

Table 2.7: Similarities between transformational leaders and Scrum masters

	Transformational Leaders	Scrum Master
Idealized influence	Strong role models to their followers and have high standards of moral and ethical conduct.	Act as coaches and advisors and assist team members in the Scrum environment.
Inspirational motivation	Motivate individuals and empower their team, and communicate high expectations.	Empower and motivate the team members during the adoption of Scrum.
Intellectual stimulation	Push their followers to be creative and innovative and to challenge their beliefs.	Help the team members to be creative and to create good products.
Individualized consideration	Provide a supportive climate where the leader listens to the needs of the team members. They coach and mentor them and help them grow and achieve more.	Assist the team to understand Scrum and listen to their concerns regarding the process.
Extraversion	These types of leaders are usually extroverted and are social.	An extroverted personality is important, along with assertiveness, because they need to ensure that the team is working and delivering the result.
Neuroticism	This is a negative trait related to anxiety issues and a person like this is likely to shrink away from transformational leadership responsibilities.	The Scrum master cannot be vulnerable as the complex process calls for resiliance. He/she needs to be stable and confident while addressing the tasks at hand.
Openness to experience	Open to creative expression and innovativeness. This trait can help a transformational leader build vision and see the bigger picture.	This trait is important for a Scrum master who needs to be open to ideas proposed. This is vital as the client can change their minds in the agile process and the Scrum master should be able to cope with that.
Agreeableness	The transformational leader requires charisma and should be able to influence the team and these qualities are the abilities of people who possess agreeableness.	Altruism is an important trait for as it helps in the motivation of the team. When the Scrum master is able to influence the team and looks after their well being that helps to build a good working atmosphere.
Conscientiousness	A transformational leader needs to be conscientious and possess a good sense of direction in order to lead the way and act as a strong role model to the team.	For the Scrum Master, this trait is seen as highly relevant because achievement is closely followed by self-discipline which is required to lead a self organising team in an agile process.

Despite this categorization of teams, a specific sort of virtual group that has received huge research consideration is the **global virtual group**, recognized in light of the fact that it draws individuals who work and live in various nations and are socially different (Powell et al., 2004).

Virtual teams

Virtual teams are defined as a group of employees scattered geographically within same or different time zones, and united by data and technology advancements to fulfil a company's undertakings (Powell et al., 2004).

Geister S. and Hertel G (2006) define virtual teams as two or more individuals interacting from diverse geographical locations, working together towards a common goal, hence communicating through technology.

Virtual teams are usually brought together on a need basis to collaborate on particular expectations, or to satisfy particular client needs. Key elements of virtual groups are their dominant dependence on IT to speak with each other, their agile structure, and their capacity, if needed, to negotiate traditional organizational limits. Virtual teams are usually created to meet specific needs and, more often than not, they are temporary (Powell et al., 2004). This is not always a feature of the virtual teams, but instead is a result of what they usually serve for.

Tirmizi (2008) provides another definition, describing virtual teams as teams that are created mainly electronically with a minor face to face interactions. In contrast to self-managed teams, members in virtual teams are less independent, however they still possess a high level of self-governance. Also, in comparison to formal and self-managed teams, virtual teams' members tend to be less reliant on each other because of the different virtual correspondences and the assortment of associations that can be included. Globalization and wide access to different means of technologies facilitating communication among virtual team members has led to a growth of virtual teams and organizations (cited inTirmizi, 2008).

Advantages of virtual teams

- Allow flexible hours so employees can invest more time with their families. This leads to people being happy, thus having a positive impact on their performance.
- Support cross-functional and cross-divisional interaction.
- Reduce travelling cost and time to and from work. If the number of people travelling to work everyday decreases, it directly reduces pollution.
- Benefit individuals who could not be part of traditional teams, like people with physical challenges, to become vital members of organizations working mainly via telecommunications.
- There is a less need for big offices space and parking spaces. It also results in reduction of utility bills.
- Successful team membership makes location less important, by enabling companies worldwide to hire and retain employees.

Disadvantages of virtual teams

- Communication among members of virtual teams tends to be challenging, leading to communication breakdowns. Therefore, members need to have linguistic accuracy in their communication since they cannot use any expressive gestures.

- Technophobia – a significant number of individuals are still uncomfortable with using technology.

- Working in virtual teams leads to being part of more than one team and that can create a stressful working environment. That is why it is important for companies to not overstretch members of virtual teams.

Culture

Culture is a universal concept that represents the social behaviour and norms of human societies. Looking at its broad ethnographic sense is quite perplexing as it incorporates knowledge, norms, arts, beliefs and habits acquired by individuals; being part of a particular society with the intention to shape the history of the future Culture has evolved significantly throughout the years and it has been viewed and defined differently by many authors.

Hofstede's (2011, p. 3) definition of culture is:

" *the collective programming of the mind that distinguishes the members of one group or category of people from others*".

According to Hofstede (2011), culture is not inherited but is learned, and it originates from an individual's social environment not from his/her genes.

Organizational culture – which is different from the individual culture of employees – plays an important role in the overall performance of a company, where it doesn't only facilitate the employees' daily objectives, but also helps companies to adjust fast enough to keep up with on-going external changes (Zieba and Schivinski, 2015). Organizational culture is an essential component of business competency that should be aligned with the strategic objectives, and contribute to the improvement of employees' behaviours, perceptions and emotions in order to adapt to the external environments. One of the most popular definition of organizational culture is by Schein (1990, p.16) who describes it as:

"a pattern of basic assumptions invented, discovered and developed by a given group as it learns to cope with its problems of external adaptation and internal integration that has worked well enough to be considered valid and is therefore taught to new members as the correct way to perceive, think about, and feel in relation to those problems."

Organizational culture indirectly has an impact on a company's performance by affecting the behaviour of its employees, resulting in automatically influencing the leaders' behaviours and also leading to the assumption that there is a strong linkage between culture and leadership. It is a dual assumption, where it is believed that leaders contribute to shaping cultural identity, and organizational culture contributes to shaping leaders' behaviour.

Emotional intelligence (EI)

Emotional intelligence (EI) is defined as the ability of certain individuals to process high level information about emotions and then apply this sort of information as a guide to shaping their thinking process and behaviour (Mayer et al., 2008). However, from the time when this concept was first presented, there has been a division in the areas that researchers were focusing on. A group of researchers were looking at EI as mental abilities, and some others were looking at constructive traits like contentment, optimism and self-confidence. Salovey and Mayer (1990) define EI as a person's ability to identify their emotions and be able to manage and comprehend those sentiments, keeping in mind the end goal to intellectual and emotional development. They also define EI as the process of making sensible decisions by employing intuition and logic.

The idea of EI has an extraordinary potential to create positive change. If people are able to build up their own EI, it will directly have a positive impact on their efficiency at work, as everything required for team performance, management and culture commences within a person's feelings. Emotional intelligence has historically been viewed as two opposing or non-complimentary ideas. People used to think that emotions would disrupt them from accomplishing their goals; the thought of being intelligent about the emotional side of life did not make sense. However, the concept of EI implied a completely different view where emotions play a crucial role in adapting to intellectual practices.

EI is a result of psychological research that has developed over more than forty years. This research was mainly dedicated to two areas. The first was focused in understanding how emotional processes (such as happiness, anger, fear, mood swings) play a role in improving the thinking process, and the second was based on the development of models of EI.

The Mayer and Salovey model of emotional intelligence (1997)

This model of EI developed by Mayer and Salovey (1997) describes four distinct mental capabilities, which are as below:

- Perception of emotion
- Utilization of emotion to encourage thought
- Comprehension of emotion
- Management of emotion

These four capabilities are organized progressively with the end goal that more fundamental mental procedures, like understanding emotions, are at the roots of the model and the more developed ones, like the intelligent control of emotions, are at the higher level.

Perception of emotion – The essential aspect of this is about being able to understand emotions by understanding body expressions and people's way of thinking. The more complicated aspect includes the ability to identify emotions in individuals by using colours, languages, appearances and behaviour.

Utilization of emotion to encourage thought – This is the exploitation of emotions to enable intellectual activities like problem solving, interpersonal communication and logical thinking, mainly by looking at the external environment and people's behaviour. This helps in producing emotions that encourage better judgment, and foster different moods, which help in dealing with different situations.

Comprehension of emotion – This involves understanding the importance of emotions and their root causes. It is linked to being able to understand where different sort of emotions, like sadness, happiness and anger, derive from. For instance, happiness can result from accomplishing a goal, or sadness as a consequence of a loss of an opportunity. There is also a focus in understanding a mix of feelings taking over an individual at the same time.

Management of emotion – This includes being able to control the emotions by reducing, avoiding or adjusting an emotional response. The very basis of this element requires one individual to accept both pleasant and unpleasant feelings; while the more evolved capability involves being able to connect or disconnect from emotions depending on the situation.

Advantages of emotional intelligence

Many advantages of EI have been identified and they are listed below (Salovey and Mayer, 1990; Druskat and Wolff, 2001):

- Development of leadership
- Improved communication
- Enhanced conflict management
- Enhanced team performance (output)
- Better decision making and problem-solving abilities
- Improved negotiations Skills

Downey, Roberts and Stough, (2011) have identified the incentives of EI. They are:

- **Emotionality:** The noticeable behavioural and physical component of emotion. It is the result of an individual's emotional response to a stimulus. Other people can see the majority of these reactions, however sometimes they can only be observed by the individual undergoing this feeling.
- **Sociability:** The ability of individuals to build social relationships, which helps in boosting their confidence.
- **Well-being:** The positive state of mind of an individual, which includes them being happy and fulfilled.
- **Self-control:** The power of being able to control one's needs by having the capability to control emotions and the level of stress.

Disadvantages of emotional intelligence

However, EI it is exposed to some limitations and those would be (Brackett, Rivers and Salovey, 2011; Goleman, 1998):

- **Ambiguity about an individual's values and competences** – If an individual lacks confidence it will lead to experiencing personal insecurities and directly having a negative impact on their job performance.

- **Deficiency of self-discipline** – If people are lacking self-control they will not be able to motivate and manage themselves.

- **Inability to adapt** – People need to be flexible and adapt to the environments they are part of. We live in a fast-moving world where changes are applied on a daily basis, hence why individuals need to be agile.

- **Mental health and well-being** – The right management of EI supports people in being aware of their emotions and hence being healthier. Once people are able to identify and manage accordingly their emotions, they will succeed in having a healthy mind and body, thus low risks of suffering from anxiety and depression.

- **Lack of reliability/trustworthiness** – Lack of reliability is a negative characteristic, as it will lead to people not taking responsibility for their own actions, not confessing their mistakes, lying and hence causing unethical behaviours.

- **Lack of initiative** – This includes people lacking motivation in getting involved in problem solving or challenging themselves by jumping into the unknown.

- **Absence of achievement focus** – This describes people's inability to motivate themselves in order to fulfil their goals and objectives. This usually happens when people don't have a clear goal and when they lack focus on accomplishing their ambitions and dreams.

Relationship between culture, communication, EI and trust in virtual team performance

Cultural adaptation in virtual teams

Chang, Chuang and Chao (2011) explain how cultural adaptation impacts people's perceptions on similarity, hence affecting their interpersonal attraction. This is described through the theory of similarity and attraction, which explains how individuals are more attracted to and influenced by people who are similar to them in terms of demographic characteristics.

Virtual teams are a clear example of teams that would be highly unlikely to work together if they were to be put under traditional circumstances. Cultural differences that exist among these teams can be the cause of a prolonged 'storming' phase. These cultural differences are reflected in the way people communicate between each other, their problem solving approaches, work ethics and their overall behavioural attitudes. Many organizations provide some cultural training workshops with the intention of overcoming these cultural challenges and helping multicultural teams to work more effectively. Chang et al. (2011) define cultural adaptation as "a dynamic procedure between the virtual team where changes are anticipated to fit the practices, norms and conduct of another culture". The first step for such adjustment is being able to comprehend the culture of fellow team members. Operating and working with members from different cultures necessitates the comprehension of cultural differences in that particular environment. Keeping in mind the end goal of having a great collaboration, will require team members to make changes in order to adapt to each other's ways of behaving. The other step of cultural adaptation happens when one party tries to gain as much from the other party by incorporating components of the other culture into their own (Lin, 2004).

Communication quality in virtual teams

Chang et al. (2011) place a lot of emphasis on the importance of efficient communications and the distribution of knowledge between team members. The elements of communication present in face-to-face teams and virtual teams are very similar. It is crucial for virtual teams to have leaders that enable communication among the members, and to ensure that no one is having problems in meeting their timelines due to poor communication or misunderstandings (Chang et al., 2012). Also, virtual teams tend to have better performance when there are efficient communication channels in place, including different sort of technologies that enhance communication among members. Poor communication among team members will lead not only to conflicts but also impact the timeline of delivering the projects. Good communication will result in high performing teams, and will enhance employees working closely and reducing gaps in their understanding. There is a lot of discussion as to whether face-to-face communication is needed in virtual teams, however the ability to communicate through different tools has reduced the need for communicating in person and still allows teams accomplish great results (D'Souza, 2016).

Emotional intelligence and good communication go hand in hand and work towards effectiveness of teams. Interpersonal relationships, communication skills and emotional intelligence are vital for success of teams and leadership.

Communication involves (Eriguc and Kose, 2013):

- setting relationships with meaning,
- being aware of ones own feelings,
- regulating ones own feelings
- empathy.

The abilities of individuals to communicate can help with their success at their workplaces and personal lives (Can et al., 2006). Communication skills are the basic requirement for members in any organization, and managers require this ability to express themselves and their ideas and notions to the rest of the team without hesitation (Whitworth, 2006).

Trust in virtual teams

In order for virtual teams to perform collaboratively, a high level of trust is needed amongst their members. Developing relationships that are based on strong trust is very essential, not only in virtual teams but in any other sort of involvement with human beings (Chang et al., 2011). Trust will enable team growth and productivity as well.

According to Gurung and Prater (2006), trust is defined as one of the key elements that leads to the success of virtual teams; on the contrary, if there are trust issues among members of a team, the communication of information will be interrupted and lead to many disagreements. Lack of trust will also lead to the failure of virtual teams, hence why strong relationships built on trust permit individuals to participate in risk related activities that cannot be controlled (Daim et al., 2011). Interpersonal trust is recognized as an important factor for improved team performance. Trust in leaders helps in productivity, in results, and in the quality of communication, and problem-solving improves as well. (Dirks and Ferrin, 2001; Dirks, 1999, 2000). Trust has impact on leadership, and employees that trust their leaders demonstrate growth (Krafft et al., 2004). Also, trust and respect enhance relationships and yield positive outcomes such as commitment from the team, performance efficiency, extra effort, creativity and the satisfaction of employees (Barbuto and Wheeler, 2006; Schaubroeck et al., 2011; Dannhauser, 2007; Hungwei and Heng-Yu, 2011). Leaders who are emotionally intelligent help motivate the team members and in turn help them increase their effectiveness, build trust amongst each other and work towards the shared vision (D'Souza, 2016). Trust is built into emotions because if an individual trusts and respects the leader or a fellow member, that person will work to the best of their abilities and build a relationship. (Prati et al., 2003).

Development of trust in teams has been described through five different theories: Time, Interaction and Performance Theory (TIP), Media Richness Theory, Social Presence Theory, Social Identification/Deindividualism Theory (SIDE) and Swift Trust Theory.

The **TIP theory** looks into three main areas of team activity: problem solving, supporting other members and high interaction, and how these produce wellbeing in the team. These functions should be implemented by the teams in the beginning of a project, the problem solving stages, conflict resolution and the delivery of the project (McGrath, cited in Daim et al., 2011).

Media Richness theory implies that technology-based communication will lead to the dismissal of the elements of communication that people use to build trust. Nonetheless, Walther (cited in Daim et al., 2011) argues that the **SIDE theory** believes that face-to-face communication does not differ from technology communication when it comes to exchanging information. On the other hand,

Swift Trust is very common in virtual teams where trust is kept within the high-level actions that occur in teams. Swift Trust is different from the traditional trust as Swift Trust imports trust instead of building it.

It has been observed that virtual teams do not really need high level of trust but a 'swift trust' is required, which is more task-oriented and helps in having a good performance.

Performance of virtual teams

Virtual teams are dependent on technology, however successful ones depend more on the individuals that make the team rather than the technology. Individuals' concerns need to be addressed, primarily in order for the technology to work adequately. It is also essential to have the right environment for the existence of the virtual teams, as they require certain types of management styles and leaders.

Four related factors to gauge the execution of worldwide virtual teams were identified: fulfilment with the basic decision-making processes, quality of decision, cooperative peaceful promotion style and perceived interest. According to research conducted in the past, higher levels of cooperative strife with respect to administration style will increase the level of contribution in the team and members will be fulfilled in regards to the leadership styles in place (Kirkman et al., 2004). In conclusion, it is expected that a cooperative conflict management-oriented environment will increase the amount of support by the individuals within virtual teams.

Case 2.1: Virtual teams – A case study from Dubai

The following section reflects on a recent study conducted by the authors on professionals who have experience working with virtual teams, mainly in financial services sector in the ME, however the study also included professionals with no experience with virtual teams, involved in different industries and geographical areas to see if there is any correlation. and also to compare the two groups.

Culture

The findings suggest that culture has a big impact on people's perceptions on similarity, thus affecting their interpersonal attraction and hence the way they behave with their team members, indirectly impacting the overall team performance (Chang et al., 2011).

Some past research sees cultural diversity more as a disadvantage which can lead to a prolonged phase of team formation and also to many conflicts among team members when differences are not understood. Moreover, these difference can have an influence on how people communicate with each other, their approach to problems and decision making processes, which indirectly would have a negative impact on team performance. Hence, why many organisations provide some cultural training workshops which can help in overcoming these cultural diversity issues.

However, the findings gathered from this research show that cultural diversity has a positive impact on virtual team performance, where multi-cultural teams are seen as an asset for the company as they bring many advantages. According to the data collected, having diverse teams means having individuals with different cultural backgrounds, which have different ways of thinking and problem-solving techniques. When you have such a big mix of cultures, the team can only be more open, learn more and improve their way of thinking, as it will give them a broader view on how others think and approach various situations. In the UAE, there are many international companies with offices all around the world, hence the teams are very diverse, which helps them to understand how to operate in different markets due to the available in-house knowledge. Thus, this can only lead to a higher position on the learning curve, which will improve the way teams operate and contribute to the overall team performance.

Emotional intelligence

Previous research conducted shows that there is an impact of emotional intelligence on virtual team performance. As stated by Salovey and Mayer (1990) emotional intelligence has many advantages such as:

- improved communication,
- enhanced conflict management skills,
- enhanced team performance (output),
- more effective leadership,
- improved negotiations skills,
- enhanced decision making and problem-solving capabilities.

All these advantages combined together will have a direct impact on team performance. If individuals exhibit good levels of emotional intelligence they will be able to manage situations better, and this leads to good virtual team performance. However, if individuals are characterised by low levels of emotional intelligence it will make it more challenging for all the afore-mentioned advantages to work cohesively and produce a team with good performance.

The data collected from this research proved that emotional intelligence has an impact on virtual team performance. The findings showed that when individuals are aware of their own emotions and able to manage them accordingly, this impacts positively on their day to day activities. People who are able to control their emotions and not let them impact their productivity or transfer negative feelings to the rest of the team, are known to have high levels of emotional intelligence, which provides the team with a good advantage as they can learn from such individuals and start displaying the same sort of behaviours. The study highlighted the need for augmented attention to emotional intelligence at the group level, which shapes emergent conditions and outcomes of work teams. If a virtual team has individuals who exhibit these attitudes and behaviours, this will bring benefits and contribute positively to the overall virtual team performance.

The study concluded that a relationship was established showing that culture and emotional intelligence impact virtual team performance. Virtual teams depend greatly on technology, however, the success of a team depends more on the team members than on the technology. Individuals' concerns need to be addressed in order for the technology to work adequately. It is also essential to have the right environment for the existence of the virtual teams, as they require a certain type of management styles and leaders (Chang et al., 2011).

Summary

There is a strong relationship between culture, emotional intelligence and virtual team performance. Having people with different cultural backgrounds provides a broader way to approach problems and different ways of thinking which are seen as benefits for a team. Also, having emotionally intelligent individuals as part of a team helps to improve team performance, as these individuals are considered skilled at managing and controlling their emotions without impacting their day to day activities.

2

End of chapter questions

1 Compare the different types of Project Teams

2 Discuss how Self-Orgainsed Teams operate within Agile Projects Management methodologies

3 List the most significant factors that impact Virtual Teams in Project context.

4 Discuss the relationship between Culture, Emotion Intelligence and Virtual teams' Performance

5 Discuss the impact of trust and communication on Virtual Team's success.

References

Abilla, P. (2006).Team dynamics: Size matters redux. http://www.shmula.com/team-dynamics-size-matters-redux/182/. [Accessed: 29th July 2016].

Anderson, L., Alleman, G.B., Beck, K., Blotner, J., Cunningham, W., Poppendieck, M. and Wirfs-Brock, R. (2003). Agile management - an oxymoron? : Who needs managers anyway? In OOPSLA '03, 275–277, New York :ACM.

Augustine, S., Payne, B., Sencindiver, F. and Woodcock, S. (2005). Agile project management: steering from the edges. *Communications of the Association of Computing Machinery*, **48** (12), 85–89.

Backblaze Inc. (2015). Application of Scrum Methods to Hardware Development. www.backblaze.com/blog/wp-content/uploads/2015/08/Scrum-for-Hardware-Development-V3.pdf

Barber, E., and Warn, J. (2005). Leadership in project management: from fire-fighter to firelighter. *Management Decision*, **43** (7/8), 1032-1039.

Barbuto. Jr., J.E. and Wheeler, D.W. (2006). Scale development and construct clarification of servant leadership. *Group and Organization Management*. **31** (3), 300-326.

Brackett, M.A., Rivers, S.E. and Salovey, P. (2011). Emotional intelligence: implications for personal, social, academic, and workplace success. *Social and Personality Psychology Compass*, **5** (1), 88-103.

Bustamante, A. and Sawhney, R. (2011). *Agile XXL: Scaling Agile for Project Teams*, Seapine Software, Inc.

Can H., Aşan, Ö. and Aydın, E. M. (2006). *Organizational Behavior*. Istanbul.

Chang, H.H., Chuang, S.S. and Chao, S.H., (2011). Determinants of cultural adaptation, communication quality, and trust in virtual teams' performance. *Total Quality Management*, **22**(3), 305-329.

Chang, J.W., Sy, T. and Choi, J.N., 2012. Team emotional intelligence and performance. *Small Group Research*, **43**(1), 75–104.

Chau, T. and Maurer, F. (2004). Knowledge sharing in agile software teams. Logic versus approximation. *LNCS* 3075, 173–183.

Chow, T. and Cao, D. (2008). A survey study of critical success factors in agile software projects. *Journal of Systems and Software*, **81**(6), 961–971.

Cockburn, A and Highsmith, J. (2001). Agile software development: The people factor. *Computer*, **34**(11), 131–133.

Cotter, C. (2014). Strategic and impactful events management. www.slideshare.net/ CharlesCotter/strategic-and-impactful-events-management. [Accessed 15th Aug 2016].

Cribari, L. (2013). The Role and Importance of Feedback in Building a High Performing Organization. Philanthropy New York Foundation Administrators Network Meeting.

Daim, T.U., Ha, A., Reutiman, S., Hughes, B., Pathak, U., Bynum, W. and Bhatla, A., (2012). Exploring the communication breakdown in global virtual teams. *International Journal of Project Management*, **30**(2), 199-212.

Dannhauser, Z. (2007). Can the Positive Impact of Servant Leaders be associated with Behaviors Paralleling Followers' Success? Servant Leadership Research Roundtable.

Dirks, K.T. (1999). The effects of interpersonal trust on work group performance. *Journal of Applied Psychology*. **84**, 445-455.

Dirks, K.T. (2000). Trust in leadership and team performance: Evidence From NCAA Basketball. *Journal of Applied Psychology*, **85** (6), 1004-1012.

Dirks, K.T. and Ferrin, D.L. (2001), The role of trust in organizational settings, *Organization Science*, **12**(4), 450-67.

Downey, L.A., Roberts, J. and Stough, C. (2011). Workplace culture emotional intelligence and trust in the prediction of workplace outcomes. *International Journal of Business Science and Applied Management*, **6** (1), 31-40.

Druskat, V.U. and Wolff, S.B. (2001). *Building the Emotional Intelligence of Groups*. https://hbr. org/2001/03/building-the-emotional-intelligence-of-groups. [Accessed: 17 Jul 2016].

D'Souza, J. (2016) Establishing Relationships between Emotional Intelligence, Culture, Leadership and Self-organizing Team Performance within Scrum. Unpublished MSc Dissertation, Heriot Watt University.

Erigüç, G. and Köse, S.D. (2013). Evaluation of Emotional Intelligence and Communication Skills of Health Care Manager Candidates: A Structural Equation Modeling. *International Journal of Business and Social Science*, **4** (13), 115-117.

Goleman, D. (1998). *Working with Emotional Intelligence*. New York: Bantam Books.

Gurung, A. and Prater, E. (2006). A research framework for the impact of cultural differences on IT outsourcing. *Journal of Global Information Technology Management*, **9**(1), 24–43.

Han, S.J. and Beyerlein, M., (2016). Framing the effects of multinational cultural diversity on virtual team processes. *Small Group Research*, **47**(4), pp.351-383.

Hertel, G., Geister, S.and Konradt, U. (2005) Managing virtual teams: A review of cur- rent empirical research. *Human Resource Management Review,*15, 69–95.

Hoda, R., Noble, J. and Marshall, S. (2010). Organizing self-organizing teams *Proceedings - International Conference on Software Engineering*, **1**, 285-294

Hofsteade, G. (2011). Dimensionalizing Cultures: The Hofstede Model in Context. *Online Readings in Psychology and Culture*. **2** (1), 3-26.

Hung Wei, T. & Heng-Yu, K. (2011). The relationships between trust, performance, satisfaction and development progressions among virtual teams. *Quarterly Review of Distance Education*, **12**(2).

Kirkman, B.L., Rosen, B., Tesluk, P.E. and Gibson, C.B. (2004). The impact of team empowerment on virtual team performance: The moderating role of face-to-face interaction. *Academy of Management Journal*, **47**(2), 175–192.

Krafft, P., Engelbrecht, A.S. and Theron, C.C. (2004). The influence of transformational and transactional leadership on dyadic trust relationships through perceptions of fairness. *Journal of Industrial Psychology*. **30** (1), 10-18.

Larsen, D. (2004). Team agility: exploring self-organizing software development teams. *Industrial Logic, and The Agile Times Newsletter.*

Lin, X. (2004). Determinations of cultural adaptation in Chinese-US joint ventures. *Cross Cultural Management*, **11**(1), pp.35–47.

Mataj, M. (2017) Establishing Relationships between Culture, Emotional Intelligence and Virtual Team Performance within the Financial Services in the UAE. Unpublished MSc Dissertation, Heriot Watt University.

Mayer, J. D. and Salovey, P. (1997). What is emotional intelligence? In P. Salovey and D. J. Sluyter (Eds.), *Emotional Development and Emotional Intelligence: Educational Implications* (pp. 3–34). New York, NY: Basic Books, Inc.

Mayer, J.D., Salovey, P. and Caruso, D.R., (2008). Emotional intelligence: new ability or eclectic traits? *American Psychologist*, **63**(6), 503.

Paul, R., Drake, J.R. and Liang, H., (2016). Global virtual team performance: the effect of coordination effectiveness, trust, and team cohesion. *IEEE Transactions on Professional Communication*, **59**(3), 186-202.

Powell, A., Piccoli, G. and Ives, B., (2004). Virtual teams: a review of current literature and directions for future research. *ACM Sigmis Database*, **35**(1), 6-36.

Prati, L.M., Douglas, C., Ferris, G.F., Ammeter, A.P. and Buckley, M.R. (2003). Emotional intelligence, leadership effectiveness and team outcomes. *The International Journal of Organizational Analysis*. **11** (1), 21-40.

Salovey, P. and Mayer, J.D. (1990), Emotional intelligence, *Imagination, Cognition and Personality*. **9**, 185-211.

Schaubroeck, J., Lam, S.S.K. and Peng, A.C. (2011). Cognition-based and affect-based trust as mediators of leader behavior influences on team performance. *Journal of Applied Psychology*, **96**(4), 863-71.

Schwaber, K. (2009). *Scrum Guide*. Scrum Alliance Resources.

Schwaber, K. and Sutherland, J. (2014). *The Scrum Guide: The Definitive Guide to Scrum: The Rules of the Game*, 3-15.

Sharp, H. and Robinson, H. (2008). Collaboration and co-ordination in mature extreme programming teams. *International Journal of Human-Computer Studies*, **66**(7), 506–518.

Thite, M. (2000). Leadership styles in information technology projects. *International Journal of Project Management*, **18**(4), 235-241.

Wageman, R. (2001). Critical success factors for creating superb self-managing teams. *Organizational Dynamics*, 49-51.

White, W.S. (2002). *Leadership: Nine Challenges for Transformation*. Charles Stewart Mott Foundation.

Whitworth, E. (2006). *Agile Experience: Communication and Collaboration in Agile Software Development Teams*. M.A Carleton University, Canada.

Wolff, S.B., Druskat, V.U., Koman, E.S. and Messer, T.E. (2001). The Link between Group Emotional Competence and Group Effectiveness. https://www.researchgate.net/publication/228368502_The_link_between_group_emotional_competence_and_group_effectiveness

3 Sustainable Leadership in Multi-Cultural Teams

Ahmed Salih and Mohamed Salama

Learning outcomes

By completing this chapter the reader should be able to

- Discuss the difference between leaders acting global and being global.
- Discuss the concept of cultural intelligence in the context of leadership.
- Explain the main components of the adaptable and sustainable leadership framework
- Demonstrate the ability to implement the framework for sustainable and adaptive leadership

Introduction

The current shift towards digital transformation that guides the building blocks of the digital economy, has made it imperative to review some of the current theories, frameworks and paradigms. This applies to the different contexts of business management, where effective leadership is crucail, including project management and more so, sustainable project management. The authors' current work, which is directed at both academics and practitioners, calls for a new paradigm in approaching Sustainable Leadership Effectiveness, that brings aspects from three knowledge domains (Anthropology, Sociology and Psychology) which are important for understanding human behaviors (in response to Murdock, 1971). The new paradigm and approach take leadership effectiveness practice, training and development into new dimensions, and embed them within an intelligent process with the Douglasian Cultural Framework (DCF)-based Cultural Intelligence at the center. Leaders focus should harness past and present experience to make a better future (Senge, 2008 cited in Tideman et al., 2013). This implies that for leadership to be considered sustainable, it must be formed around two important factors: adaptability and intelligence (Tideman, 2013). Accordingly, the journey that readers will be guided through in this chapter, is about novelty in thinking and practicing leadership which is different from the mainstream of leadership and Cultural Intelligence discourse and practice. The aim is to have managers and leaders not only understanding how to be effective, but how to behave intelligently in a challenging global context. In the introduction, the chapter presents the debate about leadership from the globalization lens, illustrating the obstacles that leadership research is facing. The chapter then provides the reader with a general review about Cultural Intelligence showing the dilemmas that the construct is facing, leading to the main theme of this chapter where the leadership adaptability framework is presented.

Historical background

Leadership has passed through a difficult trajectory since the end of the nineteenth century until today (Van Seters and Field, 1990). It starts with the personality era moving to the influence era, behavioral era, situation era, contingency era, transactional era, anti-leadership era, culture era and transformational era. An important observation one can notice is that, in the focus of most of the eras, leadership research reacts to leaders' traits or behaviors in different contexts. There is no comprehensive theory of leadership that can be applied at all times in all contexts. The era of global leadership is not so different from those in the past.

The shift in mindset: The difference between acting and being global

Management scholars such as Cabrera and Unruh (2012) have been calling for the development of global leaders, in the era of the global economy, where the whole world is interconnected and tremendously complex. These scholars argue that being global is no longer an option if companies decide to work outside their homeland environment, rather it is an imperative. Cabrera and Unruh (2012) also refer to a dilemma that individuals and organizations face nowadays in getting prepared to deal with others across national borders. There is a difference between acting global and being global: a difference that must touch people's behaviors and not only their thinking; a difference that manifests in listening to and understanding others in other contexts, instead of applying Western-oriented frameworks (Biermeier-Hanson et al., 2015); and finally, a difference between judging others' actions according to our own set of values and suspending our judgement to learn from others in context-specific encounters. Basically, a shift in the mindset of individuals and organizations must happen in order to achieve this (Cabrera and Unruh, 2012).

Other scholars such as Gupta and Govindarajan (2002) define global mindset as the ability to utilize and interpret criteria and performance across a wide array of cross-cultural contexts (cited in Biermeier-Hanson et al., 2015). Once again, Biermeier-Hanson et al. (2015) describe how reactive leadership continues to be, while there is a need to create leaders with global mindsets who can respond to global market needs. The authors argue that this is backboned by technology advancement, and hence, organizations find themselves obliged to change their behavior to cope with it.

In response to the globalization phenomena, many scholars started developing parameters and competencies taxonomies for global leaders, so that companies can start deploying them. Caligiuri (2006) identifies four areas of focus: knowledge, skills, abilities and other personality characteristics (KSAO) for potential global leaders. Such competencies are viewed as prerequisites for somebody to succeed in specific jobs, occupations, or roles (Campion et al., 2011; Shippmann et al., 2000 and Stevens, 2012 cited in Mendenhall et al., 2017). Silong et al. (2015) argue that those who are culturally intelligent have better potential to become global leaders due to their understanding of global diversity. Caligiuri (2013) adds contextual factors to global leaders' competencies list. This includes: effectively managing complex global environments; the capabilities to negotiate cultural challenges and conflicts; and also understanding regulatory conflicting requirements, unforeseen costs and stakeholders' diversity (cited in Silong et al., 2015). Other scholars call to create a model for global leadership that considers a set of competencies that focuses on personality traits, general self-efficacy and intrinsic motivation drivers to push people to work abroad (Chattanooga Model, 2001, cited in Mendenhall et al., 2017).

Cultural Intelligence (CQ)

The concept of Cultural Intelligence (CQ), which is considered as a competency of the effective leader (Rockstuhl et al., 2011), in its current form and structure failed to provide practitioners with the tools that it promised. The reason behind this dilemma is CQ's reliance on astatic culture, based on national background and race. This dilemma led to scholars (Blasco et al, 2012) arguing that CQ as a construct failed to achieve its goal and did not permit those who work outside their homeland to benefit from it. Blasco et al. (2012) also reached a conclusion that one can only understand culture as a product of social interaction, or as physical experiences and their interpretation, as opposed to knowledge. This approach becomes the crucial factor in CQ (Blasco et al., 2012). Other scholars argue that the CQ construct fails to clarify or present the mechanism required to perform the metacognitive processes, i.e. planning, reviewing and checking, and to question the capability of CQ to be useful to practitioners (e.g. Salih, 2017).

Main components of the adaptable and sustainable leadership framework

Leading in a sustainable manner implies that leaders must have deep awareness about themselves in relevance to the world around them, according to the definition given by the Sustainability Leadership Institute (2011 cited in Visser and Courtice, 2013). Moreover, the Institute calls for profound changes in the area of leaders' interactions with politics, economy, stakeholders and society (Visser and Courtice, 2013).

In response to the gaps illustrated in the introduction, the following section will be providing insights into the main components of our framework for sustainable and adaptable leadership, starting with Hamlin's (2004) Model for Leadership Effectiveness and Ineffectiveness, meta-cognitive dimension of Cultural Intelligence and then finish with the autonomous culture of the Douglasian Cultural Framework.

Hamlin's Generic Model of Managerial and Leadership Effectiveness

Hamlin's 'Generic Model of Managerial and Leadership Effectiveness' is the outcome of several meta-level analyses. Hamlin and colleagues conducted three empirical factor-analytic studies focusing on the criteria of managerial/leadership effectiveness, and applied these criteria within three different types of public sector organizations in the UK. The model was then formed according to those studies. The organizations involved in the three studies ranged from secondary education schools in the UK, the Anglia Executive Unit of HM Customs and Excise, which is a Department of the British Civil Service, to finally an NHS Trust hospital. Each study deployed both qualitative and quantitative research methods within a common subjectivist/interpretive research design and grounded theory mindset (Hamlin, 2002). The model is not tested in the Middle East area except one comparative study lately conducted in Egypt and UAE to examine Hamlin's model (Patel and Salih, in progress). The Behavioral Statement (BS) findings of Hamlin and colleagues studies derived from a 'generic model' (see Hamlin, 2004) of eleven positive and negative behavioral indications of managerial/leader behaviors: of which six were positive, and five were negative. This model with its BSs has been compared and contrasted against findings resulting from various 'single-organization' replication studies carried out in other public sector organizations in various culturally diverse countries, as well as in the UK. In Patel and Hamlin (2012), however, the resulting list was longer and consisted of 10 positive and 9 negative Behavioral Statements. Moreover, the study recently conducted by Salih (2017) showed, for example, that in UAE there are a total of 40 discrete Behavioral Statements, of which 12 are indicative of effective and 28 of ineffective managerial behaviors (see Tables 3.1 and 3.2 below).

Table 3.1: List of 12 positive behavioral statements

1	The manager supports the subordinates
2	The manager organises the workload and resources
3	The manager encourages subordinates to learn, and to develop their skills and competencies
4	The manager offers explicit rewards (salary increase, bonus) to subordinates when they do a good job
5	The manager offers tacit rewards (appreciation, recognition, encouragement) to subordinates when they do a good job
6	The manager builds personal relations with the employees and shows caring
7	My manager knows how to handle mistakes (his own and those of subordinates)
8	The manager supports team members when faced with criticism/demands from a third party
9	The manager treats his subordinates politely and respectfully
10	My manager manages conflict situations/contradictions well
11	The manager ensures a fair performance appraisal/evaluation
12	The manager makes decisions swiftly, while simultaneously sharing the decision making with subordinates

Table 3.2: List of 28 negative behavioral statements

1	The manager does not manage workload or resources well
2	The manager overloads subordinates with excess workload
3	My manager procrastinates on important matters and reacts only when the situation has escalated
4	The manager does not provide the necessary resources, tools, information or guidance for the task
5	The manager does not recognize the contribution of other team members and takes credit himself
6	The manager does not manage conflicts well
7	The manager shouts and publicly humiliates the subordinate
8	The manager is disrespectful to the subordinates
9	The manager discriminates between employees and treats them unequally/unfairly
10	The manager does not/cannot ensure a fair performance appraisal/reward allocation
11	My manager does not appreciate the work done by his subordinates
12	The manager does not help the subordinates grow or develop
13	The manager does not keep his word
14	The manager does not care about his employees
15	The manager often displays negative affect
16	The manager often reacts negatively without fully checking the fact
17	The manager compromises the team spirit in the department
18	The manager is not open to ideas different from his own
19	The manager does not support the subordinate in front of a third party
20	The manager is not open to new ideas from subordinates or to involving subordinates in decisions affecting them
21	The manager is overly negative or critical about work/non work related matters
22	The manager does not handle mistakes (his own and those of the subordinates) well
23	The manager allows his personal biases to supersede what is good for the company
24	The manager does not build human bonds or trusting relationships with the employees
25	The manager displays dishonest, exploitative, and manipulative behavior
26	The manager himself does not respect the rules of the company
27	The manager does not communicate effectively
28	The manager does not delegate authority/give space or freedom to subordinates

Hamlin's approach comply with Walley and Whitehead (1994) in creating "tools of greening" in organizations to ensure success. This is reflected in realizing and applying long-term good behaviors and eliminating bad ones as detailed by McCann and Holt (2010). This however will be further enriched by adding the dynamicity and adaptability aspects to it, as discussed later in this chapter.

Cultural Intelligence's metacognitive dimension

As the objective of this chapter is not to indulge in reviewing Cultural Intelligence (CQ), which is rooted in psychology, as a construct and how it progressed since its conception; the review will instead be confined to the meta-cognitive dimension of CQ. However, it is important to clarify to the reader that, in this approach, the presented thoughts are not following the mainstream of CQ discourse where national cultural represents the core of the construct. Instead this approach follows Salih and Patel (2015), with their new transactional approach to CQ which incorporates Douglasian Cultural Framework (DCF) or Douglasian Cultural Theory as an alternative to national culture.

CQ's meta-cognitive is defined as "thinking about thinking, hence, including the processes of monitoring and adjusting one's thoughts and strategies as one learns new skills" (see Triandis, 1995 cited in Mor et al., 2013). Furthermore, it refers to an individual's level of conscious cultural awareness and executive processing during cross-cultural interactions (see Ang and Van Dyne, 2008 cited in Van Dyne et al., 2012). People make use of this dimension to prepare and plot the plans and strategies necessary for any future cultural interaction. They also check their behaviors in an iterative mode and make the required adjustments to those behaviors. The available CQ mainstream research, practice and exams, however, fall short of explaining to both academics and practitioners where meta-cognitive process happens and how, or what mechanism is used. Lately, Salih and colleagues conducted several studies and provided an attempt toward solving this dilemma (e.g. Salih, 2017). This is done by the link made between CQ's meta-cognitive dimension and DCF's autonomous culture (hermit). This chapter builds on the work of Salih and colleagues and considers their framework of CQ, not the traditional one. CQ offers three sub-dimensions that branch from the meta-cognitive dimension: planning, awareness, and checking.

The first pillar of the meta-cognitive dimension is **planning**. Planning is defined as the process of strategizing before a culturally different encounter (Bell and Kozlowski, 2008; Jacobs and Paris, 1987 cited in Van Dyne et al., 2012). It means thinking thoroughly about a certain culture and what a person needs or plans to do before any cultural interaction. This may relate to ones personal direct need by asking the question (what can I do to achieve what I want?); or what others need to achieve (what can they do to achieve what they want?); and finally to a more comprehensive question to include the context (how might our actions affect what we can achieve in this context?) (Van Dyne et al., 2012). Plotting the necessary plans carefully and predicting the behaviors of other individuals in a particular cultural context, enhances understanding and increases the level of awareness at the individual level, primarily when a person acquires new experiences (Endsley, 1995; Schmidt and Ford, 2003 cited in Van Dyne et al., 2012).

Second is **awareness**. This is defined as the individual's knowledge of cultural thinking, about himself, and about others that interact with him in real time (e.g., Flavell, 1979; Ridley et al., 1992 cited in Van Dyne et al., 2012). Awareness includes being conscious of one's cultural habits and how to use own cultural knowledge when interacting with others from different cultures (e.g., Haller et al., 1988; Sitzmann et al., 2009; Sitzmann and Ely, 2011 cited in Van Dyne et al., 2012). It also involves the concept of mindfully suspending judgment about a situation or a person until enough information is received so that the individual can make sense of intercultural interactions (Triandis, 2006; Van Dyne et al., 2012). In a proactive process, awareness considers that the individual becomes conscious of himself, of the others that interact with him, and the specific cultural context where the interaction process is happening (Van Dyne et al., 2012).

Finally, Van Dyne et al. (2012) define the concept of **checking**, as revising the assumptions that individuals make about others and adjusting mental maps according to the real experience that happens in the outside context, especially when it is different from what the individual expects (e.g., Bell and Kozlowski, 2008; Jacobs and Paris, 1987 cited in Van Dyne et al., 2012). Checking also means that individuals always compare their plans or expectations about others' behaviors with what is occurring on the ground during inter-cultural interactions. This may lead to considering it as a function of conscious reflection and unconscious associative learning (Van Dyne et al., 2012). Following the same sense in the planning part, checking will also imply to revisiting and adjusting personal assumptions, assumptions made by other culturally diverse individuals, and the outcomes in a specific context (Van Dyne et al., 2012).

The Douglasian Cultural Framework (DCF)

Before we present DCF's fifth culture, we will briefly discuss the Douglasian Cultural Framework to set the scene for a better understanding of concepts. For more details, readers should refer to extant literature (e.g. Thompson et al., 1990).

Different from conventional geo-ethnicity based approaches to culture, DCF comes from the transactional school of anthropology (see Barth, 1967). Accordingly, DCF scholars explain that cultures do not represent countries, customs, myths, races, or ethnicities. Instead, cultures emerge through social interactions which are continually tested for social viability (see Thompson and Wildavsky, 1986). DCF attempts to free cultural studies from geo-ethnic limits or even national boundaries by focusing on social interactions. Mary Douglas, the British social anthropologist introduced the DCF or the Grid Group Typology (GGT), in her book *Natural Symbols* (Douglas, 1970) and further elaborated on it in *Cultural Bias* (Douglas, 1978). Shortly after, many researchers from different management and scientific fields adopted it.

In its original format, DCF began by responding to people's need for classification as emphasized in *Natural Symbols* (Douglas, 1970). Douglas offered two social dimensions where people focus their ideas and interests, which are 'Group' and 'Grid'. Draw this on a matrix, the X-axis or the horizontal coordinate represents 'Group', while the Y-axis or vertical coordinate represents 'Grid'. The group axis measures the degree to which people are tied to their community, and restricted in thought and behavior by their commitment to their social unit (Gross and Rayner, 1985). A collective type of mind can be found at the right-end side of the axis, where community boundaries are of paramount importance. People at this end devote a lot of their time to interacting with other unit members, which requires a long-term commitment. Each is expected to act or behave on behalf of the collective whole, while the unit is expected to act in the normative interest of its members. Individuals experience a hierarchical culture (Gross and Rayner, 1985). The ties to the group become weaker as we move toward the left-end side of the X-axis. Individuals at this end enjoy freedom from group ties and boundaries. They can negotiate their culture independently without being constrained by, or reliant upon, any significant group. The low group experience is a competitive, entrepreneurial culture (Gross and Rayner, 1985 cited in Patel and Rayner, 2012).

On the Y-axis grid, we find an index that measures the extent to which individual behavior is constrained by role differentiation, regardless of any enrolment or membership in any group (Gross and Rayner, 1985 cited in Patel and Rayner, 2012). When moving to the top end of the grid axis, we find rules and classifications governing gender, age, and family. These rules define how people relate to one another and therefore limit their life chances and opportunities; here, people experience strong grid cultures. This limitation is attenuated when moving down the grid axis, where people have the freedom to find jobs based on their merits; here, people experience weak grid cultures (Mars, 2008). Figure 3.1 shows the distribution of DCF's five cultures across grid and group axes based on the distribution made by Thompson (2008).

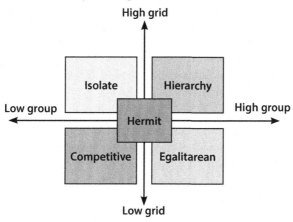

Figure 3.1: The distribution of DCF's five cultures across grid and group axes based on the distribution made by Thompson (2008 cited in Salih, 2017).

The autonomous culture (hermit) in DCF

The hermit, as elaborated by Thompson et al. (1990: 7): "escapes social control by refusing to control others or to be controlled by others". As individuals move toward any of the four cultures they get more of what they want, but they also become more involved in controlling social relations. In such circumstances, it is possible to become disenchanted with all these binding social relations, and to want less of them. In this case, individuals might want to revert back to an 'absolute zero' – a point where transactions are minimized (Thompson, 2008). Figure 3.2 shows Thompson's (2008) conceptualization of the hermit as a fifth culture.

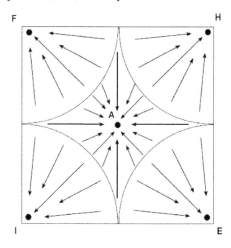

Figure 3.2: Thompson's (2008) imagination of the hermit as a fifth culture. The 'A' in the center stands for the 'autonomy of the hermit'. Also, since Thompson referred to the competitive culture as the 'individualist', the bottom left-hand quadrant is labelled 'I'.

Another important aspect of DCF to emphasize is the dynamic nature of the construct. When it was initially formulated, DCF was a static framework, and this was changed later by Thompson (1996) who introduced the dynamic aspect which potentially existed within it. Thompson (1996) explains that followers of hierarchical, egalitarian and competitive cultures compete with one other to reach their dominant position in the system. It is important to clarify that despite the ongoing competition among members of these cultures, these members also depend on each other for survival.

In the traditional approach to CQ, the meta-cognitive process remains a mental one and CQ scholars do not clearly inform, where this process happens. Planning, awareness, and checking are processes proposed by CQ scholars to assist individuals to rebuild their strategies and remedy their weaknesses after or during cultural encounters. However, CQ does not specify where these processes take place and what mechanism enables individuals to think, analyze, plan, and check their plans and actions before each encounter. DCF's autonomous culture (i.e. the hermit), which was first distinguished by Thompson and Ellis (1997) as a fifth culture, provides the desired mechanism; it is characterized by a deliberate withdrawal from social influence and is in the center of the grid-group matrix (Thompson and Ellis 1997 cited in Patel, 2014). Thompson et al. (1999) describe the hermit culture as curious because it stabilizes itself by deliberately avoiding all coercive involvement (Patel, 2014; Thompson, 2008).

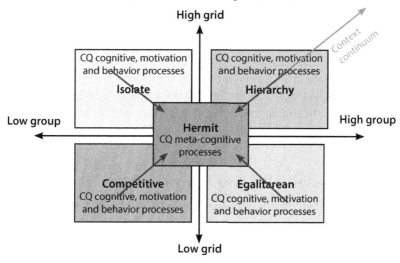

Figure 3.3: CQ dimensions placement within DCF's cultures (cited in Salih, 2017).

Different from the other four cultures, in the hermit space transactions are minimized by a deliberate withdrawal from all social involvement. Thompson further strengthened the dynamic nature of DCF by introducing the hermit as a neutral zone where individuals can drive change in their behavior. The continuous change process cannot be explained without the existence of the hermit (Thompson, 2008). 'Behaving rationally' is what makes individuals move back to the neutral zone or the 'absolute zero'. This implies that individuals check their previous actions and plot new plans for the future, based on the information they have acquired in the past about others or about contexts. This strongly corresponds with CQ's meta-cognitive processes mentioned above. While this happens, it will trigger people to move into new cultures. The change properties, as Thompson et al. (1990, p. 32) argue, can only be found in this "absolute zero" (see Figure 3.3).

The evolution of a new approach

Salih (2017) studied the link between the three components: Hamlin's (2004) Model for Leadership Effectiveness and Ineffectiveness, CQ's Meta-cognitive Dimension and DCF's autonomous culture (hermit), to understand and explain leaders' cultural adaptability and hybridity (following Patel and Rayner, 2012). The outcome of this combination leads to crafting a new behaviorally or culturally dynamic framework of leadership that calls for a new paradigm linking the three domains of knowledge; anthropology, sociology and psychology to understand human behavior (in response to Murdock, 1971).

Also, through the intelligent process that our framework adopt, organizations and individuals will have the right tools to learn better and faster in a global context. This, in turn, will put organizations in a more flexible, adaptable and change-embracing position against their competitors (McCann, 2010). However, this intelligent process must be efficient internally and externally. While leaders looking for opportunities in the global context might show flexibility to adapt to different situations, employees within the organization may not feel the same urge or may not be able to see the merit of this pursuit, and hence, resist the change. Therefore, from a sustainability point of view, engaging internal employees in the decision making process is vital so that the organization is perceived as an intelligent, learning and living one (McCann and Holt, 2010). In the next section, a case study from Dubai, UAE will be used to illustrate the development of this new framework.

Framework for sustainable and adaptive Leadership

For the purpose of this work, we selected a multinational / cosmopolitan city. Dubai has gained a global reputation and has grown rapidly during the past two decades. This in turn exposes a dialectic relationship between the forces of globalization, (economic, political and cultural), and localization (e.g. environment, demography, history and ideology), in the production of the urban environment (Smith, 2001; Newman and Thornley, 2005: cited in Pacione, 2005).

A multi-national company called Dubai_Burj, a company with more than 6000 employees and offices scattered around the world, was chosen as the sample. With Dubai_Burj, the employees come from different national backgrounds. Moreover, the national background mix is further magnified by having many of the staff holding double nationalities. Dubai_Burj is among few companies who made it during the global crisis occurred in 2018.

In the following section, the details of the study conducted in the UAE are presented and discussed leading to deduced conclusions that should help project managers and practitioners, in general, towards a better understanding and the successful implementation of the suggested framework. The findings of the interviews are presented followed by some useful reflections by the researchers.

Case 3.1: A case study from Dubai

Phase One

In this section, we describe the two phases of data collection conducted in this study. In both phases, interviewees were requested to select a specific manager or leader who had been working with the company for a long time. This provided richer data on these leaders as their behaviors was described by employees at different levels of the company, different age groups, different genders, and finally different years of experience with these managers. Our request found a listening ear from the majority, who discussed incidents with managers who have worked at the company for years, while some insisted on talking about other managers due to political and personal reasons.

In Phase One, we obtained concrete examples of observed effective and ineffective manager/ leader behaviors as exhibited by middle and first-line managers within the organization (Hamlin et al., 2006; Hamlin and Patel, 2012). The focus of Phase One was on understanding effective and ineffective managerial and leadership behaviors. This was done by exploring the behaviors related to the every-day 'managing' and 'leading' activities, as manifested by 'managers' at various levels of the organization as observed by their peers and subordinates. A total number of 401 critical incidents (CIs) were initially collected from 45 interviews conducted in this phase. The interviewees included mid-level managers (heads of departments, heads of sections, construction managers and project managers), senior architects, senior engineers, architects, engineers, human resources staff and secretaries, in addition to the engineering regulations follow-up team. The sample also includes employees from every nationality in the company – Iraq, Iran, Egypt, Syria, Oman, Palestine, Lebanon, the Philippines, Pakistan, India, Canada, Ukraine, and the United Arab Emirates. In addition, the sample features a gender mix. An interview schedule was prepared and agreed upon, in coordination with the organization's human resources department

The UAE dataset reveals that some managers display a moderate to good level of adaptability or flexibility to move from one mindset/culture to another, based on the situation they are in, or the extrinsic motivators that drive them (Price and Thompson, 1997). However, our study reveals two extremes to this observation. The first appears in the case of a manager who shows a significant level of malleability to change his behavior according to the situation he is facing (Van Dyne et al., 2012). On the other end, we found that some managers possess conditional malleability which appears only when they want to achieve certain goals or defer a threat to their own interests. The third type of malleability found is the negative one, which managers used to protect their image, status and survival. This is basically due to the dominance of a fatalistic mindset which makes it harmful to all those who work under this manager. The case is different with other managers, where their malleability is associated with a balanced kind of hybridity between the hierarchical and egalitarian cultures. We found that this confirms Thomas et al.'s (2008) argument that a culturally intelligent person is a positive and noble person, and therefore the manager who shows a negative malleability is not considered a culturally intelligent one.

Considering an example manager from UAE dataset, and looking at the flexibility of this manager to change his behavior and adapt to others' cultures, the dataset shows that he lives in a hybrid mode, i.e. during the day, he may adopt more than one culture (dominantly hierarchical and egalitarian) and this depends on the context on one hand, and his evaluation of the outcomes (i.e. applying meta-cognitive processes) on another hand. Interviews reveal that he entertains a degree of conditional malleability (Van Dyne et al., 2012) that allows him to achieve the kind of balanced hybridity that he entertains. This manager's behaviors shows a clear mix of the hierarchical and egalitarian cultures. Which one dominates, depends on the situation as noticed from the dataset. However, the UAE dataset also shows that he has broken company rules in many instances. Some of these instances are perceived as positive by employees, while others consider some cases as negative when he slips into a competitive culture. This happens when the manager feels threatened by someone or when he wants to pursue his own goals.

Case Study 1

While in case of a manager called M2, malleability is associated with a balanced hierarchical egalitarian hybridity, the second extreme found in our study, manager M1, demonstrates a different type of malleability; one that is used to build M1's own image or career, which makes working under M1 harmful for his staff. According to Thomas et al. (2008), we can now categorize managers into culturally intelligent and non-intelligent. Those who affect others positively or use their CQ capabilities to benefit others and show them respect are considered culturally intelligent, such as M2 and M4 in addition to other managers. On the other hand, those who use their flexibility or malleability to harm others are not considered as culturally intelligent managers; such is the case of M1. Below are extracts showing how M2 and M1 are perceived by their employees (E):

M2:

"A significant characteristic about my manager is his flexibility which goes hand in hand with his ability to follow management regulations...this gives him the chance to adopt the best suitable culture to handle the situation to achieve the goals successfully rather than maintaining rigid outlook or set of beliefs" and *"usually not taking him much time to plan for the change but rather he plans to be spontaneous"* (E5).

"High level of flexibility to adapt to different behaviors. It is very common that we start discussing formal issues related to work, and then immediately he jumps into subjects related to my personal life trying to help me with them even if this needs to compromise some of the rules" (E10, 6th May, 2015).

"When my manager receives information, he distributes it and works on it to ultimately enhance the company procedures and to drive a change companywide" (E5).

M1:

"He categorizes information seeking personal benefit from it without considering the overall benefit for the team or group" (E5).

"But at the end he adopts the one that is serving his plans and settings and ensuring that he receives the satisfaction of management" and *"he can show flexibility to change and adopt another culture to pursue a certain goal but he quickly goes back to his original beliefs and adopted culture so the change is temporary and only lasts for a short time"* (E5).

*"For years, this manager was planning and fighting to get promoted into his current position and showed great resistance to his boss when his **current** manager was selected and has taken that position from him. It is worth mentioning that the day his current manager was promoted to the position, M1 immediately showed public compliance and obedience to him. This however did not stop M1 from harnessing each opportunity to raise himself and sell his capabilities to the management to prove that he is a better fit for this position"* (author's remarks).

The time factor is important to this manager and it explains how profoundly he drives his meta-cognitive processes when he enters the hermit space.

Further, there is evidence that this manager adopts an autonomous way of life (hermit) where he sometimes profoundly prepares strategies to suit his next move for the best of his interests, whether to move from egalitarian to any other culture (Thompson et al., 1996 and Thompson, 2008). He, in this case, enters into a neutral space where he does not do any transaction. Instead, in this neutral zone, he performs all the analysis, planning, building the information database (from the repertoire he processes) necessary to implement the change to his behavior in order to serve him better in the next encounter. As we saw earlier, for years, he used to act in an egalitarian way when he was an employee and then he changed into strong competitive and sometimes fatalistic once he got promoted. We believe that such change in behavior does not happen overnight. Rather, this manager used to plan and act explicitly and implicitly to become the manager of the department and he succeeded in his goal at the end. This kind of planning and action over years required that he put extensive time and efforts to achieve his goal.

Case Study 2

In some cases, we find evidence that this manager adopts an autonomous culture (hermit) where he profoundly prepares strategies for his next move from one culture to another (Thompson et al., 1996; Thompson, 2008). This manager explicitly enters into a neutral space where he does not do any transaction. All information that he receives from others is secretively kept and processed, and based on that, this manager performs all the analysis, planning, and knowledge-building necessary to implement change to his behavior or inspire others to change. We noticed that this manager may take a month after receiving lead information to decide his next move:

"Sometimes he takes one month studying a subject before he calls for a meeting to discuss the matter with us. Time is important and well-utilized. He collects the necessary information prior to any encounter" (E9).

*"Planning is very important for this manager. This is obvious from the way he climbed the management ladder until he became the **manager**… This manager uses time as a vehicle to create and implement his strategies to achieve his goals. Such goals also lead to creating many successful procedures in the company besides his personal goals" (E13).*

"All our meetings are planned with him and we get instructions to this regard. I believe that he wants to educate everyone to follow the rules and be like him. His instructions and directions in all meetings flow in this direction. This is clear from his questions that show that he wants us to think the way he wants, "our company and our way"… I can see that he plans strategies to win each situation" (E1).

"This is a significant feature in M4's professional life and explains how he climbed up the ladder in such a family business organization from a mechanical engineer to become at the end a partner and top manager. M4 has not allowed anybody to become a deputy for him so that he can eliminate any competition on his position or the rights that he gained by his extensive planning. He plans a lot when he deals with those who represent a threat to him. You find him taking time to prepare prior to dealing with them although they might be normal employees but they have innovative ideas that may let them shine beyond his

control. In such cases, you find him paying attention to their ideas and in a few months he introduces it under his name. In such cases, he cares less how the employee may feel because this might seem like a threat to his authority" (Author's remarks)

Subsequently, and based on the points discussed above, there is evidence that some managers enter a neutral culture- the hermit or the autonomous culture, before changing their stances from one culture to another. In this space, managers perform all meta-cognitive processes before they engage in future encounters which lend support to the argument made by Thomas et al. (2008). This goes hand in hand with our assumption that in the neutral zero space or the hermit, managers do the same. Moreover, finally, it confirms the connection between the autonomous culture (hermit) and CQ's metacognitive dimension is apparent in the dataset.

Phase Two

In Phase Two, we conducted interviews with fourteen managers and subordinates. Interviewees were requested to provide two managerial examples about the effect of cultural encounters on employees. Note that here, 'cultural' does not refer to 'national culture' but to DCF's cultures. Interviewees are provided with an indirect introductory awareness paragraph or questions about DCF's grid-group typology and CQ dimensions. This introduction or guidance was made in the form of informative directions to the cultural preferences of the leaders/managers, which they need to take into consideration when describing leader/manager behaviors. Interviewees were requested to select a critical encounter that best conforms to one or more of the paragraphs provided. Examples of such information are; "Which cultural/behavioral preferences does your manager adopt? Does he/she change his behavior according to the situation? Is he/she team oriented (cares about the team, protects the team, promotes the team, does allow others to interfere with the team…) or does he/she only abide by rules and regulations to protect her/himself, or both, or none", "Is you manager aware of his/her own cultural/behavioral characteristics? What about the culture of others? Do you believe your manager is aware of them?", or "Does your manager know how to apply his/her knowledge about other cultures in different situations? Does she/he plan for her/his actions?". These statements and questions only served as a guide and did not need to be answered by the interviewees, the same was clarified at the interview outset. Each statement or question refers to one or more DCF culture including hermit and CQ meta-cognitive dimension.

Afterwards, the author's observations were incorporated as applicable to provide more depth to the collected data, and to support and explain the information provided by interviewees.

Recommendations to organizations, leaders and managers

Our framework for sustainable and adaptable leadership provides the necessary thinking, orientation and tools to organizations and individuals to make them not only win work but also win their employees. Typically, project managers working within the context of a temporary organisational structure face even more challenges in the pursuit of effective leadership. These challenges are magnified further when trying to embrace the principles of sustainability in managing projects that involves multi-cultural teams.

First, our framework and its derived taxonomy can form the base for more effective guidance and training to leadership education institutes around the world by training the trainer. By doing that, we reckon to speed up the adaptation process of managers/leaders around the globe and help them achieve their assignments successfully.

Second, the adaptability to cultural changes detailed in this chapter would benefit both organizations and individuals to create what Peter Senge calls the 'learning organization'. This is done through the emphasis on the importance of the hermit role. Driving the change or living in a continuously changing world make it essential for leaders to go through the neutral zone, or the hermit, as a major step in understanding and implementing cultural or behavioral transformations. In other words, if people wish to behave in a culturally intelligent manner while they work globally, they need to apply meta-cognitive processes such as reviewing their past actions and planning future strategies. This requires them to spend some time in this neutral zone to obtain the necessary fuel to evaluate the past experience that they went through, consider the positive and negative points in their behaviors, and how to change these behaviors to suit future encounters better. In this case, people may spend a good deal of time planning for future events, while others can change their culture quickly. By doing so, the hermit as space would assist leaders positively to balance the behavior of their teams' members and guide them toward becoming more rational, more calculated, and more culturally intelligent. This may lend support to Thomas et al.'s (2008) argument that: a culturally intelligent person is a noble person with good intentions to benefit himself and the others. By encouraging people to enter into a neutral zone to think about their strategies, organizations can influence those under training periods to take advantage of this important feature. Therefore, we believe that the role of the hermit, when integrated with the meta-cognitive dimension of CQ, is essential in building leader sustainable capabilities.

Finally, our current work attempts to craft a new leadership adaptability model based on integrating Leadership Effectiveness and Ineffectiveness taxonomies resulted from replicating Hamlin's (2004) work in the UAE, CQ's meta-cognitive dimension and DCF's autonomous culture. In doing that, we enrich Hamlin's (2004) model with new behavioral taxonomies that related to leaders cultural transformation and cultural hybridity. Table 3.3 presents those positive and negative taxonomies:

Positive behavioral patterns
Staff highly appreciates managers who process a balanced and calculated hybridity of hierarchical and egalitarian mindsets in the context of our private sector UAE company.
Managers who are aware of the impact of their actions on subordinates, managers who carefully analyze their actions before any encounter are perceived effective managers.
Managers who plan for their actions before interacting with others to create healthy work environment and avoid conflicts,
Managers who appreciate acquiring information sharing it openly with others and using it to implementing cultural change within the workplace
Managers who are flexible to changing their behavior based on the situation for the benefit of work and staff are positively perceived
Managers who enter an autonomous space to positively plan for their next moves before interacting with people are perceived as effective managers.

Negative behavioral patterns
Once the fatalistic culture is added to any mix, it immediately leads to a negative perception by subordinates, and this is how it impacts on those adopting a competitive culture, for example. Even if managers add the hierarchical culture to their cultural mix they would still be perceived as ineffective due to the adverse effects of the competitive or fatalistic stances that they adopt.
Managers who are aware of the impact of their actions on subordinates but do not seem to care, or managers who are not conscious of the impact of their actions on subordinates and thus repeat the same mistakes in each encounter, are seen as ineffective.
Managers who do not create a knowledge repertoire of the positive and negative behaviors emerging after each encounter because they end up repeating the same mistakes.
Managers who plan their actions prior to interacting with others only for their own self-interest and self-gain
Managers who plan their actions for the purpose of protecting themselves and achieving self-survival, managers who appreciate acquiring information but they neither use it properly nor share it with others
Managers who do not bother about acquiring information and show rigidity to change their behavior when interacting with others, are all perceived as ineffective managers. This is because such managers enter into an autonomous space explicitly to plot strategies that serve their own plans and then move into a competitive or fatalistic space.

Table 3.3: Taxonomy or list of perceived positive and negative behaviors due to cultural hybridity and adaptation

Conclusions

The concepts and practice of sustainability and adaptability to dynamic changes have become the focus for many organizations and individuals in the 21st century – especially those who work diligently to maintain their success and sustain their positions in the global market. This, however, requires all leaders and managers in those institutions to act intelligently and stay in a learning mode to achieve their targets and KPIs. Moreover, in their approach to implementing changes, organizations need to have buy-ins from all employees by engaging them in the decision-making process. This implies that leadership is required to be built at all levels. By doing so, the adaptability level of the organization becomes higher and resistance to change becomes less.

3

This chapter calls for a new paradigm in approaching leadership thinking and practice primarily to practically help leaders in accomplishing their goals. The management domain and the leadership field in particular have been dominated by research that connects leadership to national culture. Although this has benefited leadership studies for decades, it has now turned into a handicap in the face of globalization in the 20th and 21st centuries. The leadership domain is also dominated by the discussion of traits, generalizations and contingency, while leadership effectiveness receives less attention from scholars, and studies about leadership ineffectiveness are scarce. Therefore, our current emic research comes to partially addresses the paucity of indigenous studies of management/ leadership, and more specifically of 'managerial effectiveness' and 'leadership effectiveness,' in UAE; a successful example of developing countries in pursuit of sustainable development. It contributes to understanding better the issue of perceived managerial and leadership effectiveness by describing 12 broad categories of positive managerial behaviors and 28 broad categories of negative managerial behaviors. This could be thought of as a two-dimensional behavioral 'lay model' of perceived managerial and leadership effectiveness examined and proved working within the UAE private sector.

Although CQ as a construct was promising for academic research about culture as an established area in business and overall management literature, and represented a paradigm shift through its call to focus on the individual, that is on the psychological aspect of human behavior against the aggregate or anthropological one. However, the development of the new construct was constrained since scholars continued to employ static and geo-ethnicity based conceptualizations of culture. Hence CQ does not provide an adequate explanation for behavioral changes. Moreover, CQ utilizes meta-cognition to describe the 'thinking about thinking' but it does not advise on the mechanism that make thinking or strategizing processes happen to make behavioral change. Therefore, there is a need for alternative ways of conceptualizing culture that are free from geo-ethnic boundaries and are capable of explaining cultural change, cultural adaptability and cultural dynamicity. Cultural transformation/adaptation, in our current work is satisfactorily done by reviving the role of the commonly neglected fifth culture of DCF, the hermit.

Moreover, the suggested framework links the hermit with CQ's meta-cognitive aspect to provide theoretical and practical solutions that give a better understanding for how and where people build their plans and strategies that help them succeed in future cultural interactions. By addressing the mentioned points, our study thus addresses significant knowledge gaps in extant CQ literature. The sustainable adaptive leadership framework further enhanced Hamlin's taxonomy of Leadership Effectiveness and Ineffectiveness by providing longer list of positive and negative behaviors. This can be seen as a first step towards a new adaptive framework / model of leadership effectiveness model that relies on transactional and interactional CQ as a leadership effectiveness competency. This competency takes into consideration that leaders or organizations that operate outside their homelands need to liberate themselves from the dilemma of losing the absolutes defined by CQ scholars (Gelfand et al., 2008).

The new approach to global and adaptable leadership relies on a transformation within fixed number of cultures that leaders need to learn: the DCF cultures. This approach opens the doors wide to individuals and companies' HR departments to provide necessary training for their employees and get them prepared to successfully work in any place around the globe without the need for extensive knowledge about local or national cultures.

This becomes particularly vital in the case of project managers leading multicultural teams and more so in the case of virtual teams as mentioned in the previous chapter. The suggested paradigm shift is an attempt to respond to the calls from various professional bodies such as PMI that indicated, in the sixth edition of the PMBoK, the the need for more attention to the project manger's soft skills in shift towards sustainablility.

End of chapter exercise

Table 3.4 provides the students or practitioners with an opportunity to apply the contents of this chapter by evaluating their direct managers. Readers should use this script to conduct the interviews, then analyse the collected data in light of the concepts delivered in this chapter with the emphasis on the case study. If needed, students can seek advice, guidance and support from the authors by reporting back the collected data for analysis and discussion of findings.

Table 3.4: Assignment: Understanding manager behavior - questionnaire. Try to explain and provide an example in response to each question

	Questions asked to understand manager's behavior
1	Interviewee to provide background about the manager
2	Which cultural/behavioral preferences your manager adopts? Is she/he team oriented (cares about her/his team, protects her/his team, promotes them, and does allow others to interfere with them…) or she/he only abides by rules and regulations to protect her/himself, or both, or none.
3	Is you manager aware of her/his own cultural/behavioral characteristics? What about others' cultures? Do you see her/him aware of them?
4	Does your manager know how to apply her/his knowledge about the others cultures in different situations? Can she/he describe the differences of others' cultural/behavioral backgrounds?
5	Is planning important to your manager? And Why?
6	Do you think that time is of value to her/him when she/he plans how to succeed in next encounters?
7	In any encounter happen, is your manager aware of the outcomes impact on others and how can she/he overcome the negative aspects of it in the future or is awareness important at all? And why?
8	Do you think that your manager check she/he is behavior in order to enhance it in the future? Is checking her/his behavior important to him?
9	Does your manager change her/his cultural/behavioral preference from one encounter to another depending on the situation?
10	Is information important in general to your manager? Does she/he use it as a repertoire to improve future experiences? Or to introduce change to the department or the company in general?
11	What drive your manager's behavior? Do you think that she/he externally motivated in a sense that she/he looks to be promoted, noticed by management or get a raise. Or, does she/he have an internal drivers that push her/him to adopt a certain culture/behavior? Or both?
12	Does your manager appreciate communicating his ideas with others at all?
13	Does your manager focus on verbal communication when he interacts with others?
14	What about non-verbal communications such as emails and letter?
15	Is this manager committed to adapt to other cultures when there is a need to do so?
16	How do you categorize your manager's behavior? Is it effective or not? Why? And what its outcomes on you as an employee

3

References

Ang, S. and Van Dyne, L. (2008). Conceptualization of cultural intelligence: Definition, distinctiveness, and nomo- logical network. In S. Ang and L. Van Dyne (Eds.), *Handbook of Cultural Intelligence: Theory, Measurement, and Applications* (pp. 3–15). Armonk, NY: Sharpe.

Barth, F. (1966). *Models of Social Organization* (No. 23). Royal Anthropological Institute of Great Britain and Ireland.

Bell, B. S. and Kozlowski, S. W. (2008). Active learning: Effects of core training design elements on self-regulatory processes, learning, and adaptability. *Journal of Applied Psychology*, **93**(2), 296–316.

Biermeier-Hanson, B., Liu, M. and Dickson, M. W. (2015). Alternate Views of global leadership: applying global leadership perspectives to leading global teams. In J. L. Wildman and R. L. Griffith (Eds.), *Leading Global Teams* (pp. 195–223). New York, NY: Springer.

Blasco, M., Feldt, L. E. and Jakobsen, M. (2012). If only cultural chameleons could fly too A critical discussion of the concept of cultural intelligence. *International Journal of Cross Cultural Management*, **12**(2), 229-245.

Cabrera, A. and Unruh, G. (2012). *Being Global: How to think, act, and lead in a transformed world*. Harvard Business Press.

Caligiuri, P. (2006). Developing global leaders. *Human Resource Management Review*, **16**, 219-228.

Campion, M. A., Fink, A. A., Ruggeberg, B. J., Carr, L., Phillips, G. A. and Odman, R. B. (2011). Doing competencies well: Best practices in competency modeling. *Personnel Psychology*, **64**, 225 262.

Chattanooga Model of Global Leadership Development. (2001). *Unpublished document*. J. Burton Frierson Chair of Excellence in Business Leadership, College of Business, University of Tennessee, Chattanooga.

Douglas, M. (1970) *Natural Symbols*, London: Barrie and Rockliffe.

Douglas, M. (1978) *Cultural Bias*, Occasional paper, London: Royal Anthropological Institute, 35.

Endsley, M. R. (1995). Toward a theory of situation awareness in dynamic systems. *Human Factors: The Journal of the Human Factors and Ergonomics Society*, **37**(1), 32-64.

Flavell, J. H. (1979). Metacognition and cognitive monitoring: A new area of cognitive–developmental inquiry. *American Psychologist*, **34**(10), 906.

Gelfand, M. J., Imai, L. and Fehr, R. (2008). Thinking intelligently about cultural intelligence. In S. Ang and L. Van Dyne (Eds.) *Handbook on Cultural Intelligence: Theory, Measurement and Applications*, 375-388. Armonk, NY: M. E. Sharpe

Gross, J. L. and Rayner, S. (1985). *Measuring Culture: A paradigm for the analysis of social organization*. New York: Columbia University Press.

Gupta, A.K. and Govindarajan, V. (2002), Cultivating a global mindset, *The Academy of Management Executive*, **16** (1), 116-126

Haller, E. P., Child, D. A. and Walberg, H. J. (1988). Can comprehension be taught? A quantitative synthesis of 'metacognitive' studies. *Educational Researcher*, **17**(9), 5-8.

Hamlin, R. G. (2002d). *Towards a generic theory of managerial and leadership effectiveness: A meta-level analysis from organisations in the UK public sector*. Unpublished PhD Thesis. The University of Wolverhampton, UK

Hamlin, R. G. (2004) In support of universalistic models of managerial and leadership effectiveness *Human Resource Development Quarterly* **15**(2), 189-215.

Hamlin, R. G., Ellinger, A. D. and Beattie, R. S. (2006). Coaching at the heart of managerial effectiveness: A cross-cultural study of managerial behaviours. *Human Resource Development International*, **9**(3), 305–331.

Hamlin, R. G. and Patel, T. (2012). Behavioural indicators of perceived managerial and leadership effectiveness within Romanian and British public sector hospitals. *European Journal of Training and Development*, **36**(2/3), 234-261.

Jacobs, J. E. and Paris, S. G. (1987). Children's metacognition about reading: Issues in definition, measurement, and instruction. *Educational Psychologist*, **22**(3-4), 255-278.

Mars, G. (2008). Corporate cultures and the use of space: an approach from Cultural Theory. *Innovation: The European Journal of Social Science Research*, **21**(3), 185-204.

McCann, J. T. and Holt, R. A. (2010). Defining sustainable leadership. *International Journal of Sustainable Strategic Management*, **2**(2), 204-210.

Mendenhall, M. E., Weber, T. J., Arna Arnardottir, A. and Oddou, G. R. (2017). Developing global leadership competencies: a process model. In J. S. Osland, M. Li, and M. E. Mendenhall (Eds.), *Advances in Global Leadership* (Vol. 10, pp. 117–146). Emerald Publishing Limited.

Mor, S., Morris, M. W. and Joh, J. (2013). Identifying and training adaptive cross-cultural management skills: The crucial role of cultural metacognition. *Academy of Management Learning and Education*, **12**(3), 453-475.

Murdock, G. P. (1971). Anthropology's mythology. *Proceedings of the Royal Anthropological Institute of Great Britain and Ireland*, (1971), 17-24.

Newman, P. and Thornley, A. (2011). *Planning World Cities: Globalization and urban politics*. Palgrave Macmillan.

Pacione, M. (2005). Dubai. *Cities*, **22**(3), 255-265.

Patel, T. and Salih, A. Muhamad (in progress). Cultural Intelligence: A dynamic and interactional framework. *Journal of International Studies of Management and Organizations*.

Patel, T. (2014). *Cross-Cultural Management: Towards alternative tools for cultural sensemaking*. Routledge, Oxford, UK.

Patel, T., and Hamlin, R. G. (2012). Deducing a taxonomy of perceived managerial and leadership effectiveness: a comparative study of effective and ineffective managerial behavior across three EU countries. *Human Resource Development International*, **15**(5), 571-587.

Patel, T. and Rayner, S. (2012). Towards a transactional approach to culture: Illustrating the application of Douglasian Cultural Framework in a variety of management settings. *European Management Review*, **9**(3), 121-138.

Price, M. F. and Thompson, M. (1997). The complex life: human land uses in mountain ecosystems. *Global Ecology and Biogeography Letters*, 77-90.

Ridley, D. S., Schutz, P. A., Glanz, R. S. and Weinstein, C. E. (1992). Self-regulated learning: The interactive influence of metacognitive awareness and goal-setting. *The Journal of Experimental Education*, **60**(4), 293-306.

Rockstuhl, T., Seiler, S., Ang, S., Van Dyne, L. and Annen, H. (2011). Beyond General Intelligence (IQ) and Emotional Intelligence (EQ): The Role of Cultural Intelligence (CQ) on cross-border leadership effectiveness in a globalized world. *Journal of Social Issues*, **67**(4), 825-840.

Salih, M. A., (2017). *The Role of Managerial and Leadership Effectiveness/Ineffectiveness and DCF-based Cultural Intelligence Framework in Assisting Organizations To Succeed in UAE*. Grenoble Ecole de Management.

Salih, A. M. and Patel, T. (2015). *Conference: AIBMENA 5th conference: Bridging the Divide - Cognitive dissonance between management theory and practice - Developing relevant and impactful research in the Arab Middle East. Dubai, UAE (best paper nominee)*.

Schmidt, A. M. and Ford, J. K. (2003). Learning within a learner control training environment: The interactive effects of goal orientation and metacognitive instruction on learning outcomes. *Personnel Psychology*, **56**(2), 405-429.

3

Senge, P.M. (2008). *The Necessary Revolution: How Individuals and Organizations Are Working Together to Create a Sustainable World*, Doubleday, New York.

Shippmann, J. S., Ash, R. A., Batjtsta, M., Carr, L., Eyde, L. D., Hesketh, B., Kehoe, J., Pearlman, K., Prien, E. P. and Sanchez, J. I. (2000). The practice of competency modeling. *Personnel Psychology*, **53**(3), 703 740.

Sitzmann, T., Bell, B. S., Kraiger, K. and Kanar, A. M. (2009). A multilevel analysis of the effect of prompting self-regulation in technology-delivered instruction. *Personnel Psychology*, **62**(4), 697-734.

Sitzmann, T. and Ely, K. (2011). A meta-analysis of self-regulated learning in work-related training and educational attainment: what we know and where we need to go. *Psychological Bulletin*, **137**(3), 421.

Smith, M. (2001) *Transnational Urbanism: Locating Globalization*. Blackwell, Oxford.

Stevens, G. W. (2012). A critical review of the science and practice of competency modeling. *Human Resource Development Review*, **12**(1), 86 107.

Tideman, S. G., Arts, M. C. and Zandee, D. P. (2013). Sustainable leadership: Towards a workable definition. *The Journal of Corporate Citizenship*, **49**, 17-33.

Triandis, H. C. (1995). *Individualism and Collectivism*. Westview Press.

Triandis, H. C. (2006). Cultural intelligence in organizations. *Group and Organization Management*, **31**(1), 20-26.

Thomas, D. C., Elron, E., Stahl, G., Ekelund, B. Z., Ravlin, E. C., Cerdin, J. L., Poelmans, S., Brislin, R., Pekerti, A. Aycan, Z., Maznevski, M., Au, K. and Lazarova, M. B. (2008). Cultural intelligence domain and assessment. *International Journal of Cross Cultural Management*, **8**(2), 123-143.

Thompson, M. (1996). *Inherent Relationality: An Anti-Dualistic Approach to Institutions* (LOS Centre Publication, Bergen).

Thompson, M. (2008). *Organising and Disorganising*. Devon: Triarchy Press Limited.

Thompson, M. and Wildavsky, A. (1986). A cultural theory of information bias in organizations. *Journal of Management Studies*, **23**(3), 273-286.

Thompson, M., Ellis, R. and Wildavsky, A. (1990) *Cultural Theory*, Boulder, CO: Westview Press.

Thompson, M. and Ellis, R. J. (Eds) (1997) *Culture Matters: Essays in honor of Aaron Wildavsky*, Boulder, CO: Westview Press.

Thompson, M., Grendstad, G., and Selle, P. (eds) (1999) *Cultural Theory as Political Science*, London: Routledge/ECPR Studies in European Political Science.

Van Dyne, L., Ang, S., Ng, K. Y., Rockstuhl, T., Tan, M. L. and Koh, C. (2012). Sub-dimensions of the four factor model of cultural intelligence: Expanding the conceptualization and measurement of cultural intelligence, *Social and personality Psychology compass*, **6**(4), 295-313.

Van Seters, D. and Field, R. (1990). *The Evolution of Leadership Theory* (Vol. 3).

Visser, W. and Courtice, P. (2011). Sustainability leadership: linking theory and practice. *SSRN Working Paper Series*

Walley, N. and Whitehead, B. (1994). It's not easy being green. *Reader in Business and the Environment*, **36**, 81.

4 Eco-Innovation:
Lean Startup approach to Sustainable Business Model Innovation

Alberto Peralta, Jorge Castellote and Mohamed Salama

Learning outcomes

By completing this chapter, the reader should be able to:

- Understand the concept of eco-innovation in the context of business models
- Understand the building blocks of the Lean Startup (LS) methodology
- Compare and contrast Lean Startup and the corporation models
- Explain how to apply Lean Startup (LS) to create sustainable business models

Introduction

Business model innovation (BMI) has emerged as a key root cause of competitive advantage. This is vital for organizations seeking to achieve the set strategic objectives through projects, particularly New Product Development (NPD) projects. However, there is limited attention among scholars and practitioners about sustainable BMI and its methods. Eco-innovation efforts (including the environmental, social and economic dimensions of innovation) concentrate on triple bottom line goals, but to date there seems to be a deficit of academic and practitioner literature on the effect of this type of innovation on new business models.

Scholars has been trying to address this gap, mostly focused on eco-innovation from a product-centric perspective where the product is the cornerstone of the new sustainable business models. And this is how conventional sustainable business model innovation is being developed.

Lean Startup is a novel approach towards business model innovation. This chapter aims to show how its concepts and tools are deeply rooted in sustainable concepts and how eco-innovation, under this new approach, is developed a step further, considering not only the product but the whole business model as the unit subject to eco-innovation.

Eco-innovation and business modeling

Eco-innovation is being addressed extensively, acknowledging stakeholder engagement, long-term sustainability (based on the triple bottom line) and the impact of public and private governance on how corporations are integrating it in their strategies (most of them from a supply-side, He et al., 2017). A very few reviews on eco-innovation have considered the relationship with new business model development as worth mentioning. Most eco-innovation studies connect their constructs with the development of goods, services, processes and even organizations to improve corporate competitiveness, but disconnect eco-innovation from the ways organizations create, deliver and capture value, and prevent leaving value uncaptured (Yang et al., 2017). Moreover, other authors (Evans, Bocken, Geissdoerfer) who connected sustainable innovation and business models focused on theorizing and integrating eco-innovated products, services and processes with working business models (BMs) to achieve a healthy triple bottom line. To date, there is a clear gap in the literature if we consider eco-innovation of business models as driven by value holders' needs and interests, not by products or extended value proposals.

Lean Startup and eco-innovation

This chapter aims to answer the following question:

How can Lean Startup (LS) serve as a process to create sustainable business models?

It may be the first effort to present LS as a novel sustainable BMI methodology that effectively integrates sustainable goals and eco-innovation since the inception of any new business model (BM). This is of importance, since conventional BMI methodologies address sustainability at late stages and always from a product perspective, which may cause high rates of failures.

LS as a BMI is method that places the customer and the rest of the value holders front and central, and sets a process for testing BM assumptions about every element of the new business model (Blank and Dorf, 2012; Boschet al., 2013; Dennehy et al., 2016). Consequently, the value proposal is treated as just one piece of a new business model among others waiting to be discovered, tested and falsified.

The next sections will help understand the basics of sustainable BMI.

Sustainability perspectives on business modeling

In their seminal paper on Sustainable Business Models, Stubbs and Cocklin (2008) acknowledge that sustainability was itself a contested concept. It still is. They rightly cited the World Commission on Environment and Development (WCED) report, which referred to environmental, social, and economic aspects of sustainable development, as an effort to agree on a common definition of the concept. But its implementation has resulted on its two most common, and different, perspectives:

1   The neoclassical economic worldview sees sustainability as a secondary, instrumental, concept to be pursued only if it maximizes shareholder's value, advocates for the company's self-interest, or is imposed by legislation or pressure from stakeholders (namely, customers) to retain credibility/legitimacy. This neoclassical understanding fosters a production cycle that reflects a "linear take-make-waste approach", which could in turn favor a linear way of innovating organizations and their business models.

2   The ecological modernization (EM) perspective sees sustainability as an alternative to achieve economic growth through environmental innovation and use of new technologies. BMs developed under EM are ecology-inspired and environment-induced. They have transformed their core practices to be profitable, improving the welfare of stakeholders and minimizing the environmental impact. BMs developed under this perspective would then take into consideration the interests of all stakeholders, including the future ones. They, for example, compensate harmful activities, usually by considering closed-loop processing and 'coopetitive' approaches. Under this perspective, BMs not only, or preferably, act for shareholders' interests. In this paper we adopt this latter perspective.

Eco-innovation of business models: a review of the conventional product development process

Sustainable business models (SBM) are relatively new in the academic literature. Citing Stubbs and Cocklin (2008), Geissdoerfer et al. (2016) trace back the first reference of SBMs to 2008. According to these latter authors, SBMs are a simplified visual representation of the elements forming a business model (BM), the interrelation of these elements, and the interactions of those elements (or thanks to those elements) with its stakeholders as they together produce the flow of value among them. That visualization then helps understand how the BM produces, delivers and captures value (Osterwalder, 2010) for its success, measured through impact and growth rates.

What is a business model?

The term business model (BM) has been present in scientific discussions for over fifty years now. Several differing perspectives have emerged. Osterwalder and Pigneur (2010) describe a BM as the ways an enterprise creates and delivers value to customers and others, and captures value and "converts this into profit". They describe nine elements of a BM: customer segments, customer relationships, channels, revenue streams, value proposition, key resources, key activities, cost structure and partnerships. In this paper we adopt this perspective of BMs.

Zott and Amit (2010) regard the BM as an activity system, more of a network, and describe its activities ('what'), its structure ('how'), and who performs the activities ('who') (2010, p. 38). They advocate for the development of BMs with a network-centric rather than a single firm-centric perspective. Value seems no longer created by individual models acting autonomously, but by acting together with parties external and internal to the model through informal or formal commitments.

The BM can also be understood as a link between future planning (strategy), and the operative implementation (process management). In this way, the BM is not a static entity, but a dynamic and evolving one. This dynamic nature calls for change and reinvention, in what is being known as BMI. SBMs build on the triple bottom line approach (Stubbs and Cocklin, 2008), and that defines SBMs' purpose and helps measure their performance along these three dimensions. SBMs' success is established by the value they provide to conventional stakeholders, to the environment (internal and external), and society (internal and external) as stakeholders.

In summary, SBMs produce, deliver and capture economic, social and environmental values from and for a wide range of stakeholders. The benefits from deciding for such type of BMs are widely described in the literature, ranging from improved efficiency, resilience to external shocks, better relationship with employees and communities, to higher profitability (Sachs, 2015) and survival rates.

How can sustainable business models integrate eco-innovation?

As with BMs, SBMs face change. SBMs (and BMs) seek adaptation to their markets and stakeholders. In the SBMs' case, they want to succeed and grow using a triple bottom line approach, adding to the challenges that conventional BMs have. In short, they should look for eco-innovation of their BMs.

BMI could be acknowledged as a "fundamental shift in the purpose of business and almost every aspect of how it is conducted" (Bocken et al., 2013), although less radical forms of BMI should be included in this definition. And if we consider the eco-perspective of innovation, Bocken et al. (2013) help us understand that innovation of a SBM "offers a potential approach to deliver the required change [to address triple-bottom-line goals] through re-conceptualizing the purpose of the firm and the value creating logic, and rethinking perceptions of value".

Eco-innovation and sustainability: the triple bottom line

Broadly speaking, if innovation refers to changes on how something is done, eco-innovation refers to changes that improve the environmental performance (Carrillo-Hermosilla et al., 2009). This does not mean that the motivation for eco-innovation needs to be only environmental. It certainly can depart from socially and/or economically motives. But with eco-innovation, the changes also benefit the environment.

The eco-innovation concept builds on the case of improving "economic success through voluntary social and environmental activities" (Schaltegger et al., 2012) According to these authors, there is a 'traditionalist' view of innovation, arguing that companies trade-off between "(better) environmental or social performance on the one hand and (worse) economic performance or competitiveness" on the other. But there is an alternative perspective on eco-innovation where voluntary sustainability efforts and corporate economic success can be produced together, fostering the possibility of win-win or triple-win potentials. This latter expands the idea of a triple bottom line (TBL), which in its simplest terms makes companies' eco-innovation efforts focus on economic, environmental and social value added (or destroyed) (Elkington, 2013). The dimensions of eco-innovation (Carrillo-Hermosilla et al., 2010) use a complementing, maybe more comprehensive approach than the TBL, as they examine the changes in BMs along four perspectives: design, user, product-service and governance aspects.

Eco-innovation of business models' strategies

If a BM needs to be eco-innovated, the advisable strategy seems to follow systematic, on-going processes to create new business models that aim for sustainability (Schaltegger et al., 2012). And this can happen through several alternatives ranging from the creation of positive (or less negative) impacts for the business, the environment (internal and external) and the society (internal and external), to changes in the way a BM creates, delivers and/or captures value. This means that a team willing to eco-innovate a BM, whether renovating it or creating one complementary (or several) new BM, can opt for eco-strategies, conventional market strategies, or both.

In the cases of existing BMs or SBMs willing to improve their current success or growth rates through sustainability, they can opt for either or both of two basic complementary sustainable innovation alternatives: (1) using existing approaches to sustainability to continuously adapt specific aspects of their BM design and delivery; and (2) new SBM creation in corporations willing to add new SBMs to their existing BMs. Both may be key to holistically improving sustainable performance and creating greater economic, environmental and social value, as suggested by Stubbs and Cocklin (2008), Porter and Kramer (2011) and FORA (2010). Figure 4.1 depicts the decision map towards SBMI.

SBM innovation theoretical approaches are not common (He et al., 2017) and again *"focus only on individual phases of the innovation process or specific types [of value propositions] such as the Product Service Systems (PSS)"* (Geissdoerfer and Jan Hultink, 2016). Evans et al. (2017) provided an initial attempt at describing a SBM innovation process. Theirs is an approach that integrates sustainability into the value proposition, and from a solid and sustainable value proposal they develop SBMs (Evans et al., 2017).

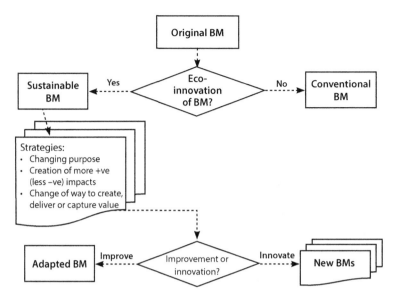

Figure 4.1: Decision map based on alternatives for eco-innnovating a business model.

The Cambridge Business Model Innovation Process

Based on the framework of Evans et al., Geissdoerfer et al. developed the Cambridge Business Model Innovation Process (CBMIP) (Geissdoerfer and Jan Hultink, 2016) which helps understand how SBM innovation might be deployed by innovators. The model builds a conceptual bridge over the Design-Implementation Gap (D-IG), which prevents companies from actually creating new successful SBMs. This bridge creates SBMs departing from a potential problem/solution (value proposal) misfit, and "consists of eight sequential but iterative phases or steps" grouped into three stages: Concept Design, Detail Design and Implementation.

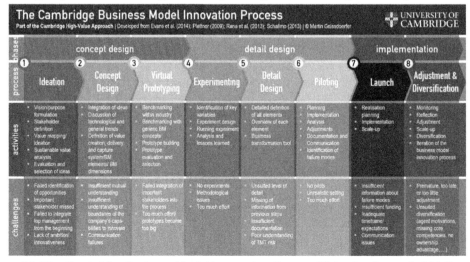

Figure 4.2: The Cambridge Business Model Innovation Process (Geissdoerfer et al., 2016)

In each of the steps or stages the CBMIP identifies corresponding activities and challenges, in an effort to visually map the planning and execution of new SBMs in different industries, companies, and operations.

The CBMIP is usually well understood by researchers and practitioners as it reflects the 'conventional' way of developing new business models. It represents the Product Development Process, or PDP. This representation of the conventional PDP sequentially integrates eco-innovation tools like Evan's five-step process (Evans et al., 2017), value mapping, Sustainable Value Ideation (Geissdoerfer et al, 2016), or the business model canvas (or BMC, Osterwalder and Pigneur, 2010).

Although the original model covers a broad spectrum of challenges, grouped by steps, it could be strengthened with the addition of two contributions from Carrillo-Hermosilla et al., (2010) and Bocken et al. (2014): The eco-innovation dimensions, and the archetypes for new SBMs.

4

Conventional product development and eco-innovation dimensions

Carrillo-Hermosilla et al. (2010) elaborated different eco-innovation dimensions, which can help organize the challenges that eco-innovation poses on a new or revised BM. These dimensions (design, user, product-service and governance), through the challenges they bring, would also drive the activities in each step of the CBMIP, aligning them with the corresponding goals set for each challenge/dimension. Table 4.1 shows the proposed relationship of the dimensions of eco-innovation and the phases of CBMIP. Each of the phases integrates the dimensions into the conventional innovation process by means of challenges and activities.

Table 4.1: Proposed relationship of the dimensions of eco-innovation and the phases of CBMIP. Developed from Carrillo-Hermosilla et al. (2010) and Geissdoerfer and Jan Hultink.(2016).

Eco-innovation aspects	Eco-innovation dimensions	CBMIP phases affected by eco-innovation dimension
Design	Component addition	Concept design , Detail design
	Sub-system change	Detail design
	System change	Detail design, Implementation
User	User development	Concept design
	User Acceptance	Detail design, Implementation
Product/service	Change in product service deliverable	Concept design
	Change in product service process	Concept design
Governance	Government-level changes	Concept design, Implementation
	Company-level changes	Implementation

New sustainable business model archetypes

Bocken et al. (2014) proposed archetypes of new sustainable business models that surely help the process of embedding sustainability into the CBMIP. Their eight archetypes, (Table 4.2), could be used as aids when planning specific sustainable strategies (the result of the business strategy is a business model, according to

Casadesus-Masanell and Ricart, 2010) to reformulate incumbent firms' corporate strategy, or complement the creation of new market entrants' overall strategy.

Table 4.2: Proposed relationship of the sustainable business model archetypes and the relevant phases of CBMIP. The table shows which phase is primarily acted upon in each BM type. Developed from Bocken et al. (2014) and Geissdoerfer and Jan Hultink (2016).

Business model archetype	Type of business model innovation	CBMIP phase affected by type of BMI
Maximize material and energy efficiency	Technological	Concept design
Create value from waste	Technological	Concept design
Substitute with renewables and natural processes	Technological	Concept design
Deliver functionality rather than ownership	Social	Concept design
Adopt a stewardship role	Social	Implementation
Encourage sufficiency	Social	Implementation
Repurpose for society/environment	Organizational	Implementation
Develop scale up solutions	Organizational	Implementation

Lean Startup for sustainability

Lean Startup offers an alternative way to develop new business models, considering all stakeholders from design

Since its inception as a methodology to develop new business models (Ries, 2008) LS addressed two key ideas: A new business model should not resemble or model the characteristics of an established and growing business (Blank and Dorf, 2012); and a new business model's initial steps are plagued by uncertainties (Ries, 2008), which in most cases result from knowing nothing about the elements forming the business model, but how those elements interrelate with each other (whether supporting, contradicting or being neutral to each other). Both ideas are at the root of what Blank, Dorf, Ries and Maurya, the authors who gave empirical consistency to LS, consider a fallacy that deeply affects founders and entrepreneurs: These types of innovators believe to be true the hypotheses they build after models of established companies, and disregard the uncertainties and disconnections these hypotheses are plagued with.

With that in mind, Ries named and designed a new methodology called 'Lean Startup' in 2011 (Ries, 2011) grounding it in Blank's customer development process, Agile software development, and design thinking (Eisenmann et al., 2011). It was then a methodology by practitioners and for practitioners, with little to no academic grounding. Since then, and given its success as a method to develop new business models, some attempts have been made to establish the theoretical foundation of the methodology. Blank (2013), Mansoori (2017) or Frederiksen and Brem (2017) have, in our opinion, successfully explained most of the theory behind the method. But there are still some gaps that need to be addressed that mostly relate to the complexity of the process of building a new business model if it is to become sustainable.

Building blocks of LS

To introduce the concepts of LS, Blank, Dorf, Ries and Maurya concentrated on describing how the LS approach favors experimentation over planning; customer feedback and stakeholder data over intuition; and iterative design over traditional business planning (Rasmussen and Tanev, 2016). Table 4.3 shows a non-comprehensive list of the concepts firstly introduced by these four authors. It is just a portrait (a complete, fully comprehensive list of LS concepts and their implications for BMI is out of the scope of this work) of the initial concepts that were described and integrated in LS. Our qualitative research on LS seems to point out that practitioners and scholars approaching LS without having tested the methodology tend to think of LS as "old wine in a new bottle" (Eisenmann et al., 2011), but the introductory concepts listed in Table 4.3 certainly differentiated it from the conventional, product-centric BMI (Eisenmann et al., 2011):

4

1 LS approaches the creation of business models from the inception of the business idea, and not as one of the final steps of the development of that business idea, when the idea is rounded and ready to be launched (marketed).

2 To realize the creation of a business model at such an early state of the development of the business idea, LS needs to adopt speed, flexibility (through a tactic called 'pivoting'), and experimentation (through another tactic called 'minimum viable product', or MVP). Those usually result in the development of several business models at the same time (even contradicting, or radically different from each other) serving the same business vision, not just one (as in 'one-size fits all') as proposed by the conventional approach.

3 There has always been a concern among practitioners and scholars about how to form the founder's vision (the business model's ultimate purpose). Conventional wisdom refers to a 'distorted view of the reality' as the grounds for the innovators' efforts, and the reason of the final success/failure (Blank, 2010) LS is about testing and reformulating that vision continually, based on market feedback (Eisenmann et al., 2011).

Blank and Ries have since then written extensively about how these concepts serve to continuously review the vision of the founders. They recognize that there are many options (business models) that can achieve the same goals. But most importantly, there are many influences and modifiers that affect the success of a business model before others.

LS, thanks to its theoretical structure, can integrate those influences as the business model progresses. At times, it would be through a systematic adaptation of the 'get customers' cycle (Blank and Dorf, 2012); at times it would be through validation of a payment method; other instances may demand finding funding for the next round; or a subtle inclusion of a control that prevents 'technical debt'. And all these changes are backed up by systematic learning from the valueholders around the business model, and throughout its growth (or decline).

Table 4.3: Building blocks of Lean Startup up to date.

Concept	Introduced by	Year of introduction
Business model creation	Blank / Ries	2003 / 2011
Minimum viable product (MVP): High and low fidelity	Ries / Blank, Dorf	2011 / 2012
Market feedback	Blank / Blank, Dorf	2003 / 2012
Business model design based on Business Model Canvas (Osterwalder et al)	Blank	2012
Customer development	Blank	2003 / 2012
Avoiding waste and spending until model is proven	Ries / Blank	2011 / 2012
Agile development	Ries	2011
Build-measure-learn loop	Ries	2011
Pivot, iteration	Ries	2011
Validated learning (hypothesis-driven entrepreneurship, Eisenmann et al)	Ries / Blank, Dorf	2011 / 2012
Business model design based on Lean Canvas	Maurya	2013
Problem / solution fit, Product / market fit	Maurya	2013
Search vs. execution	Blank	2003
Horizons of innovation	Blank	2015
Ambidextrous organization	Blank	2015
Investment readiness level	Blank	2014
Growth engines	Ries	2011
Innovation accounting	Ries	2011
Corporate / strategic innovation	Blank	2014

The valueholder concept in LS: Prioritizing stakeholders at growth

LS addresses growth based on a very simple conceptual premise, which is very hard to put into practice. Growth is based on how sustainable the new business model is. The business model will grow if it can create, deliver and capture value from its valueholders. As the business model is able to repeat, and speed-up that cycle, growth would be a consequence. (For different reasons, this growth is temporary and usually demands other complementary business models.)

The 'valueholder' concept is our language for a reality we have witnessed in our research. It is based on the 'stakeholder' concept (Geissdoerfer and Jan Hultink, 2016) which are those groups the new business model "creates, delivers, captures, and exchanges sustainable value and collaborates with/for" to achieve growth. When considering the impact (importance) of each group of stakeholders at each stage of the development of the new business model, then the stakeholder groups become less important, and only those valueholders relevant to succeed at each stage are considered.

Then, probably forcing the evolution of the business model, and following a snowballing process, the current valueholders give way to the next set of value holders initiating a new stage, usually with unique needs to address, different channels to be accessed, or different price tags, to name a few. Table 4.4 shows an example of valueholders of the Customer Discovery cycle, or first step of the Customer Development process (Blank and Dorf, 2012).

LS addresses value holders by design. By means of its validated learning, and departing from the initial hypothesis about the business model, it quickly sheds light on different valueholder groups. Table 4.4 shows a summary of the value-holders for a B2B startup Customer Discovery cycle. And as validation progresses, both new valueholders, and refinement of the original, produce the evolution of the initial business model design (through pivots and iterations) and the upsurge of other designs and differing business models.

LS as a sustainable business model innovation methodology

Geissdoerfer et al. (2016) identified the characteristics that a methodology or a process has to have to be identified as a sustainable way to innovate a business model. In their words:

> *"… We define sustainable business model innovation as the analysis and planning of transformations to a more sustainable business model or from one sustainable business model to another. This comprises both the development of an entirely new business model and the transformation of an existing business model."* (Geissdoerfer et al., 2016)

Other authors point out the importance of satisfying the stakeholders' needs (value network) (Bocken et al., 2014), and the importance of identifying value uncaptured and the creation of models aiming at higher sustainable value (Yang et al., 2017) when referring to sustainable innovation methods.

LS is designed as a BMI method that places the customer and the rest of the val-ueholders front and central and from there sets a process for testing assumptions about every element of the new business model (Blank and Dorf, 2012; Dennehy et al., 2016). But unlike conventional eco-innovation methods, LS has integrated the product, whether new or reused, within the value proposition a new business model would deliver (Blank, 4steps). And this value proposal is treated as just one piece of a new business model. From inception, the new business model is considered a collection of hypotheses waiting to be discovered and tested. Among those, the hypotheses related to the solution of a problem worth solving are a group of technical requirements called 'product' (or service), as in conventional eco-innovation. But first, they are not deemed top priority (this would be assessed quickly down the customer discovery process); and second, they are entangled with other important value-proposal assumptions that allow the creation, deliv-ery and capture of sustainable value. At the same time as the founders create the value proposal hypotheses, they non-linearly build the hypotheses about partners, resources, revenue sources, and about the rest of the elements of the new business model (Osterwalder and Pigneur, 2010).

Lean Startup and eco-innovation dimensions

Eco-innovation in Lean Startup then adopts a different perspective, complementing the product-centric one. The aim of LS is to allow the new business model to grow to achieve a triple objective, which holds together the successful business model. The product is not the centerpiece, and the customers (or the conventional stakeholders) are not the only valueholders, nor necessarily the most relevant. It is the whole business model that becomes eco-innovated. And quite unlike conventional sustainable BMI (product-centric), LS imposes the eco-innovation of the business model from its inception.

New business model challenges and Lean Startup

Eco-innovation in LS follows a different path to conventional sustainable business model design (He et al., 2017) It acknowledges that on Day 0 a new business model is nothing more than a series of hypotheses (Blank, 2013), which do not even complement each other to create a comprehensive picture of a way to create, deliver and retrieve value. To ease the selection of hypotheses leading to a sustainable business model, we suggest again the use of the eco-innovation dimensions to identify and organize the potential challenges the new business model is to face. These dimensions summarize the challenges (goals), or "internal and external factors influencing the innovation process" (Carrillo-Hermosilla et al., 2010).

Tables 4.4 and 4.5 organize the generic challenges a lean startup might face, from an eco-innovation perspective, along the Search stages of the Customer Development process. Once the challenges are identified, the gaps among challenges and dimensions could be addressed. Departing from there, LS leads the eco-innovators to test these assumptions for validation using three main processes: Business Model Design (Osterwalder and Pigneur, 2010); Customer Development (Blank and Dorf, 2012) and Agile Development (Beck and Al, 2001). Using these processes, start-ups translate their challenges, goals and ideas into falsifiable business model hypotheses, and integrate these into different business models designs (not just one, which is typically the outcome with product-centered methods) or canvases, in a process called Business Model Design (Osterwalder and Pigneur, 2010). Later, each business model canvas and its building blocks are swiftly tested using a prioritized backlog of item/hypothesis, through rapid cycles of experiments aimed at learning about valueholders, and their relevance for growing each model, by means of a series of constructs called 'minimum viable products' (MVPs), using a process of Customer Development (CustDev). This is a series of cyclical stages that seeks to achieve repeated sales and sustainable growth (Blank and Dorf, 2012) of the business models it produces. CustDev stages continuously produce new business model components, refine / replace original components, and redesign original interrelations among the building blocks of the initial business models, resulting in discarding some of them and building up new ones. This process is called Agile Development, as it is characterized by speed, quick learning and agile development of MVPs for testing hypotheses.

Table 4.4: Challenges following the dimensions of eco-innovation in the Customer Discovery stage of a LS model development (Carrillo-Hermosilla et al., 2010; Blank and Dorf, 2012).

Eco-innovation aspects	Eco-innovation dimensions	Eco-innovation dimension challenges in Customer Discovery stage
Design	Component addition	Some related to the product/market fit and MVP development
	Sub-system change	Some related to the basic development of the first hypothesis of the initial business models
	System change	Few related to founding team, funding and compliance with regulations/norms
User	User development	Many to know their needs and jobs to be done
	User Acceptance	Critical at the end of this stage to address repeatability of sales
Product/service	Change in product service deliverable	Some to build first get-keep-grow cycles
	Change in product service process	Some to integrate agility/cascade production Some to control for technical debt
Governance	Government-level changes	Critical to address sustainability (particularly social and environmental issus) Legality and illegality
	Company-level changes	Few related to organization building and founding team consolidation

Table 4.5: Challenges following the dimensions of eco-innovation in the Customer Validation stage (Carrillo-Hermosilla et al., 2010; Blank and Dorf, 2012).

Eco-innovation aspects	Eco-innovation dimensions	Eco-innovation dimension challenges in Customer Validation stage
Design	Component addition	Some related to sales and collateral materials, and metrics
	Sub-system change	Some related to the development of the sales cycles and matching the Market Type
	System change	All related to the definition of the sales roadmap, channels, retention cycles and company positioning
User	User development	Refinement of activation of users
	User acceptance	Product positioning and traffic partners
Product/service	Change in product service deliverable	Test growth, deliverable metrics, financial model
	Change in product service process	Optimize get, keep and grow customers

Governance	Government-level changes	Critical to address sustainability (particularly social and environmental issus) Legality and illegality
	Company-level changes	Sales organization building Founding team consolidation Advisory board Analytics lead

Lean Startup and sustainable business model archetypes

The sustainable business model archetypes are also helpful to understand how LS develops sustainable BMs. But to clarify the connection we must attend to the governing components of each type of BM, according to this classification. Table 6 shows our proposed connection, reflecting the CustDev stage each archetype reaches in its conceptual maturity. In other words, each archetype reaches a certain degree of maturity (CustDev stage) which forces the founding team to cycle again, or pivot, to find another, more successful BM to pass that stage. Success here means a new BM that is able to grow and repeatedly reach balanced triple-bottom line goals.

Table 4.6: Maximum Customer Development stage reached by the sustainable business model archetypes (proposed). The Table shows potential gaps for the two execution stages of Customer Development. Developed from Bocken et al. (2014) and Blank and Dorf (2012).

Business model archetype	Type of business model innovation	Maximum Customer Development stage by type of BMI
Maximize material and energy efficiency	Technological	Customer Discovery (search)
Create value from waste	Technological	Customer Discovery (search)
Substitute with renewables and natural processes	Technological	Customer Discovery (search)
Deliver functionality rather than ownership	Social	Customer Validation (search)
Adopt a stewardship role	Social	Customer Validation (search)
Encourage sufficiency	Social	Customer Validation (search)
Repurpose for society/environment	Organizational	Customer Validation (search)
Develop scale up solutions	Organizational	Customer Validation (search)

Case 4.1: Eco-innovation using Lean Startup at an established corporation

This case study is about C2. This is a national energy company, on its way to act globally (it already has global operations but is currently in an internationalization effort to further expand those operations). The corporate intrapreneurship program currently in place is quite recent and establishes the SBMI strategy right from the CEO down. Like many similar corporate programs, this includes an internal development, aiming at employees to deliver value for the company through the creation of their own enterprises from their business ideas, and an external (open) innovation program that covers the value created by other external entrepreneurs. The current agreement for research with C2 is concentrating in the intrapreneurship program that is being led by the VP of Sales of the corporation.

C2 launched their BMI program 2 years ago, after a mandate of the CEO (approved by the board) who explicitly stated it as goals for the 2 parallel programs. The overall challenges for the intrapreneurship, new business model development, program at C2 are both organizational (first) and business (second) oriented, and can be described as:

1 Development of entrepreneurial and business-oriented culture:
- Growth and efficiency
- Focusing on new strategies for C2 industry (locally and internationally)

2 Development of corporate startups
- New business models (internal startups) using the current market, financial and technical strengths of C2
- Incubation and acceleration of external startups
- Activation and more efficient use of current assets

3 Promotion of use of the main product of C2
- For consumers
- For SMEs

The program is being run by an independent unit under the lead of the Corporate VP of Sales, and is routinely supervised by the CEO. The resources allocated to this independent unit are minimum, as the whole project is under lean constrains: First results, then scaling. That unit runs across the current business lines, and gets its support from all of them (top managers) who integrate in the program at one stage or another. Involvement of the employees with the intrapreneurship activities is voluntary, but once one new business model is approved, employees affected (and their business units) become bound by the obligations set for the success of that new business model. This research team has witnessed the current level of support provided to the program from senior management, mostly ruling in favor of the intrapreneurs, in cases of contradictions against fixed organizational or business rules, norms or limitations.

As of the time of this writing, the intrapreneurship program has produced 60+ new business ideas from employees (all of them presented in a business model proprietary format), out of which three have already been incorporated as limited liability companies, with the employees leading the execution and taking equity of their respective firms, and four are on their incubation (development) stage.

Table 4.7: Comparison between Customer Discovery (LS) first stage and Pre-Incubation and Incubation: Activities

Lean Startup/Customer Development	C2 intrapreneurship program
State hypothesis Market size Value proposal 1: Product / Benefits / MVP Customers: Who / problem / job to be done / pain Channels Value proposal 2: Market size Cust. relationships: Get / keep / grow Key resources Partners Revenue / pricing	**Pre-Incubation** Identification of Startup Board Identification of Startup Team Creation / review of intrapreneurship program: goals, processes, deployment. Staffing of contest teams Lessons learned Idea selection, semifinal and final Contest final event. Final presentations. Selection of winners
Test problem Design tests Customer contacts Problem understanding Customer understanding Market knowledge	**Incubation: Steps 1-2** Meetings with external mentors Meetings with internal mentors Meetings with potential customers Collecting evidences that market exists Development of market research documents Creating sales plan Designing of business model Identifying key players Networking with agents & innovators within industry of reference
Test solution Update Business Model and team Create solution presentation Test solution with customer Update business model again 1st advisory board members **Pivot or proceed**	Designing of business model Training on skills and market opportunity selection Training on Business Model Canvas and Lean Startup Team description Performing Steering committee evaluation
Verify: product / market fit Verify: Customers and how to reach them Verify: Can we make money? Pivot or proceed	**Step 3** Producing financial plan Defining the market opportunity Training on pitching the company Mentoring sessions on finance & integration within C2 Training on financial plan and analysis Redesigning of business model Defining industry fit Defining team roles and commitment Performing steering committee evaluation

The C2 study case shows preliminary results of how a large, conservative firm, dominant in its market develops a process to create new business models thanks to a specific (expanding) market situation. It also supports the idea of an independent unit running a BMI program, in parallel to the current business operations. Also, as a particularity of this program we found that being led by the VP of Sales has an impact on the final achievements and selection process of the new business models. From the case study point of view, C2 is developing its innovation program based on a conventional way of corporate innovation, but very much spontaneously.

Its evolution from launch day, for both the program and the startups being generated with it, illustrates Lean Startup sustainable concepts in a conventional innovation environment.

Comparison between the Lean Startup and the corporation models

C2's BMI process splits the BMI activities in three stages:

1   Pre-incubation

2   Incubation

3   Acceleration

Our subject of study in this case has been the most innovative aspects of the creation of a new business model, namely the pre-launch stages, or the first and second stages of C2 program. Certainly, this may be one of the biggest differences between the corporation's models and LS: C2 models have a set of activities and challenges prior to launch time, whereas LS launches from day 0. According to this, and to ease the comparison, we have considered here only the two first steps of the Customer Development process:

1   Customer Discovery

2   Customer Validation

We then have built comparison tables where we have presented the similarities and differences between the two models (Table 4.7 is an example for reference). In the first column, we have stated the original items of the LS model. In the second column, we have introduced C2 comparative items. The main difference between the two models is that LS do all those activities in the same stage, cycling over each step continuously until a working (can sell) and scalable business model is established (pivot or proceed decision)

Conclusions

With this document we have approached a novel way of developing new business models like LS from a sustainable perspective. We can conclude that this methodology is apt for this type of business innovation, from a conceptual perspective. The evidence presented in the case study argues for further investigation on the relatedness of how corporations develop their new business opportunities and how Lean Startup is enacted, intentionally or not, in that search.

The review in this chapter offers valuable conceptual insights to understand how LS integrates different groups of valueholders (including the social and planet effects), at the time their interests and needs really impact the growth of a new business model. This is not always understood, particularly the way in which valueholders interact with the new business model and the effect of that interaction (or lack of it) in the overall success of the new business. LS seems to address those interests first, by detecting who the valueholders are at each moment of time, and second, by prioritizing those interests and valueholder groups that can support or oppose the business model success as it gains momentum and grows.

End of chapter questions

1 Conventional business model innovation activities address the creation of sustainable business models:

   a. Early in the process, when stakeholders' interests are learned.

   b. Late in the process, when all product requirements can really be taken into consideration, according to the conventional method.

   c. Early in the process, when shareholders' interests are really understood.

   d. None of the above is valid.

2 The value proposal seems a central concept for Lean Startup:

   a. And it is valued as much as in the conventional way of innovating a business model.

   b. But it needs to be complemented by other elements, such as partners, supply chain components, which are secondary to it.

   c. Not really. The value proposal would appear relevant depending on the type of valueholder group that drives the stage of creation of the new business model.

   d. None of the above is valid.

3 According to our paper, business models and sustainable business models are:

   a. Simple representations that allow capturing how value flows from an organization to its stakeholders and back.

   b. Simple representations of how companies can best serve their shareholders.

   c. Simple depictions of how to implement strategies like Lean Startup.

   d. None of the above is valid.

4 Lean Startup is acknowledging that:

   a. A startup or new business should comply and act like an established company, to compete in the same market.

   b. As a method it helps reduce uncertainties and improves competitiveness of new business models.

   c. A startup is facing uncertainty and should never behave like an established company.

   d. None of the above is valid.

5 The process presented by Lean Startup is:

   a. Linear. After a series of steps the idea is to arrive to a working business model to be launched to the market.

   b. A multilinear process that evolves cyclically using validated learning to decide which hypothesis needs to be tested next.

   c. A process that takes valueholders' interests into consideration after the product requirements are identified and tested.

   d. None of the above is valid.

6 After applying Lean Startup to develop a business model:

    a. One should expect a clear, polished business model that help take on a business opportunity.

    b. Several business models will match the conditions stated at the beginning of the process, and only one should be selected according to the criteria stated at that moment.

    c. Several business models will be developed, each matching the conditions relevant to the valueholders. Depending on these value holders relevance maybe more than one business model will be enacted, at the same time.

    d. None of the above is valid.

7 The dimensions of eco-innovation:

    a. Help Lean Startup integrate sustainability considerations in the product development stages

    b. Help the Cambridge Business Model Innovation Process select the appropriate tools for sustainable business modeling.

    c. Allow the integration of sustainable business models with the archetypes of Bocken et al.

    d. None of the above is valid.

References

Beck, K. and Al, E. (2001) *Manifesto for agile software development*. Available at: http://agilemanifesto.org/.

Blank, S. (2010) *Turning on your reality distortion field*. Available at: https://steveblank.com/2010/04/22/turning-on-your-reality-distortion-field/.

Blank, S. (2013) Why the lean start-up changes everything, *Harvard Business Review*, **91**, 64–72.

Blank, S. (2015) *Lean Innovation Management - Making Corporate Innovation Work*. Forbes. Available from https://www.forbes.com/sites/steveblank/2015/06/25/lean-innovation-management-making-corporate-innovation-work/#7f86f19f7c6a

Blank, S. and Dorf, B. (2012) *The Startup Owner's Manual: The step-by-step guide for building a great company*. K & S Ranch.

Bocken, N. M. P., Short, S.W., Rana, P. and Evans, S. (2014) A literature and practice review to develop sustainable business model archetypes, *Journal of Cleaner Production*. **65**, 42–56. doi: 10.1016/j.jclepro.2013.11.039.

Carrillo-Hermosilla, J., Del Río, P. and Könnölä, T. (2010) Diversity of eco-innovations: Reflections from selected case studies, *Journal of Cleaner Production*, **18**(10–11), pp. 1073–1083. doi: 10.1016/j.jclepro.2010.02.014.

Dennehy, D., Kasraian, L., O'Raghallaigh, P. and Conboy, K. (2016) Product Market Fit Frameworks for Lean Product Development, in *R&D Management Conference 2016 'From Science to Society: Innovation and Value Creation'*, pp. 1–11.

Eisenmann, T., Ries, E. and Dillard, S. (2011) Hypothesis-Driven Entrepreneurship: The Lean Startup, *Harvard Business School Background Note 812-095*, 44(December), pp. 1–23.

Elkington, J. (2013) Enter the triple bottom line, In A. Henriques and J. Richardson, *The Triple Bottom Line: Does it All Add Up*, London: Routledge, pp. 1–16. doi: 10.4324/9781849773348.

Evans, S., Vladimirova, D., Holgado, M., Van Fossen, K., Miying Yang, M., Silva, E.A. and Barlow, C.Y. (2017) Business model innovation for sustainability: towards a unified perspective for creation of sustainable business models, *Business Strategy and the Environment*, **26**(5), 597–608. doi: 10.1002/bse.1939.

Frederiksen, D. L. and Brem, A. (2017) How do entrepreneurs think they create value? A scientific reflection of Eric Ries' Lean Startup approach, *International Entrepreneurship and Management Journal*, **13**(1), 169–189. doi: 10.1007/s11365-016-0411-x.

Geissdoerfer, M. and Jan Hultink, E. (2016) Design thinking to enhance the sustainable business modelling process – A workshop based on a value mapping process, *Journal of Cleaner Production*, (July). doi: 10.1016/j.jclepro.2016.07.020.

Geissdoerfer, M., Savaget, P. and Evans, S. (2016) The Cambridge Business Model Innovation Process, in *14th Global Conference on Sustainable Manufacturing*.

He, F., Miao, X., Wong, C.W.Y. and Lee, S. (2017) Contemporary corporate eco-innovation research: a systematic review, *Journal of Cleaner Production*. **174**, 502–526. doi: 10.1016/j.jclepro.2017.10.314.

Mansoori, Y. (2017) Enacting the lean startup methodology, *International Journal of Entrepreneurial Behavior & Research*, **23**(5), 812–838. doi: 10.1108/IJEBR-06-2016-0195.

Osterwalder, A. and Pigneur, Y. (2010) *Business Model Generation: A handbook for visionaries, game changers, and challengers*. John Wiley & Sons.

Rasmussen, E. S. and Tanev, S. (2016) *Lean start-up: Making the start-up more successful, Start-Up Creation: The Smart Eco-Efficient Built Environment*. Elsevier Ltd. doi: 10.1016/B978-0-08-100546-0.00003-0.

Ries (2011) *The Lean Startup: How today's entrepreneurs use continuous innovation to create radically sucessful businesses*. Penguin Group.

Ries, E. (2008) *The Lean Startup, Startup lessons learned*.

Schaltegger, S., Lüdeke-Freund, F. and Hansen, E. G. (2012) Business cases for sustainability: The role of business model innovation for corporate sustainability, *International Journal of Innovation and Sustainable Development*, **6**(2), 95–119. doi: 10.1504/IJISD.2012.046944.

Stubbs, W. and Cocklin, C. (2008) Conceptualizing a 'Sustainability Business Model', *Organization & Environment*, **21**, 103–127. doi: 10.1177/1086026608318042.

Yang, M. Evans, S., Vladimirova, D. and Rana, P. (2017) Value uncaptured perspective for sustainable business model innovation, *Journal of Cleaner Production*. **140**, 1794–1804. doi: 10.1016/j.jclepro.2016.07.102.

Answer to exercises

1 b

2 c

3 a

4 c

5 b

6 c

7 d

5 Sustainable Change Management:
The 12 traits of successful post-Industrial Age transformations in the volatile, uncertain, complex and ambiguous economic reality

Ed Capaldi and Mohamed Salama

Learning outcomes

By completing this chapter, the reader will be able to:

■ Understand the basic concepts of the Agile methodology using the Scrum process.

■ Compare and contrast the advantages and disadvantages of Scrum

■ Understand the concept of VUCA amid the current digital transformation and its impact on the business environment.

■ Apply the 12 traits to a business case in a step-by-step approach.

■ Reflect on the outcome and evaluate the process of change management.

Introduction

Get ready! Buckle up! This chapter is very different from the previous chapters and even the following chapters, in this textbook. It is about change, so it leads by example! A change in the writing style, the structure and the approach. Our approach in this chapter, deviates from the standard academic writing style to a more practical, hands-on, case study-based approach. Most of the content reflects on the first author's vast experience; guiding businesses to cope with the challenges amid the volatile, uncertain, complex and ambiguous (VUCA) economic environment. The main body of the chapter is based on a fictitious case study about Kimlach Shahidi, a business owner and a CEO of a struggling business, seeking to adapt her business to the new economic realities of the Digital Age to build sustainable businesses and win in the VUCA[1] reality. In telling her story, Ed Capaldi uses a free writing style that makes it easy to read and follow, and hopefully an enjoyable learning tool.

However, it was deemed appropriate that at the outset the reader gets introduced to the relevant academic concepts covered in this chapter which is presented by the second author, the editor of the textbook, and which ties well with the previous chapters, particularly the section that discusses in depth Scrum as a process, following the earlier discussion on teams in Chapter 2.

Welcome to the Digital Age: Adapt or die!

It is not the strongest of the species that survives, nor the most intelligent. It is the one that is most adaptable to change that survives. Why is this the opening line of this chapter? It is the sincere belief of the first author that we are at an inflection point in human history. **Industrial age strategizing is dead, the Digital Age is frustratingly adolescent, business & CEOs lifecycles have halved** since the turn of the century. Our hypothesis is simple. As Dylan wrote, the times are a-changing, entrepreneurs and CEOs must adapt to the new economic reality. A new mindset is required, and the strategic planning tools and frameworks that served so us well in the Industrial Age must evolve or be left behind as economies and markets that have become unimaginably complex and increasingly volatile, uncertain and ambiguous. Welcome to the Digital Age.

Given how headstrong and stuck in their ways successful CEOs and entrepreneurs can be, it's hardly surprising that they'd be reluctant to change what's always worked for them in the past. Unfortunately, inflection points are turbulent and relying on past successes will not help you evolve. It's no wonder the average lifespan of a business has, according to some studies, dropped to 10 years, and the tenure of a CEO to half what it was at the turn of the century. The rate of return on assets has fallen by 75% since 1965, and the life expectancy of Fortune 500 firms down to 15 years, and is heading towards 5 years, only 1 in 5 workers fully engaged.[2] Peter Diamandis, co-founder of Singularity University, goes further and says within 15 years many S&P 500 companies will be extinct. Adapt or Die.

So, if you've got a big audacious goal, be it in making the world a better place, or growing a high impact business, then read on and experiment with these concepts and hopefully we can help you bring it to life. There are no shortcuts, or magical promises. Evolving your mindset and strategic planning to winning in the post-Industrial Age means you've got to do a lot of hard and scary work. What we offer in this chapter is a glimpse at the new mindset.

---

1 VUCA is an acronym used to describe or to reflect on the volatility, uncertainty, complexity and ambiguity of general conditions and situations. The U.S. Army War College introduced the concept of VUCA to describe the more volatile, uncertain, complex and ambiguous multilateral world perceived as resulting from the end of the Cold War in the early 1990s. Source: Wikipedia

2 Denning, S. [Online]. Available: http://www.stevedenning.com/slides/agile.pdf and Deloitte's Center for the Edge: The Shift Index; Kauffman Foundation

The chapter presents and discuss the 12 traits of successful post-Industrial Age transformations. Our case study will cover the story of Kimlach Ajay Shahidi in her quest to adapt her business to the new economic realities of the Digital Age to build sustainable businesses and win in the VUCA reality. Her story is fiction but based on true facts gathered from the thousands who like her have managed through the chaos to rise successfully where so many have fallen.

The following sections of this chapter will present some of the key relevant concepts, then will guide you through the 12 traits and the key tools and frameworks that she used and let you play with some of them.

A change in mindset

It might be useful to start with an age-old piece of advice, recently attributed to Peter Drucker but surely dating back to the days of the Phoenicians and Romans (Figure 5.1). "The purpose of business is to create and retain a customer". This is the first key difference between the Industrial Age mindset and the post-Industrial Age mindset. The former focuses on shareholder value, the later focuses on customer delight, and this evolved mindset is the key to effective strategic planning – make this happen, make this a reality. Most MBAs, economic journals and the like, continue to proclaim the purpose of a business is not to keep and create a customer, but to make money for its shareholders.

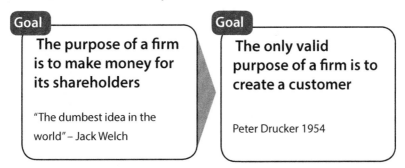

Figure 5.1: A Change in Mindset

Given Drucker is not a product of the Digital Age but as with any revolutionary idea it took time to build momentum, just like Copernicus's assertion that the Sun rather than the Earth was at the center of the universe.

Thus, putting the customer at the centre and casting making money for shareholders to the side is contrary to Industrial Age thinking and how most businesses are run, and thus revolutionary. This is a serious shift in mindset, but without this shift the tools and frameworks we discuss below will not provide true competitive advantage.

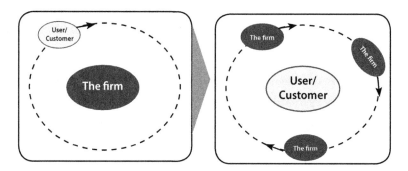

Figure 5.2: The Copernican Revolution in Management

Evolution of tools and frameworks

A great strategic plan should make it easy for the business to know where it is heading (direction), and why (purpose). Clarity of vision is central to success, and given the volatile and uncertain times, the role of leadership is to ensure clarity of vision so that all stakeholders can better plan and execute.

In what Steve Denning calls the Copernican revolution (Figure 5.2), clear vision without laser focus on delighting your customers will lead to strategic failure. Clarity of vision must be mated to clarity of the 'who', where the 'who' is a crystal-clear definition of the core customer the business must attract most of, to drive profitable sustainable growth. In the post-Industrial Age, strategic and tactical initiatives should make it easy for your core customers to find your business and make it easy for them to buy from you. In the Digital Age, you must also ensure the strategic plan is stimulating to internal stakeholders, making it easy for them to set the right priorities, to deliver insane value to your core customers and win.

That's stating the obvious, and let's face it: 90% of those highly intelligent ladies and gentlemen running businesses know this, yet CEO and business life-cycles continue their downward death march, what can we do to buck this trend? The chapter will, in its own way, attempt to answer this question in a simple and enlightening manner.

Before turning to our heroine, Kimlach Ajay Shahidi, to tell her story, we'll conclude this introductory part of the chapter with some basic concepts about Agile methodology with emphasis on the Scrum process.

Scrum

Scrum is the most common development framework that applies agile methodologies and it helps to enhance the efficiency, productivity and work quality of teams. It is a framework where people can concentrate on complicated and adaptive issues while focusing on delivering products creatively and productively. Scrum has established itself to be one of the more accepted process frameworks that are practical to use with Agile principles, and development teams have discovered success in using Agile even for hardware development. Collaborative projects are carried out by teams in the software development process and approaches that can achieve a balance between flexibility and control are needed, and this was the reason why Agile approaches were created. (Backblaze, 2015; Schwaber and Sutherland, 2014).

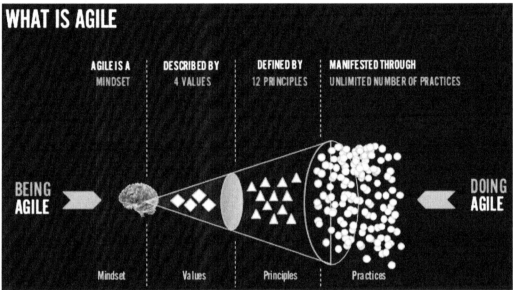

Figure 5.3: What is Agile? Image by Ahmed Sidky (Riot Games/ IC Agile)

The concept of Agile is summarized in Figure 5.3. The following list presents the 12 principles as laid down in the Agile Manifesto:

1   Our highest priority is to satisfy the customer through early and continuous delivery of customer visible value.

2   Welcome changing requirements, even late in development. Agile processes harness change for the customer's competitive advantage.

3   Deliver value frequently, from a couple of weeks to a couple of months, with a preference to the shorter timescale.

4   Business people and the delivery team must work together daily throughout the project.

5   Build projects around motivated individuals. Give them the environment and support they need and trust them to get the job done.

6   The most efficient and effective method of conveying information to and within a delivery team is face-to face conversation.

7   Customer visible value is the primary measure of progress.

8   Agile processes promote sustainable development. The sponsors, developers, and users should be able to maintain a constant pace indefinitely.

9 Continuous attention to technical excellence and good design enhances agility.

10 Simplicity – the art of maximizing the amount of work not done – is essential.

11 The best architectures, requirements, and designs emerge from self-organizing teams.

12 At regular intervals, the team reflects on how to become more effective, then tunes and adjusts its behavior accordingly. Our highest priority is to satisfy the customer through early and continuous delivery of customer visible value.

Software product releases require planning points which are explained below: (Schwaber, 2009; Backblaze, 2015; Schwaber and Sutherland, 2014).

1 **Requirements of customers -** To understand what enhancements are required for the current system.

2 **Pressure of time -** To understand the time frame required for a competitive edge.

3 **Competition -** To understand what is needed to beat the competition.

4 **Quality -** To understand the needed quality.

5 **Vision -** To understand changed needed to fulfil the vision of the system.

6 **Resources -** To understand what funding and staff are available.

In Scrum, there are three pillars that support the execution of empirical process management and they are as follows:

1 **Transparency -** This means that certain aspects of the process need to be visible to the people who are responsible for the result.

2 **Inspection -** Frequent inspection is required for progress towards a sprint in order to be able to detect unwanted variances. However, the inspection should not deter the work.

3 **Adaption -** The process should be adaptable because if the inspector requires change, then the process or material would need adjustment.

The Scrum process

The Agile Scrum process can be summarized in steps as follows: (Pries-Heje, and Pries-Heje, 2011; Ferreira et al., 2005; Backblaze, 2015).

1 The process of Scrum begins when a product backlog is created by the product owner, the team and stakeholders involved, and this is built upon the needs of the customers.

2 A meeting takes place that allows the Scrum team to add or remove items from the backlog so that they can divide the tasks according to their significance and items are filtered in this way, with some set to be looked at later. This method is continuous and takes place in each Scrum stage, so the items on the log get clearer in time.

3 Scrum projects are separated into *sprints* and these last between one to four weeks. The amount of work to be done and the team's task completion rate determine the number of sprints to take place. The sprints are arranged into four meetings called *ceremonies,* where the first one is usually the planning meeting. This takes place at the beginning of each sprint and during this meeting the top items are taken to create a to-do list for a sprint.

4   In the next step, the product owner and Scrum team together make a decision on each item in the backlog. They break down, calculate approximately and clarify the value of each item in the log until it is prepared for the sprint.

5   During the sprint, the daily Scrum begins with a meeting of about 15 minutes where each member needs to answer three questions, which are:

■   What did I do yesterday that helped the team move forward towards the goal of the sprint?

■   What will I do today that will move the team forward to reaching the goal of the sprint?

■   What obstacles do I see that could stop the team from reaching the goal of the sprint?

6   A review is conducted at the end of each sprint and the customers and stakeholders are invited to this meeting, which can go on for about two hours. Together, they review the work done, and the works not completed as well, and offer their feedback which the Scrum team uses for future sprints.

7   The Final sprint is the presentation which lasts one hour and this allows the team to look back and discuss ways in which the sprint process could be enhanced. This is an important step towards success and the team answers the following questions:

■   What went acceptably well during the sprint?

■   What could have improved?

■   What can be done to enhance the process?

Advantages and disadvantages of Scrum

The main advantages and disadvantages of Scrum have been collated in Table 5.1.

Table 5.1: Advantages and disadvantages of Scrum: Source (Ferreira et al., 2005; Pries-Heje, 2011).

Advantages of Scrum	Disadvantages of Scrum
This method can exist with other methods to fill any gaps.	Scrum requires continual modifications, monitoring and removal of obstacles by the manager to encourage support and assist teams to achieve success.
Delivery and deadlines are met rapidly so customer satisfaction is high.	Since Scrum teams are self-organizing, managers need to allow these teams to make their own decisions and sometimes fail, if required. This involves costs, in both money and time.
Agility and the Scrum master's motivation improves productivity.	The Scrum process is still a relatively new concept and people can be resistant to change. This can cause initial uneasiness where adjustment is necessary, though sometimes people are unable to adapt to Scrum at all.

Scrum is a bottom-up continuous and rapid method that caters to modifications without large demands of time or expenditure.	Scrum requires a lot from the team members and even higher authorities and this can sometimes be a daunting ordeal.
Since everyone knows what they are doing, communication and collaboration is easier.	
There are brief intervals of time amid project presentations for the customer which allows regular feedback to improve.	
A culture is created since communication is enhanced and the achievement of the process is shared amongst the team. This helps to greatly motivate team members.	

VUCA and the age of the Agile organisation

We will start with the root cause, which should now be pretty obvious, that the Industrial Age is over, and as humans are pretty bad at changing their ways, few CEOs and businesses have accepted we are at an inflection point and they need a new mindset, and new tools and frameworks to win in the new age, the Digital Age. This, coupled with the fact that digital accelerates everything, often to an exponential level, and we have the potential of a mass extinction on our hands.

How do we buck this trend? To be honest, nobody knows, inflection points in human history have never been predictable so what works today will probably not work tomorrow. That's the way of evolution in turbulent times, and right now traditional strategic planning is highly hazardous and the one emerging solution that has a track record of success at the moment is Agile. Agile enables businesses to master continuous change, and cope with today's chaotic customer driven economies. Businesses and CEOs who have mastered Agile have accelerated and scaled up in a world that is volatile, uncertain, complex and ambiguous.

VUCA, the new economic reality for businesses and CEOs

In close to 30 years of project management, strategic advisory and business coaching I have come realize, as have many others, that the world is changing exponentially. VUCA, a phrase coined by the US Military in its assessment of world order after the collapse of the Berlin Wall, has become the economic norm. We operate in an increasingly volatile, uncertain, complex and ambiguous environment and the tools and frameworks that once we held dear can no longer be relied upon; new tools and new frameworks are needed if CEOs and companies are going to survive in the post-industrial world. But why do we need to adapt to survive?

Our world is in a state of transition, as it has done so many times before. Two hundred years ago we evolved from the Agricultural Age and entered the Industrial Age; the age of kings and queens similarly gave way to the age of politics and government, and today we are faced with the chaos in transitioning from the Industrial Age to the Digital Age. Each of these inflection points resulted in massive upheavals in the way society operated; those that refused to change and adopt new modulus operandi failed to survive the transition.

In this emerging Digital Age, where VUCA is the norm, many of the tools and frameworks we have relied upon are failing to deliver value, yet like lemmings, many of us stick to what we know best. Take for example highly successful people in the domains of project management, and in strategic planning and execution. Why should they change something that's always worked for them! These highly successful people are expert in change management but now when it's looking back at them in the mirror, can they change?

In the world of IT, waterfall and traditional project management has never really delivered projects on time, to budget and to spec. How many customers of these projects are delighted by the value they gained from their IT investments? Very few, in fact something like 80% of IT projects are late, over budget and didn't deliver what the customer expected. This is painful reading, especially for me as that's what I did for years. However, CEOs, and CIOs who have embraced the new reality and are willing to adapt have turned to Agile tools and frameworks such as SCRUM. From Microsoft, SAP to local entities such as RSA Logistics, German Imaging Technologies and Al Futtaim, Agile is being embraced as an effective means to deliver value in IT projects.

Think of the annual budgeting process. If you ask any CEO or C level executive 'what's your prediction for the economy and growth of your business six months from now?' most will say that given the volatile uncertain reality they don't really know. Then ask them about their budgeting process and how it's geared towards Industrial Aged thinking – they still hold people, especially sales, to year end targets and spend vast amounts of time and effort setting annual or rolling budgets. That makes no sense at all. Others such as Statoil have introduced Agile frameworks to best manage in a time of VUCA, their standard 'Beyond Budgeting'[3] takes the process beyond the traditional command-and-control towards a management model that is more empowered and adaptive.

With so much chaos and upheaval in the business world it has been difficult to validate what works and what does not. Fortunately, there are some who have been collecting empirical data on the success of agile companies – internationally, people like Steven Denning, Arie van Bennekum, Jeff Sutherland and Luke Hohmann. It's not just in the old economies that leaders are stepping up; from Microsoft Global, ING Bank in Holland, and Kreditech in Germany, many have embraced the future and are busy charting their journeys one iteration at a time, ditching the old and figuring out the new. We are also seeing the tides of change sweep into emerging markets, where we have real examples of entrepreneurial businesses that are fearlessly experimenting with Agile. From forward thinking corporates like Mashreq Bank and Al Futtaim to high impact entrepreneurial businesses such as Ecocoast, Urbanise, ABC India Limited, SEMAC, Focus IMC,

---

3 Bogsnes, B. 2016. *Implementing Beyond Budgeting: Unlocking the Performance Potential,* Wiley

RSA Logistics, German Imaging Technologies, The Box, Intercoil, and RAW Coffee. They come from all backgrounds across all industries, but what they have in common is a hunger to adapt and grow.

Figure 5.4: The 12 traits of successful post-Industrial Age transformations - Turning vision into action and strategy into sales in today's highly volatile uncertain economic reality

The following story takes real life examples from these case studies and weaves them into the journey of one lady entrepreneur as she turns her vision into reality and strategies into sales.

Case 5.1: Kimlach Shahidi, CEO – Phaedrus Zen, LLC

It all started in closing months of the year 2020, Phaedrus Zen llc was closing another great year, in fact another stellar year! Sales had grown by 38% and the latest statistics showed an 85% global market share, their employee retention sat at 98% and gross margins were an industry-leading 40%, and all this in spite of the global meltdown in urban motorcycle sales. There didn't seem to be any complacency in the company yet Kimlach Ajay Shahidi, granddaughter of the company's founder Lord Nicholas Shahidi, felt unease. She'd attended a CEO Supper Club in Beirut and had her first encounter with the Agilitas movement. These entrepreneurs had embraced the learnings from the detested technology industry and implemented small iterative yet radical experiments in their businesses. Admittingly, most of these entrepreneurs had not kept up with the waves of disruption hitting their industries, so they had little or no choice but to experiment or get stuffed like the dodo. Yet, they all had seen rapid incremental changes in their fortunes. They evangelized like zealots, raving on and on with extreme enthusiasm of their experiments, of their successes and multiple failures. They spoke of the new way, of mastering the 12 Traits that marked the transition into the new order (Figure 5.3). These 12 Traits, from what she understood, started with forging a new mindset where the customer was at the centre of all strategic and tactical decision taking. They spoke of driving the customer versus being driven by the customer; they lectured on the importance of letting go of traditional management practices especially the annual budgeting cycle, individual appraisals and rewards; of eliminating what they called the permafrost, that middle management layer that championed the status quo and stifled agility. They spoke of 'radical transparency' and huge profit sharing schemes, and something called *scrumming the scrum* 'week after bloody week'.

She seldom drank and seeking solace she eased herself into her grandfather's worn leather armchair cupping a 1918 Armagnac, one of the last remaining bottles, distilled in the final days of the Great War by passionate artisans, who despite the incredible volatility and destruction of the times had persevered in forging the aromas of plum and vanilla that now mingled with airs of a new millennium and in perfect unison embraced her core with a warmth that took her back to a bygone era, of the time when her grandfather would sip this Armagnac and recount stories of how he'd forged the essence of their family's business. As she let herself drift in the haze of memories gone by, one emerged rising slowly out of the fog, crystalizing slowly in her mind's eye. Her grandfather had once confided in her that the key of his early success was in re-inventing his business before his competitors could catch up and well before his customers ever considered buying something else. With this, she went up to bed. She knew what she must do to take the business forward.

She slept badly that night, tossing and turning ceaselessly; her husband huffed and puffed before finally conceding defeat and retreating to the spare room. By morning she was calm, her mind now set on joining the Agilitas, to become indoctrinated into the 12 Traits, and reinvent her business now, whilst she was still ahead of the pack. After all, she might be the market leader but wasn't it bloody obvious that customers no longer wanted urban motorcycles. She needed to understand what they were employing her products for and understand what their alternatives were – pointless being the biggest fish in a shrinking pond!

She was up early, drawing open her window blinds she was dazzled by a splendid light. It had snowed overnight, the world was fresh and a clean slate awaited her design. She took to the path that would take her through the old olive grove, the ground-frost crackled underfoot and she strode purposely towards the new dawn.

She called Som Toogood, one of the ringleaders of the Agilitas movement, someone who'd broken through the shackles of Industrial Age entrepreneurship and built a passionate business which was on target to hit $3bn sales this year. He was free to meet, in fact, as she would soon find out he was always free to meet up at a moment's notice, unless he was travelling to meet a client or heli-skiing off some mountain top. She cancelled all her appointments for the day, mounted her Ducati Diavel and sped off for his chalet HQ.

5

The Transformation

By the time she arrived at Intercoil HQ Som was still freestyling down the steep heavy forested slopes that bordered his complex. She was shown inside the 'war room'[4] and plopped herself down on a chrome studded beanbag, with a shot of rocket fuel, her favorite brand of cold fusion coffee mayhem, and sat marveling at what appeared to be sticky note heaven, a room dominated by the words TO DO – DOING – DONE and below them a myriad of multi-coloured sticky notes appeared to represent a flow state of progress towards some nirvana!

The War Room

At 7:08 the doors flung open, Som and what must have been his direct reports, bursting in, destroying her calm with boisterous excitement and extreme intent. What followed was an intensive huddle, what she'd soon discover was called the daily scrum, and sticky notes moved across the TO DO – DOING – DONE boards as everyone shared with the others what they had prioritized for the day, what they'd delivered since yesterday and where they were stuck. The transparency and openness were breathtaking, a few clarification questions here or there and the anything considered an impediment to getting the work done went straight onto 'the blockage board' which recorded the date the blockage was raised, what it was and who would fix it, no time was allocated to talking about the blockage, amazing! Then at 7:20 after high-fiving one another they sped off to turn their vision into reality. The vision was crystal clear to everyone – after all it covered an entire wall of the war room. The energy was contagious, the rush comparable to opening up the Diavel on the open road. She could see why and how the Agilitas had come across as zealots, she was hooked, she wanted in.

Figure5.5: The War Room

Som, smiled, watching her stumble over her inner thoughts, containing herself from what she'd just experienced. He let her regain her composure then admonished her for the 'rocket fuel' as it was known to make you crazy!

---

4 Roberts, J. 2011. Create a Dedicated IT Situation Room: Gartner.

> ### Zenji Som Teaching: The journey begins
>
> Walking towards the veranda overlooking the mountain he'd just freestyled down, Som spoke on the great debate, how on the one side the traditionalists with years of success behind them argued the key to success was maximizing shareholder value driven by the survival of the fittest mantra, whereas he and his fellow Agilitas believed in maximizing customer delight as the number one prerogative, and given the increasingly volatile and uncertainty of the global economies to focus on creating a culture that could adapt faster and smarter to grow ever stronger and thus survive the long-haul. Playing to win, he argued, was to build adaptable systems and achieve a flow state that would give you strength and endurance, without which a business would ultimately tire and collapse into oblivion. The command and control structures of the past reduced a businesses' ability to adapt quickly and effectively in today's markets, just the Borg in Star Trek, the individuals in the company had to think together, collaborate effectively and be given the autonomy to take faster smarter decisions. A few wise men at the top of the organization could not manage the intensity of decision taking now required.
>
> The veranda was bathed in the morning sun's rays, standing side by side over a weathered cedarwood tabletop he unrolled an A3 sized black silky cloth, the cloth revealed the 12 Traits that had been at the forefront of the previous evening's supper club conversation. (Figure 5.3.)

5

How to use this case study

To maximise the benefit out of this case study, the reader should note that each of the 12 traits will be projected to Kimlach's case study with appropriate takeaways, insights and actions. Then the key reading sources appropriate for this trait will be listed. This can be a useful class exercise where groups of 3-5 can apply the 12 traits to any business case, either fictitious or from real life, over the period of the delivery of the course.

Trait 1. Clarity of vision

Som poked the black cloth, his index finger falling on the crystal ball in the top right hand corner. A leader must work tirelessly to ensure everyone understands where they are going and why. A Kaylach ship without a NorthStar will lose its way. It is not good enough to hire great technical people if they are disconnected to your vision and purpose – it's like leaving a bad apple in a basket, sooner or later the others will spoil too. In this post-Industrial Age with its highly skilled intellectualized workforce with 24 hour access to the global network, we as leaders must crystalise our vision and bring to life the core purpose of why our business exists and tirelessly communicate until every stakeholder, internal and external understands where our ship is headed and why. A ship that embarks on a voyage without its NorthStar crystal clear will never rule the seas.

Kimlach's key takeaways

Key insights:

- Never assume your team understands the purpose and vision of the business.
- Without the purpose clearly defined, you will hire the wrong people.
- A crystal clear vision and purpose attracts the right people, once on board they will think out of the box and come up with better smarter solutions in getting the work done, right.

Key actions:

- Use simple concise words, pictures and videos to hammer home the message.
- Continuously communicate the NorthStar.
- Recruit not just on technical ability – make sure people on the team believe in the vision and the purpose.

Key readings:

Collins, J. and Porras, J. (1996). *Building your Company's Vision.* An HBR article. September-October.

Sinek, S. (2011). *Start With Why: How Great Leaders Inspire Everyone To Take Action,* Penguin Group.

Denning, S. (2018). *The Age of Agile: How Smart Companies Are Transforming the Way Work Gets Done,* Amacom Books.

Trait 2. Moonshot thinking

Sum's finger slid clockwise. Moonshots! Businesses fail because they do the wrong things or are not ambitious, not because of competition, and no one changed the world by thinking small. Since Jim Collins came up with BHAGs and Google X with their Moonshot Thinking, more and more people have understood the importance of thinking audaciously and believing in making the impossible possible. Everyone at Intercoil dreams big, naysaying is frowned upon because 'big hairy audacious goals' are dreams that demand laser focus and disciplined thinking, planning and action to be turned into reality. Som stopped for a moment lost in a thought, then burst out laughing "Christ! We'd never be having this conversation today if JFK hadn't set that moonshot of putting a man on the moon and bringing him back safely in ten years. Godamnit, we'd be working down some mine under the commies!" He brought up his friend Arvind whose purpose was to wipe out child malnutrition in East Africa by providing breakfast and lunch free every day and we'd never be on track with enhancing the lives of one billion people by 2030!

Kimlach's key takeaways

Key insights:

- If you truly want to scale up fast and impact the world with your dreams, then you need a company of moonshot thinkers who believe in your vision and purpose.

- The leader must create an environment which not only attracts moonshot thinkers but allows them to work together.
- Moonshots take you outside your comfort zone and in so doing foster the environment to think outside the box and deliver great work.

Key actions:

- With a clear vision and purpose defined and understood, work with the team to set one clear long-term goal that defines in measurable terms success, then break this long-term goal into 90 day moonshots to which the teams deliver.
- Recruit and retain moonshot thinkers.
- Set a long-term moonshot for the business and champion 90 day moonshots using the OKR (Objectives and Key Results) framework.

Key readings:

Doerr, J. (2018). *Measure What Matters: How Google, Bono, and the Gates Foundation Rock the World with OKRs*, Portfolio/ Penguin.

Collins, J. BHAG – Big Hairy Audacious Goal [Online]. Available: https://www. jimcollins.com/article_topics/articles/BHAG.html

Kotler, S. and Wheal, J. (2017). *Stealing Fire: How Silicon Valley, the Navy SEALs, and Maverick Scientists Are Revolutionizing the Way We Live*, Harper Collins Publishers

5

Trait 3: Customer delight

Som continued his rhetoric. Customer delight is where the old guard get it wrong, so wrong. It's not about customer journeys and awesome design, it's more than a tick box, a meticulously designed process, it's about truly understanding the job the customer is trying to get done and their pains and unexpected gains to be had in getting it done. It's about driving the customer more than being driven by the customer, but before any of this you have to have the discipline to know who is your core customer and who is not. Your core customer, we call him 'Frank', is the one most likely to buy your product or service in the quantity required for optimal profit. Once your Frank is defined, you have to get in there close with him. I spend half my waking hours with Franks to better understand the job where they are going to use my products and services over others. Without insane focus on Frank we can't set the right 90 day moonshots that will accelerate us through the VUCA chaos. Hey let's break for lunch and order an aperitif of foamed beetroot with chilli and ginger ice, and I'll call Ted Yapaldz, he's our growth catalyst, you'll resonate with him. I love his definition of Frank, it's: *High octane visionary entrepreneurs seeking trusted advice to lead a high growth high impact business through the chaos of the VUCA economic reality*

Kimlach's key takeaways

Key insights:

- Customer delight over Shareholder value. The highest priority is to delight your core customers, in turn they will not only buy more from you they will become your key advocates.

- Find Frank in each segment you choose to play in or drift along building products and services no one really wants and will be willing to pay for.
- Know your Franks better than they do and that means getting out of the building to spend 50% of your time with them.

Key actions:

- Define Frank using the Finding Frank tool.
- Define a customer segment then use Value Proposition Canvas tool and the Lean Launchpad framework to build products and services that will fuel revenues and profits.
- Make it everybody's business to know Frank and structure the business to be laser focused on delighting Frank.

Key readings:

Capaldi, E. and Gazelles International. (2016). *The Finding Frank toolset*. [Online] Available: http://www.edcapaldi.com/sales#Frank

Osterwalder, A. and Pigneur, Y. (2014). *Value Proposition Design: How to Create Products and Services Customers Want*. Wiley Publishers.

Osterwalder, A. and Pigneur, Y. (2014). Value Proposition Canvas. [Online] Available: http://www.edcapaldi.com/sales#VPC

Christensen, C. (2016). *Competing Against Luck: The Story of Innovation and Customer Choice*, Harper Collins Publishers

Trait 4: Network of teams

Back inside, they make a detour to the retromod library where Som grabs a book and tosses it to Kimlach. "Great book this one, little dated but it championed this one important trait that distinguishes progressive organizations from their traditional industrial-aged counterparts. It takes you through how the US military had no choice but to reinvent itself in order to communicate and collaborate faster, smarter, better. This is going to be hard work for your motorcycle business, stripping out the permafrost of that 2nd level management and evolving from hierarchical command-and-control structures to a so-called Network of Teams." Seeing Kimlach's quizzed look at the strangeness of the room they are in Som explains how he got the idea of a retromod library after spending a week in Singularity University and then a summer trekking through Tibet visiting the old monasteries, and that's when he cottoned onto the idea of creating a space which welcomes deep work, a place where people can enter and chillax reading on their Surface book or grabbing a real paper book from a shelf and easing themselves into a 100 year old armchair where countless others had sat and thought before. She knew how powerful this would be over at Phaedrus Zen llc, after all her *aha* moment had come straight out of a deep thinking from her grandfather's armchair.

Som continued, explaining how the very essence of leadership was evolving. You no longer had the need to tell people what to do, if they believe in your vision and your purpose, if they had bought into and understood your BHAG and if they were laser focused on delighting the customer then you as a leader had to learn to let go. Get out of their way and support them in delivering awesome work.

"You know why I go heliskiing every morning? It's not because I'm an eccentric wierdo as some of those journalists say, and it's not just about getting me into the zone, into my flow state. It is because we have created a team of teams organizational structure and I know the teams are on track turning our vision into reality and our moonshots into sales."

A network of teams

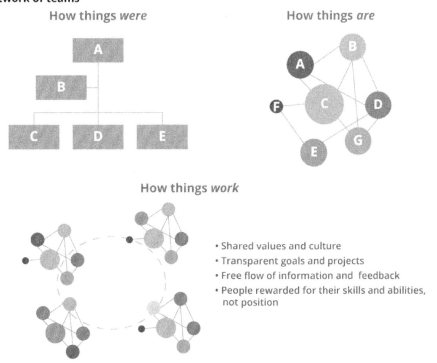

Figure 5.6: Network of Teams. From *The organization of the future: Arriving now 2017 Global Human Capital Trends* by J. Bersin, T. McDowell, A. Rahnema, Y. Van Durme. Deloitte University Press

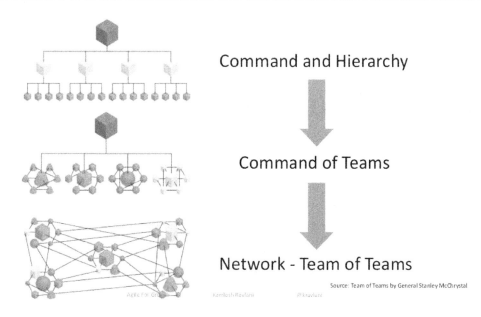

Figure 5.7: Team works(Command). From: *Team of Teams: New Rules of Engagement for a Complex World* (2015) by General S. McChrystal, T. Collins, D. Silverman and C. Fussell.

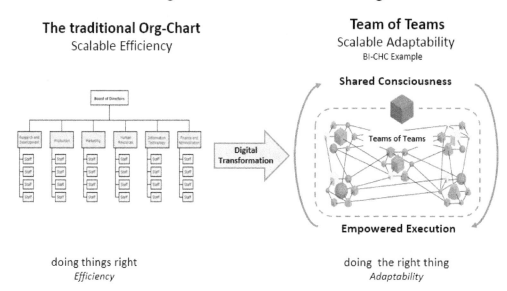

Figure 5.8: Changing management structure by moving from scalable efficiency to scalable adaptability in order to succeed. From: *Team of Teams: New Rules of Engagement for a Complex World* (2015) by General S. McChrystal, T. Collins, D. Silverman and C. Fussell.

Kimlach's key takeaways

Key insights:

- Command and control was great once upon a time but now in this VUCA reality it is insane to expect one person to have the brain capacity to take all the decisions.
- No team is an island, break down silos. All needed tasks and responsibilities lie within the teams themselves, people operating in teams/ small projects will need to work with other teams, and to do this effectively and efficiently overall goals must be clear and well communicated, everyone needs to know what others are working on.
- Empowered execution succeeds only if there is a shared culture and the psychological safety to weed out destructive behaviours. Performance management, jobs roles and accountabilities will have to evolve.

Key actions:

- Start experimenting and building Agile structures that embody interdependence over independence. Transformations are painful, so fast and incremental, is the way to go, go all-in and accept an initial dip in productivity and engagement for granted.
- Although tied to a common vison, purpose and BHAG, each team has its own clear focus on one thing that distinguishes them from other teams. Involve your people in this conversation by running collective intelligence sessions that spark debate and produce actionable plans to kick of the experiments needed to transform.
- Strip out the hierarchies starting with the permafrost layer of middle management, consider what metrics drive team positive rather than disruptive behaviours. Revaluate the role of leaders, coach them to become gardeners.

Key readings:

General McChrystal, S. and Collins, T. (2015). *Team of Teams: New Rules of Engagement for a Complex World*, Portfolio/ Penguin.

Robertson, B. (2015). *Holacracy: The New Management System for a Rapidly Changing World*, Henry Holt & Company, LLC Publishers

Laloux, F. and Appert, E. (2014). *Reinventing Organizations: An Illustrated Invitation to Join the Conversation on Next-Stage Organizations*, Nelson Parker Publishing

Trait 5: Self organising teams

Lunch at Intercoil. Som had invested in the latest and greatest technology from the Middleby Corporation, the first truly agile mega-corporate that had transitioned from the Industrial Aged strategic planning and execution without any contact with the Agilista movement but having many of the 12 Traits! Middleby is a world leader in their space, employing over 6000 employees who self-organized themselves in what appeared to be just three layers of organization. The numbers are outstanding: Som recalls attrition rates of below 2%, of market leading profitability and incredible customer loyalty. He spoke of a defining moment in his own journey of how once he'd met their COO and having done his math asked how a VP could manage 700 people, to which a rather surprised COO belted out "why the hell would I want to manage anyone?" This ethos is core to the Agilista movement, and whether by design or coincidence Som took up the story of this 5th Trait as lived by the Intercoil Canteen. As with everything else in the business the kitchen ran 90 day sprints. One team would own the canteen every 90 days; it would be formed from the business and self-organize itself delivering awesome products (menus) to their clients (the other employees of the business) in very small batch sizes. Whilst he rattled on, Kimlach chose green gazpacho, Vietnamese spring rolls and a spicy chicken noddle soup.

Sitting down at the table Som continued with the 5th Trait. Structures like these have been tried many times and often fail. Why do you think that is? I'll tell you why, it's because people try and follow these traits one by one rather than spend time understanding them as one would any complex problem, and then after gaining a holistic perspective trying through multiple experimentation and implementation, iteration by bloody iteration, small increments, baby steps that reduce the impact of failures, provide masses of learning and through these continuous step improvements achieve the new modus operandi.

Self-organizing teams in terms of structure, are not commanded by any individual. These teams are driven by the purpose – this is the anchor point from which they are rooted. They nurture their core competencies and sprout new ones where necessary. They become masters at what they do, and they have full autonomy for how they think, plan and act. But with autonomy comes discipline, and zero tolerance for failures. Excuses are not tolerated by the anyone in the team; shape up or you're out.

Kimlach's key takeaways

Key insights:

- The team of teams structure would fail unless teams are self organizing, and this means they are motivate by autonomy, mastery and purpose.

- Ultimate team size must be arrived at, maximum 9 individuals in a team. Beyond that communications breaks down and there is too much waste.

- Teams must be cross-functional and have all the skills and attributes to deliver awesome value to Frank!

Key actions:

- Review hiring process and include compatibility testing on business core values and purpose. Right people on the bus = right culture.

- Visit other Agilista organisations, and understand mechanics behind self organizing teams, refocus the business on delivering extreme delight to their Franks and organize teams behind this mindset.

■ Experiment with 90 Day strategic planning cycles using OKR frameworks and scrum weekly sprints.

Key References:

Pink, D. (2011). *Drive: The Surprising Truth About What Motivates Us*, Riverhead Books, Penguin Random House LLC.

Sutherland, J. and Sutherland, JJ. (2014). *Scrum, The Art of Doing Twice the Work in Half the Time*, Crown Business Books, Random House LLC.

General McChrystal, S. and Collins, T. (2015). *Team of Teams: New Rules of Engagement for a Complex World*, Portfolio/ Penguin.

Trait 6: Radical transparency

Having finished lunch, they were joined by Ted, Som's catalyst and coach who suggested they walk down to the lake. Taking the baton from Som, he asked Kimlach what she thought of transparency and where would transparency fit into these conversations. Transparency? No thanks, they'd tried it years ago and all it did was reinforce politics and ultimately led to people giving away corporate secrets to their competitors, and anyway do employees really care about the financials? Ted agreed, these were typical results from going transparent, however, how can a network of teams collaborate if they don't have full transparency on what each one is up to and how each fits into the vision and purpose? How can an organization adapt fast and effectively if it does not have ready access to the right metrics and data pools that are necessary for rapid decision taking? How can you have trust flourish if appraisals are hidden? In fact would you need individual appraisals if the teams are running effectively? Radical Transparency turns out to be the glue that binds many of the other traits together, without which the new modus operandi would collapse on itself. Ted flipped a stone across the lake's surface, they watched it skip six times before losing steam and sinking fast to the depths of the lake. Kimlach though to herself, well that's what we need to do, keep the momentum going, keep skipping across the face of the lake because if we don't we'll sink fast.

They paused, each lost in their own thoughts then Som motioned them back towards the base. Time to get a good look at the War Room. The War Room was named as it's where war is made, be this against one's own weaknesses, or the teams' collective intelligence at outthinking the competition, or at smashing down comfort zones and attacking the priorities of the week, of the day, of the moment. It had been a deep dive into the 12 Traits, and when they got to the War Room she realised this is where her day had started – she'd been so caught up in the stories and the learnings that she'd totally forgotten about the highly energized kick off she'd been witness to. Som was gesticulating, pointing out the Vision and Purpose statements on the far side, the 90 Day OKR tracking sheets, depicting all the key metrics that matter to Intercoil in achieving their moonshots, pointing out how each team, through weekly Red/ Amber/ Green colouring, communicated progress of their OKRs, then the weekly TO DO – DOING – DONE board that broke

5

down the progress into smaller batches of daily, and where necessary hourly, deliverables on brightly coloured Post-Its, each colour depicting a different team and how all blockages fell onto the blockage board. The blockage board was what defined peak performance; an empty board showed either a lack of trust or weak moonshot thinking, and so wherever Som saw an empty blockage board he was swift to check in with the team lead on what was going on.

Kimlach's key takeaways

Key insights:

■ Secrecy is dead, in the post-industrial VUCA reality transparency rules. Make work and track progress visibly and accessible to everyone!

■ Identify what is secret today in the business and find out why. Ask the people within the business to question if there is a good reason not to share this information. If there is no good reason and if the information is important to faster, smarter, better decision taking, then be brave and share it.

■ Individual appraisals and incentive schemes reinforce 'silo me me me' thinking.

Key actions:

■ Introduce open book management after training employees on the basics of financials, then include as part of the 90 Day OKR objective setting process.

■ Review incentive schemes and individual appraisals, consider rewarding the business for achieving its core objectives. A team focused on autonomy, mastery and purpose that is brutally transparent and delivers will review and appraise itself week after week, sprint after sprint, quarter after bloody quarter.

■ Create war rooms and set powerful effective communication rhythms throughout the organization driven by daily huddles, weekly planning and retrospectives and 90 Day transparent collaborative objectives setting.

■ Educate everyone on the beauty of 'blockage boards'.

Key reading:

Stack, J and Burlingham, B. (1992, 2013). *The Great Game of Business: The Only Sensible Way to Run a Company*, Crown Business Books, Random House LLC

Denning, S. (2010). *The Leader's Guide to Radical Management: Reinventing the Workplace for the 21st Century*, Jossey-Bass, Wiley

Lencioni, P. (2002).*The Five Dysfunctions of a Team: A Leadership Fable*, Jossey-Bass, Wiley

Trait 7: No preferences

The traits obviously put together are greater than the sum total of their individual benefits, in fact it was becoming more and more apparent that the whole model was dependent on a trial and error approach; the shorter the trials, the faster and better the learning. Moreover, it wasn't just the dramatic shift towards customer value away from shareholder value that concerned her, it was the radical style of leadership being touted that would be the key testing ground. Did she really need to change? After all, we are the market leaders and growing despite the fact that the market was shrinking; how on earth would she convince her employees to change, where was the sense of urgency, why fix what isn't broke? As soon as she voiced these concerns, Som slapped her down to reality. Who in their right mind wants to play in a shrinking market – ultimately, you'll be the absolute king of a dried worthless lake. Now, whilst you have the cash and the people, is the time to reinvent. Find Frank, figure out what is replacing urban motorcycles in getting their job done and build an organization that delivers awesome growth. Ted urges them to stay focused and Som continues with the sermon. No preferences. No gender bias, No individual bonuses, No privileged parking, No executive floors, No special privileges whatsoever! With traits such as team of teams, self-organized teams and radical transparency, it follows that some almost Marxist ideas come to play: are we moving towards 'egalitarian' entrepreneurial systems? Really? Without the privileges why would my senior mangers stay? That's the point, echoed Ted, you don't want the permafrost of middle management, you want fast, effective communications and self organizing teams pumping out real benefits regularly, to enhance the value of your products and services to your Franks. Team motivation and individuals aligned to a crystal clear vision and purpose don't need these little material extras. No it's not Marxism, or maybe it is, who gives a damn? What we have seen is that with these other traits in place it's best to remove individual preferences, and to remove them all together so the teams can stay focused on producing the awesome products our Franks actually want and will pay a premium for. If that wasn't enough to convince her, Ted asked her if she'd ever come across someone other than a boss or head of HR who was enamored with their business' performance management system and the bonus schemes that went along with them.

Kimlach's key takeaways

Key insights:

- Secrecy is dead, in the post-Industrial Age where collaboration, transparency and moonshots drive the business forward, there's no place for preferences.
- Preferences support hierarchical systems and could be disguising commitment.
- Radical Transparency will open up not only the books but salary levels, or at the very least salary bands within the business, and it would also bring to the surface any preferences.

Key actions:

- Review salaries
- Kill off any preferences

Key reading:

Denning, S. (2010). *The Leader's Guide to Radical Management: Reinventing the Workplace for the 21st Century*, Jossey-Bass, Wiley

Lencioni, P. (2016). *The Ideal Team Player: How to Recognize and Cultivate The Three Essential Virtues*, Jossey-Bass, Wiley

Sutherland, J. and Sutherland, JJ. (2014). *Scrum, The Art of Doing Twice the Work in Half the Time*, Crown Business Books, Random House LLC

Trait 8: Fair play pledge

They sat down now going through the stepped approach Som and his leadership team had taken in routing out preferences and making transparency a core discipline and value of the organization. She was flummoxed by the idea of transparent salary: would her organization be ready for this? How mature would some be? Surely the essence was not to compare oneself to another but that was bound to happen in cross functional teams. What about newly recruited, what if they are on higher salaries that those that had been in the same job there for many years? The debates and arguments would surely take everyone off track and the cost of balancing all these salaries was daunting. Som explained these things would come up, and each would need to be thought through, but just like a Catholic confession, the result was a heavy burden aired and shared and that's precisely why the 8th Trait had become mainstream in Agile transformations. The Fair Play Pledge! Surely, if the Agilista movement hadn't yet been accused as subversive Marxists raising money through the smokescreen of entrepreneurism for a modern age Doctor No, then this trait most certainly would! It was insane proposition. Who defines pay as fair? The key according to Som is to pay people fairly so that you take the question of money off the table and focus people onloving their workplace and doing great work.

Kimlach's key takeaways

Key insights:

- Before any conversations on fair pay could be opened up to the business, it was important to have open book management in place and ensure all employees have a basic understanding of financials.

- Eliminate distrust by opening up salaries and being totally transparent to internal (even external) stakeholders.

- Allowing teams to set their own salaries ensured governance as well as acceptance.

Key actions:

- Set up a voluntary committee charged with educating, and engaging the business in achieving a fair pay for everyone.

- Onboarding of all employees would include time spent across all teams to build stronger understanding of what other teams works on and deliver.

- Onboarding would include basic training in open book management.

Key reading:

Pink, D. (2011). *Drive: The Surprising Truth About What Motivates Us*, Riverhead Books, Penguin Random House LLC

Trait 9: Mutual trust and respect

It was getting late. A lot of the conversation centered on radical shifts in leadership, on cultural values that, to say the very least, were highly disruptive and unproven. Granted Som could provide case studies of successful transformations, but by and large this was all too radical. Thankfully it was winter time and the sun set late, the air was fresh penetrating deep in the lungs, stimulating the respiratory process into producing the ample quantities of oxygen her brain now required as she absorbed and churned through this day of deep learning. At least the fresh air also served to cool her brain, it was spinning almost at the rate of her Ducati!

Ted could see she was struggling with the amount of data she'd uploaded today. He enquired if it was time to bring proceeding to a close and kick off tomorrow. Kimlach would have nothing of this, she was here to learn and Som had graciously opened up his business and all that he knew for her. She had to decide today if, just like her grandfather, it was time to reinvent Phaedrus Zen llc. Som motioned them towards the hot tub, let's grab some bathing clothes and jump in, there's nothing like watching the sun sink behind the valley at this time of the year and it kind of sits nicely with the next trait. Mutual Trust and Respect! Kimlach and Ted laughed at his audacity and questioned where on earth they'd find some clothes, a quick search online and the clothes were ordered, ETA 30 mins. Enough time to get to the details of this traits.

As with everything else she'd heard today Mutual Trust and Respect was interwoven with the other traits. Radical Transparency, No Preferences and Fair Pay pledge reinforced Mutual Trust and Respect. Leaders could learn to let go and lead, giving up the shackles of management to self organizing teams when there was mutual trust and respect. But this took time; Som recounted the trials and tribulations of creating trustworthiness. It started with him having to show vulnerability, without which he could never create an environment for his peers to debate ruthlessly and candidly. He spoke of this book called the *5 Dysfunctions of a Team*, of the 5 levels leaders had to build and take the business through in order to build a high octane visionary workforce with the psychological safety required when delivering moonshots quarter by bloody quarter. Welcome to the age of trust-based leadership, which is anyways decades old right? Lead by example has been the way of the wise since the beginnings of time. If you can not lead by example how can you ever earn the respect of those you wish to lead.

He spoke of an old friend of his, Saud, who'd been promoted to a senior position in a multi-million dollar business only to find no one spoke to each other, and worked in that passive aggressive style to set each other up to fail. After three months he knew he had to find a solution or he'd lose his job. With the help of his coach he set to work on the 5 Dysfunctions of the Team and within three weeks couldn't believe the difference it had made, the team was collaborating and working together at getting things done.

Figure 5.9: Infographic by Neil Beyersdorf, in *5 Dysfunctions of a Team* by Patrick Lencioni

Kimlach's key takeaways

The Key insights:

- Core values aren't the fluffy things HR puts up on the wall that no one gives a damn about. Core values are the cultural DNA of the business, you hire and fire based on the core values and in this post-Industrial Age zero tolerance on core values is the norm.

- Without vulnerability from the leadership team you can't build trust at the fundamental level, which drives candid debate without fear of conflict and onwards towards a highly committed results focused team

- Trust and Respect without the word 'mutual' means nothing. This trait runs deep in the Agilista organization and is critical to replacing command and control systems.

Key actions:

- Determine the core values of the business, include them in the hiring and firing process.

- Bin controls, especially checking in and out, timesheets and one-to-one reviews.

- Reinforcing the daily huddle, weekly deliverables of tangible benefits and applying stretch targets to 90 Day goal setting creates the discomfort necessary to facilitate honest debate within teams.

Key reading:

Lencioni, P. (2002).*The Five Dysfunctions of a Team: A Leadership Fable*, Jossey-Bass, Wiley

Logan, D. King, J. and Fischer-Wright, H. (2011). *Tribal Leadership: Leveraging Natural Groups to Build a Thriving Organization*, Harper Business

Ferrazzi, K. (2009). *Who's Got Your Back: The Breakthrough Program to Build Deep, Trusting Relationships That Create Success - and Won't Let You Fail*, Broadway Books, The Crown Publishing Group, Random House

Trait 10: Less is More

Finally, the soft buzz of propeller shafts breaks through the peace and quiet. The black and gold drone floats into view and hovers above Som delivering the swim suits. A quick shower and change of clothes, an order of chilled aperitifs and the three of them skip across the veranda, and leaving the cold mountain breeze behind them ease with palpable "aghs" into the steaming bubbling bath. Life is good, thought Kimlach. This last trait had been important in unlocking the conundrums in her head – it was this old and critical value that would be at the core of her transformation, the mutual trust and respect everyone in her business had for her grandfather's original vision. She'd have to work hard at earning their trust and respect before she could ask them to go through this radical transformation. She'd buy that book and get stuck in straight away!

Now, 'less is more' was another familiar trait. Since the days of Toyota Quality Management, her industry had been applying this trait and when Som showed her how much of what the Agilitas did stemmed from these humble beginnings, she could see the connections between her world and this brave new world. 'Less is more' was a mindset of delivering smaller, batch-sized improvements more frequently, where each batch delivered real tangible improvements in value to the customer. Som pointed out that many didn't grasp the importance of delivering real tangible value improvements to the customer. This trait was often mistakenly deployed as faster delivery, and missing out the 'delighting customer' entirely was simply going to deliver waste and lessen competitive advantage later. He also mentioned that this is where many had deployed the Scrum framework, its daily standups, KANBAN Boards, and weekly sprints, the happiness and velocity metrics that so many loved to hate; and how overtime should be seen as another form of waste. The team had family and friends too, and overtime not only infringed on their personal time, but also implied poor planning, i.e. waste. There would always be exceptions, but small planning and execution cycles should be well managed right! For this Som's team used INVEST – an acronym used to help teams with their planning and lessen the impact of poor planning. INVEST was a checklist to help the team write out simple stories of what they had to produce and deliver in the next sprint:

Independent (of all others)

Negotiable (not a specific contract for features)

Valuable (or vertical)

Estimable (to a good approximation)

Sized to fit (so as to fit within a 'sprint' iteration)

Testable (in principle, even if there isn't a test for it yet, the requirement is a definition of 'done')

Kimlach's key takeaways

The Key insights:

- In every sprint a team needs to be laser focused on delivering something that is of tangible value to Frank, even if it is not released to Frank.
- It's just as important to have a definition of 'ready' as it is a definition of 'done' when setting the weekly plan.
- Leverage the business' core capability in Toyota Quality Management to evolve the conversation and reach buy-in quickly for the transformation to Agile.

Key actions:

- 'Less is more' ties into the weekly delivery cycle. Setting up War Rooms will provide the impetus for change by making it real, and help self organizing teams focus on delighting their customers in a disciplined structure manner.
- Apply the INVEST framework to define accurately if something is ready for the sprint, thus giving more visibility on the tasks that deliver value.
- Set up a task team to leverage TQM and small regular batches, and produce workshops helping transition to Agile.

Key reading:

Eric Ries, (2017) *The Startup Way: How Modern Companies Use Entrepreneurial Management to Transform Culture and Drive Long-Term Growth*, Currency: New York

Knapp, J and Zeratshy, J. (2016). *Sprint: How to Solve Big Problems and Test New Ideas in Just Five Days*, Simon & Schuster

Osterwalder, A., Pigneur, Y., Bernarda, G., Smith, A. and Papadakos, T. (2014). *Value Proposition Design: How to Create Products and Services Customers Want*, Wiley Publishers.

Trait 11: Measure and track everything

Great vision and purpose, held together with an awesome culture of high performing individuals being radically transparent and true to their core values, delivering small incremental batch-sized improvements to delight their customers, can only take you so far. To go faster, smarter, better you need to measure and track everything of importance. What gets measured gets done. That's really the purpose of the War Room, Som explains. It not only makes work visible – the face to face communication brings to life our emotions – it also becomes trackable. Ted felt he had to interject as he could see a case of eyes glazing over on Kimlach's face, but he need not have been concerned, by now she was in the zone. This wasn't a last grasp attempt at management to bring everything under control. This was to ensure the key metrics that mattered to the business were transparent, and by tracking them live in the daily and weekly huddles, force the team to look in the mirror and catch issues before they gained momentum and sank the ship. It was why she knew she'd drop the annual budgeting cycle and the annual offsite for setting objectives that VUCA anyways had made redundant. VUCA forced high performing teams to shift to 90 day strategic planning cycles where corporate objectives and key results would be debated and agreed and then in a matter of a week every team in the organisation and each individual therein would have set their OKRs after a solid retrospective of the previous 90 Day sprint. This brought the fluffy soft elements the Agilitas harped on about into start reality, where financial metrics became simply post-factor lagging indicators, and where cycle by cycle the business deep-dived into all the facts to ascertain which leading metrics should they focus on. Metrics from happiness, to velocity, to metrics that would make the key processes in their value streams faster, smarter and better, quarter by bloody quarter, and where customer metrics were understood as the lifeline to building awesome sustainable businesses.

Kimlach's key takeaways

Key insights:

- What gets measured gets done. Only with the right metrics can you build a highly engaged business that actively delights Frank and achieves market leading profitability. The right metrics would be arrived at through iterative and continuous improvements.

- War rooms were the nerve center of focused disciplined debate.

- In a VUCA reality, metrics need to be fewer yet more readily available. If a key metric is only available monthly that means 12 decision points per year, better to scratch beneath the monthly metric and come up with something that is available weekly or even daily.

Key actions:

- Set up a task team to investigate how best to roll out 90 day planning cycles using the OKR framework.

- Immediately kick off the War Room concept with her direct reports and start figuring out what drives the business.

- Review existing KPIs, drop all that are monthly control reports (for now) and focus on leading metrics that are trackable daily or weekly, based on Stacy Barr's PUMP framework.

Key reading:

Barr, S. (2016). *Prove It!: How to Create a High-Performance Culture and Measurable Success*, Wiley Publishers

Ulwick, A. (2016) . *Jobs to be Done: Theory to Practice*, Idea Bite Press

Trait 12: Profit Share

"OMG!!! What on earth has profit share have to do with this? What's wrong with traditional based individual and team bonuses? This is my grandfathers' business, not some pro bono lefty do gooders experiment!" A huge Cheshire cat grin sprawled across Som's face, "12 o'clock rock!" he bellowed out across the valley and into the night. "Look Kimlach, it's pretty fundamental what we're saying here. Intercoil is also my baby, my company and I own it, but we have to give back and share the spoils. The Romans did this, and every culture thereafter shared the spoils of victory with their troops! The troops got paid in salt and then if they survived and won the battle they got to take home the spoils of war! This is about ownership, if my troops are expected to go into battle every day and be top of their game then I'm willing to share 30% not 20% with every man woman and child who's contributed to our success. We all decide the split and whether or not to plough the profits back into the business, give to a charity or keep to ourselves. Let's face it, no one's every been happy with their individual and team bonus frameworks, right? Furthermore, these traditional frameworks are highly toxic for an organization that thrives on collaboration and responsiveness; we decided they should be eliminated entirely. However, fair, transparent incentives that honour collective intelligence and help our business win allow employees to participate financially in our achievements. It drives shared ownership and gives the extra ooompth and support to the other 11 traits. It's now 5 minutes to 12, if you don't get on that bike of yours, I fear it'll turn into a pumpkin!"

Kimlach's key takeaways

Key insights:

- Profit share of 30% plus builds trust between owners and employees and drives ownership across the business.
- Never implement profit share unless you've got a strong and mature Agile culture in place.
- Profits are just one dimension of success, a full and balanced view of the metrics that matter would need to be in more in place than work in progress, as would the other 12 Traits.

Key actions:

- Visit other businesses and talk to employees and owners on their experiences of profit share initiatives.
- Hold back on profit share until the transformation had built some momentum, but engage sooner rather than later in dialogue across the business.
- Get to grips testing various business models and ascertain the economic driver of the business, without which no team, no matter how proficient and honorable they be, would be able to take mid to long term decisions.

Kimlach prototypes the 12 Traits: first ever 90 Day strategic planning offsite

The dawn of the new era! Kimlach spent the next three weeks visiting every entrepreneur she could find who'd set sail lock, stock and barrel for the Agilitas's way. Every story differed, and she soon came to realise that although these 12 Traits held true, there was no one formula that could be applied, no silver bullet. She'd visited many of the grand old Industrial Age management consultants to seek their advice and had become angry how most had ready-made solutions for these transformations, when the reality was very different. Ultimately, she realised that this transformation would be iterative, built on the mantra of rapid prototyping, and it was a journey that she and all her employees would have to embrace. There was no use in engaging outside costly consultants except when needed and in very small batches. Som's coach Ted was invited in to help her and her senior team for a few days every month and Agile coaches were recruited to accelerate the process.

30 days after visiting Som, she and a hand chosen posse of Agilitas, key stakeholders in her business who'd raised their hands to lead this quest, met for a three day offsite. Ted led the thinking and they dug deep, debated like there was no tomorrow and completed their One Page Strategy Map together with their first OKRs! Massimo Grande, who'd previously been Phaedrus Zen LLC COO, took on the role of Scrum master, entrusted with their business' happiness and velocity (the measure of work a team completes during a single sprint) and Kimlach become the first ever Product owner, entrusted to reinvent her family business and win in these turbulent times.

Their War Room was up and running, the daily huddles and weekly sprint retrospectives and planning meetings took hold 42 days after that fateful CEO Supper Club. Sure there's going to be disruption ahead, and no doubt some trusted long standing employees will not have it in them to evolve and will leave, but she knew, and so did the others, that they had set a new course, an exciting one that would be revisited every 90 days and adjusted accordingly, and ultimately get them to leave behind their shrinking pond.

Figure 5.10: The Scrum Wall - A typical C-level War Room

A final word: Shu Ha Ri

Success is the sum total of all the decisions we take. Disciplined teams hold themselves to account. They will master **Shu Ha Ri** a Japanese martial art concept, that describes the stages of learning to mastery. In transforming to the Way of Agile, Preadres will first have to master the rules before you break the rules. Shu Ha Ri Aikido master Endō Seishirō stated: "It is known that, when we learn or train in something, we pass through the stages of shu, ha, and ri." These stages are explained as follows.

1 In **Shu**, we repeat the forms and discipline ourselves so that our bodies absorb the forms that our forbearers created. We remain faithful to these forms with no deviation.

2 Next, in the stage of **Ha**, once we have disciplined ourselves to acquire the forms and movements, we make innovations. In this process the forms may be broken and discarded.

3 Finally, in **Ri**, we completely depart from the forms, open the door to creative technique, and arrive in a place where we act in accordance with what our heart/mind desires, unhindered while not overstepping laws.

This is the Way of Agile. It takes courage to say "yes" to becoming a trust-based leadership team; the 12 Traits are a guide to intellectual debate and rapid cycles to test hypothesis and products alike. The 12 Traits can take you through Shu and maybe to Ha, but by then you'll know where you are going, and know what you need to do to get there, and always delivering small batches of very impressive deliverables (WOW) to your customers through short iterative Sprints ,most probably through highly audacious goals set every 90 days.

End of chapter exercises

1 Compare and contrast the advantages and disadvantages of Scrum.

2 Critically compare the 12 traits applied to Kimlach's case study with the Lean Startup (LS) concept presented and discussed in chapter 4.

3 Critically evaluate the scrum method in light of the adaptive leadership theory presented in chapter 3.

4 As a project manager what add-ons are required for the Agile methodology, particularly Scrum method, to be more adaptive to the shift towards sustainability.

6 Green ICT for Sustainable Development

Hind Zantout and Norbert Seyff

Learning outcomes

By completing this chapter, the reader should be able to:

- Demonstrate an understanding of Green ICT and the link to sustainability
- Explain the basic IT deployment models currently available
- Understand the metrics and frameworks that are currently in use
- Appreciate of the role of government and regulation in sustainability

Introduction

Almost all businesses, organizations and governments today have Information and Communication Technology (ICT) at their core. ICT enables day-to-day operations as well as assessing what has passed and planning ahead. However, ICT professionals aside perhaps, there is often little understanding of the technology and little appreciation of the link to sustainability and the impact ICT is having on the environment.

The coverage of this chapter is intended for an audience with no detailed knowledge of the various ICT specialisms, providing a broad, but high-level presentation of ICT, and discusses the various links to sustainability that are firmly established.

The discussion starts with the rapid developments since computers first were invented and then moves to energy demands that are being placed as a result of technology proliferations. We then introduce the term Green ICT, report on metrics enabling the measurement of energy consumption and discuss efforts underway to curtail energy consumption, with a focus on data centres. A view from a number of European countries is then presented, looking at how governments are addressing the issues and the barriers that are still in place for a country-wide sustainability drive in ICT. The construction project management sector is one that relies heavily on ICT services, and a brief discussion at the end presents additional issues for the project manager to consider.

Evolution of the ICT model

Information Technology (IT) infrastructure has evolved both conceptually and practically over the past sixty years. ICT is a slightly wider term as it also encompasses technologies used in communication between devices. For the purposes of this chapter, IT and ICT can be used interchangeably and the ICT landscape today is varied, offering a mix of infrastructure, equipment and devices that enable a wide range of software and applications.

The early days of ICT were characterized by one dominant central machine, the mainframe serving several users, and most of the computing power and energy consumption was concentrated in that single machine. Nowadays there many different options for where the actual processing can take place. At the one end of the spectrum we have microcontrollers that are embedded in other devices such as washing machines or cars, performing limited processing tasks. Then we have processors which are used in everyday PCs, laptops, tablets and smartphones, and at the high end there are the very powerful processors that are at the heart of servers in the Cloud and supercomputers. A widely used textbook identifies five eras so far (Laudon and Laudon, 2016) that are characterised by the domination of 1) the mainframe, 2) personal computer, 3) client-server, 4) enterprise computing and 5) Cloud and mobile computing. A sixth era is on its way, having further dramatic impact, with the rapid expansion of the Internet of Things and the concept of edge computing, where processing is pushed away from the centre to the end points in the network. Blockchain technology also seems set to expand, placing yet more demand for energy to run the large server farms that form its backbone.

In 2015 the United Nations announced 17 Sustainable Development Goals together with a framework of actions "to end poverty, protect the planet and ensure prosperity for all" (United Nations, n.d.) to be pursued for the following 15 years. Whilst none of the goals directly refer to ICT, a further report by the International Telecommunication Union (ITU, 2017) illustrates the key role that ICT is to play in reaching some of the goals. So, there is a call for leveraging ICT to eradicate poverty and help bring about a positive transformation in rural areas. ICT is also considered instrumental in delivering quality education and achieving gender equality. There are many examples of how ICT can create opportunities for the poor but also how Big Data can help better understand underlying problems in sectors such as agriculture and health, leading to more effective solutions. With such a prominent endorsement, ICT is likely to proliferate even further globally, with yet more consequences for the carbon footprint. Efforts are already underway make the accelerated use of technology sustainable, but more can and should be done.

Green ICT

The evolution of such a diverse ICT landscape is enabled by continuous advances in underlying technologies as well as the wide adoption of applications that rely on the various infrastructures mentioned above into most aspects of our daily lives, from business to government, to health, to transport and to entertainment. Within that context, today's world is one where energy is being consumed almost everywhere, be it in processing and transmission of data or the display of results. Furthermore, equipment and devices are being replaced at a very fast pace.

Green ICT is an umbrella term for agendas and solutions promoting the reduction of greenhouse gas emissions within the context of ICTs. These gases are predominantly a by-product of fossil-fuel burning in power-plants that generate energy (British Geological Society, n.d.). There are two aspects to consider. First, Greening ICT refers to the reduction of energy consumption in ICT applications and that can be provided by efficiencies of newer technologies and computing models such as Cloud computing, which will be elaborated in the next section. Recent developments also refer to sustainable software development addressing issues in the software development life cycle itself (Penzestadler, 2015). Second, Greening through ICT is the leveraging of such technologies to provide desired effects in other sectors such as video-conferencing facilities that can eliminate the need for travel. There are several stakeholders that can be identified within Green ICT and Greening ICT. Academia and non-governmental bodies such as the International Standardization Organization (ISO) and the ITU have the relevant knowledge and can develop relevant standards. Governments can then consider imposing legislation, with regulation referring to standards in order to achieve impact. Business and government can benefit from initiatives that reduce their energy bill, and business can also seize new opportunities in Greening ICT. Greening ICT will not form part of the discussion in this chapter,which will focus on two aspects of Green ICT. First, the energy consumption and lifecycle of devices will be considered, followed by a discussion of the data centres that dominate the IT scence today.

Energy consumption and life cycle of devices in ICT

When laptops or smartphones are in use, these devices consume energy, even in standby mode. The average laptop consumes about 150 Watts from the wall socket, and higher specification devices could consume twice that. As for the smartphone, typical consumption is about a single Watt, although that is dependent on which feature is currently in use; the bulk is used up by the module enabling the phone calls and screen display (Caroll and Heiser, 2010). CGI, the Canadian IT services provider, maintain that these are low numbers in comparison to other household energy needs and leaving such a device continuously on will have a limited impact on the electric bill of the average household appliances (CGI, n.d.). However, in a business environment where several hundred devices are in use, costs add up, leaving room for real savings to be made with the adoption of Green

ICT. The US Department of Energy provides guidance for simple good practice, such as not using screensavers and shutting down machines that are not in use for more than two hours (Department of Energy, n.d.).

But the International Energy Agency has a slightly different approach to the classification of home appliances where the digital television, together with its set-top box is included in the category of ICT and Consumer Electronic (CE). The UK figures for 2009 show the combined energy consumption of ICT and CE outstripping lighting and other appliances (International Energy Agency, 2009). In addition, the lines are being further blurred with fridges that incorporate television screens and cameras.

The case of Sweden, a country with a very high energy consumption overall, is possibly a good indicator of the direction of travel in the coming years for other countries. A study on the energy and the carbon footprint of ICT, Entertainment and Media sectors in that country concludes that around 2010 a major shift occurred (Ericsson, 2016). There, a sharp decrease in energy consumption started, reversing a 20-year regular increase. This decrease is happening despite a sharp increase in data usage in recent years. The use of smaller devices with smaller screens, along with better energy efficiency of new devices are cited as the major contributing factors.

However, using energy consumption metrics of devices in use only reflects part of the overall problem. Considering that the rate at which devices, especially smartphones, are being replaced is quite high, a further measure, namely embodied energy, or '*emergy*' must be taken into account, as introduced by Raghavan and Ma (2011). Calculation of energy of a device includes the energy consumed in the various stages of manufacturing. Such a calculation is not likely to be an exact figure, but it does provide an indication of the high energy requirement of that process, when compared to the wall socket energy used during its lifetime while operating and maintaining it. The biggest culprit is the smartphone. It is seen as a fashion item by many people and therefore is frequently replaced by newer models, and a real change in attitude towards mobile phones as a fashion accessory and status symbol is needed. Nevertheless, Green ICT must inevitably consider the reduction of e-waste, recycling and how to best dispose of residual material.

Motivated by principles of the circular economy, Fairphone (n.d.) is the first of its kind, and is marketed as ethical in all stages of production. It is also modular, with replaceable parts making repair and upgrade straightforward, thus extending the lifetime of the phone. In June 2017, Fairphone 2 won Gold at the Cannes Lions Festival for the category Product Design/Sustainability and Environmental Impact. Another initiative is the One For One programme of NN (NN, n.d.), an insurance and asset management company in the Netherlands that targeted the reduction of the number of mobile phones ending up in landfills all over the world. Under this scheme, a new mobile phone cannot be bought unless an old one is traded in.

The dominating data centre

In the early days of computing, universities, government entities and enterprises had full ownership of their data processing departments, with specialists to maintain the hardware and run the software. Prices of computers kept falling, accompanied by a dramatic increase in capacity and performance. This led to the concept of virtualization, where one piece of hardware is configured so that different applications could share resources seamlessly, as if each application had its dedicated hardware. The added benefit to this model of computing is energy efficiency, and studies show varying improvements that can be achieved. An investigation by the University of Greenwich (Pretorius et al., 2010) concluded that a virtualization model of the university data centres could achieve a 32% reduction in energy needs.

Virtualization also ushered in the era of Cloud computing, a model where infrastructure, platforms or services can be delivered via a private intranet or the Internet itself. The model was highly successful and despite security concerns is widely adopted today. A good example for using the Cloud in accessing software services is Salesforce, a customer relationship management solution. It is suitable for small companies since subscribers only pay for the service that is used, and do not have to concern themselves with the technical details of hardware and software, with the added benefit of scalability where more resources can be added as the company grows. There are many more examples of applications that Cloud based, such as email (e.g. Gmail), storage (e.g. Dropbox) and the vast range of social media applications in use.

This rapid expansion in Cloud computing has resulted in a large rise in the number of data centres hosting the servers that are needed for this ecosystem. Legislation imposed on citizen data having to be kept in a data centre within a country means that more data centres will be built than might be necessary in terms of data capacity. All that has contributed to a vast rise in energy demand, and today the combined footprint of data centres dotted around the globe is larger than that of many countries. However, awareness of the problem is widespread and efforts have been underway for some time now to reduce the carbon footprint of data centres.

Green data centres have been a reality for a few years now (Uddin and Rahman, 2012). Within that context, Green service level agreements were conceived such that a service provider can request from their Cloud provider a certain energy efficiency of the data centre performance, and failure to meet that could result in a penalty imposed on the Cloud provider (Amokrane et al., 2015). But to facilitate such agreements, standard metrics have to be determined and agreed, and these are continually evolving.

The Green Grid (n.d.) teams up with government and other organizations, and in its advisory capacity participates in the creation and promotion of industry metrics for data centres, issuing publications on data centre efficiency and best practice. It originally put forward the Power Usage Effectiveness (PUE) metric,

6

where the total power used by the data centre is divided by the total power consumed by the ICT equipment. With the introduction of energy efficiency measures in data centres, either by using more energy efficient ICT or by making use of the heat generated by ICT, this factor dropped gradually from a typical value of 2 down to 1.2 and edging ever closer to 1. But the PUE is a crude measure with its limitations, and the best performance is achieved with IT equipment in full use consuming maximum energy. As a result, in a 2016 white paper The Green Grid added thermal conformance and thermal resilience as two further metrics that take into account the cooling needs in normal and exceptional operating conditions. It also introduced the concept of a Performance Indicator to eventually cover more aspects of a data center's green credentials.

ASHRAE (n.d.) was founded in 1894 as the American Society of Heating, Refrigeration and Air-Conditioning, and today has a global reach with members worldwide. Originally in support of the PUE approach, ASHRAE replaced it with the Mechanical Load Component (MLC) and the Electrical Loss Component (ELC), but keeping the PUE as an option to demonstrate compliance.

Greenpeace has taken on itself the task of naming and shaming the big players that are heavily reliant on Cloud computing, calling for them to revert to renewable energy in an effort to reduce their carbon footprint, and followed this up with a league table. In 2017 (Cook et al., 2017) a company scorecard awarded grades A, B, C, D and F for the categories: Energy Transparency, Renewable Energy Commitment, Energy Efficiency, Renewable Procurement and Advocacy. In that table, Apple, Facebook and Google scored an A overall, but big companies such as Oracle and Samsung scored a D, and two Chinese companies, Tencent and Baidu, scored F grades.

European governments as adopters of Green ICT

The last few years have seen substantial developments in the technology of cars, home appliances, and also ICT devices, making them more energy efficient with less harmful impact on the environment. However, this shift was not a result of the manufacturing industry taking the initiative, but rather the result of government intervention. There are also programmes at a global level, such as the COP 21 Paris Agreement (United Nations Framework Convention on Climate Change, 2014) with 175 countries signing up to it. Committed governments are actively promoting that agenda, aligning their rules and regulation with it, with several levels of government intervention.

For example, in the EU, there are four instruments in place (Lohse, 2015). First, there are the directives and guidelines relating to the energy consumption of devices, forming a strong incentive for producers to bring ever more efficient products to market. Second, there is strict legislation on certain materials that are prohibited and cannot be used in the manufacturing processes. Third, there are incentives for innovative solutions that are helpful in reducing emissions. And finally, there are ecolabeling schemes and certifications that will help influence consumer behaviour and business attitude towards embracing Green ICT.

The key EU Directive 2009/125/EC for "establishing a framework for the setting of ecodesign requirements for energy-related products" (EU , n.d.) is implemented in different ways into the laws of the EU Member states. Any such product must carry the Conformité Européene (CE) label if the product is to trade freely in the single market. But directives are incorporated into the different national laws with different emphases, and what is achieved is harmonisation rather than strict imposition of identical laws. So rather than introducing strict legislation EU-wide, the setting of standards is delegated to expert bodies such as British Standards (BS) in the UK and the German Institute for Standardization (DIN) in Germany. Government bodies, such as Regulatory Delivery in the UK, are then given powers to enforce compliance. However, not all signatories of the Paris Agreement have bodies capable of monitoring, advising and enforcing relevant regulation.

The German Ministry for Economics and Energy is responsible for incorporation of the above-mentioned EU Directive into German law and hosts a website with all the relevant information and details about the actual legislation (Bundesministerium für Wirtschaft und Energie und BITKOM e.V., 2017). There are quite basic general guidelines on energy efficiency in the ICT sector, however, for government departments specifically, there are comprehensive and detailed regulations on procurement of ICT. In that way, government sets the benchmark for what constitutes best practice. Considering that government spend on ICT is generally quite high, this has considerable impact.

Smaller countries in the EU, such as Austria are also required to implement the EU Directive, which in Austria is ensured with the help of the "Ökodesign-Verordnung". The resulting law is documented in the Austrian legislation information system (Bundeskanzleramt, Rechtsinformationssystem, 2017). The Energy Institute for Businesses (EIW) provides more practical advice for Austrian companies. It promotes energy efficiency and climate protection, and gives support to Austrian businesses to implement sustainable solutions, e.g., by providing programmes for the practical realization of climate policy goals. In collaboration with other institutions, they published a study on Green ICT in Austria, discussing Austria's potential regarding the increase of energy efficiency (Energieinstitut der Wirtschaft GmbH, IWI Industriewissenschaftliches Institut, 2013). The report concludes that there is potential for Austria to achieve a 24% reduction in energy consumption by 2020, which translates to a reduction of 270,000 tons of CO_2 emissions compared to levels in 2010.

European awareness of the significance of Green ICT is also reflected by the activities of countries that are not part of the EU. Switzerland, for example, has an active computer society where the Green IT special interest group (Fachgruppe Green IT, n.d.) provides consultancy services for companies which are interested in this topic. The Swiss Federal Office of Energy (SFOE) also is active in analyzing the energy saving potentials of Swiss data centers. In a recent study (Amstein and

Walthert AG, 2015) the conclusion points to the potential for Swiss data centers to save up to 50% of their current energy consumption. This could be achieved through, for example, server virtualisation and the use of modern hardware such as flash technology.

Greening government and the Maturity model

In the UK, the government published "Greening Government: ICT Strategy" (HM Government, 2011) committing to the lifecycle approach as presented in Figure 6.1. It puts forward Green ICT principles that cover four areas. Not only does the energy being consumed during the operation of devices and equipment need to be taken into account, but also consideration given to the production and design stage, where consumed raw material and transport costs weigh in on the environment. When devices and equipment are no longer needed, refurbishment and reuse can be an alternative to responsible disposal.

The Strategy not only presents broad principles, but more specifically refers to compliance with Government Buying Standards (GBS) which offers statutory guidance on Sustainable Procurement for Office ICT equipment (HM Government 2012). It also includes reference to the EU Code of Conduct published by the European Commission's EU Science Hub.

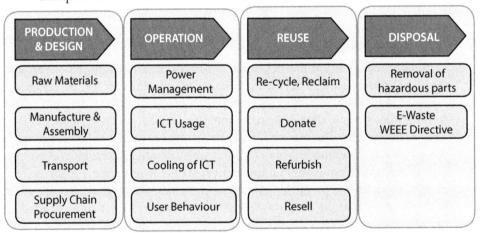

Figure 6.1: Components of published UK ICT Strategy (HM Government, 2011)

As part of the Commission's science and knowledge service, advice is provided relating to the reduction of energy consumption in technologies such as broadband communication equipment and digital television services.

Reaching out to the United States, the EU concluded an agreement on labeling office equipment so the energy efficiency can be readily assessed. Currently, the database includes computers, imaging equipment, displays, servers and uninterruptible power supplies (EU Energy Star Database, n.d.). And to complete the lifecycle, the UK strategy document cites The Waste Electrical and Electronic

Equipment (WEEE) Regulation, which controls activities related to the disposal of equipment and complying with EU law. UK Government intervention is necessary to ensure there are no breaches, otherwise infringement proceeding may be faced (HM Government, 2013). Of course, this may all become redundant with the UK deciding to leave the EU. To illustrate, in 2010, the EU Commission issued a warning to Slovakia regarding the WEEE Regulation, and in 2012 it took Sweden to the EU Court of Justice for failing to act on that. It should also be noted that these EU laws evolve over time, so for example from 2019 onwards, stricter legislation will be in place.

To measure achievements of government departments in the UK, the Green ICT Maturity Model was developed with details presented in a further document (HM Government, 2015 a). In that model, there are five levels that can be achieved from Ad Hoc (Level 0) to Foundation (Level 1) where there is an agreed plan in place; and routes for improvements are explored to Embedded (Level 2), to Practiced (Level 3), to Enhanced (Level 4) through to Leadership (Level 5), where the ICT strategy is fully implemented and outcomes can be measured. Furthermore, there are four broad areas that are presented, broken down into categories. For any government department then, each category can be individually assessed and the respective level determined. Table 6.1 lists the four main components to be assessed, together with the categories and examples of criteria to consider for Levels 1 and 5, thus providing a summary of that maturity model. The adoption of Green ICT in government departments thus follows a phased approach that starts with the creation of awareness about the issue and an inspection of the current state before any real improvements can be achieved. Buy-in from leadership of the relevant department is needed before technical solutions with real improvements can be put in place. It is also noteworthy that this maturity model is not aligned with the Commitments as laid out in the UK Government Strategy.

Annual reports on progress are published and cover all 16 government departments (HM Government, 2015 b). With a tagline "Reducing Carbon. Reducing Cost." the report presents the achievements of 2015 as depicted in Figure 6.2. Whilst some improvements can be seen, there remain gaps between desired and achieved targets on the technical side, such as disposal, but also on the nontechnical side such as governance and promotion.

Table 6.1: Main areas, categories and criteria of the Green ICT Maturity Model (HM Government, 2015 a)

Managing Services	
Governance and Promotion Level 1: Leadership and adoption of relevant Green ICT objectives into policies & identification of goals	Level 5: Full implementation of strategy and measurement of outcomes
Enterprise and Solutions Architecture Level 1: Technical team aware of need to translate adopted goals into concrete objectives such as maximizing utilization and sharing resources	Level 5: Efficient rolling out of solutions

Capacity Planning Level 1: Assessment of current and predictions of future supply and demand for ICT equipment and services	Level 5: Having in place a flexible supply that avoids environmentally costly upgrades which require new build solutions and acquisitions
End User Support Level 1: Providing phone based user support	Level 5: Tracking overall patterns and user needs enabling a proactive approach
Information and Data Level 1: Understanding the lifecycle of data and information	Level 5: Taking full advantage of technology to underpin the lifecycle and reduce the environmental impact
Disposal Level 1: Ensuring legal obligations are met and understand the waste management needs	Level 5: Re-use of equipment and reporting on waste, transport and packaging
Managing Technology	
Utilisation Level 1: Monitoring usage of services and equipment	Level 5: Workload management to optimize use of resources
Consolidation Level 1: Establish record of available assets and shared devices	Level 5: Using virtualization techniques to maximise usage of servers
Changing Services	
Investment Decisions Level 1: Include consideration of environmental costs in projects	Level 5: Introduction of environmental business case and associated benefits
Running Projects Level 1: Awareness of relevant policies related to environmental impact	Level 5: Project success factor includes consideration of environmental impact
Solution Design Level 1: Include environmental impact considerations in the ICT project lifecycle	Level 5: Green ICT policies and goals fully adopted in ICT programme management
Procurement Level 1: Understanding the environmental impact on procurement	Level 5: Meeting the highest level of Government Buying Standard (outlined separately by the Dept for Environment, Food & Rural Affairs)
Exploiting ICT	
Electronically Enabling Customer Services Level 1: Understanding the services offered	Level 5: Service offered is both effective has least environmental impact
Travel Reduction Level 1: Survey current travel needs, means and costs	Level 5: Reduction in travel budget and increased take-up of tele-conferencing facilities
Resource Optimization Level 1: Survey current usage of consumables such as paper	Level 5: Extensive use of technology, so going paperless

Energy Optimisation Level 1: Understanding current energy consumption and carbon footprint breakdown	Level 5: Complying with the EU Data Centre Code of Conduct best practice
Space Optimization Level 1: Understanding the needs for space and how usage of ICT can help reduce that need	Level 5: Realisation of strategy that meets government targets
Corporate Reporting Level 1: Basic reporting on environmental performance in place	Level 5: Extensive reporting used to drive improvements
Corporate Integration Level 1: Project related integration of travel, space and personnel requirements	Level 5: ICT leveraged to achieve high-level integration resulting in measurable reduction in carbon footprint

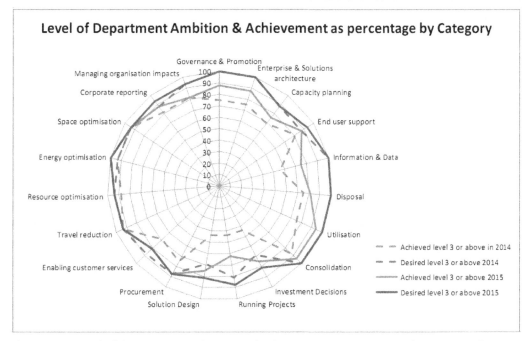

Figure 6.2: Level of department ambition and achievement as percentage by category (HM Government, 2015 b)

ICT in construction project management

One established principle in the discussion above relates to opting for a Cloud solution whenever this is available. In the construction project management sector, IT systems are widely used and often a dedicated on-site location is set up to serve a particular project, incurring overhead costs in maintaining that facility. With a location near a construction site, the facility and the data it holds is at risks of accidents, as happened recently in one of the Gulf countries where a fire resulted in the loss of project data as well as causing disruption to the project.

The levels of adoption of Cloud solutions is still evolving, and there is not sufficient literature to provide comparisons. A recent paper (Mandikac, et al, 2016) reported on the state of the adoption of Cloud solutions in construction project management in Slovakia. The average score of the exploitation level of Cloud computing in that country was 2.38/5 and is considered relatively low. Interestingly, the larger multinationals operating there had a higher score of 3.4.

The characteristics of data being collected in construction projects are changing and increasingly can be described as Big Data, so too will there be a need for solutions that can exploit the full promise that type of data can deliver. The case study on the Shangahi Tower development reports on how problems of the data lifecycle management can be resolved (Jiao et al., 2012).

The advantages of using a Cloud solution in construction project management are summarized as improved efficiency, with access to data and information processes remotely presented, as well as a positive impact on sustainability through the reduction in travel since data is available everywhere (Rawai et al., 2013). In a country like Malaysia, that aspect is highly valued.

Another effect of adopting the Cloud is that such an approach will enable the cohesion of fragmented work practices (Chong et al., 2014), although that is not straightforward, since many of the Cloud-based applications are designed to support the already fragmented tasks. Such integration is not easy to achieve because of the various stakeholders involved and the complexity and the project-based nature of the setting (Beach et al., 2013). But achieving integration can deliver important benefits. For example, there is the potential for improved safety on construction sites where real-time data analysis can have a major impact (Zou et al., 2017).

Barriers to adoption of Green ICT

Swisscom, one of the main telecommunications providers in Switzerland, has conducted a survey regarding the attitudes of people and companies to ecological issues (Swisscom AG, 2012). In particular, the focus was to determine the attitude of Swiss companies and their employees towards Green ICT. The result was that in general, the interest in Green ICT was limited in small companies and that larger companies were more aware and had actively engaged in efforts towards it. But the major deterrent was always the perception that any Green ICT initiative will be costly, with companies not prepared to commit to such expenditure.

The survey by Swisscom AG (2012) has identified motives and barriers why companies use Green ICT solutions. As main reasons for using Green ICT solutions, companies mentioned cost savings (greater efficiency, lower energy consumption, less travel); fulfilling their company's social and corporate responsibility; improving their public image; and initiatives of the management to transform their company into a 'green' organization. The study also discusses reasons against the use of Green ICT. This includes key issues, such as companies simply not considering the use of Green ICT until now, having no overview about the most efficient 'green' products and services and having no expertise regarding planning and implementation of Green ICT.

Summary

This chapter has explored the various links that exist between ICT and environmental impacts and sustainability. It highlighted legislation and guidelines already in place in different countries. These range from simple everyday tips, such as not using screensavers and switching computers off when not in use, through to detailed metrics that can be considered when implementing a Green ICT initiative. Whilst the discussion is generic, applicable across several sectors, a small section dedicated to Construction Project Management was included. The sustainability journey is well underway across many sectors, and the role of ICT is well-established and ongoing.

End of chapter questions

Only one answer is correct. Find the correct answer:

6

1   What is the sixth era of computing?

    a)   LTE-Advanced

    b)   Solid State Drives

    c)   IoT and edge computing

    d)   Quantum computing

2   What does the umbrella term Green ICT promote?

    a)   The education of ICT professionals regarding the importance of sustainability.

    b)   The reduction of greenhouse gas emissions within the context of ICT.

    c)   The development of green ICT systems.

    d)   The establishment of a green software engineering process.

3   What does the term "emergy" describe?

    a)   It is the abbreviation for "embodied energy" and describes the energy consumed in the various stages of manufacturing a device.

    b)   It is the abbreviation for "emergency" and describes the urgent need for introducing sustainable ICT systems.

    c)   It is the abbreviation for "emerging synergy" and describes the need for building sustainable ICT ecosystems.

    d)   It is the abbreviation for "emotional energy" and describes the importance of informing end-users and other potential stakeholders about an ICT system's positive and negative effects on sustainability.

4   What is the most important driver for Green ICT?

   a)   Industry intervention

   b)   End-user intervention

   c)   NGO intervention

   d)   Government intervention

5   What is the goal of the EU Directive 2009/125/EC?

   a)   Establishing a framework for the setting of ecodesign requirements for energy-related products.

   b)   Reducing the greenhouse gas emissions within the context of ICT.

   c)   Educating ICT professionals about the importance of Green ICT.

   d)   Establishing a green software engineering process.

6   What are key components of the UK ICT Strategy?

   a)   Production and design, operation, reuse, disposal

   b)   Plan, do, check, act

   c)   Conception, development, installation, evaluation

   d)   Elicitation, analysis, specification, validation

7   What is a major barrier to adoption of Green ICT?

   a)   Having no support from their government.

   b)   Having no expertise regarding planning and implementation of Green ICT.

   c)   Having no methods and tools available helping to implement Green ICT.

   d)   Having no support from their customers.

Label as true or false:

8   ICT is a slightly wider term than IT as it also encompasses technologies used in communication between devices.

9   Greening ICT is an alternative term to Green ICT.

10   Laptops and smartphones do not consume energy in stand-by mode.

11   It is recommended to switch off devices that are not in use for more than 2 hours.

12   Using a screen saver is an energy-saving feature.

13   With a Green service level agreement a service provider can request from their Cloud provider a certain energy efficiency of the data centre performance.

14   There are no advantages of using a Cloud solution in construction project management.

References

Amokrane, A. et al., Langar, R., Zhani, M.F., Boutaba, R. and Pujolle, G., (2015) Greenslater: On satisfying Green SLAs in distributed clouds, *IEEE Transactions on Network and Service Management*, **12**(3), pp. 363–376.

Amstein & Walthert (2015) Studie zur Stromeffizienz bei Rechenzentren in der Schweiz http://www.news.admin.ch/NSBSubscriber/message/attachments/40638.pdf

ASHRAE (n.d.) https://www.ashrae.org/resources--publications/bookstore/datacom-series

Beach, T., Rana, H., Rezgui, O. and Parashar, F. (2013). Cloud computing for the architecture, engineering & construction sector: Requirements, prototype & experience. *Journal of Cloud Computing*, **2**(1), 1-16.

British Geological Society (n.d.) http://www.bgs.ac.uk/discoveringGeology/climateChange/CCS/man-madeEffect.html

Bundeskanzleramt, Rechtsinformationsystem (2017). Ökodesign-Verordnung 2007. https://www.ris.bka.gv.at/GeltendeFassung.wxe?Abfrage=Bundesnormen&Gesetzesnummer=20005348

Bundesministerium für Wirtschaft und Energie und BITKOM e.V. (2017)

Caroll, A. and Heiser, G. (2010). An Analysis of Power Consumption in a Smartphone. *Proceedings of the 2010 USENIX annual technical conference*. p.21. Boston, MA — June 23 - 25, 2010. USENIX Association Berkeley, CA, USA.

CGI (n.d.) Emerging Trends in Green IT https://www.cgi.com/files/white-papers/cgi_whpr_84_emerging_trends_green_it_e.pdf

Chong, H., Wong, J. S. and Wang, X. (2014). An explanatory case study on cloud computing applications in the built environment. *Automation in Construction*, **44**, 152-162.

Cook, G. et al. (2017) Clicking clean: Who is winning the race to build a green Internet? Greenpeace Inc.

Department of Energy (n.d.). https://energy.gov/energysaver/energy-efficient-computers-home-office-equipment-and-electronics

Energieinstitut der Wirtschaft GmbH, IWI Industriewissenschaftliches Institut (2013). Studie "Green ICT in Österreich" - Potenziale und Möglichkeiten zur Steigerung der Energieeffizienz und Reduktion von klimarelevanten Emissionen. http://www.energieinstitut.net/de/vortraege-publikationen/studie-green-ict-oesterreich

Ericsson (2016). *Technology for Good - Ericsson Sustainability and Corporate Responsibility Report 2016* – ICT Footprint on Downward Energy Trend. https://www.ericsson.com/assets/local/about-ericsson/sustainability-and-corporate-responsibility/documents/2016-corporate-responsibility-and-sustainability-report.pdf

EU Energy Star Database (n.d.) https://www.eu-energystar.org/db-currentlists.htm

Fachgruppe Green IT (n.d.) http://greenit.s-i.ch

Fairphone (n.d.). The modular phone that's built to last. https://www.fairphone.com/

HM Government (2011). *UK HM Greening Government: ICT Strategy - A sub strategy of the Government ICT Strategy* https://www.gov.uk/government/uploads/system/uploads/attachment_data/file/155098/greening-government-ict-strategy.pdf

HM Government (2012). *Statutory guidance:Sustainable procurement: the GBS for office ICT equipment.* www.gov.uk/government/publications/sustainable-procurement-the-gbs-for-office-ict-equipment

HM Government (2013). *Impact Assessment of the Recast Directive 2012/19/EU on Waste Electrical and Electronic Equipment* https://www.gov.uk/government/uploads/system/uploads/attachment_data/file/186971/bis-13-763-impact-assessment-of-recast-directive-2012-19-eu-on-waste-electrical-and-electronic-equipment-weee.pdf

6

HM Government (2015 a). *Green ICT Maturity Model.* https://www.gov.uk/government/publications/green-ict-maturity-model

HM Government (2015 b). *Greening ICT 2015 Annual Report.* https://www.gov.uk/government/publications/greening-government-ict-2015-annual-report

International Energy Agency (2009). *Gadgets and Gigawatts: Policies for Energy Efficient Electronics.* OECD.

ITU (2017). Fast-forward progress - Leveraging tech to achieve the global goals. http://www.itu.int/en/sustainable-world/Documents/Fast-forward_progress_report_414709%20FINAL.pdf

Jiao, Wang, Zhang, Li, Yang and Yuan. (2012). A cloud approach to unified lifecycle data management in architecture, engineering, construction and facilities management: Integrating BIMs and SNS. *Advanced Engineering Informatics*

Laudon, K. and Laudon, P. (2016). *Management Information Systems: Managing the Digital Firm* (14th ed.) Pearson.

Lohse, E. (2015). The Law of Green IT, Chapter 4 in Dastbaz, M., Pattinson, C., Akhbar, B. and Kaufmann, M. (eds) *Green Information Technology A Sustainable Approach.*

Mandičák, T., Mesároš, P. and Kozlovská, M. (2017). Exploitation of cloud computing in management of construction projects in Slovakia. *Organization, Technology and Management in Construction: an International Journal*, **8**(1), 1456-1463. Retrieved 16 Sep. 2017, from doi:10.1515/otmcj-2016-0014

N. M. Rawai, M. S. Fathi, M. Abedi and S. Rambat, (2013). Cloud Computing for Green Construction Management. *2013 Third International Conference on Intelligent System Design and Engineering Applications,* Hong Kong, pp. 432-435.

NN (2017). Circular mobile phones. https://www.nn-group.com/Media/Article/Circular-mobile-phones.htm

Pretorius, M., Ghassemian, M., & Ierotheou, C. (2010). An Investigation into Energy Efficiency of Data Centre Virtualisation. *2010 International Conference on P2P, Parallel, Grid, Cloud and Internet Computing,* 157–163. https://doi.org/10.1109/3PGCIC.2010.28

Raghavan, B. and Ma, J. (2011). The Energy and Emergy of the Internet. *Proceedings of the 10th ACM Workshop on hot topics in networks,* 14 November, pp.1-6.

Swisscom AG (2012). The environment and Green ICT in Swiss companies – A survey regarding the attitudes of people and companies to ecological issues. www.swisscom.ch/content/dam/swisscom/en/biz/green_ict/studie/SWISS_IT_00167-03_Green_Studie_fl_e_web.pdf

The Green Grid (n.d.) https://www.thegreengrid.org

Uddin, M. and Rahman, A. A. (2012) Energy efficiency and low carbon enabler green IT framework for data centers considering green metrics, *Renewable and Sustainable Energy Reviews*, **16**(1) 4078–4094. doi: 10.1016/j.rser.2012.03.014.

United Nations (n.d.) www.un.org/sustainabledevelopment/sustainable-development-goals

United Nations Framework Convention on Climate Change (2014) http://unfccc.int/meetings/paris_nov_2015/items/9445.php

Zou, P. X. W., Lun, P., Cipolla, D. and Mohamed, S. (2017). Cloud-based safety information and communication system in infrastructure construction. *Safety Science,* **98**, 50-69.

Answer to exercises

1 c; 2 b; 3 a; 4 d; 5 a; 6 a; 7 b.

8 T; 9 F; 10 F; 11 T; 12 F; 13 T; 14 F.

7 Blockchain: A Disruptive Technology in the Sustainable Economic System

Ioannis Karamitsos, Mohamed Salama and Mohamed El Gindy

Learning outcomes

By completing this chapter, the reader should be able to:

- Discuss how the disruptive technologies relate to the digital transformation.
- Explain the basic Blockchain building blocks.
- Describe the consensus mechanisms as PoW and PoS.
- Describe how to design and implement a smart contract application.
- Discuss the benefits of Blockchain in the shared economy.
- Discuss how Blockchain can assist in sustainability energy.

Introduction

This chapter aims to provide managers in general and project managers in particular with the basic information about one of the most hyped disruptive technology concept in the shared digital economy today: *Blockchain*. Blockchain and other disruptive technologies such as Internet of Things (IoT), Artificial Intelligence (AI), and Big Data are important disruptive steps that are increasingly relevant when defining and managing projects in the sharing digital business economy.

The chapter comprises three main parts. The first part introduces the basic concept of the disruptive technologies in the digital transformation context and the main blocks required for the build of Blockchain framework. The focus is on describing each block in details applicable for any selected platform. The second part of the chapter outlines the concept of the *smart contract*. The general aim is to provide knowledge with actionable guidelines on how best to implement a smart contract using the Ethereum platform. All the components for the design, deployment, and implementation of decentralized applications (*Dapps*) are discussed. The final part discusses the benefits of using smart contract on the Blockchain technology and wraps up by two brief illustrative case studies, enlightening project managers about the Blockchain technology applications in different vertical segments; Life Cycle Assessment (LCA) leading to Environmental Product Declaration (EDA) and energy trading in pursuit of sustainable development.

Background

The parade of the new disruptive technologies has the potential to truly reshape the world in which we work and we live. All these new emerging technologies do not alter the business or the social landscape but some of them have the potential to disrupt the status quo, change the way people live and work, and rearrange the business models and the value propositions.

A report from the McKinsey Global Institute (2016) identifies five new disruptive technologies: Internet of Things (IoT), Artificial Intelligence (AI), Big Data, Cloud and Blockchain, that could drive massive economic transformation and disruptions in the coming ten years. These disruptive technologies complement each other, becoming enablers for the IT digital transformation of each organisation.

Blockchain is a fast-disruptive technology that is becoming a key instrument in the sharing economy. In recent years, Blockchain has received considerable attention from many researchers and government institutions. Blockchain is a novel disruptive technology based on decentralized computing, cryptography, security and trust-less environmental. Nakamoto (2008) showed how this technology can become the core component to support transactions of a digital currency (bitcoin). With the introduction of Blockchain, many fields such as trading energy, assets tracking, finance, accounting and healthcare will receive a positive impact using the benefits of this technology. A Blockchain is the distributed public ledger for all transactions, eliminating the need of trust between the users and the central administrator and the control is distributed among different computers/nodes in the peer-to-peer (P2P) network. Moreover, Blockchain resolved the double-spend problem using P2P technology in combination with public/private key cryptography.

One promising area is the energy market which consists of complex mechanisms involving many middlemen and clearing settlement mechanisms (Clancy 2017). The Blockchain technology provides the potential to cut out energy operators, wholesale and payment providers from the ecosystem; making the system more efficient and reducing the operational costs (OpEX) (Hasse et al., 2015). The introduction of smart metering systems and smart meters with combination of Blockchain system can be utilised to transmit payment transactions in tamper-proofed way and control electricity flow and storage via smart contracts implemented into a Blockchain infrastructure.

Blockchain has the potential to become an effective tool for sustainability into different areas such as: tracking and allocation of environmental data concerning energy consumption and waste generation, developing microgrids that use Blockchain for the local energy trading, and helping companies with Life Cycle Assessment (LCA) to develop Environmental Product Declarations (EPDs) for their products.

The potential benefits of the disruptive technologies are obvious, yet the most important are the challenges of getting prepared for the impact amid the anticipated transformation. Government institutions and business organisations should keep their organisational strategies updated in the context of the new technologies and use technologies to improve external or internal performance. Disruptive technologies can change the whole ecosystem with new models for businesses; creating new products and defining a new value chain model. Organisations will need to use digital transformation innovations to capture the value of the disruptive technologies, as discussed earlier in Chapter 4.

Disruptive technologies

Disruptive technologies are those that significantly change the way businesses or entire industries operate. Clayton Christensen (1997) popularized the idea of disruptive technologies in the book *The Innovator's Dilemma*. His defined the term disruption as "the process by which a product or service takes root initially in simple applications at the bottom of a market and then relentlessly moves up market, eventually displacing established competitors". In the beginning, the disruptive technologies have considered as innovation, tools to enable any change in the industry and organisation, transforming the whole industry ecosystem into new digital business. Each organisation or industry is starting to re-think and re-design their traditional business models and processes in the context of the today's disruptive technologies, such as IoT, AI, Blockchain, Cloud, Big Data/Analytics, and mobility 5G. While these six technologies comprise the core of the new platform for digital business, other technology enablers such as 3D printing, AR, and VR come into the industry as well. One of the keys to maximising the benefits of the disruptive technologies lies on their powerful platform combinations.

7

"Platform companies are emerging as important engines of innovation. They are increasingly at the cutting edge of rapid worldwide digital transformation."

Peter.C.Evans, The Center for Global Enterprise (Evans, and Gawyer, 2016)

Digital transformation is applied to any function of the organisation; from finance, human resource, sales and marketing using the IT enablement technology. The concept of the digital transformation is very often confused by senior management. A business may go through radical changes and significant restructuring, but it's only a transformation if it's highly visible from the outside, to its customers, and was driven by external factors.

Digital transformation - definitions

Westerman (2011) defines digital transformation as:

> *"the use of technology to radically improve performance or reach of enterprises"*

Kaplan (2010) provides a more holistic definition for the term:

> *"digital transformation can be understood as the changes that digital technology causes or influences in all aspects of human life"*

Lankshear and Knobel (2008) define digital transformation as the third and ultimate level of digital literacy that:

> *"is achieved when the digital usages which have been developed enable innovation and creativity and stimulate significant change within the professional or knowledge domain".*

Digital transformation may become successful *without* using new technology, *but* by transforming the organization to take advantage of the possibility that the new technology provides. Digital transformation (DT) is achieved only with the top-down leadership support that requires strong governance and coordination.

According to Gartner's technology hype cycle graph shown in Figure 7.1, Blockchain technology has moved significantly along the Hype Cycle since 2016 in which was at the peak of inflated expectations (as Hype July 2016) and is expected to be ready for mainstream adoption in 5 to 10 years:

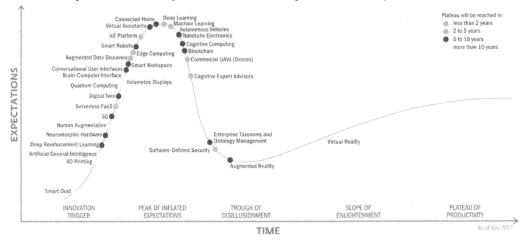

Figure 7.1: Hype cycle for emerging technologies. Source: Gartner (2017)

In the following sections the building blocks of Blockchain technology will be described in detail.

Blockchain technology

Our focus in this chapter is to explore the advanced topics in the Blockchain technology, which will revolutionize the potential application areas in the sustainable sharing economy. So, we begin this section by definitions then an introduction about the evolution and history of BC. The following sections discuss in details all the building blocks which became part of the whole Blockchain framework. .

Definition of Blockchain

According to Standard Chartered (2017):

"The technology behind Bitcoin and many other cryptocurrencies is a distributed ledger database for recording transactions, more commonly known as blocks. Blockchain technology enables users to share their ledger of transactions. The record of events gets distributed to all participants in a given network, who in turn use their computers to validate the transactions; thereby removing the need to have a third-party intermediary such as a bank or central clearing center. Blockchain records can only be updated by consensus of a majority of the participants in the system and, once entered, information can never be erased - providing a detailed audit trail of all associated events."

From Merriam-Webster dictionary:

"Blockchain is a digital database containing information (such as records of financial transactions) that can be simultaneously used and shared within a large decentralized, publicly accessible network; also: the technology used to create such a database".

Evolution of Blockchain

Even though the Blockchain technology was initially proposed for crypto-currencies, technologistss are now exploring novel areas in which Blockchain could do wonders. During the years a Blockchain evolution is performed starting from Blockchain 1.0 to Blockchain 2.0 and then Blockchain 3.0.

1 Blockchain 1.0 is the **currency**, the deployment of cryptocurrency applications related to exchange, trade and financial transactions. Blockchain 1.0 is the decentralization of money and payments.

2 Blockchain 2.0 is **contracts**, the deployment of digital assets using the concept of the smart contracts. Blockchain 2.0 is the decentralization of markets. A typical platform is Ethereum.

3 Blockchain 3.0 is **applications,** in new areas of sustainable energy, smart cities, IoT, M2M, government, health, science, and art. A typical platform is Solidity.

Emergence of Blockchain as disruptive technology

Christensen, a leading researcher on business models, cited two types of technology that impact business: sustaining and disruptive technologies. Sustaining technology allow organizations to take gradual steps towards improving their products or business offerings while industry status is maintained, unlike the disruptive technology where the technological breakthrough could challenge the existence and survival of organizations (Christenen, 1997). Disruptive technologies don't attract interest in their early beginnings, but they change the status quo over time and replace existing products. This kind of disruption has two key characteristics, which are that they develop interest over a period of time till they penetrate the market, along with increase in their adoption rate resulting in the replacement of established systems; and they rarely come from established organizations.

Blockchain satisfies these two patterns as it has been around since 2008. However, only recently has been considered one of the most interesting topics in digital transformation trends. It is the main technology underlying Bitcoin, which was introduced in 2008 by (Nakamoto, 2008) as a decentralized network for storing and exchanging information or digitized values over the internet (Mougayar, 2016). Currently, there is no such mechanism on the internet that demonstrates high level of trust and identity insurance for transactions without the validation of third parties, along with data privacy issues related to consumer data (Tapscott & Tapscott, 2016). This goes along with the increasing breach of centralized databases and data privacy issues. Consequently, it is essential to see the business implications of this technology, with the potential promises of causing unexpected industry shifts by facilitating different paradigms of doing business and interactions between individuals. In the next sections we will explore the work in progress to tap the potential of Blockchain to see the innovations and new solutions emerging. Blockchain has emerged to become a collection of technological trends that has a potential of new value generation across all industries.

History of Blockchain

It all started in the October 2008 when a white paper was published by an unknown name, Satoshi Nakamoto, under the name of "Bitcoin – A Peer-to-Peer Electronic Cash System" (Nakamoto, 2008). This email was circulated among an email list of cryptographers (Popper, 2015). Blockchain was the technology underlying Bitcoin. The cryptocurrency continued to grow as the Bitcoin market was established and the technology was tested in the real market environment over several years.

Distributed ledger technology (DLT) or Blockchain technology (BCT) was first realized by the financial industry as a potential for different applications beyond cryptocurrency when Fidor Bank set up digital currency exchange and enabled P2P Bitcoin trading. They partnered with Ripple to implement money transfer in digital currency system by allowing network participants to verify the transactions instead of mining (Kokina et al., 2017). By the end of 2013 a white paper was released by Vitalik Buterin, who had realized that the Blockchain platform had the ability to build decentralized applications (Buterin, 2013) This later became the Ethereum project; the first industry application outside the cryptocurrency.

In 2014, BCT started to emerge as a solution for enterprises in the financial industry when R3 (R3CEV, LLC), a distributed database company leading a consortium of banks was founded, and started research and development of a Blockchain database in financial firms including Barclays PLC, Banco Bilbao

Vizcaya Argentaria, S.A (BBVA), Commonwealth Bank of Australia, Credit Suisse Group, The Goldman Sachs Group, Inc., JPMorgan Chase & Co., Royal Bank of Scotland, State Street Corporation, and UBS AG (Lang, 2015; Kokina et al., 2017).

Yet 2005 was when the real industry implementation and discovery of the potential of the technology happened. Deutche Bank, Citi Bank, BNP Paribas, SCB CIO and Visa explored different approaches for implementing Blockchain in their operation process to enhance the value of their offering for their customers. The Ethereum platform gained much popularity and the "Enterprise Ethereum Alliance" was formed, supporting the platform (Higgins, 2017). This supported the evolution of the decentralized applications concept operated on a Blockchain platform, till the establishment of NASDAQ, a Blockchain based platform, and the Hyperledger project, led by the Linux Foundation, as a first push for standardization.

Blockchain technology: How it works

Blockchain Technology (BCT) or Blockchain (BC) as it is more commonly known, is considered a foundational transformation technology and one of the most influential technological trends that will impact business and society in the near future (Webb, 2015). Primarily, this is a general-purpose technology for enterprises and governments to aid transactions and information exchange, that is built on authentication and trust attributes (Yli-Huumo et al., 2016). The bitcoin system as a digital currency service has grown in value to more than $60 billion by mid-2017 since its launch in 2009. It is considered the most popular Blockchain application, and has enabled the rise of an ecosystem of innovative ideas and services that expands far beyond the financial market (Tapscott & Tapscott, 2016).

BCT is also known as Distributed Ledger Technology (DLT). DLT is based on the concept that each participant in the network has access to a shared ledger, which acts as a recording mechanism for transactions such as exchange of assets and data among network users. It is a database that is shared and is synchronized among the members of a decentralized network (Brakeville and Perepa, 2018). The idea of having an open, universally accessible ledger was born with Bitcoin, and the system provided the first solution to the problem of establishing trust in an insecure environment without relying on a third-party (Warburg, 2016).

Business operations and activities are currently taking place in networks that cross the geographic and jurisdictional boundaries. A business typically uses multiple ledgers to keep track of transactions, assets ownership and asset transfers between network participants, where they recorded on the ledgers. These networks constitute a marketplace where all stakeholders and players of the value chain exercise their rights on their assets, recorded on the ledgers within minutes and with minimum transaction fees (Brakeville and Perepa, 2018). This technology is a back-end database and can act as foundational protocol on which many decentralized applications can be interfaced and operated to act as global open sourced distributed ledger of value exchange without any intermediaries

(Mougayar, 2016). The basic idea behind the BC and DLT is that it allows those actors (called nodes) who are part of the network, to perform transactions or exchange of digital assets using a Peer to Peer (P2P) network that stores the data and the ownership of these transactions in a distributed way across the network (Back et al., 2014).

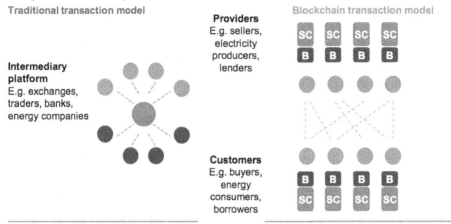

Traditional transaction model

Intermediary platform
E.g. exchanges, traders, banks, energy companies

Providers
E.g. sellers, electricity producers, lenders

Blockchain transaction model

Customers
E.g. buyers, energy consumers, borrowers

- Multi-tiered transaction model relying on a central authority
- Transaction data is primarily stored by the central authority (●)

- Transactions are carried out directly between providers and their customers
- All transaction data is stored on a distributed blockchain B, with all relevant information being stored identically on the computers of all participants
- Ideally, all transactions are made on the basis of smart contracts SC, i.e. based on predefined individual rules concerning quality, price, quantity etc.
- Largely automated, decentralized transaction model with no need for third-party intermediaries

Figure 7.2: Traditional and Blockchain transactional models (PricewaterhouseCoopers, 2016)

Figure 7.2 illustrates the traditional and Blockchain transactional models (PricewaterhouseCoopers, 2016). In steps this can be listed as follows:

1 User initiate a transaction that demonstrate value like documents, data or a contract through a user interface application from an internet connected device.

2 Digital signatures using public key cryptography is used to verify the origin, authenticity of the transaction and register the transactions, identity and the ownership on the ledger (Warburg, 2016).

3 The application sends the transaction information into a P2P network of participants computing devices, known as nodes.

4 There is consensus mechanism (protocol) to validate each transaction once entered in the P2P among the nodes in the network by confirming its legitimacy and this decision is recorded in a block (Ølnes et al., 2017).

5 Each block hold time stamped batches of valid transactions and the hash of the prior block which is used to ensure the integrity of the data while identifying required information (Yli-Huumo et al., 2016).

6 The blocks are added to the previous recorded chain of blocks in a secured locked approach in order for the latest block to maintain the latest state of agreement on the transaction (Buterin, 2014).

The cryptographic process used that is used to link the blocks received with old blocks is called 'mining', which acts as 'proof-of-work' for 'miners' who assign their computer resources and ensure their participation in the process is not free (Tapscott & Tapscott, 2016).

The concept of having several nodes storing a list of agreed-upon transactions which are continuously synchronized with the ledger eliminates the centralized point of vulnerability that computer hackers can exploit (Ølnes et al., 2017) as taking one node down will not lead to a breakdown of the chain of blocks. This P2P architecture and the consensus protocol, which could have several forms depending on the type of the transaction, enhance the security, immutability and data integrity of the transactions that are recorded in the Blockchain, though there is no guarantee of total immutability as stated by (Gervais et al., 2016) and (Narayanan et al., 2016). According to (Atzei et al., 2017) the controlling parties who set up the Blockchain network, either from citizens or public or private organizations, can decide to alter the history of the BC network.

Figure 7.3 presents another self-explanatory simple illustration that shows how the Blockchain works in six easy to understand steps using an example of a financial transaction.

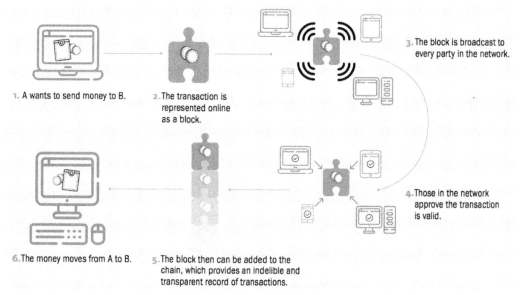

1. A wants to send money to B.

2. The transaction is represented online as a block.

3. The block is broadcast to every party in the network.

4. Those in the network approve the transaction is valid.

5. The block then can be added to the chain, which provides an indelible and transparent record of transactions.

6. The money moves from A to B.

Figure 7.3: How Blockchain works (Source: Financial Times)

Blockchain building blocks

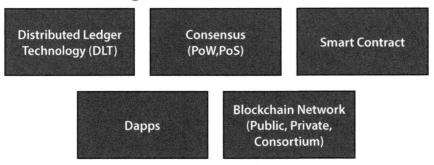

Figure 7.4: Blockchain building blocks

Figure 7.4 illustrates the building blocks for the Blockchain framework. The framework comprises the digital ledger technology (DLT), consensus algorithms; such as proof of work (PoW) and proof of stake (PoS); smart contract; decentralised applications (Dapps); and the selection of the Blockchain networks. See the Glossary at the end of this chapter for definitions of the key terms used in the following sections.

Distributed ledger technology (DLT)

Many studies forecast Blockchain as a disruptive force which could replace the legacy infrastructures for storage. In the recent years, there has been an increasing interest around the world regarding the potential of public ledger systems as a permanent solution for record keeping. The most striking feature of Blockchain that is discussed by enthusiasts and technocrats is the 'built-in asset' potential of the distributed ledger. Adding on to the authenticity, the recorded history in Blockchain is mathematically verifiable at any instance of time. This leverages the immense scope of public ledgers as a safe and stable replacement for conventional storage mechanisms.

Distributed ledgers vs traditional ledgers

Ledgers are the basic system for storing transaction details and record keeping from ancient times. When multiple parties interact, and need to keep track of complex sets of transactions, people traditionally used centralized ledgers. A centralized transaction ledger needs a trusted third party who makes the entries (validates), prevents double counting or double spending (safeguards), and holds the transaction histories (preserves). Public ledgers provide an open book-keeping system in which every stakeholder can update and view transactions in the ledger. Blockchains can be viewed as a data structure that can create and share a digital ledger of transactions, which is public and distributed across the entire network. In other words, the distributed public ledger system maintains the book-keeping mechanism of Blockchain technology by storing every transaction written into the block and in turn storing every block forming the chain. A distributed public ledger has a considerable advantage over a conventional ledger. It is generally a tamper-proof transaction database which can be shared geographically across a large network of organizations and institutions.

Conventional ledgers mainly suffer from the problem of transaction linkage and protocol enforcement. It is generally difficult and expensive to maintain all the protocols for every entry into the ledger and also to establish connection between different transactions. An error in a single transaction can spoil the entire balance sheets. Reconciliation and settlements make the ledgers more tedious to work on and consume man hours. Distributed public ledgers solve this problem with the Blockchain network, where the chain automatically creates the link between the transactions in chronological order. In addition, smart contracts can enforce the legal constraints as well as organizational protocol for connecting transactions and to control the limits of transaction. The nodes can follow a common protocol across the chain and the protocol will be distributed across the peer-to-peer network of Blockchain. The technology of concurrently validating transactions without any central authority, called *mining*, makes it simple and efficient to have any number of transactions over the decentralized platform (Kakavand and Kost De Sevres, 2016). Providing potentially faster settlements with less error and zero reconciliation improves the business with better profit. With this public, ubiquitous ledger technology, Blockchain could reduce the misconceptions created over financial networks when different intermediaries use different technology infrastructures.

In a generic terminology, distributed public ledgers are simply a huge spreadsheet that runs on thousands of computers across the world, allowing anonymous people to share data safely without worrying about trust. Every participant in the network will hold an identical copy of the ledger, with every modification in the ledger reflected to all the copies within the least time. Even though the distributed ledgers are open and public, when the transaction is validated then it is impossible to modify the transaction stored in the Blockchain. (Wall Street Journal, 2014).

The cryptographic approaches used in Blockchains use private-public key pairs to provide identity abstraction across the public ledgers. Accordingly, the identities of the individuals participating as nodes are never revealed and only the security keys (private-public keys) are used for transactions. Only the nodes with valid private keys can initiate a transaction, and the participating nodes with corresponding public keys can gain output. The identity abstraction feature provides authorization as well as authentication to nodes of the network.

Tamper-proof ledgers

In Blockchain technology. the chain of blocks containing the successful transactions will create a distributed public ledger which works in a trust-free manner over the network. In future, public Blockchains can create smart contract based permission-less ledgers, in which anyone can add transactions that solves the PoW on the network. Smart contracts can easily control the ledger entries and assign the rules for transactions. The distributed public ledgers are now preferred over centralized databases, as they are inherently harder to attack as the attacker needs to modify all the copies of Blockchain located at multiple locations over the network at the same time, which is practically impossible (DTCC, 2016). Blockchain technology also makes the public ledger tamper-proof as the modification in the ledger requires very high computational cost to redo the consensus protocol and achieve the successful proof-of-work.

Public ledger technology also improves the potential of distributed work environment and in future it can disrupt the need for corporate offices and workspaces, as anyone can perform transactions from anywhere in the world. This can also avoid much of the paperwork and complex record keeping. In future, even data warehouses will be converted to Blockchain-based distributed ledgers. Eventually, it will also provide new disruptions in data pooling and file duplication, and avoid the unnecessary redundancies in the prevailing systems. Only one copy of one file is required for the entire public ledger. As record keeping is an unavoidable part of any business, the distributed public ledger has huge potential for disruption in almost every industry in the world. Distributed ledgers promote trading of anything value-based over the network by providing a permanent and secure tool which does not requires a centralized control. This makes trading cheaper and faster through the secure public ledgers. Blockchain enthusiasts even predict the possibility of a single global distributed ledger in the future which covers all the transactions happening across the world.

Future of distributed ledgers

The distributed public ledger opens the new world of decentralized autonomous organizations (DAO) which focuses on developing autonomous agents and processes for specialized purposes. DAOs are self-reliant systems which pave the way for the future business opportunities that can automate every process and take wise decisions based on scenarios encountered. The transparency needed for DAO transactions are incorporated by the public ledgers with better integrity among the participating nodes. This also reduces the overhead of audit and the chances of disputes over transactions.

Distributed ledgers will revolutionize governmental tasks like issuing passports, collecting taxes, voting system, public distribution systems (PDS), delivering grants and other benefits, record land registries etc. They provide better monitoring and control, and ensure integrity among the various governmental services. Distributed ledgers help the government to ensure personal attention for every citizen of the country in an organized and efficient manner and to resolve the public complains through the consensus approach. Citizens will have the advantage of getting individual preferences and needs with the embedded smart contracts. The smart contracts will power the distributed ledgers to reduce the complexity and improves the efficiency of delivering services.

Decentralized apps

Decentralized apps (Dapps) are applications operated on a BC platform that serve particular purpose for the consumer as a product (Tapscott & Tapscott, 2016). These platforms will enable deploying decentralized applications on BC platforms and brings many business benefits for deployment of BC application in organizations to suit their needs. Ethereum and Hyperledger are considered one of the most famous platforms to create and deploy Dapps (Reyna et al., 2018).

Exploring the Blockchain consensus strategy

Consensus is an ancient strategy adopted by mankind for taking collective decisions over a problem. The key focus was on 'consent' made by every person to follow a procedure. Before the rise of dictatorship and governments, ancient tribes followed the consensus approach in which the decisions approved by the majority have to be accepted by all the group members.

This was considered as an efficient approach to solve disputes and to generate wise decisions. Consensus refers to a collective task where every participating individual expresses their view regarding a scenario. Eventually, these views will be synthesized to generate the best possible strategy for the scenario at the given time. Generally, the individuals can agree or disagree over a scenario but the outcome generated is based on the best need of the group. Voting is one the common and most popular approaches to achieve consensus.

Consensus strategy is used in Blockchain technology to securely maintain the immutable history of transactions without the help of a trusted third party. An important function of consensus is to protect against attacks on the Blockchain and to reach consensus if multiple instances of the Blockchain appear. This makes the distributed public ledger tamper-proof as well as transparent. Consensus plays a major role in financial services, where trades and transactions are often verified by a central authority that maintains a central ledger. Usually this process requires days to settle a transaction, and the central authority collects a fee.

Blockchain technology could eliminate that central authority by giving each bank in the network its own copy of the ledger. With the consensus mechanisms and a common Blockchain network would allow the participants to communicate with one another. Using this method, transactions could be approved automatically in seconds or minutes, significantly cutting costs and boosting efficiency (Bitcoin.org, 2009)

With the consensus strategy, the Blockchain technology can effectively solve the concurrency problem in a completely distributed manner. Instead of having a central authority that maintains a database and guards its authenticity, a copy of the entire database is distributed to every node in the network. These nodes follow the consensus protocol and compare their versions together through a continuous process of 'voting'. The version that gets the most votes from the network is accepted as authentic, and the process repeats indefinitely. In Blockchain net-

7

work, every node tends to maintain the history of transactions for the validation process and works on a peer-to-peer serverless platform to achieve the consensus strategy. This creates a new way of managing data over trust-free incentivized work platform over the distributed public ledger.

Proof of work (PoW)- a consensus algorithm

Proof of Work (PoW) is a verification process that involves solving a complex set of algorithms requiring a significant amount of computational power, as shown in Figure 7.5. Proof-of-Work is one of the most commonly used consensus approaches for Blockchains. The miner starts to build a candidate block filled with all the raw transactions competing to be added to the Blockchain. The miner then computes the hash value of his block header and checks whether it matches the current target value. If the hash value does not match, it will modify the *nonce*, usually through adding one to it, and then repeat the process. It is virtually impossible to fetch two different inputs having the same result after cryptographic hashing as the output of the cryptographic hash function changes drastically when there is a minor change to the input. Blockchains generally uses one-way Elliptic Curve Cryptography for ensuring the credibility. A nonce is a 32-bit arbitrary number that may only be used once during the mining phase. Blockchain uses a nonce to tune the difficulty of solving the hashing function.

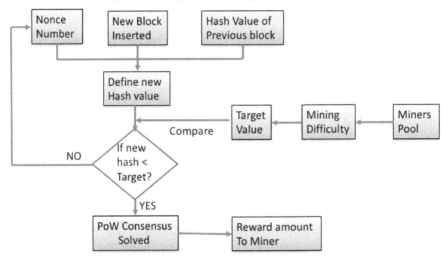

Figure 7.5: Flow diagram of proof of work mechanism

The public Blockchain network is collaboratively maintained by anonymous peers on the network, such that each block has to invest a significant amount of work in its creation to ensure that non-honest peers who want to modify past blocks have to work harder than honest peers who only want to add new blocks to the Blockchain.

The process of creating the chain of blocks in chronological order makes it impossible to modify transactions included in any block without modifying all the succeeding blocks. As a result, the modification cost for existing block increases with every new block added to the Blockchain, magnifying the effect of the proof of work.

In future, this enormous power consumption and time delay will be major barrier for using PoW for financial and non-financial applications. So, developers started thinking about faster and efficient methods like proof of stake (PoS) and proof of existence (PoE) which could save money and time.

Proof of stake (PoS)

Proof of stake (PoS) was developed as an alternative for PoW, with reduced computations and less constraints for generation of blocks. Since PoW required huge computational power, nodes with high-end Graphics Processing Unit (GPU) miners had an advantage of mining blocks over the regular nodes. Even though it would be costlier effort, this created a possibility for hacker groups for winning the consensus if they can deploy large number of enormous GPUs to gain control over the Blockchain network from the valid miners (Buterin, 2013b).

In PoS, the main mining process is related to the user's ownership stake in the system. Instead of mining power required by PoW, the probability to create a block and receive the associated reward is proportional to a user's ownership stake in the system. Any individual who has n percent of total stake creates a new block with probability n. In other words, the owners of major shares have an advantage over the others in creating the new block. The key to PoS is that individuals with the highest stakes in the system have the most interest in maintaining a secure network, as they will suffer the most if the reputation and price of the system diminishes because of attacks. Gaining the stake to obtain authority will be an expensive affair for the attacker and the chances of obtaining stakes from legitimate owners/individuals are very low.

Scope of trust-free environment

Transparency and security combine to form a major disruption that makes Blockchain a completely trust-free technology. Blockchains redefines how trust is perceived in a digital environment. The reason why Blockchain technology is considered so disruptive is that it has the ability to solve this problem of authenticity without the inclusion of any trusted intermediaries. Blockchain is secure through the immutability it gains from the hashing algorithms, when applied on the decentralized network, and transparent because anyone can look through all blocks. In essence, Blockchains have introduced a completely new type of digital trust which manifests itself in a fully distributed way without anyone having to trust any single member of the network (Mougayar, 2016). The only trust required is in that, on average, the participants of the network are behaving honestly — or more to the point, that the majority of the entire network is not colluding against the others in a coordinated manner.

Blockchain technology makes a disruption in trusted computing by providing a trustless/ trust-free computing paradigm which eliminates the need for a trusted third party. Rather than increasing the security measures and innovating on trusted platforms, Blockchain simply eliminates the need for a trusted platform. Blockchain makes it possible for users to interact with any anonymous entity in the network without any concern over the identity of the participating node. It allows anyone to verify the authenticity of transaction and data independently, without considering others' opinion, irrespective of whom or where that data came from in the network. It provides security and privacy to both the users and data being handled over Blockchain. The Blockchain uses the cryptographic hash address for every user and does not reveal the actual identity of anyone across the chain which makes personal information secure and hidden. With this, we do not need to trust anyone on the chain, as trust is incorporated by the chain in its implementation itself. The data, once stored in blocks through consensus approach, becomes immutable and the owner of data can be assured that the data remains tamper-proof.

Selection of Blockchain networks

BC is like the internet in architecture, as both have public and private versions. There are many different forms, with different properties. The main variants are either private/public permissioned (closed) BC or public permission less (open) BCs (Mainelli & Smith, 2015; Walport, 2015). A public Blockchain is a ledger that anyone can read, can send transactions to, expect to have them added to the ledger if they are valid, and participate in the consensus. These Blockchains are considered fully decentralized. A private Blockchain is a ledger where consensus permissions are restricted to specific users. Read permissions may be public or restricted depending on requirements (Jayachandran, 2017).

As shown in Figure 7.6, a variety of architectures is possible with different governance, business model and operational implications.

Public BC system

In the public system anyone can join the network. Validating the blocks is carried out by miners, and anyone can become a miner and seek out the reward. A miner may to walk away from being a node and return later and get the full account of all network activity again (Wu et al, 2017). Basically, anyone with a computer can join the system, read the chain, verify new blocks and make legitimate changes as long as they follow the rules of the system. Anyone can participate in the consensus – the process for determining what blocks get added to the chain and what the current state is. As a substitute for centralized or quasi-centralized trust, public Blockchains are secured by crypto-economics as the combination of economic incentives and cryptographic verification using mechanisms such as proof of work (PoW) or proof of stake (PoS), following a general principle that the degree to which someone can have an influence in the consensus process is proportional to the quantity of economic resources that they can bring to bear. These Blockchain are generally considered to be 'fully decentralized' or 'permission-less networks'.

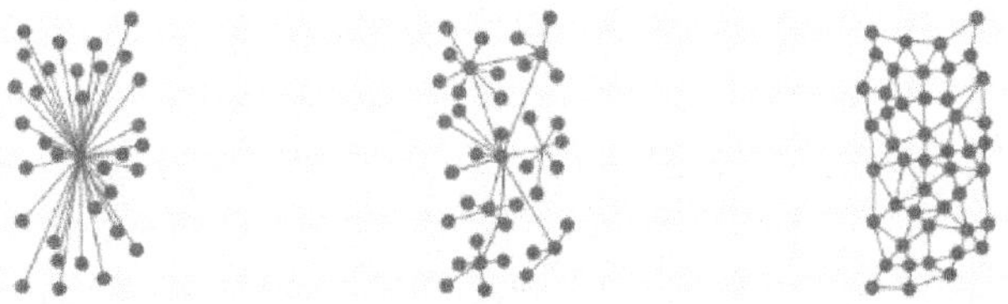

Operation	Centralized	Decentralized	Distributed
Governance/ Business Model	Centrally Controlled	Community Controlled	Autonomous
Stability/Resilience	Unstable	Bounded Stability	Stable
Scalability	Large Throughput/ Small Number of Nodes	Small Throughput/Medium Number of Nodes	Infinite
Speed of Enterprise Development	Fast	Medium	Very Slow
Architecture Evolution/Diversity	Permissioned/Private	Hybrid	Permissionless/Public
Tokenization	No	Possibly	Yes
Trust Control	High Traditional/Low Algorithmic	Medium Traditional/ Medium Algorithmic	Low Traditional/High Algorithmic

Figure 7.6: Blockchain architecture. Source: Gartner, 2018.

Permissioned (private) BC system

In this, permission is needed to read the information in the Blockchain. It also limits the parties who can make changes and restricts who can serve the network, by verifying blocks and writing new blocks in the chain (Lemieux, 2015).

One example of this is the cryptocurrency Ripple; this runs on a permissioned Blockchain. The difference from any public system is that the startup determines who may act as a validator in their network. For this cryptocurrency, some of the validators are CGI, MIT and Microsoft. Beyond these, the startup also builds its own nodes in different locations around the world. Sometimes these permissioned Blockchains may or may not involve the proof of work for mining. Among Blockchain developers there is a dispute whether private Blockchains that do not use proof of work should be called and viewed as Blockchains at all but rather as simple shared ledgers (Bauerle, 2017c).

Consortium Blockchains

Since the initial launching of the Bitcoin and consequently Blockchain technology as a public network, its use has been continuously expanding into more areas. Many financial institutions or governments are exploring alternative types of networks by creating systems that complement their existing business models and these are usually non-public networks. Another type is the consortium Blockchain. In this "the consensus process is controlled by a pre-selected set of nodes; for example, one might imagine a consortium of 15 financial institutions, each of which operates a node and of which 10 must sign every block in order for the block to be valid. The right to read the Blockchain may be public, or restricted to the participants, and there are also hybrid routes such as the root hashes of the blocks being public together with an API that allows members of the public to make a limited number of queries and get back cryptographic proofs of some parts of the Blockchain state. These Blockchains may be considered 'partially decentralized'".

Blockchain platform Hyperledger

Hyperledger project was announced on December 17, 2015, and was backed by 17 founding members. It now has over 130 members, including technology companies such as IBM, consulting and professional services companies such as Accenture PLC, and financial services companies such as JPMorgan and the Depository Trust and Clearing Corporation (DTCC). The goal is to support open source Blockchain-based distributed ledgers and advance cross-industry Blockchain technologies. Before embarking on Blockchain initiatives, organizations must first establish whether their cases merit the use of Blockchain. Organizations can use Blockchain where trust is difficult to establish between parties in a transaction value chain. Those involving multiple parties across different regions and varied systems of reconciliation, or those that require immutability and transparency into each change of state are ripe for Blockchain disruption. Blockchain is also ideal if organizations need to reduce the settlement time between parties, as it helps eliminate intermediate checks. To meet enterprise requirements, Blockchain solutions must address high-level concerns related to architectural and implementation challenges, and ensure scalability, security, and interoperability

Attributes of Blockchain

These selected attributes demonstrate what the technology could offer and how it may affect the business. The key attributes are discussed below (Mougayar, 2016):

- *Privacy*: The BC decentralized nature offers a reduced possibility of privacy breaches as there is no central authority that can control or manipulate the data. The data are stored in the form of transactions on distributed ledgers and encrypted to maintain privacy (Tapscott & Tapscott, 2016). This differs from normal centralized business networks, where there is rise in the incidents related to breaches of user privacy in the businesses that collect and control personal data. The data are under users' control and not giving the privilege of a certain institution to use this data which may have value to another external party.

- *Reduced fraud risk*: BC data is stored on distributed ledgers and copies of transaction are distributed among the nodes in the network. This gives the BC an attribute of making it almost impossible to alter the data (Cai and Zhu, 2016). This should reduce frauds and reduce business risks. However, Gervais et al. (2016) argue that a BC network is not totally guaranteed to be immutable.

■ *Transparency*: The BC ledger can be programmed to record virtually any type of information that could be represented as a code. This could be birth, death and marriage certificates, land registration deeds and titles of ownership, educational degrees, financial accounts, medical records, insurance claims or votes. BC will create a transparency culture between firms and stakeholders as data auditability becomes possible (Tapscott and Tapscott, 2016). This collaborative form of data sharing across firms can allow for more timely decisions and collaboration. This will be particularly useful to industries where real time data sharing is crucial but challenging to achieve due to fragmented systems.

■ *Security*: Security resilience is one if the greatest risks faced nowadays over the internet due to incessant attempts of different types of cybercrimes (Tapscott and Tapscott, 2016). Cyber security is becoming difficult to sustain as cyber-attacks are becoming very sophisticated. BC ledgers and networks are considered more resilient and less vulnerable to malicious attackers, since attacking multiple databases at once is challenging as they are encrypted and decentralized (Gervais et al., 2016; Tapscott and Tapscott, 2016) .

■ *Equitable access* : Nearly a third of the world's population are still excluded from access to the financial and economic system. In the developing world around two billion people don't even have a bank account, which is a gateway to financial opportunities. Lower income groups can't afford the minimum account balances, minimum payment amounts, or transaction fees to use the system. The high infrastructure costs related to financial operations make micropayments and micro accounts unfeasible to include these groups in the financial eco-system (Tapscott and Tapscott, 2016). Blockchain can help in financial inclusion. By removing intermediaries, it reduces the overheads related to financial operations and solves the problem of scaling across borders, allowing the possibility of reaching previously excluded group of customers.

■ *Speed*: In general remittance takes three to seven days to process. Stock trades take two to three to days settle whereas bank loan trades take on average a 23 days. The SWIFT network, which handles fifteen million payment orders a day globally, requires days to clear them whereas Blockchain transactions are instant or completed within minutes (Tapscott and Tapscott, 2016). This means that companies can process transactions of money, asset or information more quickly, thereby enhancing their service levels.

■ *Efficiency*: By providing a single version of all transactions across the network, Blockchain provides instant visibility. All the parties need to perform tasks throughout the product life cycle, thus improving efficiency through automation. Further, Blockchain-based systems could help drive unprecedented collaboration between participants resulting in process efficiency.

- *Productivity*: The transparent nature of Blockchain makes it possible for the organizations to use it as a platform to facilitate collaboration between different levels of administration (Tapscott and Tapscott, 2016). It ensures efficient implementation of various policies based on the terms set for different customer and suppliers through smart contracts, while keeping every relevant department appraised of the situation. A recent analysis by Australia's Commonwealth Scientific and Industrial Research Organization (2017) identified that Blockchain adoption may lead to increased productivity and innovation.

- *Quality*: Information stored in a Blockchain system corresponds to what is being represented in reality due its distributed consensus creating mechanism (Tapscott and Tapscott, 2016). This ensures that if a transaction cannot be verified by the majority of nodes, it will be rejected. The result is higher data quality. By utilizing the Blockchain to automate processes, companies may increase the integrity of data.

- *Cost savings*: Blockchain removes the need of intermediaries through transaction validation and recording of data on a distributed cloud. This makes it a network that has peer-to-peer or shared-cost basis. Experts say it is possible that the costs of using Blockchain's computing infrastructure will be as cheap as Internet access today, on a relative per-user basis (Mougayar, 2016). Costs related to transaction clearance and settlement can reduce due to removal of intermediaries (Tapscott and Tapscott, 2016; Ølnes, 2016). Fraud related costs may go down due to the immutable structure of Blockchain.

Smart contracts over Blockchain

Introduction to smart contracts

In everyday life, contracts are valuable mechanisms to uphold the promises between known or unknown individuals in a fair manner. By definition, a contract is a voluntary agreement between two or more parties creating certain obligations enforceable by law. Contracts are generally enforced to ensure smooth interaction with all the stake holders over the participating scenario without any problems and minimal need of trust. The beauty of a contract is that you have a remedy when people break their promises. By incorporating the power of physical contracts into the computing world, we could create wonders in the way we do business, with clearly outlined contractual terms, and solve disputes, if any, amicably. With all the noteworthy properties of Blockchain network, it turns out that Blockchain seems to be the perfect platform for deploying the digital contracts to run digital businesses than making physical contracts. This thought gave rise to the invention of smart contracts, the programmable digital contracts written and deployed using any Turing-complete language over the Blockchain network (Buterin, 2014).

Smart contracts are self-executing programs which run on the Blockchain and are capable of enforcing rules, consequences and computation over every transaction happening in the Blockchain. The concept of smart contracts was first formally coined by Nick Szabo in 1994. Smart contracts can take any form of data as input; perform computations over the input, based on the protocols specified in the smart contract, and can enforce decisions based on the prevailing conditions for producing the output (Szabo, 1997). This revolutionary concept automates the enforcement of contractual promises without any intermediaries or trusted-third parties and improves transparency, as every individual node in the Blockchain abides by the protocols specified in the smart contract. All the contract transactions are stored in Blockchain in a chronological order for future access, along with the complete audit trail of events. Also, the participating nodes cannot tamper with or change the contract agreements stored in the Blockchain, thus removing the chances of attack. Smart contracts make the entire network behave like a large central computer, but avoid the risk of failures, cost and trust of a centralized computing mechanism.

Like any regular legal contract or agreement, smart contracts can incorporate every possible consequence of transaction behaviour and can issue the actions to be taken for each scenario. Smart contracts make it possible to deal with all the valid and invalid transactions that can happen over a Blockchain and even trace out abnormal actions from participating nodes. Smart contracts do not store any data, instead they provide a guideline on how the data are stored in Blockchain. Rather, they have the potential to reduce and even eliminate the chances of fraud and overhead costs of many commercial transactions.

Consider a simple example of supply chain which is currently controlled by the intermediaries, mostly through a centralized platform. We have chosen this scenario since the supply chain is where middlemen play a major role in controlling the activities right from the production to distribution. Many unlawful activities like hoarding, black marketing etc. happen in the supply chains to multiply the profits of middleman, and the producers and customers suffer a lot. Before unveiling the Blockchain platform, it was practically impossible to administer and govern individual activities over the Internet without the help of a centralized governing organization to ensure that the data is not tampered or fudged by any attacker. Due to lack of a stable decentralized platform, the individuals could not confirm that a transaction had successfully been performed without relying on a trusted central body to verify that this particular transaction was genuine.

The middleman, who has played an intermediate economic role, in controlling the business between producers and consumers for many decades, will be eliminated by the potential of smart contract powered Blockchains (Figure 7.7). They provides liberty for people to perform transactions of digital assets or data across the Blockchain network, in a secure, trust-free, and immutable way. They could do wonders in the supply chain by enabling a legal set of protocols for every transaction happening in the supply chain. Moreover, the public ledger system may enhance visibility and thus fair distribution and pricing to products with less wastages.

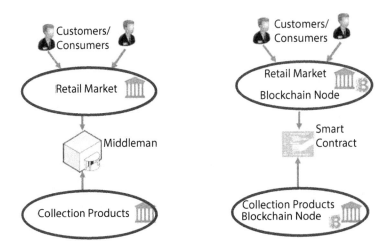

Figure 7.7: How smart contracts eliminate middleman in supply chain

Need for smart contracts

The evolution of autonomous scripts for handling any kind of business or process based upon digital assets, which can self-execute, self-verify, self-enforce and self-constrain the agreement between two parties, give rise to the thought of smart contracts. The role of the Blockchain network is to eliminate the need for a trusted third party for resolving any legal disputes that may arise between the participants of the contract. The modular and repeatable smart contracts enable the building of applications for specific uses and are encoded into the Blockchain at specific addresses known as contract addresses, which are determined at the time of deployment. Whenever the nodes initiate an activity being controlled by the contract, a transaction is sent to the contract address and the virtual machine executes the code using the data input from the transaction. In other words, smart contracts are self-executing applications that run as programmed with zero downtime, censorship, fudging or third-party interference (Buterin, 2014).

Smart contracts avoid the delays and expenses incurred by physical contracts. They can execute independently without the influence of any external entities and have the potential to take necessary actions in the event of violation of contract. Generally, the promises are hardwired into the code to create an 'unbreakable' contract. Such contracts will have zero flexibility. New programming language like Solidity, Serpent etc. are designed for writing smart contracts, which can precisely specify the outcomes with zero ambiguity in contract interpretations and can refrain any sort of violation. By agreeing to use a smart contract, the participating individuals effectively cede control over an aspect of the performance of a contractual obligation to a digitized process which cannot be reasoned with or influenced.

Implementation of smart contracts

For obtaining the desired functionalities, smart contracts need to be implemented by clearly specifying every aspect of the system. Technically, a smart contract is a program code written using any Ethereum compatible language, that the Ethereum Virtual Machine (EVM) (see below) is able to execute over the Blockchain. Once the program code has been added to the Blockchain as bytecode, the smart contract itself cannot be modified or decoded back to readable format. After this, the nodes can only perform storage and retrieval operation on the immutable contract code (Luu et al., 2016). The smart contracts deployed over the Ethereum Blockchain network will have a unique contract address and are available globally to any node over the network. A smart contract can simply invoke other smart contracts using message call statements.

Smart contracts are realized by Turing complete programming languages that can convert the contract into bytecode and execute them using EVM. Currently available programming languages that support the Ethereum platform are Solidity (Java-like) and Serpent (Python-like). Even though each smart contract has a contract address to uniquely identify it globally, it differs from the bitcoin wallet in the fact that it can execute the contract code based on the data received through transactions. For resisting different forms of attacks like DDoS, malicious codes, infinite loop problems, every step involved in the creation and execution of smart contract involves spending a certain amount of virtual currency, termed as *'gas'* or *ether* (hence *Ethereum*). The total number of computations and data storage entries of the contract bytecode generated by the EVM compiler determines the amount of gas require to run the entire smart contract.

The gas price determines the cost of every action to be performed during the execution of EVM bytecode and making transactions over the Blockchain. The gas acts as fuel for running the contracts and every node should possess sufficient fuel to run the smart contract. Usually the computational complexity of statements defines the gas needed for its executions. The simple mathematical computations such as addition, subtraction, and multiplication will cost 1 gas for every instance of execution. Generally, a start price is set for every smart contract to reward every miner for the computational power being spent by them. The gas prices are restricted only to transactions in the smart contracts, while the messages send between different contracts does not require gas for communication. The total amount of gas being spent on all the executions done of all the smart contracts initiated by any transaction should be in the limits of the 'gas field' of the corresponding transaction. Otherwise, abnormal termination of executions may arise due to exhausting the gas. Generally, a well–defined mathematical logic should be incorporated into every contract for proper estimation and utilization of gas and to deal with any critical situation such that the contract remains live globally to every participating node

7

Smart contracts using the Ethereum platform

The Ethereum project was formally announced by Vitalik Buterin in January 2014 at the North American Bitcoin Conference in Miami, Florida, USA. Buterin was a developer associated with Bitcoin and published a white paper "*A Next Generation Smart Contract & Decentralized Application Platform*" in late 2013, which describes developing decentralized applications (Dapps) on the Ethereum platform (Buterin, 2014). In the early 2014, Dr. Gavin Wood associated with Buterin and co-founded Ethereum. The Ethereum Yellow Paper was released by Wood in April 2014. This described in depth the Ethereum Virtual Machine (EVM) which could be used as the backbone of smart contracts and Dapps (Wood, 2014). Ethereum was the first Turing-complete platform for developing programmable Blockchains that could revolutionize the development of decentralized applications. Buterin considered that this next generation platform had immense potential to develop more Bitcoin-like applications in the decentralized environment. This concept is clearly specified by Buterin in the Ethereum white paper, as he suggests Ethereum as an 'alternate protocol' for developing decentralized applications (Dapps). He mainly focuses on getting faster application development time with high security and better interaction among the Dapps. The Ethereum project realizes this by building the base layer, the open Blockchain platform with a built in Turing-complete programming language that helps programmers to write smart contracts that are executable directly over the Blockchain. Moreover, a wide variety of Dapps can be directly integrated on top of the Blockchain platform that is secure and powerful. The most striking feature of programmable Blockchains like Ethereum is that they can disrupt potentially every business domain with the advent of Dapps.

The token used in Ethereum Blockchain is known as *ether*, which is used for paying transaction fees over the Ethereum network. Ether is also considered as a crypto-currency like Bitcoin, and is now traded over the crypto-currency exchanges. The current value of 1 Ether (ETH) is $ 683.39 (as of 16 May 2018).

Ethereum mining

Ethash is the proof of work used in Ethereum 1.0. Ethash is integrated into the Blockchain technology by making the creation of a new block require all members of the network undertake the proof of work based on a set of fixed resources know as DAG (Directed Acyclic Graph). The DAG will be completely updated for every 30,000 blocks, a 125-hour window called an *epoch* (roughly 5.2 days) and needs some time to generate. As the DAG depends only on the height of the block, it can be generated before the generation of block. If the DAG is not generated, the node has to wait until the process is being committed to produce a block. Consensus is achieved via incentivization for peers to always accept the longest chain of blocks in the Blockchain by distribution of a cryptographic token of value: ether. While Ethereum is currently based on PoW, it is expected to move to PoS in its next update, Serenity. Ethereum's development team is more centralized and can therefore can plan and implement PoW changes. Changes to the mining algorithm are much harder to implement with Bitcoin and aren't likely to happen. Ethereum's block time is set at 12 seconds per block, while Bitcoin blocks are found on average every 10 minutes. Ethash is the latest version of Dagger-Hashimoto, which is extensively used in Ethereum network for hashing (Ethereum, 2016). The algorithm works as follows:

1 For every block in the Blockchain, a seed value exists which is computed by traversing through the block header from genesis block till the current block.

2 A pseudorandom cache (16MB) is computed from the seed which are stored in the light clients.

3 A new dataset (1GB) will be generated from the cache such that the dataset depends only on limited number of items in the cache which exhibits a linear growth. All the nodes and miners will store the copy of the dataset.

4 From the above dataset, random pieces are sliced and hashed together by a process known as mining. The main advantage is that auditing and verification process of this mined data can be carried out with minimum amount of memory. Only the contents of cache are stored, as the cache memory can be used to recreate the sliced piece of dataset.

After every 30000 blocks, the dataset will be updated and hence the miner's computational power will be used for the reading the data rather than modifying it.

After completing the mining process (PoW) successfully, the miner who mines the winning block will gain:

■ A reward of 5 Ether as the block reward of winning block

■ The gas value spent for the block in terms of Ether equivalent depending on the current gas price.

■ For each *uncle* being included in the block an extra reward of 1/32 per uncle will be issued to the miner.

Uncles represent the stale blocks, which mean having parents which are ancestors (maximum of 6 preceding blocks) of the current block being included. In order to eliminate the consequence of network lag, the valid uncles are rewarded while dispersing the mining rewards. These valid uncles improve the security as predecessors are maintained effectively. Eventually, the initiators of each transaction will pay for the gas value spent for every transaction inside the winning block being generated by the miner (Ethereum, 2016).

Ethereum transactions

In the Ethereum Project, the 'transaction' refers to the signed data package which holds the content to be sent from an EOA (Externally Owned Account) to another account on the Blockchain. Every transaction in an Ethereum Blockchain consists of 6 fields namely:

■ The **recipient** of the transaction (either user or smart contract).

■ **Signature** of the sender for identifying and validating the message being sent.

- **Value** field: specifies the amount of wei (one trillionth of an ether) to be transferred from the sender to the receiver.

- **Data** field (optional): holds the message being sent to a contract.

- **Startgas** value: specifies the maximum number of computational steps that can be carried out by a transaction execution.

- **Gasprice** value: specifies the amount that the sender is willing to pay for gas. One unit of gas corresponds to the execution of one atomic instruction, i.e., a computational step

Ethereum Virtual Machine (EVM)

Ethereum is a programmable Blockchain platform on a peer-to-peer network, where every peer stores the same copy of a Blockchain database and runs an Ethereum virtual machine to maintain and alter its state. EVM is a virtual machine designed to be run by all participants in a peer-to-peer network, and can read and write to a Blockchain both executable code and data, verify digital signatures, and run code in a quasi-Turing complete manner. It will only execute code when it receives a message verified by a digital signature, and the information stored on the Blockchain says it is appropriate to do so.

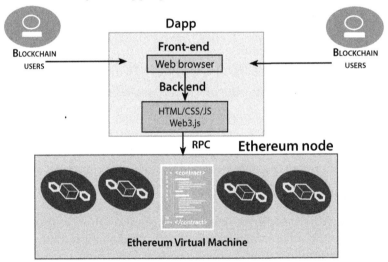

Figure 7.8: Dapp components

Figure 7.8 illustrated the EVM works in the same way as that of any other virtual machine: it will take any high level programming language designed for writing smart contracts, and can compile it into EVM bytecode that the machine can understand. EVM is typically a huge decentralized computer having millions of accounts. The accounts can be viewed as objects that have the capacity to handle an internal database, run contract code and can communicate with other accounts. The smart contract itself can be considered as an account. Private keys are used for handling the EOAs (Externally Owned Accounts); only the owners of these private keys will have the complete privilege to perform transactions and send ether using EOA (Ethereum, 2016).

Web 3: A platform for Decentralized Apps

Web 3 is actually a back end developed for the decentralized internet service upon the Ethereum platform, as depicted in the Figure 7.8. The Dapp projects built on Ethereum will leverage the Blockchain to build solutions that rely on decentralized consensus to provide new products and services that were not previously possible. As Wood (2014) noted, Web 3 will be a "zero-trust interaction system" built on decentralized platform governed by consensus strategy.

Ether and gas

Ethereum uses its own crypto-currency ether, to execute the contracts over the Blockchain. Cost of computation depends on its complexity. Every contract and transaction has a fixed start price used to pay the miner as rewards in return for the computational power spend by him. The gas price for any transaction is found by multiplying the number of computations with the current gas price, and thus giving the equation:

Gas Price for Transaction = (No. of Computations X Gas Price Current) + Start Gas Price

Ethereum project differs from Bitcoin in the fact that the miners will process random transactions from the previous blocks and produce a hash of the result for the succeeding block. This means that the smart contracts have the power to carry out any form of computational sequence while the transactions proceed, and can create the chain as per the contractual statement. Moreover, a miner should possess the entire Blockchain, so the concept of mining pools does not work same as that of Bitcoin.

Similar to the Bitcoin users, the Ethereum users also have to pay a fee to the Ethereum network for performing any transaction over the Ethereum Blockchain. The idea of this transaction fee is to protect the Blockchain from the attack of illegitimate users and malicious transactions. Those users possessing enough ether for paying the fee could perform transactions on the Blockchain. Similar to Bitcoin Blockchain, the Ethereum Blockchain charges fees for every computation step and data storage. The ether collected by the miners in the Ethereum Blockchain will be issued as reward for every valid block being mined. These rewards promote more miners to build the blocks competitively and to protect the Blockchain from attackers (Ethereum, 2016).

As we discussed earlier, the notion of gas in the Ethereum Blockchain is to incorporate a fixed value for every transaction and computation in the Ethereum network. There are several concepts associated with the gas like *gas prices*, *gas cost*, *gas limit*, and *gas fees*.

- **Gas cost** represents a static cost value for a computation over the Ethereum Blockchain in terms of gas. Gas cost is used in smart contracts to have a control over the computations over time.

- **Gas price** represents the actual cost to be spent in terms of a currency like ether. Usually the gas price will be a floating value to stabilize the value of gas, which means that with the changes in currency values, the gas price also changes to adapt to match. The gas price is set by the equilibrium price of how much users are willing to spend, and how much processing nodes are willing to accept.

- **Gas limit** specifies the maximum amount of gas that can be used per block. It is depicted as the maximum computational load, volume of transaction, or the block size, and miners can gradually change the gas limit over a period of time.

- **Gas fee** is the amount of gas needed to be paid to execute a particular transaction or contract. The miners will get paid with the gas fee based on the computational expenses incurred to build a block.

Implementation on Ethereum

In the Ethereum platform, the underlying Blockchain keeps track of the state of each account, and all state transitions happening on the Blockchain are transfers of value and information between accounts. The accounts can be generally classified into two categories:

- **Externally Owned Accounts (EOAs):** Accounts that are controlled by private key of the users.

- **Contract Accounts:** Accounts which are controlled by smart contract code and EOA can activate these contracts.

The major difference between these two accounts is that humans control EOAs – as they own the private keys which give control over an EOA. While, the contract accounts are governed by their 'smart contract code'. There are certain contract accounts that are 'controlled' by humans, and these are pre-programmed to be controlled by an EOA with a certain address, which is in turn controlled by whoever holds the private keys that control that EOA. The smart contracts get executed whenever a transaction is being sent to the contract account. Eventually, the users can create new contracts and deploy them into the Blockchain to perform specified tasks.

The EOAs initiate each activity in the Ethereum Blockchain by starting the concerned transactions. Every time a transaction is received at a contract account, its code gets executed as per the input parameters sent through the transaction. Finally, the EVM executes the contract code on each participant in the Blockchain network and ends up in creating new block.

The externally controlled accounts possess an ether balance to pay for the transactions to be carried out. They can send transactions even without the associated code. On the other hand, a contract will have an associated code along with the ether balance. The incoming transactions from various external contracts trigger the code execution, which includes operations of arbitrary complexity.

These operations can eventually reflect on the state of the system, perform storage operations or even invoke other contract codes as shown in Figure 7.9. Thus, Ethereum can be viewed as a Turing complete platform for exploring the potentials of Blockchain technology to satisfy user requirements (Ethereum, 2016).

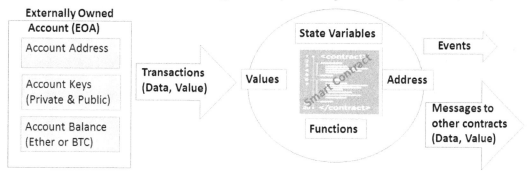

Figure 7.9: Smart contract structure

Deploying smart contracts using Ethereum in steps

1 Start the Ethereum node. Some of the important implementations of the Ethereum node are Geth, testrpc, ethersim, etc.

2 Compile the smart contract and fetch its binary file If the contract is written in Solidity, use solc compiler to get the binary. Online and offline versions of solc compiler are available.

3 Deploy the compiled smart contract into the Ethereum network. For this we need the Blockchain address of the smart contract and the ABI representation. Deployment needs a certain amount of ether (Ethereum Blockchain or test network) for connecting with the node's address. The cost of deployment depends on the contract being executed and the gas price needed for execution of various functions in the contract.

4 Use JavaScript API of web3.js to access the functions of the contract. This also requires spending a certain amount of ether as specified in the smart contract.

Applications of smart contracts

In the following sections, we present some smart contract applications. This concludes with two brief illustrative case studies about the application of Blockchain technology in the context of the sustainable economy via digital transformation.

1 Smart contracts facilitated rental and lease services will create disruption in the coming era. A simple digital key controlled by a smart contract can be used to lease vehicles, houses, rooms and other services to customers without the burden of handling the service manually. IoT powered smart control is emerging which helps to lease any service remotely without any caretaker or issuing authority. Slock.it had demonstrated a smart lock powered with IoT and Blockchain technology that can be used to rent house and rooms based on

smart contracts. Access to rooms will be disabled automatically after the specific usage time through these smart contracts. Airbnb, a peer-to-peer online homestay reservation network, is also experimenting the potential of smart contracts for leasing rooms. IBM Blockchain has demonstrated smart contract based car rental services with significant reduction in overhead costs and with higher integrity and security.

2   Smart contracts could bring tremendous changes in the e-commerce business by enabling autonomous digital markets where any individual can buy or sell anything without the need of intermediary business portals. This can reduce the market complexities and delays and help governments for better taxation through the public ledger support. IoT powered drones are also being tested currently for doorstep delivery of goods to ensure on-time and secure delivery (Sofia, 2016).

3   In the field of machine-to-machine (M2M) communication and machine learning, smart contracts can bring out extraordinary capabilities for device interaction and automation to a level perceivable by humans. Self-driving vehicles, autonomous gadgets and self-equipped devices (like ADEPT) could be realized effectively with the immense potential of smart contracts (Sofia, 2016).

4   Any case where the value needs to be released upon met conditions is an area of smart contract application. Funding (scholarship, discount, sponsorship, donation, etc.) can be automatically released once the conditions for each case are met and verified digitally. Digitally executed due diligence for start-ups can automatically release the funds as a final step of an investment.

5   In future, even betting and gambling will be powered with Blockchain-enabled smart contracts to avoid frauds and to make it legal. Smart contracts will be enabled to find the winners and to pay rewards based on the play statistics.

6   The property rights and transfer of assets to legal heirs can be digitalized with smart contracts to enable much more complex legal documents or escrow statements. This can also automate asset transfer to concerned parties when the owner dies.

Blockchain applications in the built environment

Following a systematic literature conducted by Li et, al., (2018), seven categories of Blockchain applications in the built environment were identified: smart energy; smart cities and the sharing economy; smart government; smart homes; intelligent transport; Building Information Modelling (BIM) and construction management; and business models and organisational structures. The review comprised initial searches in three databases (Scopus, ScienceDirect and Web of Science), where 534 papers were returned. After removal of duplicates and application of inclusion and exclusion criteria within the databases, 131 papers remained. Abstracts for these papers were reviewed and 32 selected for review. In addition, further searches were conducted in Google Scholar following a more traditional route and an additional 21 papers were added resulting in 53 papers being reviewed. This demonstrates how quickly the energy industry has embraced distributed ledger technologies. Most of the papers in this category provide some element of prototyping or proof-of-concept demonstrating that the research community is developing cutting-edge technologies to exploit it. (Li, et al., 2018)

BCT, aka DLT, in smart energy is changing the energy market by opening it up to allow individual homeowners who produce their own renewable energy the opportunity to trade with Major Power Producers (MPPs) through the smart grid and/or directly with their neighbours through the use of DLTs and microgrids. These prosumers generate competition in the energy market by offering alternative energy choices, which, as a side effect, is encouraging proliferation of renewable energies. Moreover, they are supporting demand response management through offering additional sources of energy that were not available previously. Different models and architectures have been proposed for the implementation of Blockchain depending on the aims and objectives of the research for smart energy ranging from implementation of new cryptocurrencies and tokenisation models as incentives to trade or as currency for energy (i.e. NRGCoin), through resource management using serious gamin, to development of end-user mobile applications integrated with DLT to make the technology more user-friendly for the general public. Closely linked to smart energy are smart cities, smart homes and smart government. These concepts are not new per se but they are constantly under development as technologies evolve and understanding and acceptance of these technologies proliferates throughout society. A key concern across these areas is the security and privacy of data; something that DLT addresses in some respects but not entirely. Any data uploaded to a Blockchain is considered to be immutable (unchangeable and everlasting) which removes people's right to be forgotten but alternative approaches to address this concern are being considered, particularly in smart government.

For example, government records can be stored off the Blockchain but pointers that they exist and where to find them are put onto the Blockchain. Key issues raised with regards to smart government are interoperability, longevity, accessibility and balance of power. Interoperability is important as records produced today should be accessible and in the right format for many years into the future. While internet connectivity, both high-speed broadband and mobile networks, has advanced significantly in recent years, there still remains a large portion of the population without reasonable connectivity – only one in seven people has access to the internet in the world's least developed countries.

Central governance is inherent in society and Blockchain technology aims to disrupt that entirely whether it be through revolutionising the finance industry by removing the need for banks or through changing the role of governments. Organisations and roles within them will change with the introduction of wholly automated and semi-automated organisations. Corporate hierarchies will become much flatter and many roles will disappear entirely with new ones coming into being. Also residing under the umbrella of smart cities is intelligent transport. This is already in operation in many major cities and arterial roads throughout countries, for example, through traffic calming and route variations to avoid congestion and improve air quality.

Like in smart energy, Blockchain technology and innovative technology companies (e.g. La'zooz) are opening up markets in the transport industry where vehicle owners now have a platform on which to monetise their idle vehicles or offer ride sharing to people travelling in the same direction. This crosses over into the sharing economy where communities are able to devise and utilise proprietary value systems for sharing information, products and services resulting in a more user-led and user-empowered society. The challenges and the opportunities facing the identified Blockchain applications specific to the built environment are part of an ongoing research study conducted by the 2nd and third authors of this chapter in response to the expected growth in business applications of BCT. Figure 7.10 provides a forecast of the business value of BC in global context from 2018-2030 adopted from a research report by Gartner (Kandaswamy & Stevens, 2018). Gartner research report states that Blockchain is the most researched term on their portal since 2017 (Kandaswamy & Stevens, 2018).

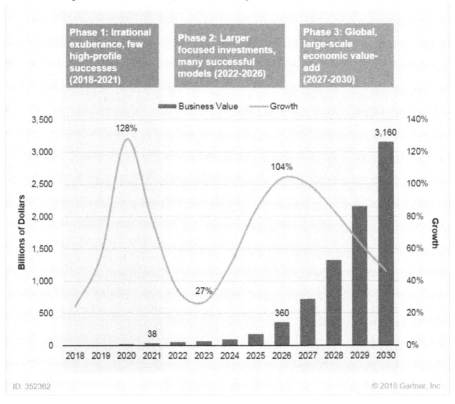

Figure 7.10: Blockchain businessvalue forecast, 2018-2030

To conclude this chapter, two brief case studies will provide further examples of BCT applications to illustrate this growing trend.

Case 7.1: The role of Blockchain in Life Cycle Assessments

For environmental protection, many industries and companies are preparing Life Cycle Assessment (LCA) techniques and developing Environmental Product Declarations (EPD) for their products. LCA studies the environmental aspects and potential impacts throughout a product's life. Following the ISO 14040/44 standard with the smart contract concept could build LCA data into a product's or asset's digital ledger. The EPD's components consist of a product's environmental data such as raw materials, energy consumption, and environmental impact, converting this in a smart report readable from the Blockchain network. The benefits of Blockchain are to provide transparency between organisations and companies, and also ensure their products are truly sustainable at every step during the product journey.

Case 7.2: Energy Trading using smart contracts

For this use, Blockchain nodes become a trading platform for local energy micro-grids, using renewable energy sources such as photovoltaic and wind. Applying Blockchain allows for trust, tamper-proof, transparent, and trackable trading of green energy without the presence of the centralised electricity operator. Energy trading is performed between various stake-holders, using the Blockchain nodes. With this technology, the local energy market can be separate from the main grid. It could also reduce costs and storage technology. An example for local energy trading is the collaboration between Siemens and LO3 Energy company. LO3 is a start-up company, based in New York, which has developed a micro-grid in the Brooklyn area and reimagined the traditional energy grid model, with the concept of a communal energy network. While the utility provider still maintains the electrical grid that delivers power, the actual energy is generated, stored, and traded locally by members of the community, for a more resilient and sustainable clean energy model using Blockchain technology.

Summary

This chapter discussed the concept of disruptive technologies in the digital transformation context. At the start the Gartner hype cycle explained how Blockchain will be built over the next 5-10 years. The following sections presented the Blockchain building blocks with emphasis on the functionality of digital ledger technology and the various types of network. This was followed by an in-depth discussion of the smart contract features using Ethereum and how to build a smart contract application. The chapter ended with some smart contract applications and two cases applicable in the context of sustainability. No doubt, Blockchain will bring a unique disruptive revolution in many industries and financial area.

End of chapter questions

1   Discuss how the disruptive technologies relate to the digital transformation.

2   Explain the basic Blockchain building blocks

3   Describe the consensus mechanisms as PoW and PoS

4   Describe how to design and implement a smart contract application

5   Discuss the benefits of Blockchain in the shared economy

6   Discuss how Blockchain can assist in sustainability energy

Test your skills

Only one answer is correct

1   What is the nonce?

   A.   A specific string used in Blockchain only

   B.   Is a number generated string?

   C.   Is a number generated number?

   D.   A random number used only once

2   What is Ethereum?

   A.   A kind of smart contract

   B.   Cryptocurrency generation engine

   C.   A Blockchain application development platform

   D.   A modified version of bitcoin technology

3   Which of the following most accurately defines Blockchain?

   A.   A centralised ledger

   B.   A distributed ledger on a peer to peer network

   C.   A database technology

   D.   A type of cryptocurrency

4   What are smart contracts?

   A.   An easy to enforce a contract

   B.   A contract which is way move smarter than traditional contract

   C.   A digital version of legal contract

   D.   A Blockchain based on programming by thousands of peers on Blockchain

5   When will you prefer a private Blockchain over public Blockchain

   A.   When we have enough trusted private miners who can mine on contract

   B.   When we need to avoid cryptocurrency indirect due to regulations

   C.   We need high availability or uptime

   D.   When corporate rules do not allow the data to go out in any possible manner

6   Can you download Blockchain?

    A. No. The Blockchain can be downloaded if the miners allow it

    B. Yes. All the public/private keys can be downloaded

    C. No. How can you download the network?

    D. Yes. But only the Blockchain ledger can be downloaded via client.

7   Which of the following is the core component of Ethereum Blockchain?

    A. Solidity/Serpent

    B. Miners

    C. Ethereum Virtual Machine (EVM)

    D. Smart Contract

8   Which of the following are not benefits of using Blockchain technology?

    A. Security

    B. Provenance

    C. Availability

    D. Compression

    E. Immutability

    F. Computability

9   Every Blockchain account has a private/public key pair

    A. True

    B. False

10   Any node can initiate the transaction in Blockchain

    A. True

    B. False

7

References

Atzei, N., Bartoletti, M. & Cimoli, T. (2017) A survey of attacks on Ethereum smart contracts (SoK), *Lecture Notes in Computer Science* (including subseries *Lecture Notes in Artificial Intelligence and Lecture Notes in Bioinformatics*).

Back, A., Corallo, M., Dashjr, L., Friedenbach, M., Maxwell, G., Miller, A., Poelstra,A., Timón, J. and Wuille, P. (2014) Enabling Blockchain innovations with pegged sidechains. Available at: https://www.blockstream.com/sidechains.pdf.

Bitcoin.org. (2009). *Bitcoin Developer Guide*. Retrieved from https://bitcoin.org/en/developer-guide

Brakeville, S. and Perepa, B. (2018) *Blockchain basics : Introduction to distributed ledgers*, IBM, https://www.ibm.com/developerworks/cloud/library/cl-Blockchain-basics-intro-bluemix-trs/index.html .

Buterin, V. (2013a). *Ethereum white paper*. Ethereum. Available from: https://blog. ethereum. org/2015/08/07/on-public-and-private-Blockchains/ [12 May 2018]

Buterin, V. (2013b). *What Proof of Stake is and Why it Matters*. bitcoinmagazine.com.

Buterin, V. (2014). *A next-generation smart contract and decentralized application platform*. Etherum White Paper. Available at: http://buyxpr.com/build/pdfs/EthereumWhitePaper.pdf.

Cai, Y. & Zhu, D. (2016) Fraud detections for online businesses: a perspective from Blockchain technology, *Financial Innovation*, **2**(1), 20.

Christensen, Clayton M. (1997) *The Innovator's Dilemma: How New Technologies Cause Great Firms to Fail*, Harvard Business School Press.

Clancy, H. (2017). The Blockchain's emerging role in sustainability. Available from: https://www.greenbiz.com/article/Blockchains-emerging-role-sustainability. [Accessed 12 May 2018]

DTCC. (2016). *Embracing Disruption: Tapping the Potential of Distributed Ledgers to Improve the Post-Trade Landscape*. Retrieved from www.finextra.com/finextra-downloads/newsdocs/embracing%20disruption%20white%20paper_final_jan-16.pdf

Ethereum (2016) Ethereum Homestead Documentation.. Retrieved from http://ethdocs.org/en/latest/

Evans, P. and Gawyer, A. (2016) *The rise of the platform enterprise: a global survey.* The Center for the Global Enterprise. Available from: htpp://thegce.net/archived-papers/the-rise-of-the-platform-enterprise-a-global-survey [Accessed 17 May 2018]

Financial Times (2018) *Technology: Banks seek the key to Blockchain*. https://www.ft.com/content/eb1f8256-7b4b-11e5-a1fe-567b37f80b64 [Accessed 12 May 2018]

Gartner (2017) *Top Trends in the Gartner Hype Cycle for Emerging Technologies, 2017*. Available from: https://www.gartner.com/smarterwithgartner/top-trends-in-the-gartner-hype-cycle-for-emerging-technologies-2017/ [Accessed 18 May 2018]

Gervais, A. Karame, G.O., Wust, K., Glynkatzis, V., Ritzdorf, H. and Capkun, S. (2016) On the security and performance of proof of work Blockchains, in *Proceedings of the 2016 ACM SIGSAC Conference on Computer and Communications Security - CCS 16*, pp. 3–16.

Hasse, F. von Perfall, A., Hillebrand, T., Smole, E., Lay, L. and Charlet, M. (2015). Blockchain-an opportunity for energy producers and consumers?

Higgins, S. (2017) R3 Blasts JP Morgan Consortium Exit as 'At Odds' With Global Banks - CoinDesk. Available at: https://www.coindesk.com/jpmorgan-exits-Blockchain-r3-distributed-ledger-consortium/ (Accessed: 25 August 2018).

Kakavand, H., & Kost De Sevres, N. (2016). *The Blockchain Revolution: An Analysis of Regulation and Technology Related to Distributed Ledger Technologies*. Academic Press.

Kandaswamy, R., Furlonger, D. and Stevens, A. (2018) *Digital Disruption Profile: Blockchain's Radical Promise Spans Business and Society*. Gartner. Available at: https://www.gartner.com/doc/3855708/digital-disruption-profile-Blockchains-radical (Accessed: 17 September 2018)

Kokina, J., Mancha, R. & Pachamanova, D. (2017) Blockchain: Emergent industry adoption and implications for accounting, *Journal of Emerging Technologies in Accounting*, **14**(2), p. jeta-51911.

Li, J., Greenwood, D. J. & Kassem, M. (2018) Blockchain in the built environment: analysing current applications and developing an emergent framework, in *Creative Construction Conference 2018*, pp. 1–10.

Luu, L., Chu, D. H., Olickel, H., Saxena, P. and Hobor, A. (2016). Making smart contracts smarter. In *Proceedings of the 2016 ACM SIGSAC Conference on Computer and Communications Security* (pp. 254-269). ACM.10.1145/2976749.2978309

Luu, L., Narayanan, V., Zheng, C., Baweja, K., Gilbert, S. and Saxena, P. (2016) A secure sharding protocol for open Blockchains, *Proceedings of the 2016 ACM SIGSAC Conference on Computer and Communications Security - CCS'16*, pp. 17–30.

McKinsey Global Institute (2016). *Five technologies for the next ten years*. Available from: https://www.mckinsey.com/industries/oil-and-gas/our-insights/five-technologies-for-the-next-ten-years [Accessed 12 May 2018]

Mougayar, W. (2016) *The Business Blockchain : Promise, practice, and application of the next Internet technology*. Hoboken, New Jersey: John Wiley & Sons.

Nakamoto, S. (2008). *Bitcoin: A peer-to-peer electronic cash system*. Academic Press.

Narayanan, A., Bonneau,J., Felten, E., Miller,A. and Goldfeder, S.(2016) *Bitcoin and Cryptocurrency Technologies: A Comprehensive Introduction*. New Jersey: Princeton University Pres.

Ølnes, S., Ubacht, J. & Janssen, M. (2017) Blockchain in government : Benefits and implications of distributed ledger technology for information sharing, *Government Information Quarterly*, **34**, 355–364.

Popper, N. (2015) *Digital Gold: Bitcoin and the Inside Story of the Misfits and Millionaires Trying to Reinvent Money*. (1st ed.). New York, NY, USA: : HarperCollins.

PricewaterhouseCoopers (2016) Blockchain – an opportunity for energy producers and consumers?, PwC global power & utilities. Available at: www.pwc.com/utilities.

Sofia. (2016). *Blockchain-Enabled Smart Contracts: Applications and Challenges*. Available from: https://letstalkpayments.com/Blockchain-enabled-smart-contracts-applications-and-challenges/ [Accessed 12 May 2018]

Standard Chartered (2017) Blockchain. Available from: https://www.sc.com/fightingfinancialcrime/av/SCB_Fighting_Financial_Crime_Deep_dive_Blockchain_August_2017.pdf [18 May 2018]

Szabo, N. (1997). *The idea of smart contracts*. Nick Szabo's Papers and Concise Tutorials.

Tapscott, D. and Tapscott, A. (2016) The impact of the Blockchain goes beyond financial services, *Harvard Business Review*. Available at: https://hbr.org/2016/05/the-impact-of-the-Blockchain-goes-beyond-financial-services.

Wall Street Journal. (2014). *The Imminent Decentralized Computing Revolution*. Available from: http://blogs.wsj.com/accelerators/2014/10/10/weekend-read-the-imminent-decentralized-computing-revolution/

Warburg, B. (2016) How the Blockchain will radically transform the economy, TED Talk. TED Summit.

Webb, A. (2015) 8 Tech Trends to Watch in 2016, *Harvard Business Review*. Available at: https://hbr.org/2015/12/8-tech-trends-to-watch-in-2016 (Accessed: 25 August 2018).

Wood, G. (2014). *Ethereum Yellow Paper*. Ethereum.

Yli-Huumo, J., Ko,D., Choi, S., Park,S. and Smolander, K. (2016) Where is current research on Blockchain technology? - A systematic review, *PLoS ONE*, **11**(10), 1–28.

Answer to exercises

1 d; 2 c; 3 b; 4 c; 5 d; 6 d; 7 c; 8 d; 9 a; 10 a

Glossary

Address: Cryptocurrency addresses are used to send or receive transactions on the network. An address usually presents itself as a string of alphanumeric characters.

Bitcoin: The first decentralised, open source cryptocurrency that ran on a global peer to peer network, without the need for middlemen and a centralised issuer.

Block: Packages of data that carry permanently recorded data on the Blockchain network.

Blockchain: A shared ledger where transactions are permanently recorded by appending blocks. The Blockchain serves as a historical record of all transactions that ever occurred, from the genesis block to the latest block, hence the name Blockchain. (https://blockgeeks.com/guides/what-is-Blockchain-technol7ogy/)

Block Explorer: An online tool to view all transactions, past and current, on the Blockchain. They provide useful information such as network hash rate and transaction growth.

Block height: The number of blocks connected on the Blockchain.

Block reward: A form of incentive for the miner who successfully calculated the hash in a block during mining. Verification of transactions on the Blockchain generates new coins in the process, and the miner is rewarded a portion of those.

Central ledger: A ledger maintained by a central agency.

Confirmation: The successful act of hashing a transaction and adding it to the Blockchain.

Consensus: Achieved when all participants of the network agree on the validity of the transactions, ensuring that the ledgers are exact copies of each other.

Cryptocurrency: Representations of digital assets, also known as tokens, (https://block-geeks.com/guides/what-iscryptocurrency/).

Cryptographic hash function: Produces a fixed-size and unique hash value from variable-sized transaction input. The SHA-256 computational algorithm is an example of a cryptographic hash. (https://en.wikipedia.org/wiki/Cryptographic_hash_function)

Dapp: An open source application that operates autonomously, has its data stored on a Blockchain, incentivised in the form of cryptographic tokens and operates on a protocol that shows proof of value. (https://blockgeeks.com/guides/dapps-the-decentralizedfuture/)

DAO: Decentralised Autonomous Organizations – corporations that run without any human intervention and surrender all forms of control to an incorruptible set of business rules.

Distributed ledger: Ledger in which data is stored across a network of decentralized nodes; does not have to have its own currency and may be permissioned and private.

Distributed network: A type of network where processing power and data are spread over the nodes rather than having a centralised data centre.

Difficulty: Refers to how easily a data block of transaction information can be mined successfully.

Digital signature: A code generated by public key encryption that is attached to an electronically transmitted document to verify its contents and the sender's identity.

Double spending: Occurs when a sum of money is spent more than once.

Elliptic-curve cryptography (ECC): An approach to public-key cryptography based on the algebraic structure of elliptic curves over finite fields.

Ethereum: A Blockchain-based decentralised platform for apps that run smart contracts, and is aimed at solving issues associated with censorship, fraud and third-party interference. (https://blockgeeks.com/guides/what-is-ethereum/)

EVM: The Ethereum Virtual Machine – a Turing complete virtual machine that allows anyone to execute arbitrary EVM byte code. Every Ethereum node runs on the EVM to maintain consensus across the Blockchain.

Fork: An alternate version of the Blockchain, leaving two Blockchains to run simultaneously on different parts of the network.

Genesis block: The first or first few blocks of a Blockchain.

Hash: The act of performing a hash function on the output data. This is used for confirming coin transactions.

Mining: The act of validating Blockchain transactions. The need for validation warrants an incentive for the miners, usually in the form of coins. In this cryptocurrency boom, mining can be a lucrative business when done properly. By choosing the most efficient and suitable hardware and mining target, mining can produce a stable form of passive income. (http://blockgeeks.com/what-is-bitcoin-mining-an-easy-guide/)

Multi-signature addresses: Provide an added layer of security by requiring more than one key to authorize a transaction. (https://en.bitcoin.it/wiki/Multisignature)

Node: A copy of the ledger operated by a participant of the Blockchain network.

Peer to peer: P2P – refers to the decentralized interactions between two parties or more in a highly-interconnected network. Participants of a P2P network deal directly with each other through a single mediation point.

Public address: The cryptographic hash of a public key. They act as email addresses that can be published anywhere, unlike private keys.

Private key: A string of data that allows you to access the tokens in a specific wallet. They act as passwords that are kept hidden from anyone but the owner of the address.

Proof of Stake: A consensus distribution algorithm that rewards earnings based on the number of coins you own or hold. The more you invest in the coin, the more you gain by mining with this protocol.

Proof of Work: A consensus distribution algorithm that requires an active role in mining data blocks, often consuming resources, such as electricity. The more 'work' you do or the more computational power you provide, the more coins you are rewarded with.

Smart contracts: Encode business rules in a programmable language on the Blockchain and are enforced by the participants of the network.
(https://blockgeeks.com/guides/smart-contracts/)

Solidity: Ethereum's programming language for developing smart contracts.
(https://blockgeeks.com/introduction-to-solidity-part-1/)

Testnet: A test Blockchain used by developers to prevent expending assets on the main chain.

Transaction block: A collection of transactions gathered into a block that can then be hashed and added to the Blockchain.

Transaction fee: Paid for cryptocurrency transactions. These fees add up to account for the block reward that a miner receives when he successfully processes a block.

Turing-complete: Refers to the ability of a machine to perform calculations that any other programmable computer is capable of. An example of this is the Ethereum Virtual Machine

7

8 New Product Development: Implementing Agility through innovation and technology

Wallace Whistance-Smith and Mohamed Salama

Learning outcomes

By completing this chapter, the reader will be able to:

■ Understand the relationship between operations management and new product development (NPD).

■ Discuss the difference between goods and services amid growing service sectors.

■ Understand the challenges to achieve sustainable competitive advantage through NPD.

■ Explain how the concept of 'Agility' facilitates new product development success.

■ Explain the benefits of integrating Agile framework with virtual and augmented technologies.

Introduction

New product development is an integral part of the project management practice. However, product design and process design have been, historically, two of the main components of the operations management theory. Operations management is the task of creating value in the form of goods and services by transforming inputs into outputs. More specifically, the techniques to create value are universal in scope and can be applied to any form of enterprise whether service-oriented or manufacturing-based. It is this operations transformation model that creates the possibility for enterprise success. The efficient production of goods and services requires an effective application of the transformative process, and it is in this transformation that value is created. Value supports the possibility for enterprise viability, and without such, there is little opportunity for sustained financial feasibility – this is particularly so in the ever-increasing competitive landscape of today's worldwide economic system. This chapter discusses the fundamentals of product and service development, in the context of sustainable competitive advantage, in the era of digital transformation.

"The design and management of operations strongly influence how much material resources are consumed to manufacture goods or deliver a service, making sure that there is enough inventory to produce the quantities that need to be delivered to the customer, and ensuring that what is made is in fact what the customer wants" (Sanders, 2017).

To create goods and services, organizations must be fully engaged in three essential, perhaps classical, functions. These functions are the necessary ingredients for continued financial viability; they are often at the heart of whether a corporation succeeds or fails – they are the manifest for organizational survival. Simply put, these functions are:

1 *Marketing*: which is the primary mechanism to generate the fundamental demand for products and services within the scope of the enterprise.

2 *Production/operations*: which is the mechanism to create products and/or services.

3 *Management / Administration:* those who not only have the vision for the enterprise, but also can organize, control, and plan as well possess the relentless focus needed to keep the financial underpinning at the forefront of daily decision making.

Although these three functions seldom create value on their own, they provisionally provide the groundwork for change. Change, along with a firm's ability to embrace new technologies, new process methodologies and new trends, enable future enterprise success.

8

Differences between goods and services

From a functional perspective, operations which provide goods or services are very alike in nature. Essentially, both goods and services must have established quality standards, and both must be designed and processed according to planned logistics and scheduling, in facilities where human resources are employed. Goods are typically considered to be: *tangible consumable products, articles, or other commodities that can be purchased by consumers in exchange for money*. These are items which have physical determination and characteristics, i.e. shape, appearance, size, weight, etc. Further, goods provide an inherent capability to provide utility and satisfaction to the consumers of such.

Services are the *intangible* economic products provided by individuals or firms that can only be delivered at a moment in time, and are by their very nature *perishable*. As such, they lack physical identity and correspondingly, services cannot be distinguished from the service provider. Moreover, services cannot be **owned**, but rather, can only be **utilized**.

Some differences between goods and services are:

- Services, for the most part, are *intangible* and have the potential to vary significantly from one service provider to another.

- Services are often *produced and consumed simultaneously* and with that said, there is typically no stored inventory.

- Services are often *unique* and may vary, even when offered by the same service provider over time.

- Services typically have *high customer collaboration* with the service provider, often contributing significantly to the uniqueness of the service.

- Services are often *difficult to standardize* or *automate*, which typically means there is a significant labour content needed to provide these services.

- Services fundamentally make a profit by *optimizing the cost of labour,* since automation is largely impossible.

- Services are *inconsistent by definition*; providers of such have good days and bad days which potentially impact on the delivery of such.

- Services typically are highly *knowledge-based* on the part of the provider, and this knowledge is often proprietary in nature.

- Services are frequently *dispersed,* often with an existing client base.

- Services typically have *lower barriers to entry* meaning that startup costs are frequently much lower than manufactured goods. Given that these barriers to entry are that much lower, logically, the competition is the much greater.

Growth of services

Services currently, in terms of contribution to the gross economic worldwide product, are on the increase – such cannot be said for manufacturing. Until the very early 1900s much of the economic sector was engaged in agriculture and related activities; manufacturing was merely in its infancy. With the introduction of technology and automation, manufacturing became increasingly important with respect to contributing to worldwide prosperity.

Manufacturing outpaced service sector growth until the early 1980s, with many claiming that the introduction of the personal computer gave new opportunities to service providers.

> *"This is likely because of automation . . . with advanced tools such as robotics to handle tasks that were previously completed by employees, the average employee is able to produce more now than in years past. Thus, firms don't need to hire as many workers to produce the same amount of output"* (Chien, 2017).

Advances in new technology also created many more options for the delivery of countless innovative services. Interestingly, manufacturing employment has decreased significantly worldwide with very few exceptions; however, workers are significantly more productive, largely because of the many new technologies that have been implemented throughout the production process.

"An alternative explanation is that we really are experiencing an inevitable shift to a post-industrial, Information Age economy where manufacturing's importance to output and jobs is declining, similar to the trend in agriculture over the last century." (Perry, 2017)

The worldwide manufacturing data as a percentage of valued added to GDP, shows the significant decrease in manufacturing as a percentage of value added to the worldwide gross domestic product. Essentially, over the last 20-year period, there has been approximately a six percent decrease in contributing value. Considering worldwide manufacturing data as a percentage of valued added to GDP, it is apparent that this percentage decreases at a consistent rate. Simply put, there is about a one percent decrease every three years.

"Manufacturing's declining share of output isn't a sign of economic weakness — it's just the opposite. It's a sign that advances in manufacturing productivity and efficiency are translating into lower prices for consumers when they purchase things like cars, food, clothing, appliances, furniture, and electronic goods." (Perry, 2017)

The worldwide service sector data as a percentage of valued added to GDP, shows the significant increase in the service sector's contribution as a percentage of value added to the worldwide gross domestic product. This increase effectively offsets the percentage loss resulting from the manufacturing sector. There is approximately a one percent increase in every two years with respect to the contribution the service sector makes to worldwide GDP. According to the World Bank:

"the demand for services is on the rise with increases in income, as people are becoming less concerned about material needs. In the consumer sector, this leads to increasing demand for services such as health, education, and entertainment. In business, companies recognize that many activities can be handled more efficiently by a service provider. Outsourcing services allow a business to concentrate on the activities that are critical to its success. These are called core activities, and they include sales and marketing, accounting, technology, quality, product and service delivery, management, human resources, finance and product development." (Linton, 2017)

Needless to say, there are many disruptive forces accelerating rapid growth in the service sector. Largely relying on innovation and new technology, an increasing amount of new services are taking advantage of the proliferation of worldwide Internet availability; further, *"the idea that innovation drives economic growth is incontrovertible, but the factors that, in turn, drive innovation are not fully understood"* (Nicholas, 2011). Innovation evolves incrementally with the refinement or the implementation of new technologies largely with a focus on empiricism. This essentially suggests that all concepts [innovations] originate in 'experience'; and all concepts [innovations] are about or applicable to things that can be experienced.

8

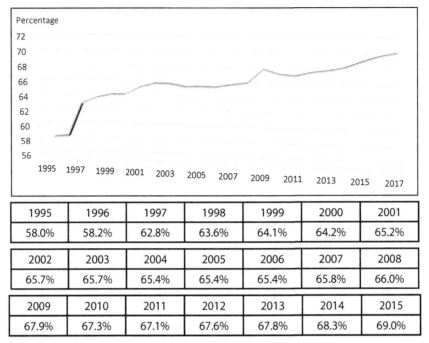

Percentage

1995	1996	1997	1998	1999	2000	2001
58.0%	58.2%	62.8%	63.6%	64.1%	64.2%	65.2%

2002	2003	2004	2005	2006	2007	2008
65.7%	65.7%	65.4%	65.4%	65.4%	65.8%	66.0%

2009	2010	2011	2012	2013	2014	2015
67.9%	67.3%	67.1%	67.6%	67.8%	68.3%	69.0%

Figure 8.1: Worldwide service sector data as a percentage of valued added to GDP.
Source: https://data.worldbank.org/indicator/NV.SRV.TETC.ZS

Furthermore, as the price of new technologies continues to decrease, the startup costs in the service sector decrease as well. Additionally,

"small business owners today are better at managing their businesses than their counterparts were 35 years ago. They are better educated and are more likely to have studied business in school. Moreover, the growth of the Internet and the popularization of academic research has exposed more small business owners to knowledge about how to run a business effectively . . . Small business owners today have access to better technology to help them operate their companies than those in business for themselves had 30-plus years ago. Today's small business owners have computers, point-of-sale terminals, inventory and financial management software, and many other tools that weren't available three decades ago." (Shane, 2017)

Whether or not these tools make today's business owners 'better' managers is debatable; however, they do afford a certain level of comfort when managing their companies, perhaps limiting, or minimizing, the chances of business-ending mistakes.

Current data suggests that more than half of the worldwide population is now on the Internet (Internet World Stats, 2017). This availability is largely a matter of very few years, having *"changed forever the way we do business and the way we communicate"* (Internet World Stats, 2017). Moreover, with availability comes innovation. *"Nowadays, there are many startups that have emerged by exploring new and innovative technology and are dedicated to further their growth using the same"* (Gupta, 2017).

New challenges

Maintaining successful daily operations, whether it be in the service or manufacturing sector is an extremely challenging task.

"Operation managers play a central role in stabilizing an organization's policies and procedures across major business areas including finance, planning and technology. In small businesses, the role of the operation manager is often assumed by the business's owner or its general manager. The job involves overseeing the company's strategic approach to its on-site operations." (Bradley, 2017)

When considering the fluidity associated with the dynamic challenging forces of globalization, the job of the operations manager is all that much more complex.

At the macro level, firms today face many diverse challenges, such as:

- **Increased global competition:** Having a larger market means there are more suppliers worldwide. Increased supplies in the distribution channel result in lower profits overall. Successful leaders recognize the need to adapt to the rapidly changing ways to do business in the global environment. These leaders seek to build competitive advantages around the core competencies of the organization, while also reducing costs to conduct their business. These organizations also understand that doing the best they do is not always enough to be on top. In order to keep a competitive position in the domestic market, they will need to acquire knowledge of other key competitors in the global marketplace. They need to stay informed of other domestic and foreign competitors' potential strategies, as well as their strengths and weaknesses (Study.com, 2017).

- **Uncertainty about the future:** Disruptive technologies can immediately change the prospects a firm faces at any moment, potentially rendering it without viable products to sell. *"Disruptive technologies can change the game for businesses, creating entirely new products and services, as well as shifting pools of value between producers or from producers to consumers. Organizations will often need to use business-model innovations to capture some of that value. Leaders need to plan for a range of scenarios, abandoning assumptions about where competition and risk could come from, and not be afraid to look beyond long-established models."* (Manyika et al., 2017)

- Organizations will also need to keep their employees' skills up-to-date and balance the potential benefits of emerging technologies with the risks they sometimes pose. *"Security, effectiveness and cost are the three biggest risk factors for the modern technologies."* (Dujmovic, 2017)

- **Financial management:** Evidence suggests that the number one reason why firms fail is due to their inability to successfully manage their finances. *"If you don't have enough cash to carry you through the first six months or so before the business starts making money, your prospects for success are not good"*. (Mason, 2017). Further, *"new business owners often don't understand cash flow or underestimate how much money they will need for startup and they are forced to close before they*

8

have had a fair chance to succeed. They also may have an un-realistic expectation of incoming revenues from sales." (Schaefer, 2017)

■ **Regulation and compliance:** At any moment, new government regulations can substantively alter the way a firm can conduct business; furthermore, compliance can protract operations which detracts from operational performance. Governments play a role in the way businesses operate. With new rules and regulations implemented by governments, businesses need to be sure they become compliant in a timely manner. Inherent competitive advantages can lie within the response time of businesses to these sweeping changes, and the faster a company can adapt, the better.

■ **Competencies and recruiting the right talent:** Attracting talent can be a costly matter; suffice to say that retaining this talent is certainly another question. With the world increasingly becoming a truly global village, a new assortment of challenges have arisen that businesses have to effectively deal with. Such challenges include: aging populations, global politics, different cultures and emerging technologies. With this set of new challenges, there is growing pressure on companies to make sure they hire the right people to deal with these issues. Therefore the process of hiring and recruiting staff are of chief importance to the firm, especially so if continued growth is to be realized.

■ **Technology**: The decision to be labour intensive and pay wages versus the cost of automation and rent to facilitate these investments can be a burdensome dilemma. *"Replacing humans with machines has been happening for over a century. People often meet change and technology with resistance, and it's usually fueled by lack of knowledge, concern for job security, or complacency with current technology. With the rise in automation and the Industrial Internet of Things (IIoT), many are still worried about job security and the ever-encroaching technology. But is this a valid concern?* "The real threat to jobs is the inability to remain competitive." *Jeff Burnstein, President of the Association for Advancing Automation (A3) explains,* "If you can't compete, you only have a few choices—you send it overseas, you shut down, or layoff." *Automation can keep jobs from moving overseas, and often, new technology wins new business, too* (Kerns, 2017)."

■ **Customer service**: Statistics indicate the cost of retaining a customer is significantly less expensive than finding a new customer, with that said, customer services need to be at the forefront of the decision-making process. Customer service is the fastest way to differentiate a business. Usually it is the only point of contact the customer has with the company. Customers are essentially the life blood of a company and it is therefore vital that this point of contact with the company be an extremely positive one.

■ **Rising cyber security threats**: Reliance on technology means an increased dependency on preventive information security, and with the increasing cost for such, this has a direct impact on the firm's financial bottom line. *"Cybersecurity spending to exceed $1 trillion from 2017 to 2021."* (Morgan, 2017) As security awareness grows among companies and their employees, it becomes more challenging for cyber criminals to trick victims into conducting fraudulent transactions, downloading malware or compromising sensitive data; however, these techniques are still amongst the most popular means available to cyber criminals today.

- **Finding capital**: Clearly, the cost of financing is a harsh reality that all firms encounter; it gets even harder with increasing interest rates and risk intolerance. *"The lack of easy access to capital results in stagnating expansion for individual social enterprises and the social enterprise sector in general. Although accessing capital is a challenge faced by many 'regular' businesses as well, there is an extra dimension for social enterprises as potential investors need to be willing to take the enterprise's financial and social mission into account."* (Hoekstra, 2017). Typically, there are two sources of funding available for growing a business – lenders who loan money for a specific period of time and look to get repaid with a return, or second, investors looking to take an equity stake in the firm, essentially purchasing a portion of the company in return for long-term capital gains when it prospers. Lenders, as a rule, are not primarily interested a vision for a 'great business', typically their interest is solely focused on risk management, and the repayment of any monies advanced to the firm. Further, *"most business require investment capital to cover start-up expenses as well as expansion. Attracting capital in a sole proprietorship can be a tricky endeavor, because the business is so closely linked to the owner's personal finances. Like virtually every other aspect of its operations, the process of attracting capital for a sole proprietorship is inextricably linked to the owner's personal resources and reputation."* (Gartenstein, 2017)

- **Virtual real estate**: There is a tradeoff that every firm must make, and that is between having a bricks and mortar location versus a more online or virtual presence. With a more concentrated online presence comes the inherent issue of offsite communications, which can lead to poor customer service. On the other hand, the cost savings associated with being more online cannot be ignored moving forward. You don't have to run your entire business over the internet to benefit from online business opportunities. Small businesses might only need an email address to communicate with their clients, customers and suppliers electronically. The many benefits of online business include:
  - ☐ global access, 24 hours a day, 7 days a week
  - ☐ improved client service through greater flexibility
  - ☐ cost savings
  - ☐ faster delivery of products
  - ☐ increased professionalism
  - ☐ opportunities to manage your business from anywhere in the world. (Business Queensland, 2017)

- **Market oversaturation**: The bandwagon effect clearly states that where profits are found in an industry, more suppliers will gravitate (thereby jumping on the 'bandwagon'). This leads to a market with an oversaturated product that

8

inherently dilutes the profit dispersion in the industry. *"The bandwagon effect is a psychological phenomenon in which people do something primarily because other people are doing it, regardless of their own beliefs, which they may ignore or override. The bandwagon effect has wide implications, but is commonly seen in politics and consumer behavior. This phenomenon can also be seen during bull markets and the growth of asset bubbles. This tendency of people to align their beliefs and behaviors with those of a group is also called a herd mentality. For example, people might buy a new electronic item because of its popularity, regardless of whether they need it, can afford it or even really want it."* (Investopedia, 2017)

- **Managing a global supply chain**: Considering the global village we now live in, it has never been easier to acquire supplies from any corner of the world. This leads to increases in complexity of logistics. *"Supply chain leaders cite the increased complexity of supply chain flow as the top challenge they face. A new report,* Managing the Complexity Paradigm, *from APICS and Michigan State University, discusses the balance between managing complexity that can increase cost but also has the potential to increase revenue."* (MHL News, 2017)

- **Rapid product development**: New additive technologies have decreased the time it takes to prototype and develop new products to a fraction of the time and cost previously associated with injection or other molding technologies which were the norms of not too many years ago. *"3D printing is a rapid prototyping technique which does not rely on drilling or cutting materials to create a product. In this process, a three-dimensional solid object is made from a digital model by laying down successive layers of the material. 3D printing, also known as 'additive manufacturing', has been welcomed by product designers and manufacturers across the globe, due to many reasons apart from being cost-effective. 3D printing rapid prototyping technology helps you take well-informed decisions about product designing. One doesn't need a functional mechanical prototype before manufacturing the actual product, which helps in reducing the rapid prototyping cost significantly."* (Outsource 2 India, 2017) Further, with additive manufacturing, *"the cost and time required to develop molds, patterns and special tools can be eliminated. The same CAD software and the printing equipment can be utilized to produce different geometries. Unlike conventional prototyping methods, such as CNC machining, the amount of waste produced is minimum, as rapid prototyping only prints the material that is actually required to build the object."* (Patel, 2017)

Achieving competitive advantage through NPD

Competitive advantage implies the creation of systems that have a unique advantage over the firm's competitors. Essentially, the fundamental idea is to create customer 'value' in an efficient and sustainable way. Various strategies to achieve such do exist; however, their potential to achieve these objectives are often at odds with one another. Developing a prevailing strategy to achieve this may reside in a combination of many methods available to the firm. *"Competitive advantage examines the economics of a firm's business, focusing primarily on its ability to generate excess returns on capital, and links the business strategy with fundamental finance and capital markets, for a longer period of time. In the end, it is a firm's competitive advantage that allows it to earn excess returns for its shareholders. Without a competitive advantage, a firm has limited economic reason to exist - its competitive advantage is its reason of life. Without it, the firm will decline. Creating a sustainable competitive advantage may be the most important goal of any organization and may be the most important single attribute on which each firm must place its most focus."* (Strategy Train, 2017)

Firms typically create an advantage by competing on product differentiation, price, or on customer needs and response. In practice, differentiation, low cost, and response can increase productivity and generate a sustainable competitive advantage as the firm plays to its unique value proposition (UVP).

Competing on product differentiation[1]

Product differentiation attempts to showcase the differences between products from one firm to another. Differentiation looks to make a product more attractive by contrasting its unique qualities with other competing products. Successful product differentiation creates a competitive advantage for the product's seller, as customers see these products as being unique or superior. Why is product differentiation important?

"For brands, the field of competition is more crowded than ever. When faced with too many choices, consumers can be overwhelmed, and often walk away rather than make a difficult decision. That is why it is imperative to find a way for your product to stand out and be considered uniquely valuable. You want it to be crystal clear to your customers what you are offering and how your product compares to competitors'. If you have other products, you also want to make sure each product has a clearly defined identity to eliminate confusion for customers. Creating a differentiated product which appeals to your target market can help to build your competitive advantage over other brands." (Aha! Staff, 2017)

The purpose of product differentiation is to create and sustain a demand for the firm's products by nurturing consumer brand loyalty. Differentiation often doesn't work because there is a tendency to lump consumers into one category, as opposed to finer segments, in the hope to make the product more attractive to this target market. Today, it is not enough just to make your product different, firms need to act quickly through successful advertising campaigns, social media, and innovation to take full advantage of this strategy.

"Finally, product differentiation may serve to act as a barrier to entry, thereby protecting existing market shares against new competition." (Farlex, 2017)

---

1 *"The term Product Differentiation was first coined by Edward Chamberlin (1933) to describe how a supplier may charge a higher price for a product in a perfect competition environment. However, if a firm in a competitive environment wants to compete in the market the least thing that it would wish to do is to increase the prices of its products. According to Chamberlain if a firm differentiates its product, that is adds value to its product, then it can charge a higher price. Here it would be more sensible if we call that resulted product a premium product rather than a differentiated product."* (Chelumbrun, 2017)."

A firm's opportunities for creating product uniqueness can rise in virtually any department, or employee working within the scope of the firm. Moreover, because most products include some service, and most services include some product, the opportunities for creating this uniqueness are limited solely by the vision of those that direct the firm.

Competing on cost

Competing on price often feels like such a 'natural' path to follow; however, in most cases, the results of such are anything but successful, and for most small businesses, it is the road to ruin. Product pricing is an important element of a marketing strategy. The concept of 'everyday low pricing' means that the company consistently tries to provide the consumer with the lowest price in the marketplace for a good or service. Having the lowest price can work to the company's advantage with respect to sustaining its customer base; but there can be many disadvantages pursing this marketing strategy. *"In the years prior to the prevalent use of the Internet in e-commerce, being the everyday low-price leader meant being the price leader in your geographic region. The Internet now offers consumers the ability to check your pricing against hundreds or thousands of online retailers. Your company stands to lose credibility among consumers if your everyday low prices are not comparable to pricing found on the Internet. [Further], the promise of everyday low pricing can work against you when it comes to discounts and pricing specials. Because your company strives to provide the lowest prices at all times, you may not have sufficient profit margin to offer occasional promotional discounts."* (Root, 2017). Pricing discounts are marketing vehicles that can be used to improve sales or gather quantitative data through algorithmic pricing. There are risks associated with this, as if you have conditioned customers to expect everyday low prices, offering further, or promotional price discounts can seem as contradictory, and may cause customers to question whether or not the business has indeed actually had the 'lowest' price.

For most small operations, 'price' should not be the main reason one would expect one's firm to be chosen from any of many other competitors. Competing on price typically only makes sense when the firm has a significant cost advantage over its competitors. With that said, many large national firms enjoy such a position, and competing on price is most certainly a very viable operations strategy. It is important to note that competing on price does not imply low value or poor quality; in fact in many cases such could not be further from reality.

Competing on customer needs and response

Flexible response may be thought of as the ability to match changes in the marketplace where design innovations in volumes fluctuate substantially. The competitive advantage generated through a reliable response strategy delivers value to the end customer, often by meeting their individual needs. *"However good your product or service is, the simple truth is that no-one will buy it if they don't want it or believe they don't need it."* (Info Entrepreneurs, 2017). Knowing and understanding customer needs is central to operational success. Every business needs a reason for their customers to buy from them and not their competitors. This is called a Unique Sales Proposition (USP). Unless you can pinpoint what makes your business unique in a world of homogeneous competitors, you cannot target your sales efforts successfully. Typically, business build their USP on their unique product characteristics, differential price structure, or their varied promotional strategies to delineate such.

Why do organizations fail?

In many ways, the word 'failure' is becoming an obsolete term; for example, is a 'merger' an example of business failure? Is a 'retirement' an example of business failure? For that matter, how does one go about measuring failure, and/or the rate thereof? At the expense of convenience, defining the word 'failure' as an economic concept, where the firm does not have the operating capital to cover expenses, the most significant of such being wages, there are many and diverse reasons for failure to occur. Typically, reasons for failure are usually much more obvious than reasons for success.

Experience shows that when firms lose their ability to stay competitive, or lack capital, the slide to closure accelerates very rapidly. There are "*numerous reasons [why] a manufacturer [fails], including neglect, inexperience, and financial. Financial reasons account for approximately 80 percent of all failures.*" (Oxley, 2017)." Although the former references manufacturing operations, the same can be said of service sector firms. "*Nobody starts a business expecting to fail, but sobering statistics indicate that many do, in fact, go under. According to the Small Business Administration's Office of Advocacy, three out of 10 new firms with employees fail to survive for more than two years and about five out of 10 close shop within five years. The survival rate is even lower for sole proprietors.*" (Polevoi, 2017)

How does the concept of 'Agility' facilitate NPD success?

What are 'Agile operations?' By analogy, "*Agile operations no longer means keeping the technology lights-on, it means making the business shine brighter; working closely with Development by applying systems-style thinking to visualize and speed a constant flow of value to customers. It also means adopting automation, tools and methods to amplify the cross-functional feedback so necessary to improve quality and the customer experience. Finally, it's about future-proofing the business—managing technology at scale, yes, but never burdening the organization with additional cost, waste and complexity.*" (Kim, 2017). This definition may seem to many as reminiscent of what has been term, 'lean' operations. Both lean and agile methodological approaches, whether in the service sector, or manufacturing sector, attempt to lower costs, improve customer service, and provide faster response time for their customers.

Both lean and agile methods are suited for modern managers who desire to increase business sustainability and revenue, embracing servant leadership while empowering teams to be self-organizing and cross-functional. Both are designed to keep companies competitive. Both affect all aspects of operations.

Agile operations represent a very interesting approach to developing a competitive advantage in today's fast-moving marketplace. These methods place an extremely strong focus on rapid response to the customer. The agile framework is all about delivering value focusing on items that cost the least and produce the most value thereby turning speed and agility into a key competitive advantage. An agile company is in a much better position to take advantage of short windows of opportunity and fast changes in customer demand.

Why is agility something to strive for? Simply put, consumers today love instant gratification and they have been conditioned for such most recently with same day product shipments from every corner of the globe. Consumers are increasingly getting used to instantaneous transactions and they are willing to pay for this. More importantly, consumers love choice. They prefer to get a product exactly as they want it, when they want it, and without compromise. Agility gives way to the fickleness of today's consumers, understanding that their interests shift in a moment and often move in unpredictable ways.

Agile operational success

Agile production began as a business concept but has turned into a new form of manufacturing that has all the potential to significantly change the production world in the future.

"There are four key elements for agile manufacturing:

- *Modular Product Design: designing products in a modular fashion that enables them to serve as platforms for fast and easy variation.*

- *Information Technology: automating the rapid dissemination of information throughout the company to enable lightning fast response to orders.*

- *Corporate Partners: creating virtual short-term alliances with other companies that enable improved time-to-market for selected product segments.*

- *Knowledge Culture: investing in employee training to achieve a culture that supports rapid change and ongoing adaptation."* (Lean Production, 2017)

These four elements are a good starting point for agile manufacturing; however, the scope of such is somewhat limited. Agile manufacturing is more than this. It is a process, along with methods and preparation required to respond swiftly to customer needs, while at the same time taking ownership of the social organizations that control cost and quality. It is a strategy for incorporating velocity and flexibility in a made-to-order production process. Based on minimizing the cost of setup and changeover times throughout production runs, the end goal is to facilitate production with high flexibility for customization.

*"Agile manufacturing is most successful in environments where specialization, customization, and configuration have a competitive edge. The **key to agile production is customer satisfaction**. This is achieved through producing products with speed and versatility while meeting customer needs"* (Robot Worx, 2017).

Agile focused production has numerous benefits to the manufacturer, such as:

- Greater ability to enjoy the benefits of associated with specialization
- Greater ability to enjoy the higher financial margins associated with customization
- Improved production flexibility
- Higher degree of responsiveness
- Lower costs
- Higher quality
- Lower inventory
- Improved inventory tracking
- Shorter setup times
- Higher reliability
- Shorter lead times

As Darrell Rigby states, *"the spread of agile raises intriguing possibilities. What if a company could achieve positive returns with 50% more of its new-product introductions? What if marketing programs could generate 40% more customer inquiries? What if human resources could recruit 60% more of its highest-priority targets? What if twice as many workers were emotionally engaged in their jobs? Agile has brought these levels of improvement to IT. The opportunity in other parts of the company is substantial."* (Rigby et al., 2016). Many suggest with the use of new technologies these kinds of results many well be possible.

Implementing agile using virtual and augmented technologies

8

Augmented reality (AR) is a technology that allows for virtual objects to be placed in the real world in real-time, enhancing the viewable information available to the user. AR uses the ability to layer detailed information over the localized (real world) viewable content while allowing the user to navigate through their perceivable "real" environment. The term "augmented reality" was first coined by Boeing researcher, Tom Caudell in 1990. Caudell was tasked with improving the expensive diagrams and marking devices used to guide workers on the factory floor. (Robinson, 2017). He proposed replacing the large plywood boards, which contained individually designed wiring instructions for each plane, with a head-mounted apparatus that displays a plane's specific schematics through high-tech eyewear and project them onto multipurpose, reusable boards. Dr. Ivan Sutherland, who is widely regarded as the father of computer graphics, created the first head-mounted display (HMD) which is now synonymous, if not defining the field of alternative realities.

Augmented Reality differs significantly from Virtual Reality (VR). AR *"enhances and expands your view of the real world with computer-generated outputs including sound, video, graphics, or GPS data"* (Baum, 2016). As the name suggests, the point of virtual reality is to persuade users that they have entered an entirely new reality (The Economist, 2016); VR *"offering a hybrid universe, submerges you in an alternative, computer-created world"* (Baum, 2016). First, VR seeks to not just enhance reality but to recreate reality in an immersive environment. In short, virtual reality is an artificial, computer-generated simulation or 're-creation' of a real-life environment or situation that the user engages in; it immerses the user by making them feel like they are experiencing the simulated reality firsthand, primarily by stimulating their vision and hearing.

This primary distinction between AR and VR is based on the current state of both technologies. Augmented reality and virtual reality are reflections of one another, with what each technology seeks to accomplish and deliver for the user. Virtual reality offers a digital recreation of a real-life setting, while augmented reality delivers virtual elements as an overlay to the real world.

In addition to the benefits associated with the Agile framework, manufacturers embracing the many advances stemming from the fields of VR and AR now can plan their production and assembly processes out in full, in a truly virtual world, making changes and viewing results instantaneously. This in turn has greatly speeded up factory and plant efficiencies, throughout all aspects of the operations. In practical terms, agile enabled virtual and augmented technologies can:

- Structure and layout production lines while optimizing process flow.
- Simulate production flow while introducing new robots or production cells, with the focus on maximize productivity and efficiency.
- Manage and reduce inventory.
- Operate and handle virtual tools and equipment through employee training.

It is this latter point that many claim harnesses the most promising aspects of these technologies.

When a manufacturing firm faces production downtime, or even slowdowns due to a broken part, or machine in need of maintenance, the ensuing costs can be astounding. By implementing an AR or VR technology solution, operators and maintenance staff can quickly react to these potential downtimes and further quickly identify the machine or part that needs attention. *"With augmented reality solutions equipped with mobile devices on the shop floor, employees can visually identify the problem that needs to be resolved."* (Brown, 2017)

The variety of Agile enabled applications based on AR and VR in the service sectors are endless, ranging from retail, hospitality, design, to virtually anything that you can imagine. The service sector is all about how it can do better for the public and allow it to have the most efficient and easiest access to what they demand. According to a study done by Krishnan and Sitaraman from the University of Massachusetts Amherst, the average person is only willing to wait two seconds for a video to load (Krishnan and Sitaraman, 2017). This fast-paced, impatient society has technology companies scrambling to provide the quickest and highest quality they possibly can. Using AR and VR, this is entirely possible. This essentially gives consumers hands-on, in real-time, results for what they desire.

Similarly, Agile methodologies through the use of AR and VR can be employed in the world of healthcare, whether to diagnose patients, for preventative care, or rehabilitation. There are various applications that employ agile focus AR methodologies such as AccuVein, a vein visualization technology to help nurses and doctors identify the locations of veins to minimize the possibility of discomfort for the patients (AccuVein, 2015).

Companies such as L'Oréal Professional have also equipped their European sales team with agile AR to show hair salon owners display stands for hair care products. L'Oréal sales representatives have the capability to choose various three-dimensional models of their merchandise in their proprietary app. They can then simulate life size products in augmented reality in their customers' salons. With this, consumers can fully visualize the impact of L'Oréal's merchandise. [2]

While the uses of associated realities has the potential to greatly assist the agile framework, the potential for usage in the real estate services is extremely promising. Current methodologies and procedures have very much been the status quo for decades. Slowly agents have begun to implement 'virtual' tours of various residential properties. However, through the use of AR and VR, industry professionals are able to give their clients the ability to take things like floor plans and bring them to life allowing clients to introduce and adapt furnishing throughout the property. Through the use of AR and VR, agents can enable clients to work with contractors to not only design properties but to find the highest and best use for the development or redevelopment thereof.

Companies like Visa are envisioning a world where augmented reality takes over the shopping experience only to enhance it. Visa Europe Collab co-founder, Hendrik Kleinsmiede, states *"Augmented reality has the potential to be transformative for the retail industry. Imagine a future where you can point your phone at a friend's new outfit with their permission, only for the app to recognize and source that outfit in your size, and give you the option of having it sent straight to your home,"* (Baldwin, 2016). This gives consumers the ability to shop in ways that have never been thought of before, with easy convenience, and instant speed it opens the world of e-commerce in a whole other dimension.

Using the Agile framework, through VR and AR in the future

Right now, virtual reality for businesses is still in its early stages of development; however, through agile methodologies it is sure that product development will improve for far less cost. Product development costs are essentially about time and money, but many of these issues can be improved substantively though the agile framework. Complicated products can be developed virtually, which helps reduce material costs. Plus, virtual models allow managers and other decision makers to assess product development early on. Further, potential customer markets will grow substantively. Consider seniors living in retirement communities

---

2 For a more detailed treatment of this topic and associated multimedia regarding AR and L'Oréal c.f., http://www.augment.com/portfolio-items/loreal/

who one might think would be obvious candidates for virtual reality experiences; as VR and AR becomes more accessible, the elderly and others with limited mobility are a large potential market. Understanding your customer base today will help you understand how to use VR and AR marketing successfully in the future.

VR and AR will impact on retail and will influence how people purchase physical products. For instance, VR will allow customers to virtually try a product before they buy. This will lead to an increase in the online sales of products which were traditionally more often purchased in a brick and mortar store. *"Recently, Entrepreneur emphasized the need for retailers to provide their customers with a content-rich experience. Today's savvy consumers have evolved in the Internet age, putting their trust in data, detailed descriptions, video reviews and social proactivity prior to purchase. Top e-Retailers have implemented a content-rich experience for their audience, and they are seeing enormous profits as a result. A comprehensive omnichannel [sic] strategy with an emphasis on user-experience solutions is a major contributor to significant sales gains across all brands, with a return on investment of tenfold or more."* (Aarts, 2017)

No matter what type of product or service you sell, VR and AR will likely be useful in some capacity. Businesses might use these technologies to create advertising and other content for customers. VR might also impact more behind-the-scenes areas such as product development and employee communications.

Conclusion

The Industrial Revolution captured the minds of economists, politicians and historians as it spurred rapid urban growth, at at the expense of immense social inequalities. For many academics, the Industrial Revolution is not just a subject for political debate, it holds the key to interpreting the effects of technological change and understanding economic growth. This era, and the ensuring technologies have fundamentally altered the way we live, work and interact with one another. All revolutions are complex, from steam power to electric power, information technology to fusion technology; however, we continue to radically rethink our approaches to progress. The crucial elements of business success are changing, and many have described our current era as the fourth Industrial Revolution. The current rate of technological change has no historical precedent and is accompanied by an increased demand for transparency, efficiency and adaptation. Collaborative, innovative models are more malleable and have a keen focus on highly motivated teams that constantly interact with the product and the customer. What we are seeing in the potential of implementing AR and VR technologies to the agile framework is nothing short of astounding.

Today's data-driven world is characterized by hyper-connectivity and we are reliant on metrics for almost every aspect of life. Modern organizations are so dependent on these metrics that it seems as though they can't operate without them. Yet, the agile framework teaches us to put customers at our highest priority. Innovative organizations like Google, Amazon and Etsy continuously deliver value to the end consumer because they adopt modern agile principles in developing their new products and services. The agile framework is unique because no prescription is incited and there is no definitive or conclusive technique on how it must (or can) be implemented. There is no 'silver bullet', no right or wrong – there is just learning through implementation. Agile is simply a general-purpose framework that can be applied to very complex situations. The true measure of progress now lies in the continuous delivery of business value.

Case 8.1: Good Buy

Good Buy is one of North America's largest and most successful retailers. The Company offers consumers a unique shopping experience with the latest technology and entertainment products, plus an expanded assortment of lifestyle products offered through its website and various e-commerce channels.

Good Buy continues to expand its operations opening stores from coast-to-coast. However, with the advent of the large aggregators such as Amazon and the efficiencies associated with these distribution channels, Good Buy now faces a variety of problems as detailed below.

- Huge competition in the sector space primarily with Amazon which offers:
    - ☐ free shipping/ logistics/
    - ☐ A variety of third party products, and
    - ☐ Product insurance at a very minimal price
- Further completion in the sector from Costco, which offers a significant variety of product, all predicated on a pricing strategy based on very low profit margins
- Further competition from Ikea, which offers furniture and appliances along with 'knock down' case goods which are not only proprietary but well below the price point that Good Buy could possibly offer.
- In order to facilitate cash flow, Good Buy now lease out space to third party suppliers which makes the location setup on supplier groupings as opposed to product groupings all of which seems to confuse the customer during their shopping experience.
- As a direct result of store layout, customer service is considered less than acceptable because workers 'seem' not knowledgeable about products throughout the store, their knowledge is limited to the supplier that they represent. As a result, consumers tend to feel that they are 'wasting time' having to browse unnecessarily throughout the store.
- In order to commit to this supplier based layout, consumers tend to claim that there is "Too much open space in the stores, and not enough product to purchase." This is further complicated by frequent stock outs.
- Consumers tend to see the stores often empty and as a result, Good Buy keeps minimal staff on the floor.
- Stores from one location to the next are all setup differently which means that there is no shared common experience for the consumer from one store to the next.

8

- Customers tend to say that the stores have a 'negative vibe' and are just not very appealing to shop in.

- Customers frequently complain that 'on sale' or 'promotional' items are not available from one location to the next.

- Customers experience stock out because there is no focused attempt to manage inventory in a meaningful way. Although there are systems in place to do such, staff have little regard for the integrity of the information provided.

- Good Buy does have a customer loyalty program; however, customers generally feel that it is 'awful' and cumbersome to use, and as a result, customers often just throw their hands up in the air when asked for the loyalty membership information.

- Lots of Good Buy's products featured on their website are available to purchase, but shipping is expensive and delivery times are often greatly protracted.

- Customers are moving away from Good Buy rapidly, preferring the ease of purchase, free and virtually instantaneous delivery offered by Amazon and other online retailers.

- Good Buy feels that it cannot compete.

Suggest appropriate measures to improve Good Buy's performance, using the Agile framework and through the implementation of new technologies such as Augmented Reality and Virtual Reality based solutions.

End of chapter questions

1   Strategy Innovation is the ability to reinvent the basis of competition within existing industries. Discuss Strategy Innovation in the context of Strategic Management and the Agile framework.

2   What businesses come to mind when you think of Strategy Innovation, and how have they appropriately applied the Agile model in terms of their effort to gain market share.

3   Using the Agile framework, discuss the changing landscape in consumer purchasing behaviour with emphasis on how consumers' purchasing behaviour is shifting and what in the market is suggesting this shift.

4   Creating strong relationships is a key cog in the system of producing a sustainable business that lasts. Discuss the importance of Relationship Management, drawing from the material cited in the chapter. Using examples, discuss the important relationships a firm must create, and using the Agile framework suggest ways of improving these relationships.

5   Using the Agile framework, propose a sustainable competitive advantage for an industry of your choice and justify your answer.

References

Aarts, P. (2017). *How Virtual Reality Is Transforming The Retail Industry*. Retrieved from Retail Touch Point: https://www.retailtouchpoints.com/features/executive-viewpoints/how-virtual-reality-is-transforming-the-retail-industry

AccuVein. (2015). *Vein visualization is emerging as the standard of care*. Retrieved 25 March 2017, from AccuVein: http://www.accuvein.com/evidence/

Aha! Staff. (2017). *What is product differentiation?* Retrieved from Aha! The Project Management Guide: https://www.aha.io/roadmapping/guide/product-strategy/what-is-product-differentiation

Baldwin, C. (2016). *Visa launches augmented reality payment technology*. Retrieved 25 March 2017, from Essential Retail: http://www.essentialretail.com/ecommerce/article/575e64c572731-visa-launches-augmented-reality-payment-technology

Baum, G. (2016). *6 things to know about augmented reality*. Retrieved from Electronic Design: http://electronicdesign.com/embedded/6-things-know-about-augmented-reality

Bradley, J. (2017). *Challenges that face operation managers*. Retrieved from Chron: http://smallbusiness.chron.com/challenges-face-operation-managers-61711.html

Brown, K. (2017). *5 ways augmented reality is changing manufacturing*. Retrieved from The Catavolt Blog: https://blog.catavolt.com/2015/08/the-augmented-reality-in -manufacturing/

Chelumbrun, J. (2017). *The concept of product differentiation in marketing*. Retrieved from: www.linkedin.com/pulse/20140721131511-199981170-the-concept-of-product-differentiation-in-marketing/

Chien, Y. (2017). *Is U.S. Manufacturing really declining?* Retrieved from Federal Reserve Bank of St. Louis: www.stlouisfed.org/on-the-economy/2017/april/us-manufacturing-really-declining

Dujmovic, J. (2017). *What risks do we face from emerging technology?* Retrieved from Market Watch: www.marketwatch.com/story/what-risks-do-we-face-from-emerging-technology -2017-02-22

Farlex. (2017). *Product differentiation* . Retrieved from The Free Dictionary by Farlex: https://financial-dictionary.thefreedictionary.com/product+differentiation

Gartenstein, D. (2017). *Attracting capital in a sole proprietorship*. Retrieved from AZ Central: https://yourbusiness.azcentral.com/attracting-capital-sole-proprietorship-12827.html

Gupta, P. (2017). *How technology along with innovation is helping entrepreneurs build successful startups*. Retrieved from Entrepreneur: https://www.entrepreneur.com/article/273841

Hoekstra, A. (2017). *Social Enterprises. How to raise capital as a social entrepreneur?* Retrieved from PWC: https://www.pwc.nl/nl/assets/documents/pwc-social-enterprises.pdf

Info Entrepreneurs (2017). *Know your customers' needs*. Retrieved from: http://www.infoentrepreneurs.org/en/guides/know-your-customers--needs/

Internet World Stats. (2017). Retrieved from Internet Growth Statistics: http://www.internetworldstats.com/emarketing.htm

Investopedia. (2017). *Bandwagon Effect*. Retrieved from: https://www.investopedia.com/terms/b/bandwagon-effect.asp

Lean Production. (2017). *Agile Manufacturing*. Retrieved from Lean Production: https://www.leanproduction.com/agile-manufacturing.html

Manyika, J., Chui, M., Bughin, J., Dobbs, R., Bisson, P. and Marrs, A. (2017). *Disruptive technologies: Advances that will transform life, business, and the global economy*. Retrieved from McKinsey Global Institute: https://www.mckinsey.com/business-functions/digital-mckinsey/our-insights/disruptive-technologies

8

Kerns, J. (2017). *What's the difference between automation and employment?* Retrieved from Machine Design: www.machinedesign.com/robotics/what-s-difference-between-automation-and-employment

Kim, G. (2017). *Agile operations and the three ways.* Retrieved from CA Technologies: https://www.ca.com/content/dam/ca/us/files/ebook/agile-operations-and-the-three-ways.pdf

Krishnan, S. S. and Sitaraman, R.K. (2017). Video stream quality impacts viewer behavior: inferring causality using quasi-experimental designs. Retrieved from Umass Education: https://people.cs.umass.edu/~ramesh/Site/HOME_files/imc208-krishnan.pdf

Linton, I. (2017). *What are the causes of rapid growth in the service industry?* Retrieved from Chron: http://smallbusiness.chron.com/causes-rapid-growth-service-industry-16007.html

Mason, M. K. (2017). *What causes small businesses to fail?* Retrieved from http://www.moyak.com/papers/small-business-failure.html

MHL News. (2017). *How to Survive Supply Chain Complexity.* Material Handling and Logistics. Retrieved from: http://www.mhlnews.com/global-supply-chain/how-survive-supply-chain-complexity

Morgan, S. (2017). *Top 5 cybersecurity facts, figures and statistics for 2017.* Retrieved from CSO - cybersecurity business report: https://www.csoonline.com/article/3153707/security/top-5-cybersecurity-facts-figures-and-statistics-for-2017.html

Nicholas, T. (2011). What Drives Innovation? *Antitrust Law Journal,* **77**(3), 787-809.

Outsource 2 India. (2017). *Does 3D Printing Reduce Rapid Prototyping Cost?* Retrieved from: https://www.outsource2india.com/eso/mechanical/articles/3d-printing-reduce-rapid-prototyping-cost.asp

Oxley, M. (2017). *Top 5 Economic Reasons Manufacturing Companies Fail.* Retrieved from Georgia Tech - Georgia Manufacturing Extension Partnership: http://gamep.org/wp-content/uploads/2014/11/TipSheet_TopFiveReasonsManufacturing CompaniesFail.pdf

Patel, N. (2017). *5 Key Benefits of Using Rapid Prototyping for Product Design & Development.* Retrieved from Medical Design Technology: https://www.mdtmag.com/article/2015/03/5-key-benefits-using-rapid-prototyping-product-design-development

Perry, M. J. (2017). *Manufacturing's declining share of GDP is a global phenomenon, and it's something to celebrate.* Retrieved from US Chamber of Commerce Foundation: https://www.uschamberfoundation.org/blog/post/manufacturing-s-declining-share-gdp-global-phenomenon-and-it-s-something-celebrate/34261

Polevoi, L. (2017). *8 reasons why small businesses fail.* Retrieved from QuickBooks Resource Center: https://quickbooks.intuit.com/r/money/8-reasons-why-small-businesses-fail/

Business Queensland. (2017). *Benefits of doing business online.* Retrieved from: https://www.business.qld.gov.au/starting-business/internet-start-ups/online-basics/benefits

Rigby, D.K., Sutherland, J. and Takeuchi, H. (2016). Embracing Agile. *Harvard Business Review,* May. Retrieved from: https://hbr.org/2016/05/embracing-agile

Robinson, A. (2017). *7 ways augmented reality in manufacturing will revolutionize the industry.* Retrieved from Cerasis: http://cerasis.com/2017/01/30/augmented-reality-in-manufacturing/

Robot Worx. (2017). Agile Production. Retrieved from: https://www.robots.com/articles/viewing/agile-production

Root, G. N. (2017). *The disadvantages of an everyday low pricing strategy.* Retrieved from Chron: http://smallbusiness.chron.com/disadvantages-everyday-low-pricing-strategy-23379.html

Sanders, N. (2017). *Operations Management Defined.* Retrieved from Pearson - Always Learning; InformIT: http://www.informit.com/articles/article.aspx?p=2167438

Schaefer, P. (2017). *Why small businesses fail: top 7 reasons for startup failure.* Business Know How: Retrieved from https://www.businessknowhow.com/startup/business-failure.htm

Shane, S. (2017). *Why small business failure rates are declining.* Entrepreneur - US edition. Retrieved from: https://www.entrepreneur.com/article/254871

Strategy Train. (2017). *Why competitive advantage is important?* Retrieved from Strategy Train: http://st.merig.eu/index.php?id=38

Study.com (2017) *What is global competition in business? - definition & challenges.* Retrieved from Study.com: https://study.com/academy/lesson/what-is-global-competition-in-business-definition-challenges-quiz.html

The Economist. (2016). *The difference between virtual and augmented reality.* Retrieved from: http://www.economist.com/blogs/economist-explains/2016/04/economist-explains-8

8

Sustainable Construction: Green Building Strategic Model

Mohamed Salama and Ashraf Hana

Learning outcomes

By completing this chapter, the reader should be able to:

- Understand the basic concepts of sustainable construction (SC)
- Compare and contrast green buildings with traditional buildings
- Discuss the challenges facing the implementation of green buildings
- Discuss the key enablers that facilitate the implementation of green buildings.
- Understand the process of developing a green building strategic model.

Introduction

Academic and policy literature over the past four decades (from as early as the 1970s) has been, and still is, concerned with understanding and articulating the core principles of sustainable development and sustainable construction or, in other words, *sustainable building and construction*, which is a holistic, multi-disciplinary approach. The increasing global concern with the maintenance and improvement of the environment, as well as the protection of the human health has become an important aspect to be considered by construction companies worldwide.

The chapter falls into two parts. The main aim of the first part is to present a critical review of the established theoretical frameworks in order to understand the topic in depth, and identify the main concepts and relevant dimensions or variables that have a crucial influence on promoting and implementing sustainable construction/green buildings practices.

The second part presents the findings of a research study conducted by the authors (Salama and Hanna, 2013) that sought to develop a strategic model for implementing the green building initiative in the UAE; Green Building Strategic Model, (GBSM – UAE). Despite being based on the UAE case, the underpinning theoretical framework and the stages of modelling used in building, training and validating the model makes this section a useful read for all parties interested in the area of sustainable construction in general, and green buildings in particular, regardless of their geographical location.

Sustainable development

The awareness of sustainable development has been growing around the globe for the last few decades. The UN Summit on Environment and Development in 1972, 'Agenda 21', the closing document of the UN Earth Summit in 1992 in Rio de Janerio, followed by many other international and national meetings and conferences show the growing concern for protecting the environment for future generations and hence introducing the sustainable development concept.

In 1987 the UN Commission on Environment and Development (the Brundtland Commission) used the term 'sustainable development' to relate the concept of sustainability to human endeavour.

The Brundtland Report defined sustainable development as: *"Development which meets the needs of the present without compromising the ability of future generations to meet their own needs"* (Brundtland, 1987). This is the most commonly quoted definition of sustainable development and it is appropriate in the context of construction works (Dresner, 2002; Purvis and Grainger, 2004; Bigg, 2004; Prasad and Hall, 2004; Murray and Cotgrave, 2007). On the other hand, the problem with the Brundtland definition of sustainable development is that it is vague and open to individual interpretation; the meaning of sustainability and sustainable development is evolving over time (Murray and Cotgrave, 2007).

A great deal of both academic and policy literature within the ten years immediately following the Brundtland announcement (World Commission on Environment and Development, 1987) was concerned with understanding and articulating the core principles of sustainable development. Two key conceptual approaches were clearly evident, namely: *strong sustainability* and *weak sustainability* (Scottish Executive Social Research, 2006).

Sustainable construction and its significance

The International Council for Innovation and Research in Building and Construction (CIB, 1999) identified the significance of construction in achieving a sustainable world within their Agenda 21 report on sustainable construction. Bourdeau (1999, p. 354) reiterates this claim.

Sustainable construction was defined as a construction process that incorporates the basic themes of sustainable development (Parkin, 2000; Langston and Ding, 2001; Said et al., 2009; Ugwu and Haupt, 2007). In contrast, the European

Commission concluded that there may never be a consensus view on its exact meaning and it is probably futile to suggest an exact definition.

Other sources (Edwards and Bennett, 2003; Graber & Dailey, 2003) support the concept of sustainable construction as an approach to building which promotes the attainment of goals associated with the triple bottom line:

■ Economic sustainability,

■ Environmental sustainability and

■ Social sustainability (Department of Trade and Industry, 2002).

The triple bottom line concept was endorsed by many views in the literature such as Baloi, 2003; Adetunji et al., 2003; Panagiotakopoulos and Jowitt, 2004; Carter and Fortune, 2006; Roper and Beard, 2006; Murray and Cotgrave, 2007; Elkington, 1998; Cole, 1998.

Miyatake (1996) suggested that there are three ways by which the civil engineering and construction industry can act to realise sustainable construction:

1 Creating built environments,

2 Restoring damaged and/or polluted environments and

3 Improving arid environments.

Vanegas et al. (1996) have drawn attention to this expanded set of belief systems for the construction industry, which was further developed by Huovila and Koskela (1998) (Figure 9.1). A new paradigm for a sustainable construction industry has incorporated these beliefs in both a model of sustainable construction, and a set of technological puzzle solutions.

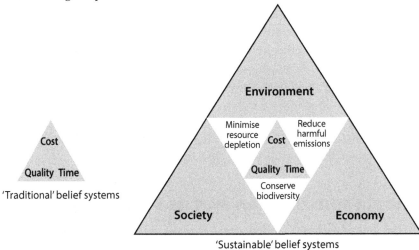

Figure 9.1: Expanded set of belief systems for a new technical paradigm (based on Huovila & Koskela, 1998)

Khalfan, in his literature review for C-Sand (2002), highlighted that sustainable construction is generally used to describe the application of sustainable development to the construction industry. Therefore, sustainable construction could be best described as a subset of sustainable development, which encircles matters such as tendering, site planning and organisation, material selection, recycling, and waste minimisation. This is endorsed by Paumgartten (2003).

The Kyoto Protocol, which was initially adopted on 11 December 1997 in Japan and entered into force on 16 February 2005, is a protocol to the United Nations Framework Convention on Climate Change, aimed at fighting global warming. Under the Kyoto Protocol, 37 industrialized countries commit themselves to a reduction of greenhouse gases (GHG) and all member countries give general commitments (UNFCC, n.d.). Almost all of the non-Annex I countries have also established a designated national authority to manage its Kyoto obligations, specifically the Clean Development Mechanism (CDM) that determines which GHG projects they wish to propose for accreditation by the CDM Executive Board.

Crowther (2006) illustrated that in the modern contemporary construction industry, the current belief system is dominated by a traditional view of delivering a building to a client with a balance of time, cost, and quality. This is a limited view that focuses primarily on economics. A new belief system that aligns with environmental sustainability would expand upon these goals to include minimising depletion of resources, conserving biodiversity, and reducing harmful emissions. These goals would then sit within a global context of environmental, social, and economic sustainability.

Crowther also pointed out that a conceptual model of sustainable construction, as part of a broader new paradigm, is essential. The recognition of this type of paradigm structure is seen in the work of Cole 2005, p.460 and Cole 1999, p.244. Hence, Crowther (2006) identified the model of sustainable construction (Figure 9.2), which can guide the implementation of technological puzzle solutions, which needs to be tempered with a regional contextual view.

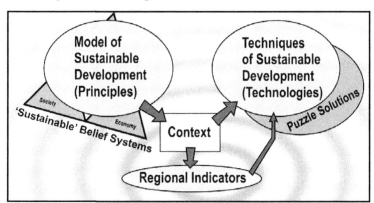

Figure 9.2: Model of a new technological paradigm for sustainable construction (Crowther 2006)

Kibert (2008) described the high-performance green building delivery system, where increasingly assessment is perceived as a necessary tool for understanding the social, economic and environmental consequences associated with the way we design, build, operate, maintain and finally dispose of buildings and their support systems (Thomson et al., 2008; El-Haram et al., 2007).

Sustainability policy

Essa and Fortune (2006) and Shelbourn et al. (2006) explained the need to have a sustainable policy as one of the key sub-processes of the generic process model of construction. It is imperative to translate the key set objectives into a clear policy that reflects the pillars of sustainability and can guide the implementation of the sought initiative. This can then be utilised in producing a generic process model of construction.

Environmental performance

Degani and Cardoso (2002) revealed the significance of environmental performance on the building process and on the building as a product. They also noted that every project is an opportunity to improve the building's environmental performance on sites, during its use and at demolition or rehabilitation stages (Doerr Architecture, 2002). Essa and Fortune (2006) highlighted that the concern for wellbeing and safety during construction is spreading to include concern for the neighbours who live around the sites and who will use the completed products.

Murray and Cotgrave (2007) stated that the UK's Building Research Establishment (BRE), in 1990, published its first evidence-based environmental performance for buildings (Baldwin et al., 1990). Since then, a number of applications have emerged describing the environmental impacts of buildings and construction, authored by professional bodies (CIOB, 2004), academics (Edwards, 1999), research institutions (CIRIA, 1994; Halliday, 1992), trade bodies (Glass, 2001), practitioners (Johnson, 1993) and charities (WWF, 2003). In other words, construction is likely to impose increasing adverse impacts on the environment and well being of people around the world (Ofori, 1998, p. 144).

Over the last several years, there has been a rapidly growing concern about environmental issues and a rising interest in sustainable practices in the United States (Turner Construction Company, 2008).

Traditional construction performance

Traditional buildings have an enormous impact on resources use and the environment and are one of the largest polluters of the environment (Weier, 1996; Johnson, 2000; Paumgartten 2003; Shen et al., 2005; Ding, 2008; Said *et al.*, 2009). Growing cities such as Dubai and Abu Dhabi in the UAE, should look at sustainable lines in order to reduce their negative environmental impacts and natural resource depletion (Al Marashi, 2006).

Cost of green buildings

Richardson and Lynes (2007) highlighted that there are mixed views in the literature regarding whether green buildings have higher initial capital costs than traditional buildings. Essa and Fortune (2008) underlined that the main source of constraint on sustainable buildings is cost. For instance, in contrast to the view held by Johnson (2000) and Orr (2004), who argued that the initial capital cost of a green building is higher, several other researchers claim that green buildings do not necessarily result in higher initial capital costs for design and construction (Bordass, 2000; Hydes and Creech, 2000; Intrachooto and Arons, 2002; Scofield, 2002; Muto, 2003; CIEF 2005a). Under the right circumstances, green or high-efficiency buildings have both an equal capital cost and lower operating and energy costs when compared to conventional buildings; a win-win situation (Bartlett and Howard, 2000; Johnson 2000; Orr, 2004). In other words, green buildings could reduce costs to the owner/occupier over the operational life-cycle of the building (Johnson, 2000; von Paumgartten, 2003).

The October 2003 report, titled *The Costs and Financial Benefits of Green Buildings*, attempts to answer the question: is green building economically justifiable? It revealed several green cost premiums, as previously outlined (Kats, 2003). Furthermore, the National Canadian Energy Code states that life-cycle costs of buildings can be reduced by 25% at the very least using an integrated team approach (Paumgartten, 2003).

The Turner Construction Company 2008 Green Building Market Barometer is an important survey that focused on green building issues in the USA. It showed that there was a broad consensus among the real estate executives (Figure 9.3) that green buildings enjoy lower operating costs and improved financial performance, while providing an environment that fosters healthier, more productive workers. Nevertheless, a perception of higher construction costs is posing an important obstacle to additional green construction.

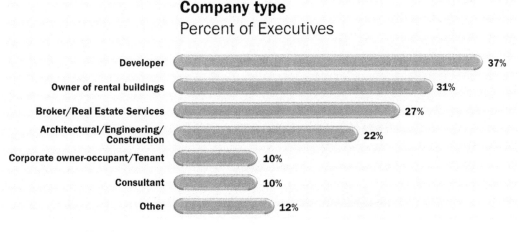

Company type

Percent of Executives

Figure 9.3: Profile of survey respondents (Turner Construction Company, 2008)

In many instances, green building did cost more because: a) the technologies being implemented were new and not widely available or mass manufactured; b) architects who specialized in sustainable design were few and thus able to charge a premium for their services; c) contractors who were unfamiliar with changes in the construction and management process experienced inefficiency and productivity losses; they may also have charged a premium for the burden; and d) the cost of commissioning and other soft costs incurred in order to obtain certification. In addition, many owner decision makers probably reacted first to the capital cost sticker shock (Langston and Mackley, 1998). They failed to take into consideration the lower lifecycle cost of the sustainably-designed facility. These costs in many cases may have offset the initial increased expenditure in part or as a whole (Nalewaik and Venters, 2009).

Growing interest in sustainable construction

The Turner Barometer Survey (Turner Construction Company, 2008) revealed that, given the benefits of green buildings, recent developments in the credit markets would not make their companies less likely to construct green buildings. The report also revealed that real estate owners are increasingly interested in green construction since many recognized that sustainable building features lead to lower operating costs and improved financial performance. Owners also found that corporate tenants are more likely to rent space in buildings that incorporate green features and corporations recognized that green buildings could be less expensive to operate due to their lower energy and operating costs, while worker satisfaction and productivity is higher.

Green buildings offer an attractive cost/benefit ratio

Costs associated with green buildings

Green construction generates potential tangible quantifiable benefits to the owner such as the life-cycle cost (LCC) savings, utilities savings, maintenance savings and savings by design. Cost benefit analysis is considered a potential tool to evaluate all the benefits throughout the life cycle of the building; even if a benefit cannot be assigned a monetary value, it should be valued using a qualitative rating system which assigns relative numerical values (Davis Langdon, 2007; Watkins, 2003; Essa and Fortune, 2006; Nalewaik and Venters, 2009).

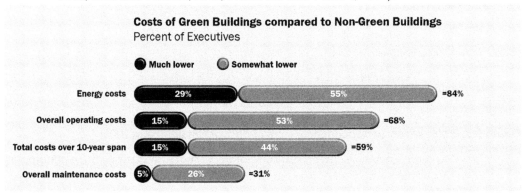

Figure 9.4: Cost of green compared to non-green buildings (Turner Construction Company, 2008)

Green buildings, having lower operating costs and generating more benefits to their owners and tenants, were considered to be less expensive than non-green buildings for several key measures of cost related to energy costs, all operating costs, total costs over a 10-year span and overall maintenance costs as shown in Figure 9.4 (Turner Construction Company, 2008). These perceptions are confirmed by other studies (Nelson, 2007; Turner and Frankel, 2008; GSA, 2008 and Salama and Hanna, 2010)

Greater Return on Investment (ROI)

While operating costs and total lifecycle costs are lower, green buildings also generate greater benefits. For instance, the Turner report (Turner Construction Company, 2008) found that green buildings have higher building values than similar non-green buildings, they command higher asking rents and provide a greater return on investment (ROI) and higher occupancy rates as shown in Figure 9.5. This was asserted by Paumgartten (2003) stating that being green substantially increases a building's performance and its market value.

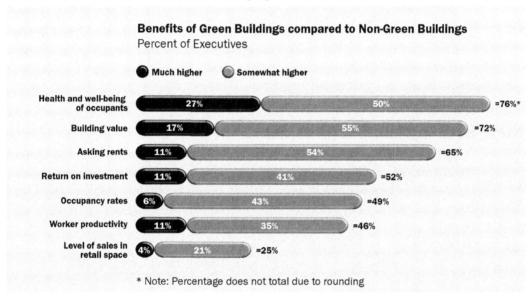

Figure 9.5: Benefits of green buildings compared to non-green buildings (Turner Construction Company, 2008)

Additional (intangible) benefits

The benefits of green buildings are not only financial. Green construction yields a number of intangible benefits in terms of improvements in human performance (including productivity gain and better health) and an increase prestige/reputation and customer satisfaction (Scofield, 2002; Benson Kwong, 2004; Richardson and Lynes, 2007; Turner Construction Company, 2008). The 'Feel-Good' factor is an important qualitative benefit which is social value; a compound function of public image, marketability, resource conservation, and corporate responsibility. However, most results regarding the effect of sustainable design on building occupants are qualitative not quantitative (Nalewaik and Venters, 2009).

Kats (2003), in his report to California's Sustainable Building Task Force, highlighted that there is growing recognition of the large health and productivity costs imposed by poor indoor environmental quality in commercial buildings – estimated variously at up to hundreds of billions of dollars per year as people spend 90% of their time indoors (US Environmental Protection Agency, 2003).

On the other hand, Roper and Beard (2006) contended that the relationship between comfort/productivity and building design/operation is complex and stated that one way to address the problem is to use a balanced scorecard approach, which can look at categories of building performance, such as the financial results associated with the cost of absenteeism and turnover.

Payback period

The Barometer Survey (Turner Construction Company, 2008) reported that, although it is believed that green buildings cost more to construct, these higher costs would be paid back through lower operating costs, with a median payback period of seven years. The findings of the survey indicated that while achieving a higher level of LEED certification (LEED, 2003, US Green Building Council, 2002) may require a greater initial investment, it is more than recouped through higher returns over time. This view is adopted by (Siddens, 2002; Kats, 2003)

Green buildings improve performance

Kats (2003) reported that the Center for Building Performance at Carnegie Mellon University has reviewed over 1000 studies that related technical characteristics of buildings to tenant responses, such as productivity, and demonstrated that better building design and performance in areas such as lighting, ventilation and thermal control correlate to increases in tenant/worker well-being and productivity (Loftness et al., 2002).

The Turner Barometer Survey (Turner Construction Company, 2008) reported that green buildings have better financial performance than non-green buildings in terms of: a) higher building values; b) higher asking rents; c) greater ROI; and d) higher occupancy rates. They also provide greater non-financial benefits to those who occupy them with respect to: a) improved health and well-being of occupants; and b) greater worker productivity (Figure 9.5).

Social and cultural values

Du Plessis (1999, p.388) was deeply critical of the way in which sustainability, at project level, was being developed without considering the social impact it had.

Ronald Rovers (2003), in the UNEP Industry and Environment report, has emphasized that sustainable building and construction (SBC) is not only about environmental concerns. In addition to securing the physical resources, SBC means paying attention to social and cultural values. The main elements receiving attention are the history and traditional values of people in different cultures and climates, which have often been overlooked in modern building and planning. He concluded that social and cultural aspects can relate very closely to environmental ones, and can even be mutually reinforcing with use of local resources, attention to the existing building stock and respect for cultural values.

Guy and Moore (2005, in Ch 4):

"The Social Construction of Green Building Codes *by Steven A. Moore and Nathan Engstrom, highlighted that the production of environmental programmes and building codes is, of course, not entirely a matter of science. Rather, it is a highly social and contentious process in which some interests are suppressed and others are reinforced. The presence of competing interests is reflected in the confusing array of codes and green building standards, such as commercial construction certification schemes like LEED, that have emerged in response to contemporary environmental conditions. "*

The four-pillar model of sustainability, shown in Figure 9.6, includes four interlinked dimensions namely:

■ Environmental responsibility,

■ Economic health,

■ Social equity, and

■ Cultural vitality.

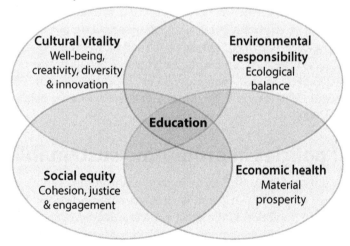

Figure 9.6: The four-pillar model of sustainability

A cultural input is reflected in evaluating the impacts of the environmental, economic, and social initiatives being implemented in cities and communities. The model recognized that a community's vitality and quality of life is closely related to the vitality and quality of its cultural engagement, and dialogue. It also acknowledged that the contribution of culture to building lively cities and communities where people want to live, work, and visit, plays a major role in supporting social and economic health (West Kootenay Regional Arts Council, 2002; Hawkes, 2001).

While the triple bottom line of sustainability, which is economic, environmental and social, was well defined and documented in community sustainability planning, the inclusion of the 'cultural vitality' as a fourth bottom line is a fairly new phenomenon in sustainable development as shown in Figure 9.7 (Sustainable Kingston, 2010).

Figure 9.7: Sustainable Kingston: The four-pillar approach of sustainability

Also, Estidama has strongly referred to the cultural aspect of sustainability since it is based on the four pillars: environmental, economic, cultural and social aiming to achieve a balance amongst them to create more sustainable communities.

The Emirates Environmental Group (EEG), a leading non-government organization (NGO) established in 1991 and based in Dubai, is working on changing the UAE's poor environmental image and spreading out the sustainable culture (http://www.eeg-uae.org/). The environmental awareness has also gained pace in schools across the UAE and some universities began to respond to the need for qualified experts in sustainable practices. This commensurate with the views of Perdan et al., 2000, pp. 267-279; Jucker, 2002, p.16; Martin, 2002, p.20; Murray and Cotgrave, 2007.

The role of policies in promoting sustainable practices

Rovers (2003), in the UNEP Industry and Environment report, expressed well the importance of policies in promoting sustainable practices. Rovers emphasized that resource depletion is the most pressing overall concern related to the built environment. Determined policy development is needed to address this concern. He also stated that developing countries face particular barriers regarding policies on the built environment. If strong policies can help industrialized countries lead society towards sustainability, such efforts in developing countries face particular barriers. He stressed that sustainability needs to be the main driver of policy development and legislation. He added that to bring about a shift in resource management would require reinvention of the current predominant economic system and the policy-making that guides it.

Carter and Fortune (2006) maintained that the registered social landlords (RSLs) had a well-developed sustainable development (SD) policy supported by a board range of guidance, but they referred to the existing gap between policy and practice.

The authorities must formulate effective ways to achieve sustainability which need to be implemented as a cornerstone for future policies. The policies should be formulated in a way that gives change to the economic market forces to govern the activities of professionals in the construction industry (Bon and Hutchinson, 2000; Kuhtz, 2007; Said et al., 2009).

Building materials / construction products and life-cycle thinking

The implementation of construction methods, materials, components, equipment and processes in projects must have a minimal effect on the built environment and be based on sound ecological principles (Abanda and Tah, 2008). Edwards and Bennett (2003), in their article in the 2003 UNEP Industry and Environment report, highlighted that construction materials and products are essential to life with respect to both buildings and infrastructure. They noted that people spend around 80% of their time, on average, in some type of building or on roads, and underlined that construction products play a major role in improving the energy efficiency of buildings and contributing to economic prosperity as well as having a considerable impact on the environment. The construction sector is responsible for 50% of the material resources taken from nature and 50% of total waste generated (Anink et al., 1996). The impact of construction products relative to the overall lifetime impact of a building is currently 10-20%. For infrastructure this value is significantly higher, greater than 80% in some cases (www.buildingsgroup.nrcan. gc.ca/projects/gbc_e.html).

A balance should be made between the desirable qualities of indigenous, traditional materials, in terms of internal comfort and relatively benign environmental impacts, and the social need for providing quickly constructed, affordable housing solutions on a mass scale. Hence, the careful selection of construction products is a feature of national green building labels such as BREEAM in the UK and LEED in the US. The challenge is how best to measure and to manage the impact of construction products. Life-cycle assessment (LCA) is an approach to measuring the environmental impact of construction products and a method for evaluating the environmental impacts of a system by taking into account its full life cycle from cradle to grave. This concept is expressed in Figure 9.8 (Edwards and Bennett, 2003).

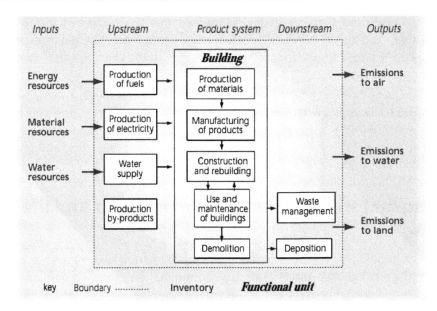

Figure 9.8: Application of LCA to construction products (Edwards and Bennet, 2003)

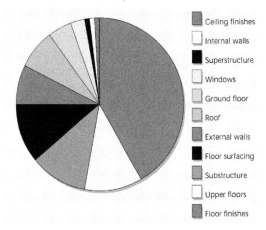

Figure 9.9: Relative contribution of different construction elements to impacts of a typical office building (Edwards and Bennet, 2003)

The Business Case for Sustainable Design in Federal Facilities published by the Federal Energy Management Program (U.S. Department of Energy) in August 2003, provided a series of case studies related to federal government facilities where recycled, durable and locally supplied building materials played an essential role in providing world-class workplaces for the federal workers, and superior value for the American taxpayer.

Egbert (2009) in his article 'Are You Leeding the Industry On?' underlined the importance of green building materials and their contribution to obtain a LEED certification. Egbert mentioned that construction activity is one of the biggest contributors that harm the environment in the Gulf Countries (GCC) and many building materials suppliers, such as BASF (http://www.basf.com), Cemex and Mapei, have begun to realise this and turn to less emitting materials and greener products. He stressed that there is no LEED certification for suppliers; it is a building rating system not a company rating system. The correct term is not 'LEED certified' but 'LEED compliant'.

Integrative design process (IDP)

The U.S. Department of Energy (2003) demonstrated the importance of employing an integrated design to produce sustainable buildings that can be constructed at the same or lower cost than conventional buildings. *The Business Case of Sustainable Design in Federal Facilities* report illustrated case studies where an integrated, multidisciplinary design approach was adopted developing a "whole building" design that best met the economic and environmental interests of all parties; the Zion National Park Visitors Centre (Figure 9.10) is a good example.

Sustainability assessment, defined as a 'process to identify, predict and evaluate the potential impacts of a range of initiatives and their alternatives on the sustainable development of a society' (Therivel *et al.*, 1992), requires to be emerged as a tool for promoting communication and learning about sustainability across the building process (Kaatz *et al.*, 2006)

Figure 9.10: Zion National Park Visitors Centre (U.S. Department of Energy, 2003)

The National Canadian Energy Code states that life-cycle costs of buildings can be reduced by 25% at the very least using an integrated team approach (Paumgartten, 2003).

Richardson and Lynes (2007) stressed that one of the main pillars for the successful implementation of green buildings on campus of the University of Waterloo is the collaborations between researchers, designers and facilities management employees to realize the design and construction of high-efficiency buildings. Hydes and Creech (2000, p. 404) contended that integrated design leads to simpler buildings which are not only robust but work better, as well (Scofield, 2002).

9

7group and Reed (2009) have explained well the philosophy, background and foundations of the integrative design process (IDP), which offers a new path to make green building decisions and address complex issues that threaten living systems. They introduced the construction industry professionals to the concepts of whole-building design and whole systems.

Insurance and risk management benefits

In his *Capital E* report to California's Sustainable Building Task Force, Kats (2003) indicated that where formal or informal self-insurance is used, risk management is particularly important, since there is no hedge (upper limit) against loss costs. He noted an important remark which is the considerable untapped opportunities suggested by the synergies between green-building technologies and risk management (Figure 9.11).

Figure 9.11: Risk management benfits of green buildings (Kats, 2003)

> - **Worker Health & Safety.** Various benefits, including lower workmen's compensation costs, arise from improved indoor environmental quality, reduced likelihood of moisture damage, and other factors enhancing workplace safety.
> - **Property Loss Prevention.** A range of green building technologies reduce the likelihood of physical damages and losses in facilities.
> - **Liability Loss Prevention.** Business interruption risks can be reduced by facilities that derive their energy from on-site resources and/or have energy-efficiency features. This includes risks resulting from unplanned power outages.
> - **Natural Disaster Preparedness and Recovery.** A subset of energy efficient and renewable energy technologies make facilities less vulnerable to natural disasters, especially heat catastrophes.

Kats (2003b) maintained that most insurers and risk managers still have to make the connection between green buildings and reduced risk, and referred to instances where insurance companies offered premium credits in the order of 10% for insured parties implementing selected energy savings strategies (Mills, 2003). However, he concluded that little was done to quantify or monetize the benefits. He also provided an interesting and important addendum by Evan Mills (2003) to his report, Appendix K, which included a more specific characterization of the potential insurance benefits of green buildings where benefits were plotted onto the credits of the LEED system (Version 2.0).

Gonzalez and Sangar (2009) discussed how to avoid legal risks associated with green buildings. They mentioned that in spite of their environmental benefits, green buildings pose many legal challenges and in order to avoid them, specific measures need to be taken.

The U.S. Department of Energy (2003) reported that, with the explosion in mold-related claims, for example, insurance companies began to take defensive action with mold exclusion clauses and premium rate hikes. On the other hand, some insurance companies were willing to offer lower insurance premiums for buildings and facilities with positive environmental effects (Mills, 2003b).

Challenges to green construction

The Turner Barometer report (Turner Construction Company, 2008) identified eight challenges / issues potentially discouraging the construction of green buildings (Figure 9.13). At the top of the list was the amount of documentation and additional cost to have a building become LEED-certified. Two issues relating to the cost of green construction came next: higher construction costs and the length of the payback period. Generally, an overview of the literature revealed the higher initial capital costs to be the main barrier to the implementation on green buildings (Richardson and Lynes, 2007; Essa and Fortune, 2006).

The payback issue was raised by Kimmet and Wikstrom (2005) who emphasized that the research on understanding and measuring sustainability payback for business must be significantly developed in terms of people, profit and planet tri-partition to illustrate the threefold dimension of the sustainability 'triple bottom line'.

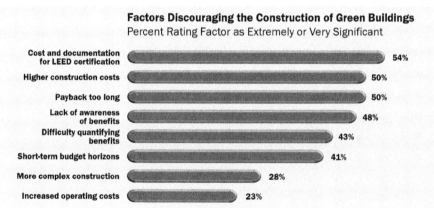

Factors Discouraging the Construction of Green Buildings
Percent Rating Factor as Extremely or Very Significant

Cost and documentation for LEED certification — 54%
Higher construction costs — 50%
Payback too long — 50%
Lack of awareness of benefits — 48%
Difficulty quantifying benefits — 43%
Short-term budget horizons — 41%
More complex construction — 28%
Increased operating costs — 23%

Figure 9.12: Factors discouraging the construction of green buildings. (Source: Turner 2008)

Another obstacle is 'short-term budget horizons' where companies often focus on budgets that don't take account of savings that green buildings achieve over time. This approach may lead an owner to decide not to build a green building that will easily pay for itself through lower operating costs over a longer time-frame (Turner Construction Company, 2008).

The lack of understanding of the life-cycle costing and related key issues, lack of green education, affordability and the lack of a comprehensive framework to support the consideration and assessment of sustainability are also barriers to be considered. All the benefits accrued with green building occur over the economic or design life of a building with a typical time horizon of 20-50 years (Kats, 2003; Sponge, 2004; Kimmet and Wikstrom, 2005; Roper and Beard, 2006; Murray and Cotgrave, 2007; Turner Construction Company, 2008).

Deakin et al. (2002) maintained that the lack of a comprehensive framework to support the consideration and assessment of sustainability restricted the ability of practitioners to interact positively in this regard, which refers to the difficulty of quantifying the benefits of sustainable construction. In contrast, Singh et al. (2009) stated that there is sufficient effort to measure sustainability with an integral approach that encompasses its environmental, economic and social aspects.

Challenges and Critical Success Factors

Asurvey conducted in summer 2014, that covered 500 practitioners from the UAE construction industry and attracted 243 responses, showed there was a clear lack of awareness and that the availability of specifications was one of the key challenges, despite the specifications in the form of the systems currently available and implemented by the UAE government both in Abu Dhabi and Dubai. A detailed list of all the factors was collated from the literature (Tagaza & Wilson, 2004; Hakkinen & Belloni, 2011; Zou & Zhao, 2014) and others, and put to the surveyed sample to give a score to indicate importance. The findings of the analysis of the data set, as shown in Table 9.1, revealed the most and least influential challenges / CSF, with the weighted average score, as perceived by the sample, before factor analysis was applied to the data set, to yield the following components (categories).

The statistical analysis identified five main categories of challenges facing the implementation of green building in the UAE. Those included:

■ Availability of specifications;

■ Awareness;

■ Organisational factors;

■ Environmental factors and

■ Contractual factors.

In addition, four main categories of CSF that can enhance the implementation of green building in the UAE. Those included:

■ Socio-environmental factors;

■ Organisational factors;

■ Economic factors and

■ Financial factors.

Due to the nature of the UAE demographic context, where the majority of the population are expats who do not view the UAE as their home country and see that their stay in the UAE is for a limited period of time, the majority would opt for renting rather than buying property. This meant that those who own are different from those who use the building. In other words, the owner is not reaping the whole life (long term) savings due to green building reduced consumption of energy and water, typically paid by the tenant. On the other hand, there is no evidence that green buildings attract higher value for rent in the housing market that would entice owners to create demand. The interviewed experts suggested that until this changes the driver for and awareness of green buildings will be limited. In the UAE, the word of mouth is very effective and this has to be utilised in promoting the green building concept. However, there must be incentives and this perhaps needs government actions

Table 9.1: Most important challenges/ CSF

S.N.	Description	Freq. %	CSF No	Description	Freq. %
C10	Availability of materials based on their renewability/recyclability	72.8	5	Available technology	74.9
C13	Adopting green practices or procedures (eg waste management)	72	12	Project members' technical skills	74.5
C14	Availability of green product inform-ation from reliable sources/databases	70.8	2	Social awareness of GB benefits	73.3
C11	Awareness of green performance assessment of buildings	70	15	Government's role in sustainable development strategy planning	70.8
C8	Availability of advanced green technol-ogy for construction purposes	67.9	3	Clear legislation enforcing GB	70.4
C23	Greater communication and interest are required amongst project team members	67.5	11	Effective leadership	69.5
C18	Higher costs for green construction practices and green material	65.4	4	Availability of required GB material	69.1
C26	Lack of awareness of the concept and benefits of green buildings	64.6	14	Clients, project managers and energy companies' awareness of the sustainable development theory	69.1
C3	Implementing environmental regula-tions via contractual framework	64.2	1	Stable economic environment	67.9
C24	More time is required to implement green construction practices onsite and complexity of construction	64.2	6	GB experience level amongst project team	67.5
			7	Project scope clearly defined	67.5
Least Influential challenges/ least important CSF					
C4	Conflicts of interest (e.g. suppliers providing specifications)	51.7	26	Project change control mechanism	58.8
C5	Bias towards particular products or processes	51	27	Accurate measurement and verification of as-built works	58.8
C17	Availability of verifiable green performance criteria for performance based specifications	40.9	9	Site and location limitations	57.2
C7	Risk of using green specifications	39.1	18	Awareness of financing institute of Energy Performance Contracting EPC and GB in general.	56.8
			21	Savings share amongst stakeholders	56.8

9

The conclusions of the study suggested that to enhance the implementation of green building, the government has to provide significant incentives in the form of reduced energy and water tariffs for green buildings that would stimulate the market and entice the shift towards green building in the private sector .

Commitment

Kats (2003) referred to the commitment shown by several Sustainable Building Task Force member agencies whom their resources and staff support helped to increase the collective knowledge of the true costs and benefits of green building. In addition, he recognized the contributions of the Undersecretary and Senior Consultant of the State and Consumer Services Agency, due to their leadership, as well as their commitment which made the Capital E report to California's Sustainable Building Task Force possible. On the other hand, Baloi (2003) indicated that the empirical evidence showed that the most significant challenge associated with environmental management is the lack of commitment.

UAE Green Building Strategic Model (UAE – GBSM)

The following section will reflect on the findings of research studies conducted by the authors on the implementation of the green building initiative in the UAE. The study aimed at developing a strategic model for green buildings in the UAE (Salama and Hana, 2013). The full details of the underpinning theory, how the model was developed, verified and tested can be found on the companion website: http://www.goodfellowpublishers.com/sustprojman

The UAE Green Building Strategic Model (UAE GBSM) as shown in Figure 9.13 and 9.14 consists of four key pillars namely 1) Leadership, 2) Financial Vision, 3) Sustainability Objectives/Targets and 4) Communication & Collaboration. Each pillar has the shape of a triangle pointing towards the 'Green Building in the UAE' circle which is in the centre of the model. Each pillar has a triangular shape outlining the evolution and challenges of the sustainable construction concept in a global context, which is not only dominated by the construction industry traditional view focusing mainly on economics in terms of handing over a building with a balance of time, cost and quality but also includes minimizing depletion of resources, conserving biodiversity, and reducing harmful emissions and emphasizes on the three main corners of sustainability namely environmental (environmental quality), social (social equity and cultural vitality), and economic (healthy sustainable economy). The triangular shape emphasizes on the fact that each pillar contributes to the global context of sustainability. The four pillars are embraced by 'Abu Dhabi & Dubai Sustainability' Policies under the umbrella of a UAE Federal Green Legislation.

The clockwise and anti-clockwise arrows as well as the vertical and horizontal ones, indicated in green, emphasize on the dynamism of the process and ensure the flexibility of the model. The four pillars complement each other and work in parallel not in a sequential manner. It is the linkages and integration among the measures and themes of each pillar and within the four pillars that will support the model in becoming more sustainable. Given the current status of the green building concept in the UAE, the four pillars should have similar (equal) weighting, but meanwhile could be kept flexible. They are equally important as a basis for sustainable design. The weights are not static but dynamic depending on the nature and priorities of the entity (category) looking at the model, the evolution of the model with time and in response to any particular project.

The 'social equity and cultural heritage' corner of the global context sustainability (the triangular shape) is replaced by 'social equity and cultural vitality' since the culture heritage is an element of the culture vitality, which comprises four themes namely 1) arts, creativity and environment, 2) history and heritage, 3) active citizenship and 4) diversity (Focus Kingston, 2010). The 'cultural vitality' dimension is underlined and indicated in bold red to stress on the key role it plays and the core influence it has on the triple bottom line of sustainability: environmental, economic and social.

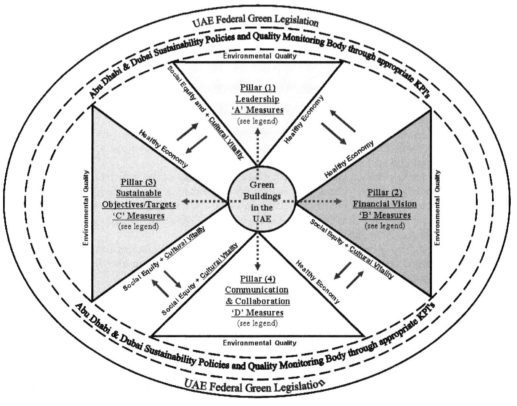

Figure 9.13: UAE Green Building Strategic Model (UAE GBSM), diagram.

LEGEND

Pillar (1) - Leadership - 'A' Measures

- Clear and concise vision of the UAE Government.
- Holistic definitive strategies.
- Collaborative working amongst Authorities.
- Strong Leadership from the UAE Government and Authorities.
- Open attitude towards innovative designs.
- Financial and non-financial incentives from the local governments.

Pillar (2) - Financial Vision - 'B' Measures

- Minimizing both the upfront capital and lifetime operation costs of a building against a conventional one.
- Setting an operational structure that rewards building designs with life-cycle cost, long-term budget horizon, lower energy costs and higher water and emissions savings.
- Life cycle costing (LCC) as a contribution to sustainable construction.
- Financial incentives.
- Payback period and return on investment (ROI).

Pillar (3) - Sustainable Objectives/Targets - 'C' Measures

- Quantifiable targets set by the UAE Government addressing the most pressing sustainability issues to the UAE and reflecting on Estidama (Abu Dhabi) & LEED (Dubai).
- Quantifiable targets to set goals and to assess the success of the building once it is operational (quantify progress).
- Key Performance Indicators (KPI's) to be set to monitor and measure the progress towards achieving these objectives.
- Green project stakeholders to use these targets/objectives for educational purposes, to give guidance through the design process and monitor and quantify progress.

Pillar (4) - Communication & Collaboration - 'D' Measures

- Effective communication amongst construction industry key Stakeholders (clients, designers, facilities management, contractors and suppliers) / Holistic Approach - Worth of Integrative Design (IDP).
- Effective communication and collaboration between the construction industry key stakeholders and the EGBC making effective use of its expertise and knowledge.
- Effective communication and collaboration between the construction industry key stakeholders any green Non Governmental Organization (NGO), i.e. the Emirates Environmental Group (EEG).
- Culture Vitality – a cultural input should be reflected in evaluating the impacts of the environmental, economic and social initiatives that are implemented in Abu Dhabi and Dubai communities.
- Education of the construction industry to increase knowledge and awareness on sustainability in general and sustainable construction (green building) in particular.
- Education of the society (end users) about sustainability is paramount to implant the right values and sense of responsibility towards the environment and the planet's limited resources.

The four pillars should have similar equal weighting but meanwhile could be kept flexible (the weights are not static but dynamic depending on the nature and priorities of the entity (category) looking at the model)

Figure 9.14: UAE Green Building Strategic Model (UAE GBSM), legend.

Summary

This chapter introduced the topic of sustainable construction (SC) with emphasis on green buildings. The chapter can be divided into four main parts; the first part introduced the reader to a wide range of literature on SC from different lenses. The second focused on the green buildings as one of the key elements required to shift towards SC. This included a discussion of the debate in the literature about the cost and costing of green buildings as well as the other benefits and challenges. The third part presented a critical review of the findings of a number of studies conducted by the authors on the area of green buildings over the past 8 years in the UAE. This included identifying the main challenges facing the shift towards green buildings as well as the critical success factors that would enable the successful implementation of this initiative. The chapter ended by introducing the steps used to develop the UAE Green Building Strategic Model; utilizing two well defined frameworks from the sustainability literature as the underpinning theory.

End of chapter questions

1   Compare the cost of green building with that of traditional building for the same category of building.

2   Discuss the different views on sustainable construction as mentioned in the literature.

3   Discuss the main challenges facing the implementation of green building.

4   Critically evaluate the UAE GBSM that was developed and presented in this chapter. Your critique should link to the relevant literature to support your argument.

References

7 group and Reed, B. G.,(2009). *The Integrative Design Guide to Green Building: Redefining the Practice of Sustainability*. New Jersey: John Wiley & Son

Adetunji, I., Price, A., Fleming, P. & Kemp. P. (2003). The application of systems thinking to the concept of sustainability. In Greenwood, D. J., (Ed), *19th Annual ARCOM Conference*, 3-5 Sept, University of Brighton, Association of Researchers in Construction Management, **1**, 161-70.

Al Marashi, H., (2006). Facing the environmental challenge: encouraging sustainable urban development in the United Arab Emirates. *Global Urban Development Magazine*, **2** (1). Retrieved from http://www.globalurban.org/GUDMag06Vol2Iss1/Al%20Marashi.htm

Baldwin, A., Leach, S., Doggart, J. and Attenborough, M., (1990). Building Research Establishment Environmental Assessment Method Version 1/90. An Environmental Assessment for New Office Designs, BRE, Watford.

Baloi, D., (2003). Sustainable construction: challenges and opportunities. In: Greenwood, D., J., (Ed), *19th Annual ARCOM Conference*, 3-5 September, University of Brighton, Association of Researchers in Construction Management, Vol. 1, 289-97.

Bartlett, E. and Howard, N., 2000. Informing the decision makers on the cost and value of green building. *Building, Research and Information*, **28**(5/6), 315-24.

9

Benson Kwong, P.C.(2004) *Quantifying the Benefits of Sustainable Buildings*. AACE International Transactions, Washington, DC, AACE International.

Bigg, T., (2004). *Survival for a Small Planet: the sustainable development agenda*. London: Earthscan.

Bon, R. and Hutchinson, K.,(2000). Sustainable construction: some economic challenges. *Building Research and Information*, **30** (2), 83-94.

Bordass, B. (2000). Cost and value: fact and fiction. *Building, Research and Information*, **28** (5/6), 338-52.

Bourdeau, L. (1999). Sustainable development and the future of construction: a comparison of visions of various countries. *Building Research and Information*, **26**(6), 355-67.

Brundtland, G. H., (1987). *Our Common Future: Report of the World Commission on Environment and Development*. New York.

Carter, K. and Fortune, C.(2007). Sustainable development policy perceptions and practice in the UK social housing sector. *Construction Management and Economics*, **25**, 399-408.

CIB, (1999). *Agenda 21 on Sustainable Construction*. CIB Report Publication 237, CIB, Rotterdam, July, 1999.

CIEF, (2005a). *Socially Responsible Construction: Key Design Aspects. Construction Industry Environmental Forum Seminar Report*, CIEF, Glasgow.

CIOB, (2004). *Sustainability and Construction*. Chartered Institute of Building, Ascot.

CIRIA, (1994). *Environmental Impacts of Materials*, Special Publication 116, Volumes A to F. Construction Industry Research and Information Association, London.

Cole, R. J., (1998). Emerging trends in building environmental assessment methods. *Building Research and Information*, **26**(1), 3-16.

Cole, R. J., (1999). Building environmental assessment methods: clarifying intentions. *Building Research and Information*, **27**(4/5), 230-246.

Cole, R. J., (2005). Building environmental assessment methods: redefining intentions and roles. *Building Research and Information*, **35**(5), 455-467.

Crowther, P., (2006). Sustaining a Subtropical Response. In *Proceedings Subtropical Cities 2006*, Brisbane, Australia. Retrieved from http://eprints.qut.edu.au/5378/1/5378_1.pdf

Davis Langdon Management Consulting (2007) Life cycle costing (LCC) as a contribution to sustainable construction: a common methodology.

Deakin, M., Huovila, P., Rao, S., Sunikka, M. and Vreeker, R. (2002). The assessment of sustainable urban development. *Building Research and Information*, **30** (2), 95-108.

Department of Trade and Industry (DTI), 2002, Profiting from Sustainability, BRE. London. Retrieved from www.2006conference.crcci.info/docs/.../P57_Foulis_R.pdf

Doerr Architecture (2002) Definition of Sustainability and the Impacts of Building. Colorado, EUA. Retrieved from doerr.org/html/GreenChecklistResidential.doc

Degani, C. M. and Cardoso, F. (2002). Environmental Performance and Lean Construction Concepts: Can we talk about a 'Clean Construction'? In: 10th *Conference of the International Group for Lean Construction*. Gramado, Brazil 6-8 August. Retrieved from http://www.pcc.usp. br/fcardoso/Lean%20Construction%202002%20Degani%20Cardoso.pdf

Ding, G. K. C. (2008). Sustainable Construction – The role of environmental assessment tools. *Journal of Environmental Management*, **86** (3), 451-464.

Dresner, S., (2002). *The Principle of Sustainability*. London: Earthscan.

Du Plessis, C., (1999). Sustainable development demands dialogue between developed and developing worlds. *Building Research and Information*, **27** (6), 319-90.

Edwards, B., (1999). *Sustainable Architecture: European Directives and Building Design*. 2nd Ed. Oxford: Architectural Press.

Edwards, S. and Benett, P. (2003). Construction products and life-cycle thinking. *UNEP Industry and Environment*, **26** (2-3), 29-32. Retrieved from http://www.uneptie.org/media/review/vol26no2-3/005-098.pdf

Egbert, C. (2009). Special Report 'Leed Compliant: Are You Leeding The Industry On?' *Construction Week Magazine*, Oct. 31-Nov. 6, 38-40.

Elkington, J., (1998). *Cannibals with Forks: The Triple Bottom Line of 21st Century Business*. Gabriola Island, BC: New Society Publishers.

Essa, R. and Fortune, C. (2006). Project price forecasting processes and pre-construction evaluation of sustainable housing association projects. In: Boyd, D., (Ed), *Proceedings of 22nd Annual ARCOM Conference*, 4-6 September, Birmingham, UK, Association of Researchers in Construction Management, 543-552.

Essa, R. and Fortune, C. (2008). Pre-construction evaluation practices of sustainable housing projects in the UK. *Engineering Construction and Architectural Management*, **15**(6), 514-526.

Estidama. (n.d.) Retrieved from http:// http://estidama.org/

GSA – General Services Administration (2008) *Assessing Green Building Performance: A Post Occupancy Evaluation of 12 GSA Buildings*. Public Buildings Service, June.

Glass, J. (2001). *Ecoconcrete – The Contribution of Cement and Concrete to a More Sustainable Built Environment*. British Cement Association, Crowthorne.

Gonzalez, C. and Sangar, A. (2009). *Green buildings: Opportunities and risks*. ConstructionWeekonline.com. Retrieved from http://www.constructionweekonline.com/article-6061-green-buildings-opportunities-and-risks/

Graber, S. and Dailey, C. (2003). *Environmentally Sustainability in Building Construction: Implications and assessment tools*. Final year research project, Swinburne University of Technology, Victoria. Retrieved from http://www.abcb.gov.au/documents/research/Environmental_Sustainability_in_Building_Construction.pdf

Guy, S. and Moore, S. A. (2005). Sustainable architectures: Cultures and natures in Europe and North America. In *The Social Construction of 'Green Building' Codes: Competing models by industry, government and NGOs*. New York: Spon Press, 51-70.

Halliday, S. (1992). *Environmental Code of Practice for Building Services*. Building Services Research and Information Association, Bracknell.

Hawkes, J. (2001). *The Fourth Pillar of Sustainability: Culture's essential role in public planning*. Melbourne: Cultural Development Network & Common Ground Press. Retrieved from http://www.culturaldevelopment.net/downloads/FourthPillarSummary.pdf

Huovila, P. and Koskela, L. (1998). Contribution of the principles of Lean Construction to meet the challenges of sustainable development. *Sixth international conference of the International Group for Lean Construction*, Guarujá, Brazil, 13-15 August. Retrieved from http://www.ce.berkeley.edu/~tommelein/IGLC-6/

Hydes, K. R. and Creech, L. (2000). Reducing mechanical equipment cost: the economics of green design. *Building Research and Information*, **28**(5/6), 403-7.

Intrachooto, S. and Arons, D. (2002). Nurturing green innovations for academic institutions. *International Journal of Sustainability in Higher Education*, **3**(2), 155-63.

Johnson, S., (1993). *Greener Buildings – The Environmental Impact of Property*. Macmillan, London.

Johnson, S. D. (2000). The economic case for high performance buildings. *Corporate Environmental Strategy*, **7**(4), 24-35, 350-61.

Jucker, R. (2002). Sustainability – never heard of it. Some basics we should not ignore when engaging in education for sustainability. *International Journal of Sustainability in Higher Education*, **3**(1), 8-18.

9

Kaatz, E., Root, D. S., Bowen, P. A. and Hill, R. C. (2006). Advancing key outcomes of sustainability building assessment. *Building Research and Information, 34*(4), 308-320.

Kats, G. (2003). *The Costs and Financial Benefits of Green Buildings: A Report to California's Sustainable Building Task Force*. Retrieved from http://www.cap-e.com/ewebeditpro/items/O59F3259.pdf

Khalfan, M. A. (2002). *Sustainable Development and Sustainable Construction: A Literature Review for C-Sand*. Loughborough University. Retrieved from http://www.c-sand.org.uk/Documents/WP2001-01-SustainLitRev.pdf

Kibert, C. J. (1994). Establishing principles and a model for sustainable construction. In: *Proceedings of the First International Conference of CIB Task Group 16 on Sustainable Construction*, November 6-9, Tampa, Florida, USA, pp. 3-12. Retrieved from http://www.cce.ufl.edu/rsc06/PDFs/SC04.pdf

Kibert, C. J. (2008). *Sustainable Construction: Green Building Design and Delivery*. 2nd ed. New Jersey: John Wiley & Sons.

Kuhtz, S. (2007). Adoption of sustainable development schemes and behaviours in Italy – barriers and solutions – what can educators do? *International Journal of Sustainability in Higher Education, 8* (2), 155-169.

Langston, C., and Mackley, C. (1998). The Role of Environmental Economics in the Cost Management of Projects. AACE International Transactions, Cincinnati OH.

Langston, C. A. and Ding, G. K. C. (2001). *Sustainable Practices in the Built Environment*. Oxford: Butterworth-Heinemann. Second edition.

LEED (2003) Green Building Rating System Committees, US Green Building Council. Retrieved from https://www.usgbc.org/Members/members_committees.asp

Loftness, V. et al. (2002) Building Investment Decisions Support (BIDS). ABSIC Research 2001-2002 Year End. Retrieved from http://nodem.pc.cc.cmu.edu/bids

Martin, S. (2002). Sustainability, systems thinking and professional practice. *Planet*, Special Edition **4**, 20-1.

Mills, E. (2002). Climate change, buildings, and the insurance sector: technological synergisms between adaptation and mitigation. *Building Research and Information* **31**(3-4), 255-277

Mills, E. (2003). *The Insurance and Risk Management Industries: New Players in the Delivery of Energy-Efficient Products and Services*. Energy Policy. Lawrence Berkeley National Laboratory, Report No. LBNL-43642. Retrieved from http://eetd.lbl.gov/emills/PUBS/Insurance_Case_Studies.html

Miyatake, Y. (1996). Technology development and sustainable construction. *Journal of Management in Engineering*, 12(4), 23 – 27.

Murray, P. E. and Cotgrave, A. J. (2007). Sustainability literacy: the future paradigm for construction education? *Structural Survey*, **25**(1), 7-23.

Muto, S. (2003). The public sector spurs green building. *Real Estate Journal of WSJ/Dow Jones*, July.

Nalewaik, A. and Venters, V. (2009). Cost engineering: Cost benefits of building green. *The AACE International Journal of Cost Estimation, Cost/Schedule Control, and Project Management*, 5(1), 28-34.

Nelson, A. J. (2007). *The Greening of U.S. Investment Real Estate—Market Fundamental, Prospects, and Opportunities*. Rosenberg Real Estate Equity Funds Research.

Orr, D. W. (2004). Can educational institutions learn? The creation of the Adam Joseph Lewis Center at Oberlin College, in Barlett, P.F. and Chase, G.W. (Eds), *Sustainability on Campus: Stories and Strategies for Change*. MIT Press, Cambridge, MA, pp. 159-75.

Panagiotakopoulos, P. D. and Jowitt, P. W. (2004). Representing and assessing sustainability in construction. In: Khosrowshahi, F. (Ed.), *20th Annual ARCOM Conference*, 1-3 Sept, Heriot Watt University. Association of Researchers in Construction Management, Vol. 2, 1305-11.

Parkin, S. (2000). Context and drivers for operationalizing sustainable development. *Proceedings of ICE Civil Engineering Journal*, **138**, 9-15.

Paumgartten, P. von (2003). The business case for high performance green buildings: Sustainability and its financial impact. *Journal of Facilities Management*, **2**(1), 26-34.

Perdan, S., Azapagic, A. and Clift, R. (2000). Teaching sustainable development to engineering students. *International Journal of Sustainability in Higher Education*, **1**(3), 267-79.

Richardson, G. R. A., Lynes, J. K. (2007). Institutional motivations and barriers to the construction of green buildings on campus: A case study of the University of Waterloo, Ontario. *International Journal of Sustainability in Higher Education*, **8**(3), 339-354.

Roper, K. O. and Beard, J. L. (2006). Justifying sustainable buildings – championing green operations. *Journal of Corporate Real Estate*, **8** (2), 91-103.

Rovers, R. (2003). The role of policies in promoting sustainable practices. *UNEP Industry and Environment*, **26** (2-3), 29-32. Retrieved from http://www.uneptie.org/media/review/vol26no2-3/005-098.pdf

Said, I., Rashideh, W. M., Osman, O., Razak, A. R. and Kooi, T. K. (2009). Modeling of Construction Firms Sustainability. Universiti Sains, Malaysia. Retrieved from http://eprints.usm.my/16094/1/Ilias_Said_4.pdf

Salama, M. and Al Saber, T. (2013) Imposing Green Building Regulations in Dubai. In: Smith, S (Ed.), *29th Annual ARCOM Conference*, September, University of Reading. Association of Researchers in Construction Management. http://www.arcom.ac.uk/-docs/proceedings/ar2013-1309-1320_Salama_AlSaber.pdf.

Salama, M. and Hana, A. R. (2010) Green Buildings and sustainable construction in the United Arab Emirates. In: Egbu, C. (Ed), D. J. (Ed.) *Proceedings of 26th Annual ARCOM Conference*, 6-8 September, Leeds, UK, Association of Researchers in Construction Management, 1397-1405.

Salama, M. and Hana, A. R. (2013) Green Building Strategic Model for UAE. In: Smith, S (Ed.), *29th Annual ARCOM Conference*, September, University of Reading. Association of Researchers in Construction Management. http://www.arcom.ac.uk/-docs/proceedings/ar2013-1321-1330_Salama_Hana.pdf.

Salama, M. and Salama, O. (2017) The Implementation of Green Building in the UAE: Challenges and Critical Success Factors. In Awad et al.,(Ed.), *International Conference on Sustainable Futures - ICSF*, Kingdom of Bahrain

Scofield, J. H., (2002). Early energy performance for a green academic building. *ASHRAE Transactions*, **108**(2), 1214-30.

Shelbourn, M. A., Bouchlaghem, D. M., Anumba, C. J., Carillo, P. M., Khalfan, M. K. and Glass, J. (2006). Managing knowledge in the context of sustainable construction. *Journal of Information Technology in Construction*, **11**, 57-71.

Shen, L. Y., Wu, Y. Z., Chan, E. H. W. and Hao, J. L. (2005). Application of system dynamics for assessment of sustainable performance of construction projects. *Journal of Zhejian University Science*, **6A**(4), 339-349.

Siddens, S. (2002), Verdant Horizon. *Consulting – Specifying Engineer*, October, pp. 30-34. Retrieved from http://www.syska.com/Sustainable/news/index.asp

Singh, R. K., Murty, H. R., Gupta, S. K. and Dikshit, A. K. (2009). An overview of sustainability assessment methodologies. *Ecological Indicators*, **9**(2), 189-212.

Sponge (2004). *Sponge Survey of Sustainability in the Construction Industry*. Sponge, London.

9

Sustainable Kingston (2010) Four Pillars of Sustainability. Retrieved from http://www.sustainablekingstone.ca/community-plan/four-pillars-of-sustainability

Thomson, C. S., El Haram, M. A., Hardcastle, C., Horner, R. M. W. (2008). Developing an urban sustainability assessment protocol reflecting the project lifestyle. In: Dainty, A. (Ed), *24th Annual ARCOM Conference*, 1-3 September, Cardiff, UK, Association of Researchers in Construction Management, 1155-1164.

Turner Construction Company (2008). Green Building Market Barometer. Retrieved from http://www.usgbc.org/ShowFile.aspx?DocumentID=5361

Ugwu and Haupt, T. C. (2007). Key performance indicators and assessment methods for infrastructure sustainability – a South African construction industry perspective. *Building and Environment*, **42**(2), 665-680.

UNFCC (n.d.) The Kyoto Protocol. Retrieved from https://unfccc.int/process/the-kyoto-protocol

U.S. Department of Energy (2003) *The Business Case for Sustainable Design In Federal Facilities*. Federal Energy Management Program (FEMP), in collaboration with the Interagency Sustainability Working Group.

US Green Building Council (2002) LEED Rating System, Version 2.1. Retrieved from http://www.usgbc.org/Docs/LEEDdocs/LEED_RS_v2-1.pdf

Vanegas, J. A., DuBose, J. R. and Pearce, A. R. (1996). Sustainable technologies for the building construction industry. *Proceedings of the Symposium on Design for the Global Environment*, Atlanta, USA, November 2-4.

Weier, J. (1996). Reaping What We Sow, referring to a study by the World Resources Institute. Retrieved from http://www.earthobservatory.gov.

Watkins, T. (2003). *Introduction to Cost Benefit Analysis*. Retrieved from http://www2.sjsu.edu/faculty/watkins/cba.htm

10 Sustainable Logistics and the Supply Chain

Shereen Nassar and Mohamed Salama

Learning outcomes

By completing this chapter, the reader will be able to:

■ Discuss the importance of logistics and supply chain management (SCM) for business success

■ Understand the role of logistics and SCM in the context of project management

■ Discuss the key attributes of sustainable logistics and SCM in green ports and maritime logistics

■ Discuss the application of the integrated framework for sustainable port and maritime logistics

Introduction

In today's global business environment, logistics has become one of the key determinants of sustainable competitive advantage. In the context of sustainable project management, every project will have to embrace a sustainable logistics system. Port and maritime logistics is classified as the most significant logistics system since it is considered to be the backbone for facilitating global trade. Around 80% of the world trade by volume, and 70% by value, is done by sea and is managed by seaports across the globe. It is evident that managing the pressures of sustainability is one of the critical challenges for creating value and ensuring growth across all businesses. Port and maritime industry is required to ensure high level of accountability and transparency on sustainability concerns including waste management, climate change and global warming, energy efficiency, employee health, safety and security, impacts on local society and coastal and local environmental health. Because of the global nature of the port and maritime sector, it encounters more challenges in improving sustainability performance. This chapter covers sustainable port and maritime logistics. It starts by presenting an overview of logistics, supply chain management and maritime logistics. The second section discusses sustainability in the context of supply chain and logistics management. The third section explicates green port and maritime logistics aspects. The fourth identifies sustainability issues and introduces an integrated framework for sustainable port and maritime logistics. It wraps up with a brief section on suggested areas for future research.

Logistics, SCM and maritime logistics

Logistics is an essential function for various types of businesses. It encompasses all the activities involved in managing the flow of inventory throughout a supply chain including raw materials, work in progress and final products. These activities incorporate order fulfillment, inbound and outbound transportation management, fleet management, inventory management, warehousing, material handling, third-party logistics service (3PL) management, product returns, supply and demand planning and logistics network design. The logistics process is extended to cover information management, supplier integration, environmental management, customer service, maintenance, quality and human resources management. Logistics is defined as *"the process of planning, implementing, and controlling procedures for the efficient and effective transportation and storage of goods including services, and related information from the point of origin to the point of consumption for the purpose of conforming to customer requirements"* (Mangan et al., 2012). Logistics is included in all levels of planning and implementation including strategic, tactical and operational.

Supply chain is a broader term than logistics. It encompasses the coordination between organisations involved via upstream and downstream linkages in a network, in various processes and activities that produce customer's value (Chopra and Meindl, 2007). The Council of Supply Chain Management Professionals (CSCMP, 2018) defines the supply chain management (SCM) function as:

"the planning and management of all activities involved in sourcing and procurement, conversion, and all logistics management activities. Importantly, it also includes coordination and collaboration with channel partners, which can be suppliers, intermediaries, third party service providers, and customers. In essence, supply chain management integrates supply and demand management within and across companies."

Rushton, et al. (2010), identified four main features of SCM which support successful planning and implementation of logistics operations. The four factors incorporate the following:

- The supply chain is seen as a single unit in which suppliers and end users are part of the planning process of integrated functions including procurement, manufacturing and logistics;
- Supply chain management is seen as a strategic planning process which deals with strategic decisions;
- Supply chain management considers inventory as a means to balance the flow of product through the chain;

■ Visibility of product demand in the downstream supply chain and stock levels in the upstream supply chain supported by integrated IT infrastructure is a key success factor.

Logistics and SCM: competitive drivers

Since 2000, logistics and supply chain management have been considered key factors for business success. The logistics objective is to get the right product in the right way, in the right quality and quantity, in the right location at the right time, at the right cost for the right customer. To this end, logistics management is seen as an integrated function through which all logistics activities, as well as other activities encompassing sales, marketing, finance, manufacturing and information technology, are coordinated and optimized.

Over the last two decades, the role of logistics activities in managing business performance has maximized and the logistics function has shifted from cost center to profit center. (Christopher, 2011). A number of factors has contributed to this shift including:

■ Supply chain competition rather than individual firm competition,

■ Globalisation of industry,

■ Industrial deregulation, personalization and customers taking control.

The transformation in business models has also been driven by the advancement in information communication technology, supply chain applications and industrial automation, including smart mobility, sensors, robotics and 3D printing, which have changed the competition drivers towards speed and short lead-time (Chartered Institute of Logistics and Transport, 2018). Figure 10.1 illustrates examples of sources of pressure on logistics systems.

Figure 10.1: Sources of pressure on logistics systems.

The logistics management system is one of the major determinants of today's competition which requires managing responsiveness, reliability, resilience and relationships. Figure 10.2 depicts the role of logistics in supporting various types of competitive positions.

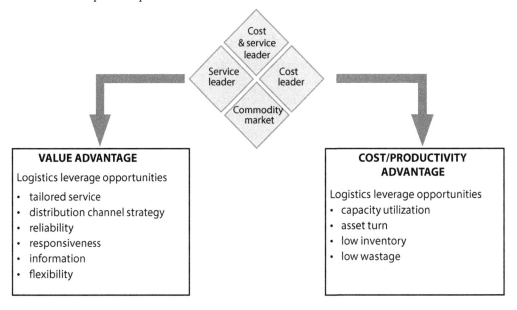

Figure 10.2 : The role of logistics in gaining a competitive advantage. *Source*: Rushton et al. (2010)

The role of logistics and SCM in the shift towards sustainable project management

Following the discussion about the crucial role of logistics and supply chain management in pursuit of sustainable competitive advantage, it becomes imperative that the project manager should be acquainted with the basic concepts of this area of knowledge. Project management methodologies have been historically introduced as a generic set of tools and techniques that can be applied to different types of project in various sectors, for example, new product development (NPD), which has been discussed in previous chapters.

The argument might be that logistics and SCM tend to lean more towards the strategic project management domain, that is the programme and portfolio level, managed at the corporate or business unit level rather than at the operational, individual project level. This does not eliminate the need for project managers at the appropriate level to have adequate knowledge of the key concepts and the relevant skills to design and manage the required activities to achieve an effective logistics and supply chain management system. This should be no different from the pursuit of, for example, a robust quality management system or an efficient risk management system, as well established constituents of the current project management methodologies.

Transportation is a key activity in logistics and supply chain management. Freight transport encompasses different modes, including maritime, air, rail and intermodal as well as road freight. Maritime transport is recognized as the backbone for facilitating world trade. Around 80% of the world trade by volume and 70% by value is done by sea and is managed by seaports across the globe (Cheng et al., 2015). The following section introduces port and maritime logistics as the core of this chapter.

Port and maritime logistics

Maritime logistics is a relatively new discipline which incorporates economic, managerial and operational aspects of shipping, ports and logistics (Song and Panayides, 2015). Traditionally, maritime transport was seen as a primary mode for global transportation of finished products and parts, and its role was limited to facilitate loading and discharge operations. Maritime logistics is a concept which has evolved due to the introduction of intermodal and multimodal transport, specifically the physically integrated transport modes as the outcome of introducing containerization intermodalism (D'Este, 1996). Such physical integration of various transport modes has triggered the need for organizational integration for enhanced economic performance (Panayides, 2002). Maritime logistics encompasses supply chain and logistics management as integrated concept (Panayides, 2006). Recently, more attention has been given to maritime logistics management by both academics and practitioners.

There are a number of factors contributed to the importance of maritime logistics from supply chain and logistics perspective, including globalization, outsourcing and off-shoring. In addition, technological advancement and smart applications in the transport sector encompassing logistics integration, containerization and the expansion of maritime industry, have reshaped the functional role of shipping and ports to meet the demand of enhanced value-added logistics services at global supply chain and logistics level. As a result, the need for more integrated transportation modes, e.g. multimodal and intermodal transport systems has augmented. The performance of maritime operations is greatly influenced by the ability to provide high quality logistics services along with the efficient and effective integration of transport and logistics activities (Song and Panayides, 2015).

Maritime logistics is an integrated part of the global logistics systems that encompasses transport and other logistical services. Sea freight occupies a major role in international and regional trade which is known as seaborne. At the macro level, nearly 90% of the international trade is shipped by sea (Rushton et al., 2010). The last decade witnessed a fast increase in global trade due to novel developments, fierce competition and deregulation, which resulted in restructuring the world maritime industry. Additionally, supply chain integration supports the business to business model, which in turn has altered the mode of transportation of cargo and international trade.

Maritime logistics and maritime transport are used interchangeably; however the former is more comprehensive and incorporates operational and service

10

aspects. Scholars and practitioners have recognized the need to integrate supply chain and logistics management concepts and perspective in managing maritime transport operations. Accordingly, maritime logistics should manage and integrate the physical flows of maritime transport as well as the associated information and financial flows. Implementing maritime logistics tools and strategies from supply chain and logistics management perspective help companies to improve their operational and financial performance (Panayides and Song, 2013). Port efficiency is one of the four dimensions of trade facilitation, along with customs environment, service sector infrastructure and regulatory environment (Wilson et al., 2003) . Operational efficiency in terms of minimal costs, emissions and fuel consumption and shorter lead-time, as well as service effectiveness through flexible, responsive and reliable services, are key indicators for the performance and value of maritime logistics system (Gudehus and Kotzab, 2012). Increasing the value of maritime logistics is a strategic goal of maritime industry, that in turn contributes to the value of the global logistics system. The development of port and maritime facilities and their related operations has a significant impact on the growth of maritime industry, coastal countries' economic development and the employment in the region (Paipai, 1999). As part of a supply chain and logistics network, ports have set of effects, and aim at reconciling short term goals, social and economic objectives and public and private interests (Dooms et al., 2012). Although, ports play an important role in economic growth, the development of port and maritime activities has an adverse impact on the environment causing various negative environmental impacts (Gupta et al., 2005, Dinwoodie et al., 2012, Kroger et al., 2006). This will be discussed in detail in this chapter.

The following section focuses on addressing sustainability in supply chain and logistics management.

Sustainable logistics and SCM

In today's business environment, sustainability is an important buzzword and a hot topic. Sustainability can be defined as the capability of being sustained in relation to, for example, energy sources, community well-being, economic development, etc. It might also refer to the capability of being able to maintain sustainable development without causing severe ecological damage or exhausting natural resources (Collins English Dictionary, 1998). Sustainable development is *"a development that meets the needs of the present without compromising the ability of future generations to meet their own needs"* (WCED, 1987). Sustainability is also connected to corporate social responsibility (CSR), which goes beyond environmental issues to cover aspects related to, for example, fair labour conditions, fair trade and ethical relationships with suppliers, customers and other stakeholders. Taking a more comprehensive approach, Hassini, et al. (2012) defined supply chain sustainability as *"the management of supply chain operations, resources, information, and funds in order to maximize the supply chain profitability while at the same time minimizing the environmental impacts and maximizing social well-being".*

A number of factors have contributed to the amplified concerns about sustainability, including issues related to climate change via global warming; the nature of energy demand and supply and the impact on energy consumption and prices; technology advancement in the area of renewable energy; the scarcity of non-renewable energy; concerns related to improving quality of life; and the growing pressure on businesses for more environmental and social transparency and accountability (Carter and Rogers, 2008, Kleindorfer et al., 2005, Carter and Liane Easton, 2011, Christopher, 2011). There are various parties who are seen as the source of sustainability pressure, including customers (external and internal), stakeholders, regulatory entities and NGOs (non-governmental organisations). Supply chain and logistics decisions might have a positive or a negative environmental and social impact when considering the selection of the supplier, carrier and modal choice, location decisions, vehicle routing and packaging selection.

The literature has addressed the main trends in supply chain management and logistics; some of them might significantly impact sustainability including globalisation, relationships and outsourcing, technology, lean versus agile systems and under-developed reverse flow of supply chain and logistics management (Christopher, 2011, Bowersox et al., 2000). The following section discusses the triple bottom line view which identifies the key sustainability dimensions of the impacts of business decisions.

Triple bottom line (TBL) perspective

The triple bottom line (TBL) concept was first introduced by Elkington (1997). This concept emphasises the significance of assessing the effect of business decisions on three main dimensions including environmental (e.g. climate change, pollution, depletion of non-renewable resources, etc.), Economic (e.g. business profitability, impact on citizens' financial security, etc. and social (e.g. better working and living conditions, good employment practice, etc.). Figure 10.3 draws examples of the impacts of business decisions on the three dimensions of sustainability.

Environmental	Economic	Social
• Climate change • Ozone depletion • Water management • Air pollution • Soil pollution • Pollution and live stock • River/sea/ocean pollution and fish stock • Water/hazardous chemical usages and discharges • Biodiversity management	• Gross Domestic Product • Return on investment • Labour and wages • Tax • Corruption • Business Ethics • Poverty lessening • Risk management • Consistent, profitable growth	• Health • Education • Human rights • Equal opportunity • Labour standards • Access to services and products • Diversity • Impact on community

Figure 10.3: Triple bottom line concept. Adapted from Christopher (2011)

10

In considering the TBL viewpoint, Seuring and Müller (2008) define sustainable supply chain management as

> *"the management of material, information and capital flows as well as cooperation among companies along the supply chain while taking goals from all three dimensions of sustainable development, i.e., economic, environmental and social, into account which are derived from customer and stakeholder requirements."*

Supply chain and logistics business environment has traditionally developed from single-channel systems, through bricks and mortar stores, moving to multiple-channel systems and online to offline (O2O) community services. As a result, stakeholders are able to closely monitor companies' sustainability related actions (Denktas-Sakar and Karatas-Cetin, 2012, Notteboom and Rodrigue, 2005). Sustainability is a concept which combines corporate social responsibility in a way that puts pressures upon businesses to actively respond to customers' and stakeholder's green and social concerns. Dinwoodie et al. (2012) recommend that organisations need to alter the way they delineate the logistics and supply chain and introduce a proper framework of environmental scanning. According to the UK's Department of the Environment, Transport and the Regions, a sustainable distribution system should comply with the following principles (DETR, 1999).

> *"[. . .] minimise pollution and reduce greenhouse gas emissions; reduce noise and disturbance from freight movements; manage development pressures on the landscape (both natural and manmade); and reduce the number of accidents, injuries and cases of ill health associated with freight movement. "*

According to the *Future of Transport – a network for 2030*, this freight policy was updated to move away from considering individual types of transport separately when addressing the specified objectives to have a more holistic view of various transport modes (DfT, 2004).

In the context of supply chain and logistics, TBL philosophy is adopted to identify that sustainability can ensure long term endurance and viability of the business as well as adding to the future well-being of the community and society. It is argued that these two goals are mutually supportive, in other words by implementing supply chain sustainability strategies, cost reduction can be achieved over the long term due to better use of resources (Christopher, 2011). Supply chain and logistics management is seen as an appropriate perspective to enhance sustainability. The main objective is to achieve greater effectiveness and efficiency in the business, which are aligned with sustainability goals and offer opportunities for sustainability improvement.

Carter and Rogers (2008) introduce a theoretical framework for supply chain sustainability which relied on the TBL theory that considers the interaction of social, environmental and economic performance. The specified framework has identified four facilitators of sustainable supply chain management. It combines integrated sustainability strategy, which should ensure the alignment of sustainable supply chain management initiatives; risk management, including contingency planning for both the upstream and downstream supply chains; organisation culture, which promotes sustainability values and ethics, and organisational citizenship; and transparency and visibility of supply chain activities, including supplier operations. Other literature has focused on corporate social responsibility, e.g. (Dyllick and Hockerts, 2002); green logistics, e.g. (McKinnon et al., 2015) and environmental logistics, e.g. (Aronsson and Huge Brodin, 2006). It is argued that sustainable logistics and supply chains require developing reverse logistics capabilities, measuring of emissions and greening of logistical and supply chains activities, including transportation, infrastructure network and vehicles, sourcing, design of product and packaging and green buildings (Grant et al., 2017) .

The following section identifies the key challenges for sustainable logistics which are related to carbon footprint and greenhouse gases emissions.

Greenhouse gases challenges and sustainable logistics

Climate change due to global warming and its impact on increasing the height of flood water and rising sea levels, are among the major environmental concerns, which continuously add more pressure on businesses to decarbonise their activities. Greenhouse gases are one of the major sources for potential environmental harm; these include carbon dioxide, nitrous oxide, methane and various fluorocarbons. Since these emissions are related to an activity, they can be referred to as its carbon footprint. The tremendous upsurge of economic activities around the globe resulted in a massive increase in the level of these gases over recent years. It is estimated that the current levels of greenhouse gases are around 430 parts per million (ppm) which indicates a more than 50% increase compared to the levels before the Industrial Revolution, when it was around 280ppm (Christopher, 2011).

Supply chain and logistics activities can be seen as major causes of greenhouse gas through manufacturing and transport. Globalisation of logistics and supply chain operations has resulted in moving products and parts longer distances, which has a real impact on their carbon footprint. It was estimated that logistics contributes 5.5 % of global greenhouse gas emissions, which is distributed among freight transport modes and logistics buildings (World Economic Forum / Accenture, 2009). The introduction of carbon taxes, emission trading schemes and regulatory change requires a proactive approach by supply chain and logistics managers to work on alternative strategies. Developing and executing realistic and feasible carbon mitigation strategies for the logistics sector is a challenge. The following section introduces the idea of integrated framework for minimising supply chain and logistics footprint.

An integrated framework for decarbonising logistics

The core focus of carbon mitigation strategies is freight transport, which contributes by 80-90% of logistics-related carbon emission. McKinnon et al. (2010) have identified six dimensions of carbon-mitigation efforts, which focus mainly on logistics activities and operations. These dimensions include:

10

1   Reducing the transport-intensity of supply chains

2   Using less carbon-heavy transport modes

3   Maximising vehicle utilisation

4   Improving the energy efficiency of the operations of freight transport

5   Decreasing the carbon intensity included in the energy used in freight transport

6   Reducing the carbon intensity involved in warehousing operations.

Christopher (2011) argue that minimising a supply chain's footprint should not be limited to greenhouse emissions, but must consider the broader impact of supply chain decisions on resources generally. In considering a firm's value chain, each decision which is taken at every stage has an impact on resource requirements and the broader environment. Table 10.1 provides examples of these decisions which have environmental implications.

Table 10.1: Examples of supply chain and logistics decisions which affect resource footprint. Adapted from (Christopher, 2011).

Stage	Related decisions
Design	Physical features of the product; Materials for the product and the packaging; Recycling and reuse
Source	Selection of suppliers; Locations of suppliers; Environmental impact of supply source
Make	Enhancing the efficiency of energy; Elimination of the emissions and pollutions; Minimising waste, scrappage and rework
Deliver	Reconsidering the mode of transport; Optimising network configuration; Minimising transport intensity
Return	Developing closed-loop supply chain; Managing end of product's life; Developing reverse logistics capabilities.

In the following section, green port and maritime logistics issues, as the core of this chapter, are discussed in detail.

Green port and maritime logistics

Green maritime logistics is defined as *"an attempt to attain an acceptable environmental performance in the maritime transport supply chain, while at the same time respecting traditional economic performance criteria."* (Psaraftis, 2016). Maritime emission and the efficient use of energy are the core of this section. Green maritime logistics is a strategic goal which is not easy to attain since it involves socio-economic elements. Therefore, it requires various trade-offs which need to be examined and assessed to come up with feasible and practical solutions.

This section starts by addressing the main environmental impacts of port and maritime logistics. Then, detailed discussion on aspects related to green port and maritime logistics is introduced.

Environmental effects of ports and maritime logistics

One of the key ecological effects generated by ports is the emissions of greenhouse gases causing air pollution and global warming (Lashof and Ahuja, 1990). Ships are key source of various air pollutants including CO_2, CO, SO_2, etc. It is stated that container ships are the key source of CO_2 emissions in the shipping industry (Psaraftis and Kontovas, 2009). Health problems (e.g. athma, lung cancer, cardiovascular disease, premature mortality and other respiratory diseases) are another important factor, which affects local residents surrounding ports (Bailey and Solomon, 2004).

In addition, landside activities, especially cargo operations occurring at terminals, constitute another source of air pollution. Air quality is also affected by dust emissions due to handling bulk cargo, consumption of electricity, trucks, emission from cargo handling vehicles and cranes (United Nations, 1992). Inland transport which is used to connect shipments moved at ports to hinterland emit greenhouse gases.

Water pollution is another crucial ecological concern which greatly impacts marine ecosystems. Shipping operations might intentionally or accidently harm the environment in terms of destroying natural habitats, as well as negatively affecting ports' related economic activities (Talley, 2006, Heaver, 2006). Sources of water pollution include ballast water, waste disposal of ship's operations, cargo residue as well as residue of fuel oil (Ng and Song, 2010). Water pollution is caused by operational activities and might be catastrophic in the case of oil spillage, which causes health hazards (Gupta et al., 2005). Coastal and marine ecology is impacted by marine pollutants, since they might harm natural habitants surrounding port waters and damage fish stock and coastal ecology (United Nations, 1992). In addition, large ships need upgrading and maintenance of the infrastructure of the maritime access that might lead to contaminated sludge due to dredging to widen and deepen the navigation channel. Natural geographical characteristics and the sea floor might be altered, resulting in a disruptive effect on marine ecosystems from civil operations and dredging (Peris-Mora et al., 2005).

Waste disposal (including liquid, solid and hazardous) of ports and maritime logistics causes significant impact on marine ecosystems, and comes from industrial activities, port operations and construction projects. Careful attention should be paid to industrial waste management, as the waste is mostly toxic. In addition, solid waste, consignments operations waste and waste lubricant are other pollution sources. Disposal of the polluted and toxic materials on land has harmful impact on plants, from leakage of polluted materials, smell and unpleasant views. Poor waste management has a harmful impact on the marine ecosystem and surrounding area.

10

The environmental effects of ports are not limited to existing ship, port and transport operations in their hinterland, but extend to cover the development and extension of existing ports, which should ensure sustainable development. Ports' environmental sustainability is seen as imperative and requires various trade-offs to make it economically feasible (Lam and Notteboom, 2014).

Issues related to green port and maritime logistics

Maritime logistics, as part of the logistics system, is dealing with the above-mentioned environmental concerns, which have grown due to recent environmental maritime disasters including oil spillages and harmful emissions. In addition, future environmental plans add more pressure on maritime logistics industry. The EU white paper published in 2011 has announced challenging targets for transport greenhouse gases emissions by a minimum of 60% reduction against 1990 levels that should be achieved by 2050. In considering maritime logistics, the target is to diminish EU CO_2 emissions from maritime bunker fuels by 40% (if feasible by 50%) (EU, 2011).

As a result, great attention was paid to address these concerns by regulatory bodies, scholars and practitioners. The approach followed to manage maritime environmental concerns is more comprehensive as it targets emissions reduction as a reactive operational approach, as well as a more proactive strategic approach through adopting green logistics and transport concept across a supply chain. To do so, supply chain and logistics, as integrated unit of business analysis, should be considered (Fahimnia et al., 2015, Song and Parola, 2015). There are three dimensions of the raised maritime environmental concerns, including operational, technical and economic. In their study, Davarzani et al. (2016), Roh et al. (2016) and Psaraftis, (2016) provide the following examples of these concerns:

- Regulatory bodies raised a concern related to the effect of burning large amount of sulfur fuel at sea on busy inhabited areas that resulted in the introduction of Emission Control Areas (ECAs) which requires ships to shift to low sulfur fuel (As per regulation 14 of the IMO[1], less than 0.1% sulfur by weight compared to 3.5% outside ECAs). In addition, other indicators are employed including the use of scrubbers, slow steaming in the coastal area, and converting to cleaner fuels, such as liquified natural gas and diesel (Zis et al., 2014).

- In considering ship technology and construction, as per the Energy Efficiency Design Index (EEDI), some ships' design and technology are greener and more environmentally friendly compared to others. New designs and modes of ships are greener in terms of energy efficiency. Cleaner technology is used in the design of the hull and engine. In some ports, EEDI was considered in deciding the port fees as a means of promoting more energy efficient shipping. Route optimisation, focusing on currents and weather, is also considered by shipping lines to save energy. Additionally, trim and ballast might be improved

---

1   http://www.imo.org/en/OurWork/Environment/PollutionPrevention/AirPollution/Pages/Sulfur-oxides-(SOx)-%E2%80%93-Regulation-14.aspx (Accessed 4/1/2018).

for more efficient use of fuel[2]. It was concluded that gas is better in terms of environmental performance compared to diesel, suggesting the usage of bio-fuels as a means to diminish the shipping impact on climate change and global warming (Bengtsson et al., 2012). In addition to ship type, ship size has been found to be another important factor in determining emissions (Walsh and Bows, 2012). It is argued that due to growing global environmental and green awareness, it is highly expected that shipping companies are going to implement green practices and to have more environmentally friendly systems and operations (Yang et al., 2013). The chief challenge which shipping companies face is the economic feasibility of these practices (Cheng and Tsai, 2009).

■ As an operational concern which impacts environment, at berth ships are encouraged to switch off their generators and engines and use the port's local electricity supply. This process is called *cold ironing* (Zis et al., 2014). For the purpose of automated cargo handling and movement of containers, the port's local electricity can be used to power equipment and cranes. Here, there is a possibility of using renewable energy relying on the introduction of regenerative technology (assuming that most ports are located in windy areas) which might result in 30% reduction in the consumption of crane energy. Current studies examine the feasibility of using batteries to charge cranes and vehicles for moving containers in ports. Progress in this area will contribute towards diminishing emissions and maximising energy efficiency and in turn environmental performance of the ports and maritime logistics.

■ To diminish the environmental effect and pursue green operations over the long term, Roh et al., (2016) discuss a number of legislations and regulations related to ports' construction and extension which have been developed at both national and international levels for the purpose of incorporating environmental and green issues into the main port development strategies, relying on stricter standards. Here are some examples of these legislations:

　　□ In the EU there are related legislations (i.e. Classification Societies – Regulation (EC) No 391/2009, Ship-Source Pollution – Directive 2000/59/EC, Marine Equipment – Directive 96/98/EC and Directive 2014/90/EU),

　　□ USA (i.e. Diesel Emission Reduction Act (DERA),

　　□ Singapore (i.e. Environmental Protection and Management Act (Cap.94A), etc.),

　　□ Australia (i.e. Environmental Protection Act 1986 (WA),

　　□ New Zealand (i.e. Resource Management (Marine Pollution) Regulations).

It is argued that going green in ports and maritime logistics has a competitive edge (Dinwoodie et al., 2012). Environmental and ecological aspects are seen as great incentives for potential investors and trading partners (Lee and Lam, 2012).

10

2　IMO study of GHG emissions, http://www.imo.org/en/OurWork/Environment/PollutionPrevention/AirPollution/Pages/GHG-Emissions.aspx (Accessed 4/1/2018).

However, ports encounter incremental challenges to go green, particularly when global buyers put pressures on ports operators and service providers to ensure environmentally friendly operations and practices, which are a requirement in their supply chains. Although, the great awareness of green ports and maritime logistics is largely observed, academic research in this area is still underdeveloped (Davarzani et al., 2016, Denktas-Sakar and Karatas-Cetin, 2012, Notteboom and Winkelmans, 2001, Notteboom and Rodrigue, 2005). In addition, there is a gap in extant literature in relation to examining green ports and maritime logistics in a wider sustainability context.

Green port and maritime logistics and sustainable development

Lai et al. (2011) claim that green port and maritime logistics are concerned with more efficient utilization of port resources, including human, operational and natural resources. Although efficient activities are expected to reduce costs, there is a lack of empirical evidence of the impact of greening port and maritime activities on environmental performance (Lai and Wong, 2012). Pazirandeh and Jafari (2013) and Kohn and Huge Brodin (2008) come up with the same conclusion. McKinnon et al. (2010) argue that current ports' methodology is to evaluate the environmental impact after implementing optimization of conventional objectives, e.g. minimizing cost (McKinnon et al., 2010). They identified the need for robust and explicit environmental measures during the optimization process, simultaneously with traditional objectives. Ports and maritime logistics managers perceive the importance of how greening port and maritime logistics may affect the measurement of effectiveness and efficiency (Pazirandeh and Jafari, 2013).

The empirical findings show that green logistics and maritime business are the corporate strategies through which sustainable growth and competitive advantage can be achieved. The green logistics approach has proved its concept in a number of developed countries, which is not the case in many developing countries (Lam and Notteboom, 2014, Notteboom and Winkelmans, 2001). In addition, sustainable growth, which is linked to greening port and maritime logistics, varies from one country to another in considering the significance of the related ports to the rest of the globe.

The following section will discuss the wider ports and maritime logistics sustainability context, focusing on triple bottom line concept and ending by introducing an integrated framework for sustainable port and maritime logistics.

Sustainability of port and maritime logistics

Supply chain sustainability concept applies to ports and maritime logistics, as a sub-context of the wider supply chain and logistics management context, that incorporate sustainable operations and resources to minimise environmental emissions, and maximise social well-being and profitability. The port and maritime logistics sector provides global supply chain services as it represents a significant node in the seaport network where the tasks are performed. Ports and maritime logistics are an important determinant of supply chain sustainability (Denktas-Sakar and Karatas-Cetin 2012). In satisfying economic demands and industrial activity, port authorities, which vary in activity profile, geographical surrounding and size, have to ensure sustainable development, cost reduction, risk mitigation and compliance with legislation (Puig et al. 2014). Hence, there is a need to evaluate sustainability dimensions of port and maritime activities that should inform ports' decision makers for optimal decisions and support future sustainable development strategies. Recently, sustainable port and maritime supply chain and logistics have received more attention from scholars and practitioners. Port sustainability is defined as *"business strategies and activities that meet the current and future needs of the port and its stakeholders, while protecting and sustaining human and natural resources."* (AAPA (America Association of Port Authority) 2007). This requires integration of organizational units of maritime (including shipping, ports, companies, etc.) throughout a supply chain, and coordination of physical flow of materials (e.g. bulk, container and general cargoes), financial and information flows. The main objective is to enhance the competitiveness of a supply chain as one unit, through satisfying customer demands in a way that ensures sustainable environmental, social and economic performance. In her recent study to design a sustainable maritime supply chain, Lam (2015) identified the four key customer requirements including

1 Price and cost competitiveness

2 Pollution elimination,

3 Efficient consumption of resources and fuel; and

4 Health, safety and security.

It is argued that extant literature has paid more attention to green and environmental aspects and impacts rather than economic and social ones (Gupta et al. 2005, Dinwoodie et al. 2012, Hassini et al. 2012, Roh et al. 2016).

Supply chain sustainability aims at delivering a value package to the end user through collaboration with supply chain partners, e.g. suppliers and logistics service providers. The interrelationship between port and maritime players, such as terminal operators, port authorities, private and public shipping companies, import and export companies, and other partners highlights the important role of stakeholders in achieving sustainability (Davarzani et al. 2016). The growing concerns over some important issues like greenhouse gases and global warming, biodiversity loss and health issues, drive sustainability to be at the strategic level of corporations, taking into account the long-term goals of operations and the stakeholders' expectations (Lam and Notteboom 2014).

Sustainability entails concurrent balancing of the environmental, economic and social dimensions in performing business functions at both strategic, tactical and operational levels. Therefore, ports' sustainable development strategies must consider the limited environmental resources, including space and the high-impact

10

interactions with the associated hinterlands. This chapter adopts an integrated approach in discussing sustainable ports development, which addresses the three key aspects of sustainability, encompassing environmental, social and economic.

Sustainable green port and maritime logistics

It is evident in port and maritime activities that a sustainable development strategy and related business plan must incorporate environmental management as an essential component of any operation, which is efficient, sustainable and compliant with legislation (Puig et al., 2015). The adoption of green marketing strategies and environmental programs result in enhanced environmental performance and competitive position (Gimenez et al., 2012, Zhu and Sarkis, 2004). In addition, the implantation of ISO 14001 standards would contribute to better environmental performance (Yang et al., 2013).

Port and maritime partners, including port authorities and shipping companies, need to work together to eliminate environmental damage produced by their operations. It is stated that ports have special harbour dues for ships with voluntary speed limits or with emissions which contain low sulfur content (Puig et al., 2014). For the container shipping industry, CO_2 emission reduction is a core concern in attaining economic and environmental sustainability (Qi and Song, 2012). Green/environmental practices in the shipping industry might include the use of clean burning fuels with low sulfur, green design for ships and green materials and equipment which have positive impact environmental performance and company's competitive position (Yang et al., 2013). Ports' projects need to be assessed by the urban authorities to ensure there are no negative impacts on residents around the port's location to avoid any future conflict with the surrounding community (Daamen and Vries, 2013).

Regular actions are required to eliminate environmental damage caused by ports' operations, including monitoring programs to avoid unethical behaviour or illegal environmental or social actions by ports and maritime partners, and these actions have a positive effect on green performance (Carter and Rogers, 2008, Yang et al., 2013). Besides, regular ship inspection by port authorities is essential for ports' sustainable development.

Employee education, training, and welfare programs are important in environmental management, and result in diminishing the harmful environmental actions and in turn enhancing green performance (Gimenez et al., 2012).

Sustainable social port and maritime

Sustainable social performance of the port and maritime supply chain focuses on the requirements of corporate social responsibility (CSR). In the port and maritime industry, implementing CSR includes improving employees' job satisfaction, partners' relationship, customer loyalty, authorities, community and economic performance (Fafaliou et al., 2006). Literature has confirmed the positive impact of CSR on economic and non-economic performance (Lu et al., 2009). It is widely confirmed that socially responsible companies which add economic and ethical values to their local community and society are more likely to increase their profit and enhance their reputation (Drobetz et al., 2014). Environmental programs have positive impacts on society and local communities. Environmentally friendly operations and activities improve the employees' working conditions and the quality of life for the internal and external community (Gimenez et al., 2012). It is argued that a company's reputation and social performance can be improved through ensuring employees' health and safety, improving working conditions and providing support to society's projects (Roh et al., 2016). Promoting a positive image and establishing relationship based on trust with the local community and the wider society require port authorities to exert substantial efforts (Puig et al., 2015). In addition, positive financial impacts can be achieved through better transparency, relying on increased CSR reporting which offers low cost information for various stakeholders (Drobetz et al., 2014). In considering the supply chain and logistics context, Lam (2015) addressed the importance of including the concerns of stakeholders in attaining social sustainability. The literature indicates that more investigations are required on how to improve social performance to achieve sustainable development in the port and maritime industry (Lam, 2015).

Sustainable economic port and maritime

The port and maritime industry has always a strong focus on economic performance. Liner shipping companies endeavour to maximise their financial and operational efficiencies (Carter and Rogers, 2008). It is stated that using more green processes and materials has a positive effect on the efficient use of resources and in turn cost reduction (Gimenez et al., 2012). It is contended that the integration of a company's environmental responsibility into their financial strategies can lead to cost savings through greater efficiency, and higher revenue from an enhanced brand image and better stakeholder relations (Hoffman and Ventresca, 1999). Sustainable port and maritime industry, within the supply chain context, needs to be economically viable and to be able to generate and enhance profitability. Profitable companies have the financial capabilities to invest in a sustainable manner in green processes and activities which allows them to improve their environmental performance (Stefan and Paul, 2008).

Port and maritime optimisation aims at synchronising the processes and actors who are involved in the maximum profit gained (Lam and Van de Voorde, 2011). Economic benefit is the main driver for achieving a high level of supply chain integration which is applied to port and maritime logistics. This requires a high level of collaboration among the port and maritime supply chain's partners, as the main driver for enhanced environmental practices that can have positive effect on environmental performance and businesses' competitive position (Gotschol et al., 2014, De Giovanni and Zaccour, 2014). In their recent paper focusing on the dynamics in sustainable port and hinterland operations, Hou and Geerlings (2016) concluded that the major challenge for the shift towards sustainable ports in relation to hinterland transport system is not to install new technology, but to develop novel governance arrangements.

Environmental management can diminish the negative impacts of non-green activities on the environment and improve a company's competitive advantage. It is contended that successful environmental management can enhance a firm's image and offers real opportunities for companies to improve their capabilities (Hansmann and Claudia, 2001). It is also evident that enhanced environmental risk management practices are able to diminish the probability of the occurrence of environmental natural and man-made disasters, that have a negative impact on the company's anticipated liquidity and cash flows, including fines, lawsuits, reputation damage and clean-up costs of environmental accidents, etc. (Sharfman and Fernando, 2008).

An integrated framework for sustainable port and maritime logistics

Extant literature showed a number of frameworks for sustainable port and maritime logistics. It is claimed that ports' sustainability performance varies from one port to another, even in the case of implementing a global sustainability framework (Denktas-Sakar and Karatas-Cetin, 2012). It is useful for port management and stakeholders to have a generic and structured framework for port and maritime sustainability which incorporates the key indicators of port's sustainability performance. Figure 10.4 presents an integrated framework for port sustainability relying on the triple bottom line view.

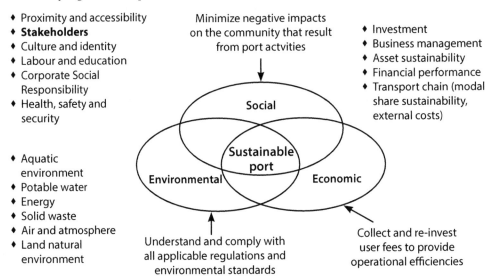

Figure 10.4: An integrated framework for sustainable port and maritime. *Source*: Denktas-Sakar and Karatas-Cetin, (2012)

It is evident that managing the pressures of sustainability is one of the critical challenges for creating value and ensuring growth across all businesses. The port and maritime industry is required to ensure a high level of accountability and transparency on sustainability concerns, including waste management, climate change and global warming, energy efficiency, employee health, safety and security, impacts on local society and coastal and local environmental health. Because of the global nature of the port and maritime sector, it encounters more challenges in improving sustainability performance and managing sustainability risks. These challenges include poor coordination in legislation and regulations at global, regional, and local policy levels and the highly fragmented nature within port and maritime industry itself (Coady et al., 2013).

Further research

Cheng et al. (2015) stated that although there is substantial academic effort in the field of port and maritime sustainability, there are various areas in the port and maritime supply chain which require investigation, including:

- Sustainability measurement and indicators;
- Cost and profit sharing of sustainability initiatives;
- Sustainable network design;
- Coordination and relationship issues in managing sustainable development;,
- Cultural issues.

Summary

This chapter shed the light on sustainable port and maritime logistics as one of the important topics within the supply chain and logistics context. The chapter started by providing an overview of logistics, supply chain management and maritime logistics concepts. Then, it explained sustainability within supply chain and logistics management field. After that, the chapter discussed in detail the green and environmental aspects of port and maritime logistics. Finally, detailed discussion on sustainability in port and maritime logistics was presented and wrapped up by introducing a number of topics for future research.

10

End of chapter questions

1   In the design stage, supply chain decisions which impact resource footprint include…

   A.   Location of suppliers

   B.   Optimising network configuration

   C.   Enhancing the efficiency of energy

   D.   Materials for the product and packaging

2 The following factors are related to social dimensions of triple bottom line concept except…

A. Labour standards

B. Impact on community

C. Business ethics

D. Human rights

3 Decarbonisation of freight transport includes…

A. Reducing the intensity of carbon in warehousing operations

B. Using less carbon-heavy transport modes

C. Maximising vehicle utilisation

D. All of the above

4 The following actions are required to reduce the environmental damage caused by ports' operations except…

A. Regular ship inspection

B. Monitoring programmes to avoid unethical behaviour

C. Local environmental policies and regulations

D. Employees training programmes and welfare

5 To design a sustainable maritime supply chain, the following customer requirements should be identified…

A. Efficient use of resources

B. Pollution elimination

C. Implementation of ISO 14001

D. Health, safety and security

6 The challenges of green initiatives in ports and maritime logistics include…

A. Global buyers' pressure for green operations

B. Lack of legislations and regulations

C. Underdeveloped academic research on green ports and maritime

D. A & C

7 The following drivers contribute to the importance of maritime logistics except…

A. Innovative technology

B. Off-shoring

C. On-shoring

D. Outsourcing

8 Sustainable supply chain management requires the following enablers except…

A. Risk management

B. Agile system

C. Visibility of supply chain activities

D. Organisation culture

9   The challenging targets for 2050 for sustainable freight transport in European Union (EU) combine...

    A. A reduction of EU CO_2 emissions from maritime bunker fuel by 40% - 50%

    B. A reduction of greenhouse gases emissions by 40% against 1990

    C. A and B

    D. None of the above

10   The following are the technical aspects of maritime environmental concerns except...

    A. Route optimisation

    B. Improving trim and ballast for efficient use of fuel

    C. Using batteries to change crane and vehicles for moving containers in ports

    D. Green design of modes of ships

References

AAPA (America Association of Port Authority) (2007). *Embracing the concept of sustainability as A standard business practice for ports and the association.* http://aapa.files.cms-plus.com/PDFs/sustainability_resolutions.pdf.

Aronsson, H. & Huge Brodin, M. (2006). The environmental impact of changing logistics structures. *The International Journal of Logistics Management,* **17** (3), 394-415.

Bailey, D. & Solomon, G. (2004). Pollution prevention at ports: Clearing the air environmental impact. *Assessment Review,* **24,** 749-774.

Bengtsson, S., Fridell, E. & Andersson, K. (2012). Environmental assessment of two pathways towards the use of biofuels in shipping. *Energy Policy,* **44,** 451-463.

Bowersox, D. J., Closs, D. J. & Stank, T. P. (2000). Ten mega-trends that will revolutionize supply chain logistics. *Journal of Business Logistics,* **21** (2), 1-15.

Carter, C. R. & Liane Easton, P. (2011). Sustainable supply chain management: evolution and future directions. *International Journal of Physical Distribution & Logistics Management,* **41** (1), 46-62.

Carter, C. R. & Rogers, D. S. (2008). A framework of sustainable supply chain management: moving toward new theory. *International Journal of Physical Distribution & Logistics Management,* **38** (5), 360-387.

Chartered Institute of Logistics and Transport (UK); (2018). *Professional development: Developing professional performance.* https://ciltuk.org.uk/Portals/0/Documents/PD/2018/CILT_Prof_Dev_20pp_A4_0318_no_marks_HR_WEB.pdf.

Cheng, T. C. E., Farahani, R. Z., Lai, K.-H. & Sarkis, J. (2015). Sustainability in maritime supply chains: Challenges and opportunities for theory and practice. *Transportation Research Part E,* **78,** 1-2.

Cheng, Y. H. & Tsai, Y. L. (2009). Factors influencing shippers to use multiple country consolidation services in international distribution centers. *International Journal of Production Economics,* **122** (1), 78-88.

Chopra, S. & Meindl, P. (2007). *Supply Chain Management: Strategy, planning, and operation,* New Jersey, NJ, Pearson Prentice-Hall.

Christopher, M. (2011). *Logistics and Supply Chain Management,* London, 4th edn. London: Financial Times Prentice Hall.

10

Coady, L., Lister, J., Strandberg, C. & Ota, Y. (2013) *The role of corporate social responsibility (CSR) in the international shipping sector*. The Northern European Symposium on CSR in Shipping Copenhagen, Denmark.

Collins English Dictionary (1998). HarperCollins, Glasgow, p. 1543.

CSCMP (Council Of Supply Chain Management Professionals) (2018). Glossary of terms, Available at: https://cscmp.org/CSCMP/Educate/SCM_Definitions_and_Glossary_of_Terms/CSCMP/Educate/SCM_Definitions_and_Glossary_of_Terms.aspx. Last accessed 29/03/2018.

D'Este, G. (1996). An event-based approach to modelling intermodal freight systems. *International Journal of Physical Distribution and Logistics Management*, **26**, 4-15.

Daamen, T. A. & Vries, I. (2013). Governing the European port-city interface: institutional impacts on spatial projects between city and port. *Journal of Transport Geography*, **27** (1), 4-13.

Davarzani, H., Fahimnia, B., Bell, M. & Sarkis, J. (2016). Greening ports and maritime logistics: A review. *Transportation Research Part D: Transport and Environment*, **48**, 473-487.

De Giovanni, P. & Zaccour, G. (2014). A two-period model of closed-loop supply chain. *European Journal of Operational Research*, **232** (1), 22-40.

Denktas-Sakar, G. & Karatas-Cetin, C. (2012). Port sustainability and stakeholder management in supply chains: a framework on resource dependence theory. *The Asian Journal of Shipping and Logistics*, **28** (3), 301-319.

DETR (1999). *Sustainable Distribution: a Strategy*, Department for the Environment, Transport and the Regions, London.

DfT (2004). *The Future of Transport – a network for 2030*, White Paper CM 6234, Department for Transport, London.

Dinwoodie, J., Tuck, S., Knowles, H., Benhin, J. & Sansom, M. (2012). Sustainable development of maritime operations in ports. *Business Strategy and the Environment*, **21** (2), 111-126.

Dooms, M., Verbeke, A. & Haezendonck, E. (2012). Stakeholder management and path dependence in large-scale transport infrastructure development: the port of Antwerp case (1960-2010). *Transport Geography*, **27**, 14-25.

Drobetz, W., Merikas, A., Mrika, A. & Tsionas, M. G. (2014). Corporate social responsibility disclosure: The case of international shipping. *Transportation Research Part E*, **71**, 18-44.

Dyllick, T. & Hockerts, K. (2002). Beyond the business case for corporate sustainability. *Business Strategy and the Environment*, **11**, 130-141.

Elkington, J. (1997). *Cannibals with Forks: The Triple Bottom Line of 21st Century Business*, Capstone Publishing.

Eu (2011). *White Paper on Transport: Roadmap to a Single European Transport Area – Towards a competitive and resource efficient transport system*. European Commission.

Fafaliou, I., Lekakou, M. & Theotokas, I. (2006). Is the European shipping industry aware of corporate social responsibility? The case of the Greek-owned short sea shipping companies. *Marine Policy*, **30** (4), 412-419.

Fahimnia, B., Sarkis, J. & Eshragh, A. (2015). A tradeoff model for green supply chain planning:A leanness-versus-greenness analysis. *Omega*, **54**, 173-190.

Gimenez, C., Sierra, V. & Rodon, J. (2012). Sustainable operations: Their impact on the triple bottom line. *International Journal of Production Economics*, **140** (1), 149-159.

Gotschol, A., De Giovanni, P. & Esposito Vinzi, V. (2014). Is environmental management an economically sustainable business? *Journal of Environmental Management*, **144**, 73-82.

Grant, D. B., Wong, C. Y. & Trautrims, A. (2017). *Sustainable Logistics and Supply Chain Management: Principles and practices for sustainable operations and management*, Kogan Page Publishers.

Gudehus, T. & Kotzab, H. (2012). *Comprehensive Logistics,* 2nd ed. Berlin: Springer.

Gupta, A. K., Gupta, S. K. & Patil, R. S. (2005). Environmental management plan for port and harbor. *Clean Technologies and Environmental Policy,* **7** (2), 133-141.

Hansmann, K. W. & Claudia, K. (2001). Environmental management policies, in Sarkis, J. (Ed.), *Green Manufacturing and Operations: From Design to Delivery and Back,* Sheffield, Greenleaf.

Hassini, E., Surti, C. & Searcy, C. (2012). A literature review and a case study of sustainable supply chains with a focus on metrics. *International Journal of Production Economics,* **140** (1), 69-82.

Heaver, T. (2006). The evolution and challenges of port economics, in Brooks, M.R. and Cullinane, K. (eds.), *Devolution, Port Governance and Port Performance,* Amsterdam:, Elsevier Ltd.

Hoffman, A. J. & Ventresca, M. J. (1999). The institutional framing of policy debates: economics versus the environment. *American Behavioral Scientist,* **42** (8), 1368-1391.

Hou, L. & Geerlings, H. (2016). Dynamics in sustainable port and hinterland operations: A conceptual framework and simulation of sustainability measures and their effectiveness, based on an application to the Port of Shanghai. *Journal of Cleaner Production,* **135**, 449-456.

Kleindorfer, P. R., Singhal, K. & Wassenhove, L. N. (2005). Sustainable operations management. *Production and Operations Management,* **14** (4), 482-492.

Kohn, C. & Huge-Brodin, M. (2008). Centralised distribution systems and the environment: How increased transport work can decrease the environmental impact of logistics. *International Journal of Logistics Research and Applications,* **11**(3), 229-245

Kroger, K., Gardner, J. P. A., Rowden, A. A. & Wear, R. G. (2006). Long-term effects of a toxic algal bloom on subtidal soft-sediment macroinvertebrate communities in Wellington Harbour. *New Zealand. Estuarine, Coastal and Shelf Science,* **67** (4), 589-604.

Lai, K.-H., Lun, V. Y., Wong, C. W. & Cheng, T. (2011). Green shipping practices in the shipping industry: Conceptualization, adoption, and implications. *Resources, Conservation and Recycling,* **55** (6), 631-638.

Lam, J. S. L. (2015). Designing a sustainable maritime supply chain: A hybrid QFD–ANP approach. *Transportation Research Part E: Logistics and Transportation Review,* **78**, 70-81.

Lam, J. S. L. & Notteboom, T. (2014). The greening of ports: a comparison of port management tools used by leading ports in Asia and Europe. *Transport Reviews,* **34** (2), 169-189.

Lam, J. S. L. & Van De Voorde, E. (2011). Scenario analysis for supply chain integration in container shipping. *Maritime Policy Manage,* **38** (7), 705-725.

Lashof, D. A. & Ahuja, D. R. (1990). Relative contributions of greenhouse gas emissions to global warming. *Nature,* **344**, 529-531.

Lee, C. K. M. & Lam, J. S. L. (2012). Managing reverse logistics to enhance sustainability of industrial marketing. *Industrial Marketing Management,* **41** (4), 589-598.

Lu, C. S., Lin, C. C. & Tu, C. J. (2009). Corporate social responsibility and organisational performance in container shipping. *International Journal of Logistics Research and Applications,* **12** (2), 119-132.

Mangan, J. J., Lalwani, C. C., Butcher, T. & Javadpour, R. (2012). *Global Logistics and Supply Chain Management,* Chichester, John Wiley & Sons.

McKinnon, A., Browne, M., Whiteing, A. & Piecyk, M. (2015). *Green Logistics: Improving the environmental sustainability of logistics,* Kogan Page Publishers.

McKinnon, A., Cullinane, S., Browne, M. & Whiteing, A. (2010). *Green Logistics: Improving the Environmental Sustainability of Logistics* London, Kogan Page.

10

Ng, A. K. Y. & Song, S. (2010). The environmental impacts of pollutants generated by routine shipping operations on ports. *Ocean & Coastal Management, 53*, 301-311.

Notteboom, T. E. & Winkelmans (2001). Structural changes in logistics: how will port authorities face the challenge? *Maritime policy and management, 28* (1), 71.

Notteboom, T. E. & Rodrigue, J.-P. (2005). Port regionalization: towards a new phase in port development. *Maritime Policy & Management, 32* (3), 297-313.

Paipai, E. (1999). *Guidelines for Port Environmental Management*, Report SR 554, London: Department of the Environment, Transport and the Regions.

Panayides, P. M. (2002). Economic organization of intermodal transport. *Transport Reviews, 22* (4), 401-414.

Panayides, P. M. (2006). Maritime logistics and global supply chains: towards a research agenda. *Maritime Economics and Logistics* 8(2), 3-18.

Panayides, P. M. & Song, D.-W. (2013). Maritime logistics as an emerging discipline. *Maritime Policy & Management, 40* (3), 295-308.

Pazirandeh, A. & Jafari, H. (2013). Making sense of green logistics. *International Journal of Productivity and Performance Management, 62* (8), 889-904.

Peris-Mora, E., Diez Orejas, J. M., Subirats, A., Ibanez, S., & Alvarez, P. (2005). Development of a system of indicators for sustainable port management. *Marine Pollution Bulletin, 50* 1649-1660.

Psaraftis, H. N. (2016). Green Maritime Logistics: The Quest for Win-win Solutions. *Transportation Research Procedia, 14*, 133-142.

Psaraftis, H. N. & Kontovas, C. A. (2009). CO2 emission statistics for the world commercial fleet. *WMU Journal of Maritime Affairs, 8* (1), 1-25.

Puig, M., Wooldridge, C. & Darbra, R. M. (2014). Identification and selection of Environmental Performance Indicators for sustainable port development. *Marine Pollution Bulletin, 81* (1), 124-130.

Puig, M., Wooldridge, C., Michail, A. & Darbra, R. M. (2015). Current status and trends of the environmental performance in European ports. *Environmental Science and Policy, 48*, 57-66.

Qi, X. & Song, D. P. (2012). Minimizing fuel emissions by optimizing vessel schedules in liner shipping with uncertain port times. *Transportation Research Part E, 48* (4), 863-880.

Roh, S., Thai, V. V. & Wong, Y. D. (2016). Towardssustainable ASEAN port development: challenges and opportunities for Vietnamese ports. *The Asian Journal of Shipping and Logistics, 32* (2), 107-118.

Rushton, A., Croucher, P. & Baker, P. (2010). *The Handbook of Logistics & Distribution Management*, The Chartered Institute of Logistics and Transport, Kogan Page.

Seuring, S. & Müller, M. (2008). From a literature review to a conceptual framework for sustainable supply chain management. *Journal of Cleaner Production, 16* (15), 1699-1710.

Sharfman, M. P. & Fernando, C. S. (2008). Environmental risk management and the cost of capital. *Strategic Management Journal, 29* (6), 569-592.

Song, D.-W. & Panayides, P. (2015). *Maritime Logistics: A Guide to Contemporary Shipping and Port Management*, (2nd ed.), Kogan Page, London.

Song, D.-W. & Parola, F. (2015). Strategising port logistics management and operations for value creation in global supply chains. *International Journal of Logistics Research and Applications, 18* (3), 189-192.

Stefan, A. & Paul, L. (2008). Does it pay to be green? A systematic overview. *The Academy of Management Perspective, 22* (4), 45-62.

Talley, W. K. (2006). Port performance: an economic perspective, in Brooks, M.R. and Cullinane, K. (eds.), *Devolution, Port Governance and Port Performance*, Amsterdam, Elsevier Ltd.

United Nations (1992). *Assessment of the Environmental Impact of Port Development*, UN:New York, NY.

Walsh, C. & Bows, A. (2012). Size matters: Exploring the importance of vessel characteristics to inform estimates of shipping emissions. *Applied Energy*, **98,** 128-137.

WCED (World Commission on Environment and Development) (1987). *Our Common Future*, Oxford: Oxford University Press.

Wilson, J., Mann, C. & Otsuki, T. (2003). *Trade Facilitation and Economic Development: Measuring the impact*, World Bank Working Paper. #2988, World Bank, Washington, DC.

World Economic Forum / Accenture (2009). *Supply Chain Decarbonisation: the Role of Logistics and Transport in Reducing Supply Chain Carbon Emissions.* Geneva:WEF.

Yang, C. S., Lu, C. S., Haider, J. J. & Marlow, P. B. (2013). The effect of green supply chain management on green performance and firm competitiveness in the context of container shipping Taiwan. *Transportation Research Part E,* **55,** 55-73.

Zhu, Q. & Sarkis, J. (2004). Relationships between operational practices and performance among early adopters of green supply chain management practices in Chinese manufacturing enterprises. *Journal of Operations Management,* **22** (3), 265-289.

Zis, T., North, R., Angeloudis, P., Yotto Ochieng, W. & Bell, M. (2014). Evaluation of cold ironing and speed reduction policies to reduce ship emissions near and at ports. *Maritime Economics and Logistics,* **16** (4), 371-398.

Answer to exercises

1 d

2 c

3 d

4 c

5 c

6 d

7 c

8 b

9 a

10 c

10

11 Sustainable Tourism: Towards Sustainable Development

Ljubomir Janjusevic and Mohamed Salama

Learning outcomes

By completing this chapter, the reader will be able to:

- Discuss the concept of sustainable tourism
- Understand the goals of sustainable tourism
- Explain the contribution of tourism to sustainable development
- Discuss the effective governance, policies and tools required for sustainable tourism
- Reflect on real-life case studies of sustainable tourism projects, in pursuit of sustainable development

Introduction

Following the previous two chapters on sectorial applications of sustainable project management, the tourism sector has been identified as one of the most influential contributors to the economic growth of many developing countries. The growing influence of the tourism sector as an economic powerhouse and its potential as a tool for development are irrefutable. The available data indicates that the sector contributes to more than 10% of global gross domestic product (GDP) and provides for one in ten jobs in the world. Not only does the tourism sector spearhead growth, it also improves the quality of people's lives, supports environmental protection, champions diverse cultural heritage and strengthens peace in the world

The necessary shift from the traditional tourism practice to sustainable tourism is a change which can very appropriately utilize the concepts, frameworks and methodologies of sustainable project management, presented and discussed in depth in the earlier chapters of this textbook. This starts from the higher level of applying eco-innovation concepts discussed in Chapter 4, in defining the business model, in the era of digital transformation, that would translate the set strategy of sustainable tourism into SMART objectives to be broken down into well-defined deliverables. Agile methodologies using Scrum tools and the 12 traits of sustainable change management, as discussed in Chapter 5, can be useful in managing this process amid the VUCA economic reality. The use of the technology will be imperative to manage such change with the urgent need for tools such as Smart Contracts on Blockchain as discussed in Chapter 7. In order to do so, the project manager seeking to contribute to this vital sector of the economy needs essential background about the basic concepts of the sector, with emphasis on the definition, attributes, goals, policies and tools of sustainable tourism.

This chapter aims to provide the reader with these basic concepts. It start with a general background about the tourism sector leading to the concept of sustainable tourism in light of the 17 Sustainable Development Goals set by the UNDP, (2015). The benefits of sustainable tourism are discussed in the context of sustainable development. The chapter then presents a detailed discussion of the attributes, governance, policies and tools for implementing sustainable tourism. It wraps up with eight real-life case studies from different parts of the world, about how sustainable tourism has a significant impact on sustainable development. Each case study is in fact a project, so it should make an interesting learning tool for project managers working in the tourism sector.

Background

Tourism can be defined as: travel for pleasure or business; the theory and practice of touring; the business of attracting, accommodating, and entertaining tourists; and the business of operating tours. Tourism may be international, or within the traveller's country. The World Tourism Organization defines tourism more generally, in terms which go *"beyond the common perception of tourism as being limited to holiday activity only"*, as people *"traveling to and staying in places outside their usual environment for not more than one consecutive year for leisure, business and other purposes"*. Tourism can be domestic or international, and international tourism has both incoming and outgoing implications on a country's balance of payments.

Today, tourism is a major source of income for many countries, and affects the economy of both the source and host countries. Tourism is an important, even vital, source of income for many regions and countries. The growing interest for the development of the tourism sector is explained primarily by the fact that the tourism industry produces numerous positive economic effects: (i) on the social product and national income and their territorial redistribution, (ii) on the activity of the tourist industry, (iii) on the employment, (iv) on balance payment. Tourism is seen as a factor of economic development.

In the second half of 20th century, in many tourist countries the concept of the tourism development that was focused exclusively on achieving economic goals

11

and making as much profit as possible was applied. However, even though economic interests are still priority, many countries have started to pay more attention to the ecological interests of destinations. That is the result of adopting and implementing the new concept of tourism development, which is the *sustainable development of tourism*. The goal of the following sections of his chapter is to present an overview of the scope of current and potential contribution tourism, and particularly sustainable tourism, has towards sustainable development.

Sustainable tourism from the perspective of the United Nations Development Programme

In 2015, leaders from 193 countries created a plan called the Sustainable Development Goals (SDGs). This set of 17 goals imagines a future in just 15 years with no poverty and hunger, and safe from the worst effects of climate change. The United Nations Development Programme (UNDP) is one of the leading organizations working to fulfil the SDGs by the year 2030 and is present in nearly 170 countries and territories. To harness tourism's impressive potential to advance sustainable development, it is imperative to stress it can contribute to all 17 SDGs. Tourism is specially included as target in Goals 8, 12 and 14 on inclusive and sustainable economic growth, sustainable consumption and production and the sustainable use of oceans and marine resources, respectively, making the pursuit of these targets actionable rather than solely aspirational.

Critical attention must be paid to the way tourism is managed. While countries strive to maximize the sector's positive impact as a generator of economic activity, a provider of jobs and source of foreign exchange, this must be juxtaposed against the need to mitigate some of the current and potential risks including, inter alia, tourism overcrowding and climate change. The evidence from the 2017 tropical hurricane season, which has been one of the most intense and destructive in recent memory, not only forces us to confront the overwhelming scientific evidence that these events are largely due to the changes to our climate and are likely to increase in frequency and ferocity, but to also consider the importance of mainstreaming the issue of resilience in all tourism planning, so that we are in a better position to mitigate these impacts.

There is an increasing evidence of the emergence of a more responsible tourist; one that demands tourism products and services better geared towards environmental protection and beneficial to local communities. Managing sustainable tourism for development also highlights the need to focus on developing and strengthening existing partnerships between government and the private sector, as well as those involving local communities, local stakeholders and tourism authorities, and partnerships among the international tourism community.

Despite its importance there is still a need for a better understanding of how the sector can surmount current challenges and capitalize on opportunities, and how to measure tourism's role in sustainable development, including its economic, environmental and social dimensions. Very often tourism development is seen as a development which creates fewer negative effects on environment. However, although environmental protection is only one dimension of sustainable development, sustainable tourism should include much more. Therefore, in this paper we will try to present all elements of sustainable tourism development: environment protection, sustainable economic growth, culture, diversity and heritage, social inclusion, employment and poverty reduction, resource efficiency and climate change, as well as some cross-cutting elements such as governance, policies and tools for sustainable tourism development.

Sustainable tourism is an economic activity towards sustainable economic growth, so before digging deeper in the details of sustainable tourism, the following section will review the definition of the sustainable economic growth.

Sustainable economic growth

Sustainable economic growth is economic development that attempts to satisfy the needs of humans but in a manner that sustains natural resources and the environment for future generations. In fact, an economy cannot exist without it. The ecosystem provides the factors of production that fuels economic growth: land, natural resources, labor, and capital (which is created by labor and natural resources). Sustainable economic growth is managing these resources in a manner that they will not be depleted and will remain available for future generations.

While many economists and people disagree about the importance of the environment regarding economic activity, the following facts are seldom disputed (UNWTO, 2016):

- The extraction and depletion of natural resources, as well as pollution and permanent changes made to the landscape, are caused by economic activities and can harm the environment.

- Many of the costs of the harm created by economic activities are not born by those who cause it but by other people who neither obtain the benefits from the economic activity or agree to pay the costs related to it. Pollution is a perfect example. Businesses are permitted to pollute to a certain degree (less now than in the past). They don't have to pay for the pollution, but society does by dirty air, water, and contaminated soil that affect the quality of our air, water, and food. This pollution can lead to serious health effects, which may reduce the quality of life and health of the population. We call a cost borne by someone who did not agree to bear it an *externality*.

- Humans live in an ecosystem and cannot survive without it. If we destroy the environment, we will eventually destroy ourselves.

Sustainable development is based on interrelated systems (social, economic and environment) and the goal is to establish a balance between the development of society, economic resources and environmental requirements. Environment protection ensures overall conservation of environmental quality, natural wealth

11

and is the basic condition for healthy lifestyle and sustainable development. Environmental economics is used in determining environmental policies at local, regional, national and international level. For the purpose of development and growth, it is necessary to establish an environmental and economic balance. Achieving such development requires that the costs of environmental pollution have their place in the prices of goods and social level, and the use of market based instruments and instruments of environmental policy. Modern environmental policy should be created in a way to achieve sustainable development goals of economic and social systems, protection of particular ecosystems and permanent conservation of biological diversity, ecological stability etc.

Sustainable development is meaningful if it helps demographic and economic survival and a certain, at least a gradual, increase in the quality of life. Of course, economic sustainability and entrepreneurial success are in vain if they damage the natural foundations of life. Thus, sustainable development is generally considered as a type of development that is intended to be self-sufficient, as well as maintained and reproduced in the long run. The principles of sustainable development are: prevention, precaution, integrity, respecting rules, values of natural resources and biodiversity, substitution or compensating for other activities, paying for the costs of public pollution and participation.

Tourism, seeking to be sustainable and successful in the long run, must embrace the principles of sustainable development planning and development despite the conflict that is most likely to occur between the economic and social development of tourism (e.g. increase in the number of tourists, overnight stays, income, capacity, employment, involvement of the local population) and development of tourism from environmental perspective (e.g. protection of natural, cultural, historical and other resources).

The UNDP 17 goals are promoting sustainability in all spheres of human life. They pay attention to social inclusion, employment poverty, towards environment protection, combating climate change, peace and cooperation. In next part of this chapter we will see how tourism influences all those aspects of human life and in which way it should be organized to make tourism development sustainable.

Sustainable tourism development
Defining sustainable tourism

The World Tourism Organization defines sustainable tourism as resource management, achieving economic, social and esthetical needs in order to respect cultural integrity, basic ecological processes, biodiversity and the systems on which life is based, creating welfare and well-being for the entire society, taking into account the needs and tourists and their hosts.

In order to better understand the sustainable development of tourism, it is first necessary to define sustainable development. Sustainable development is defined as development in which processes of change, resource use, direction of intervention, technological development and institutional changes are being carried out, in accordance with the needs of today's and future generation (CREST, 2016).

Sustainable development also means that economic and social growth is in line with the ecosystems in which it operates, and as such it is sustainable in the long run (Mihalic, 2016). Sustainable development today is one of the most common concepts in science, media and civil society. However, there is still great space for improvement when it comes to the implementation of all mentioned in reality.

The concept of sustainable development rests on satisfying the needs of current, but especially future generations, so that all resources remain preserved and uninhabited. When it comes to tourism and sustainable development, it should be emphasized that these are two interrelated dependent and mutually conditioned variables. The concept of sustainable tourism development is based on the protection and sustainability of all tourist resources and on meeting the needs of all generations.

If not handled properly, tourism, together with industry and urbanization, is seen as one of the strongest pressure factor on the environment. It creates environmental damages like pollution of air, water, sea, soil, noise and waste growth; degradation of the natural and man's environment such as landscaping and shore; traffic crowding and hospitality crowds; disruption of cultural and historical values; spatial deviations; increasing some types of crime, and the like.

The solution to these problems is located in managing tourism resources in a way that ensures development within the supporting capacity of destinations. Sustainable tourism development ensures that the ecological system is maintained and cultural sustainable integrity obtained, while at the same time meeting ethetical, social and economic needs.

Thus, sustainable tourism development implies the ability of the tourist destination to remain in balance with the environment, and in the same time to remain competitive on the market, despite the emergence of new and less-visited destinations, and to attract equal number of new and returning visitors (Mihalic, 2016). The term 'responsible tourism' is often used, and includes tourism that maximizes positive effects for the local community, minimizes negative social and natural effects and helps local people preserve their culture and environment (Figure 11.1). It is noticeable that the concept of sustainable development in tourism is about increasing positive effects of tourism, both for the local community and for the whole national economy.

Negative consequences on the environment, society and the economy, created by the arrival of a large number of tourists in the certain point of the year to relatively limited spatial units of the tourist destination should be reduced. The fundamental requirements that responsible sustainable tourism should satisfy are: environmental awareness, education, information and ethics, stakeholder participation, their mutual cooperation, consensus and clear leadership with a defined vision, and ultimately the pleasure of tourists visiting the destination.

11

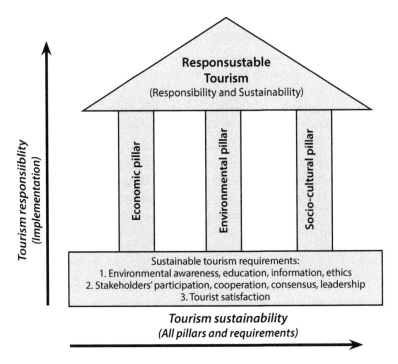

Figure 11.1: Responsible tourism based on three basic pillars and requirements (Mihalic, 2016.)

In national and global terms, tourism is developing and taking place in a highly competitive environment, bringing together a large number of private and state entities that offer a wide range of products and services for the different segments in the tourism market (Reige and Perry, 2000). In this context, tourism should be viewed as a large and complex system, and not as a simple process of exchanging goods and services between providers of products and services to tourists.

Sustainable tourism development implies:

- Optimal use of natural resources while preserving ecological processes, natural heritage and biodiversity;

- Respecting the social and cultural values of the community, preserving cultural heritage and traditional values with intercultural understanding and tolerance;

- Long-term planning for improving economic opportunities and alleviating poverty with a constant contribution to social conditions within the community.

Many countries recognize the importance of incorporating the principle of sustainable development into strategic national documents, but the question is to what extent they are implementing these principles from the national to the local level. Tourism is an sector that can bring economic benefits to the local community and preserve the natural and cultural heritage, but only with proper planning and development. Sustainable tourism is not just another form of selective tourism; it is actually a holistic approach that is fully taking into account current and future economic, social and environmental impacts and the needs of visitors, sectors, the environment and destinations. Sustainable tourism should be the foundation for the future development of all forms of tourism, because it uses the natural and cultural heritage in a way that it is preserved for future generations. It contains environmental (ecological), economic, cultural and social components that imply long term growth and development, both for the present and future generations.

Sustainable tourism development goals

There are 12 main goals of sustainable tourism development, defined the UN World Tourism Organization (UNWTO) publication *Making tourism more sustainable: a guide for policy creators*:

1 **Economic sustainability**: Ensure sustainability and competitiveness of tourism destinations and businesses to be able to provide the benefit over long period.

2 **Improving the local community**: maximize the contribution of tourism to the economy of the destinations, including the locally retained share of visitors' spending.

3 **Quality of jobs**: improve the quantity and quality of local jobs created for and maintained by tourism, including salaries, conditions of labor and accessibility to all without discrimination on grounds of gender, race, disability or any other basis.

4 **Social justice**: establish a comprehensive and just distribution of economic and social benefits of tourism throughout the entire destination, including increased opportunities, income and services available to the poor.

5 **Visitor satisfaction**: Provide a safe and satisfying experience for visitors, available to everyone without discrimination regarding gender, race, disability or any other basis.

6 **Local management**: give a voice to local communities and involve them in planning and decision-making on the management and future development of tourism in their area, in cooperation with other stakeholders.

7 **Enjoying community**: maintain and improve the quality of life of local people, including social structures and access to resources, benefits and life-sustaining systems, and avoiding any form of social degradation or exploitation

8 **Cultural wealth**: respect and improve historical inheritance, authentic culture, tradition and peculiarity of the destination

9 **Physical integrity**: maintainand improve the quality of landscapes, both urban and rural, and avoid physical and visual degradation of the environment

10 **Biodiversity**: support the preservation of natural areas and habitats, and plant and animal world, and minimize their damage.

11 **Efficient use of resources**: minimize the use of rare and non-renewable products in the development and operation of tourist facilities and services.

11

12 Environmental cleanliness: minimize the level of air, water and land pollution, and the creation of waste that is caused by tourism companies and visitors.

Social inclusiveness, employment and poverty reduction

Social inclusion is usually defined as an affirmative activity on changing conditions that have led to social exclusion. The Center for Economic and Social Inclusion (n.d.) defines social inclusion as a process that seeks to ensure that everyone, regardless of their experience and circumstances, can achieve their full potential of life. In order to achieve inclusion, income and employment are important, but not sufficient. The company that seeks to include all citizens is characterized by efforts for reduced inequality and the balance between individual rights and duties increased social cohesion.

Regardless of the different approaches, exclusion is often regarded as the vicious circle that it has three components:

- Exclusion from the labor market due to unemployment and / or low employability (marginalization on the labor market labor market),
- Poverty,
- Social isolation.

Tourism, above all, is a people-centred activity. It is a major source of employment, estimated to provide one in eleven jobs worldwide. The sector is also notable for employing higher proportions of women and young people than are represented in the global workforce as a whole. Overall, it is widely held to offer accessible and flexible opportunities for inclusive participation, alongside socio-economic benefits for a wide range of individuals, including the disadvantaged and the vulnerable (World Travel and Tourism Council, 2013).

Direct employment in tourism companies has several advantages as a mechanism for inclusive development and poverty reduction. It provides a large number of people with job security, regular payment and access to social insurance. As a service-oriented workforce, the interface for employee-visitor is critical in providing non-economic services benefits from both sides, depending on the nature of the offered labor contract.

However, the ability of tourism to encourage 'decent work' (Stacey, 2015) is a more complex issue. In advanced and advanced developing economies, employment in tourism – compared with other sectors – is often characterized by higher job turnover levels and greater proportions of long working hours, and seasonal and temporary jobs. To what extent this is problematic is debatable, as it can be argued that such employment allows workers to diversify and supplement their income or continue their education. More problematic is that, in some cases, tourism jobs may be low paid, with limited training and career prospects, poor workers rights and poor employment conditions, including a long working day and a limited number of free days. Such circumstances do not meet the definition of 'decent work' according to the International Labor Organization (ILO).

Some multinational companies may also favor the employment of foreigners in managerial positions rather than capacity building locals to fill those roles.

Therefore, the priorities for action must be focused on two key areas (Stacey, 2015):

■ Governments, trade bodies, working bodies and individual tourism companies should cooperate to ensure and implement the necessary frameworks or regulations, while promoting good practices, in order to ensure that tourism-related employment provides an adequate level of pay and conditions, meeting international relations human rights and ILO requirements.

■ There should be training and capacity building for all employees, and professional training in tourism should strengthen. Training programs should be informed by an assessment of needs and skills shortages, for which training bodies need to work closely with stakeholders in the tourism sector.

Even in countries where the tourism sector has grown significantly, the need to improve education and skills of workers is recognized. Private sector involvement is essential for relevance and quality of training. For example, the Maldives College of Higher Education's Faculty of Hospitality and Tourism Studies provides tourism training. Skills development facilitates employment opportunities. Learning opportunities must be open to the poor and groups like women and ethnic minorities who often face discrimination. In addition, skills development intervention does not have to focus only on direct employment in the hospitality industry. One of the most promising areas for poverty reduction is the strengthening of the supply chain that serves the tourism sector. The production of quality food, for example, combined with on-time delivery, can multiply the economic benefits of tourism, without relying on increasing tourist arrivals. Developing and improving skills in the supply chain requires coordination between different vocational training institutions and accompanying programs.

Supplying goods and services to poorer tourist companies, or companies using the poor, is one of the channels through which tourism contributes to efforts to reduce poverty. Linkages between sectors are necessary to promote growth and growth broad-based development in the least-developed countries, where internal markets are often small and industrial clusters are not competitive in the world markets. The tourism sector can have strong links with agriculture, fisheries, construction and manufacturing, among others. Modern holiday homes require high quality products. While in the past there was excessive reliance on imports, corporate social responsibility has persuaded hotel chains to invest in local sources. Other relationships occur in the creative industry, including cultural products and craft activities. Encouraging poverty reduction through sustainable supply chain management is probably one of the largest areas of potential for achieving poverty reduction (See Chapter 10 for more on sustainable supply chain management).

The 'Gambia is Good' programme is an example of linkages between tourism enterprises and agricultural suppliers. Under this programme, local farmers supply half of all fresh fruits and vegetables required by the country's tourism sector. The Association of Small Scale Enterprises in tourism in Gambia sponsors a programme that encourages handicraft and batik producers to develop new designs and otherwise vary their product offering to increase visitor spending. *(For details of this, see the first case study in this chapter)*

Social inclusion is an integral part of the sustainable tourism development approach: by bringing together local communities, governments, and private sector partners, economic benefits can be shared equitably. In Colombia, ecotourism community organizations are strengthened by engaging remote indigenous reserves (*resguardos*), Bogota investment bankers, artisanal gold miners, and world-class scientists. In the Dominican Republic, regional and industry-level public-private partnerships has been established in the tourism sector that created local economic opportunities, enhanced competitiveness, and improved the lives of vulnerable populations.

Resource efficiency, environmental protection and climate change

Environmental and climate change policy promotes strong action on climate change prevention and sustainable development, to protect the environment for present and future generations. It is based on preventive action, the 'polluter pays' principle, the suppression of ecological damage at source, shared responsibility and the integration of environmental issues and climate change into other policies. Moving to low levels of emissions and climate-resistant economies in line with the Paris Agreement will require strong reforms in all economic sectors, in particular energy, transport and agriculture, among others. In addition, a strong and well-equipped administration at the state and local levels is an imperative for its implementation.

Environmental protection and sustainability are put at the forefront of the work to reduce tourism's environmental impact and raise awareness about conservation. Many programs all around the world in this sector have created local environmental stewardship councils, launched eco-tourism investment zones, crafted ecotourism economic development plans, and supported local businesses to become more 'green'. Through these activities, eco-friendly enterprises are encourage to appeal to tourists' interests and imaginations.

Responsibility for the environment is a basic requirement for sustainable development. Not only is environmental sustainability embedded in Agenda 2030, it is a special concern of six sustainable development goals. Tourism has multiple impacts on the natural environment, and environmental issues have significantly affected the sustainable development of tourism in the short and long term. As a sector that depends so much on the natural environment, tourism has a special responsibility towards the planet, and should promote conservation. This section examines the relationship of tourism to resource efficiency; protection of the environment and of biodiversity; and climate change. It seeks to better understand how tourism can mitigate adverse environmental impacts and contribute to protecting the invaluable natural resources of our planet.

The relation between tourism and the natural environment is complex. On the one hand, tourism depends – directly and tangibly – upon natural assets. It is a sector that is very largely based upon the world's natural resources, different ecosystems and rich biodiversity. In the end, a quality environment is the natural capital of tourist destinations, and revenues from tourism provide a financial return on investment on that capital.

Particularly concerning is the impact of tourism on natural resources. Although the sector uses a small share of global water consumption, tourism can be a burden on freshwater resources in areas of scarcity (UNWTO, 2014). Levels of water use vary considerably between types of accommodation – from 100 to 2,000 liters per guest, per night – and are often far greater than the amount of water used by local populations. The supply of the food is another major concern in the sector that serves around 73 billion meals around the world (Cole and Browne, 2015). The Food and Agriculture Organization of the United Nations (FAO) estimates that one-third of the food produced is lost or consumed within the food supply chain, Especially at the end of the supply chain, in hotels and restaurants. This has significant implications on the ability of tourism to improve sustainable patterns of production and consumption.

The rapid expansion of tourism offers great opportunities for economic growth, but it is a significant challenge to sustainably manage this growth, within the emission targets necessary to combat climate change, and without imposing unacceptable pressure on the use of land, water and other resources. Addressing this challenge must be a key part of the sustainable tourism development agenda; one that should be taken into account by governments, the tourism sector, individual businesses and tourists.

Although many businesses are highly efficient in resource management, efficiency should become more widespread in the tourism sector, especially among small businesses. This will require the use of different approaches and tools, selected according to what is most appropriate in different circumstances. Priorities for action to make tourism jobs more efficient in terms of resources include:

- Application of appropriate legislation and licensing;
- Encouraging higher levels of company disclosure and reporting;
- Economic instruments, including tax incentives and subsidies in relation to green materials and practices;
- Information and guidance, supported by easily accessible and well-promoted training and capacity building;
- Work through existing business associations and establish new networks, thus enhancing the impact of business and mutual support;
- Support and involvement from the body at the destination-level related to promotion and marketing.

11

Tourism plays an important role in mitigating the effects of climate change. The 2015 Paris Agreement, adopted by the UN Framework Convention on Climate Change (UNFCCC, 2015), will require joint actions to reduce greenhouse gas emissions in all sectors, including tourism, in line with the primary objective of maintaining an increase in global average temperatures significantly less than 2°C above the pre-industrial level and efforts to limit the increase to 1.5° C above. A number of approaches can be used to reduce emissions and net contributions to climate change while presenting particular opportunities for certain sub-sectors, such as aviation. These approaches may include, among others:

- Emissions trading schemes;
- The use of new and improved technologies;
- Improvements in operational efficiency; and
- The use of offsetting schemes.

Regardless of the outcome of mitigation, climate change will have more and more serious consequences for tourist destinations in many parts of the world, especially in coastal areas. The damage from rising sea levels, desertification, extreme weather conditions and more specific impacts on the visitor experience – such as coral bleaching – is already appearing. As climate change picks up pace, these effects will become more pronounced. In accordance with the Paris Agreement, priorities for climate change adaptation activities include:

- Climate risk management through adaptation, based on a strengthened and coordinated approach across areas and sectors;
- Improving awareness of the threats and opportunities of climate change, so as to enhance the measurement and monitoring of environmental changes as they relate to tourism;
- Using this strengthened understanding to build practical adaptation measures into future tourism strategies and physical master plans – with implications for product development, operations, activities and markets – as well as to publicize and share good practice.

Cultural values, diversity and heritage

The global wealth of cultural heritage – tangible and intangible – is one of the main motivations for travel. Tourism is largely based on cultural interaction – such interaction, in turn, encourages dialogue, and dialogue builds mutual understanding. Numerous links between tourism and culture can contribute to catalyzing inclusive and sustainable development. Tourism presents significant opportunities for preserving the rich cultural heritage in the world, and culture offers innovative means to achieve socio-economic benefits through tourism. This section reflects the current role of tourism in the preservation and promotion of culture, before considering how to increase this contribution – including the promotion of cultural tourism; preserving tangible heritage; and support for immaterial, living culture and creative industries.

Before discussing the relationship between tourism and culture and its wider implications for a sustainable development program, it is necessary to define key concepts in this area. UNESCO (2015) defines cultural heritage as *"the inheritance of physical artifacts and non-material attributes of a group or society that are inherited from the past generations, held in the present and for the benefit of future generations."* This heritage includes:

- **Material cultural heritage:** physical representation of culture, including underwater locations, buildings, monuments, landscapes, works of art and other items that should be preserved for the future.

- **Intangible cultural heritage:** practices, expressions, knowledge and skills, as well as related objects and cultural spaces – that are transmitted through generations and are constantly recreated, providing people with a sense of identity and continuity.

- **Contemporary culture:** creative expression, processes and outputs, through music, theatre, visual arts, design, fashion, architecture, and other creative activities.

Cultural diversity has become the main catalyst for tourism since travelers are increasingly seeking new cultural experiences. A recent survey estimates that 40% of international arrivals are 'cultural tourists', or travelers participating in cultural visits or activities as part of their stay. Tourists for whom pre-determined cultural activity or experience is the primary motivation for their journey form a smaller percentage of arrivals, but cultural tourists overall still represent the main economic power. The same survey suggests that the number of cultural tourists is constantly increasing compared to the total number of travelers.

Tourism generates substantial economic returns from investments made to safeguard cultural heritage, which can, in turn, be used to support conservation, local employment and prosperity. For instance, a 2011 UNWTO study found that tourism offers a powerful incentive for preserving and enhancing intangible cultural heritage, since the revenue it generates can be channeled back into initiatives to aid its long-term survival. The end benefit is not merely economic – intercultural dialogue lies at the heart of cultural tourism, entailing wider experiential and educational benefits for both visitors and communities.

To bolster the relationship between tourism and the world's cultural values, heritage and diversity, with a view to stimulating more inclusive, sustainable development, action is required on the following key issues (UNWTO, 2012):

- Positioning and championing cultural tourism as a tool for sustainable development;

- Safeguarding and promoting cultural heritage – tangible and intangible;

- Linking tourism to living, contemporary culture and the creative industries.

In order to further strengthen the synergies between tourism and culture in the context of sustainable development, priorities for action include:

11

■ Closer integration of cultural and tourism policies and planning, at all levels – within communities, provinces, countries, regions and globally;

■ Further quantification and case studies on sustainable development outcomes from cultural tourism, including through enhanced collaboration with academic institutions, civil society and the media;

■ Creating and expanding collaborative structures, networks and programmes which link tourism and culture at the national, regional and international levels;

■ Increasing knowledge-sharing and data exchange between the cultural and tourism sectors at the national, regional and international levels;

■ Encouraging inter-ministerial approaches and improving partnerships between tourism and culture stakeholders within governments at a national and local level, whether or not these issues are covered by the same ministry; and

■ Strengthening private sector engagement – as well as engagement by conservation bodies, academia, civil society and local communities – in policy formation and implementation, with respect to tourism and culture.

Cross-cutting issues: governance, policies and tools for sustainable tourism

Effective governance, policies and tools are the basis of sustainable tourism – essential for making the contribution of tourism to sustainable development. The cross-cutting issues of governance which shape tourism's role in sustainable development are particularly relevant to SDG 17, which cover the means of implementation of sustainable development. It has separate sections on finance, technology, capacity-building, trade and systemic issues. The latter include policy and institutional coherence, multi-stakeholder partnerships, data, monitoring and accountability. All of these topics are relevant to the effective implementation of sustainable development through tourism.

A large number of necessary actions for planning, promoting and managing sustainable tourism development must occur at the local level. Local destinations may be cities or wider areas, including significant rural and coastal areas, with a coherent brand identity and significant groups of products and services in the functional value chain of tourism. Local authorities play a key role in providing leadership and a wide range of functions necessary for the successful development and promotion of tourism, as well as the management of its impacts. For the purpose of efficient local governance, the following are included (UNWTO, 2016):

■ **Effective coordination**: As with national governments, local authorities must ensure effective coordination between their functions – in terms of development, promotion and tourism management – and should provide the necessary structures to ensure such coordination.

- **Governance and management structures for different stakeholders**: These bodies, which include tourism companies and other interest groups of stakeholders, play a key role at the target level. This role is increasingly played by destination management organizations (DMOs). One of the biggest challenges is to ensure that such bodies deal with planning, development and management issues, including the sustainability of destinations, rather than focusing exclusively on marketing. The engagement of local authorities in DMOs and their support is essential.

- **Financial and human resources**: A common problem, especially in developing countries, may be the lack of funding and insufficient human resources and skills to provide effective destination management. To solve this needs the introduction of a range of public and private funding opportunities and capacity building and training for relevant staff.

- **Community engagement**: Some aspects of governance and sustainable tourism management should be 'on-ground' within destinations, including the engagement of local communities in tourism planning and management in their respective areas. Processes of participation and consultation of local communities are particularly necessary.

Globally agreed development priorities emphasize the need for policy frameworks and tools for tracking and managing sustainable tourism. In 2015, the Third International Conference on Financing for Development's action agenda, provided for the elaboration and implementation of *"tools for sustainable development, as well as monitoring the impact of sustainable development for various economic activities, including sustainable tourism."* SDG 12 on sustainable consumption and production, in particular Target 12.B, refers to the need to *"develop and apply tools for monitoring the impact of sustainable development for sustainable tourism"*.

The vital elements needed to support sustainable tourism development are as follows:

- Policies and plans;
- Data collection, analysis and monitoring;
- Tools to influence tourism development, investment and operations; and
- Issues of funding.

A wide range of tools can be used to influence tourism development and operations, so as to achieve more sustainable outcomes. These include:

- **Ensuring compliance with regulations**: A range of regulations are important in ensuring compliance with environmental and social legislation. A key principle is to ensure that all regulations, as well as related compliance assessments and inspections, are purposeful and clear. Crucially, they must also be fairly and consistently applied.

- **Land-use planning**: Such planning, alongside associated development control and requirements for impact assessments, is arguably the most important form of regulatory control for sustainable tourism development. As well as

11

being used to prevent damaging and intrusive development, positive planning processes should be used to stimulate and guide appropriate investment. They can do so by identifying suitable locations for new development and encouraging high quality, sustainable design and construction.

- **Key economic tools**: These include the provision of discretionary financial assistance, tax incentives and other forms of commercial advantage, such as promotional coverage, for certain forms of development and operations. Further research-based evidence and examples are required about their influence in terms of stimulating more sustainable tourism development.

- **Voluntary standards and certification schemes**: Voluntary tools include the setting of sustainability standards, coupled with schemes to certify the compliance of tourism businesses – and more recently of destinations – with these standards. For instance, the Global Sustainable Tourism Council has established a set of Global Sustainable Tourism Criteria, which are being used to guide the sector generally, while strengthening consistency in the standards and processes used by sustainability certification schemes. Certification schemes have proved successful in influencing sustainability performance among those who sign up to them. Nevertheless, overall levels of engagement remain low. Initiatives to strengthen awareness of current standards and certification options should be pursued, in order to strengthen cohesion and increase participation in such schemes. Similarly, although voluntary reporting by tourism businesses on their sustainability performance and actions has risen, it remains lower in the tourism sector than in many other sectors. Levels of reporting by enterprises, and the visibility of such reporting, should be strengthened.

- **Codes of good practice**: These have been used successfully to influence the behaviour of tourism operators and visitors, so as to reduce the negative impacts of certain tourism activities, such as wildlife watching.

- **Marketing and social media**: In general, visitor awareness of sustainability issues can be most simply influenced through marketing messages, information, and personal interactions during their travels. Social media presents a potent vehicle for spreading messages, not only via individual posts but also through the work of bloggers, which supplements more traditional travel media. However, it must be acknowledged that there is a wide gap between awareness and consequent behavioural change. Concerted efforts are needed to truly change behaviours, backed by consumer research and the application of incentives and tools.

Case studies of sustainable tourism development

Tourism is included as part of three SDGs – Goal 8 on economic growth and jobs; Goal 12 on sustainable production and consumption and Goal 14 on Life below water. Yet, sustainable tourism can and must play a significant role in delivering solutions through the framework of all 17 SDGs. The case studies compiled to accompany this chapter showcase nine examples of projects that witnessed good practice on how sustainable tourism can contribute towards these universal goals, and its potential to advance the SDGs in all around the world.

The cases are available at: https://www.goodfellowpublishers.com/sustprojman.

There are many independent projects and initiatives all over the world for sustainable tourism development. The majority are related to the environmental dimension, organizing tourism in a way so that it has minimum negative effects on environment. However, there are also examples which are focused on other dimensions – social and economic. Below are some countries and cities which are recognised as positive examples in sustainable tourism development. Indeed, these can be seen as good examples of projects that have contributed to the sustainable development agenda, regardless of the geographical location.

It will be up to readers (particularly project managers) to reflect on these case studies in light of the concepts presented and discussed earlier, and whether these projects could have been even better delivered if some of those concepts, frameworks, methods and tools had been applied within these projects.

Conclusion

Capitalization of the strong economic potential of tourism depends on the creation of a favourable business environment, characterized by stability and supportive policies. This will require efforts to address existing constraints on a weak business environment, especially in developing countries – including work and skills deficiency; limited access to finance; and low level of investments including FDI. Reform of policy, legal, institutional and regulatory conditions governing business activity is an important first step. This has to go hand in hand with raising awareness of tourism among investors and support services, encouraging them to invest and integrate tourism into trade policies and agreements. Investing in human capital is equally necessary in order to bridge the significant skills gap in the sector. It is also necessary to strengthen connectivity, in particular traffic links, visa regimes and access to the Internet. Innovations and new technologies can be useful allies on the path to an inclusive sustainable tourism sector. Risk and crisis management will also need to be effectively applied to support the sector's resilience to shocks of all kinds.

In order to exploit the potentials of tourism for inclusiveness, employment and poverty eradication, a holistic approach to inclusive growth should be achieved – through effective policies, planning and action – to ensure that the dividends of prosperity that are generated by tourism are fairly distributed in all societies. This will ultimately depend on nurturing 'decent work' and entrepreneurship opportunities, which will address sectoral skills shortcomings, while at the same time ensuring fair and productive employment. It is necessary to focus on women and young people, taking into account the significant perspectives that the sector offers for their employment and empowerment. Similarly, local communities must be at the heart of sustainability, to secure benefits through direct employment and business opportunities, as well as through indirect and collateral resources such as investment in local infrastructure. Universal accessibility is equally crucial for ensuring inclusiveness and providing an approach to non-discrimination that benefits both visitors and residents.

In accordance with the Paris Agreement of 2015, the tourism sector requires stricter efforts to monitor, report and reduce resource use and emissions, through strategies for separating tourism growth from environmental degradation and excessive use of resources. Resource efficiency can be facilitated by impact assessments; careful planning; water and energy management; and replication of good practices in areas such as retro-fitting. Access to reduction, reuse and recycling is needed to address food waste and the overuse of resources. It is equally necessary to improve waste management and waste treatment. In addition to engaging tourists in order to cause ecological changes in behaviour, conservation of biodiversity must be balanced with creative opportunities for sustainable use and management of ecosystems. This sector also has to adhere to internationally agreed climate change mitigation goals, while implementing innovative strategic means to reduce carbon emissions.

The positioning of cultural tourism as a tool for sustainable development requires greater integration between cultural and tourism policies at all levels, facilitated cooperation structures, networks and programs. Strategies for the preservation and promotion of cultural heritage should be complementary both to the preservation of the integrity of cultural assets and to the provision of support for conservation. Engaging the community is necessary to ensure that their concerns are reflected in all aspects of tourism planning and management. Formal recognition of the location and heritage at the national or international level, together with appropriate protection strategies, such as load assessments, are vital to preservation. Given the rapid growth of creative industries, it is time to connect contemporary culture and creative cultural activities with tourism to enrich the tourist offer, ease urban regeneration, encourage the interaction of domestic guests and promote local creativity.

The transformative power of tourism, which deals with human activities, can be used as a force for peace. Smart, educational experiences can help create and maintain the conditions for a culture of peace through 'tourism in a sensitive world' - marked by significant interaction between visitor and host, cross-cultural encounters, and sensitive interpretations at peace and conflict sites. The development of tourism can be an agent for peace, improvement of local prosperity, strengthening of cultural and territorial identity and self-esteem, and providing incentives for dialogue and reconciliation in post-conflict environments. In tandem, it is necessary to maintain security in the sector, through cooperation between and within countries; integrating tourism into systems of international and national security; and providing timely, accurate, updated travel advice.

End of chapter questions

Select the one and only correct answer

1   The World Tourism Organization defines sustainable tourism as:

a. resource management, achieving economic, social and esthetical needs in order to respect cultural integrity, basic ecological processes, biodiversity and the systems on which life is based, creating welfare and well-being for the entire society, taking into account needs and tourists and their hosts.

b. achieving economic and social needs in order to increase revenues no matter the cultural integrity,

c. Having basic ecological processes, biodiversity and the systems on which life is based, taking into account needs and tourists and their hosts to make the optimal level of the profit increase

d. none of the above

2   Sustainable development is related to:

a. development in which processes of change, resource use, direction of intervention, technological development and institutional changes are being carried out, in accordance with the needs of tourism industry profit goals.

b. development in which processes of change, resource use, direction of intervention, technological development and institutional changes are being carried out, in accordance with the needs of today's and future generation.

c. Development which makes the highest level of income from tourism sector.

d. None of the above

3   The fundamental requirements that responsible sustainable tourism should satisfy are:

a. environmental awareness, education, information and ethics,

b. stakeholder participation, their mutual cooperation, consensus and clear leadership with a defined vision

c. the pleasure of tourists visiting the destination

d. All of the above

4   Tourism plays an important role in mitigating the effects of climate change.

a. True

b. False

5   In order to further strengthen the synergies between tourism and culture in the context of sustainable development, priorities for action include:

a. Closer integration of cultural and tourism policies and planning, at all levels – within communities, provinces, countries, regions and globally;

b. Creating and expanding collaborative structures, networks and programmes which link tourism and culture at the national, regional and international levels;

11

  c. Increasing knowledge-sharing and data exchange between the cultural and tourism sectors at the national, regional and international levels;

  d. All of the above.

6 The vital elements needed to support sustainable tourism development are as follows:

  a. Policies and plans;

  b. Data collection, analysis and monitoring;

  c. Tools to influence tourism development, investment and operations; and

  d. All of the above

References

Center for Economic and Social Inclusion, (n.d.) http://www.cesi.org.uk

Cole, S. and Browne, M. (2015) Tourism and water inequity in Bali: A social-ecological systems analysis, *Human Ecology*, **43**(3), 439- 450.

CREST, (2016) Our mission, Available at: http://www.responsibletravel.org/home/about.html

Mihalic, T., (2016) Sustainable - responsible tourism discourse – Towards responsible tourism, *Journal of Cleaner Production*, **111**, 461.-470.

Reige, A.M. and Perry, C., (2000) National marketing strategies in international travel and tourism, *European Journal of Marketing*, **34**(11/12), 1290.-1305.

Stacey, J. (2015) Supporting quality jobs in tourism. *OECD Tourism Papers*, 2015/02. Paris: OECD.

United Nations Development Programme (UNDP), (2015) Sustainable Development Goals. available at: http://www.undp.org/content/dam/undp/library/corporate/brochure/SDGs_Booklet_Web_En.pdf

United Nations Educational, Scientific and Cultural Organization (UNESCO), (2015), Tangible Cultural Heritage, Paris, Available at: http://www.unesco.org/new/en/cairo/culture/tangible-cultural-heritage/

United Nations Framework Convention on Climate Change UNFCCC, (2015) *Paris Agreement*, Available at: https://unfccc.int/files/meetings/paris_nov_2015/application/pdf/paris_agreement_english_.pdf

United Nations World Tourism Organization UNWTO (2016), *International Recommendations for Tourism Statistics 2008 Compilation Guide*, Available at: https://unstats.un.org/unsd/tradeserv/tourism/E-IRTSComp-Guide%202008%20For%20Web.pdf

United Nations World Tourism Organization (2012) *World Tourism Day 2012. Tourism – Linking Cultures*. Available: http://wtd.unwto.org/en/content/about-theme-tourism-linking-cultures

Answer to exercises

  1 a

  2 b

  3 d

  4 a

  5 d

  6 d

12 Renewable Energy for Sustainable Development

Mohamed Salama, Mutasim Nour, Adel Haloub and Yara Al Jundi

Learning outcomes

By the end of this chapter the reader should be able to:

- Compare the different types of renewable energy technologies (RETs)
- Appreciate the importance of RETs for sustainable development
- Discuss the key features of a Biofuel Refinery Plant Project as an example of sustainable development projects in the energy sector.
- Understand how to conduct a feasibility study to build a waste-to-energy (WTE) incineration plant as an example of sustainable recycling project.

Introduction

This chapter aims to introduce the reader in general, and project managers in particular, to the basic concepts and applications of renewable energy (RE) with emphasis on the various renewable energy technologies (RTEs), emerging as an alternative to traditional energy sources, in an applied, practical and project-focused context. The chapter builds on academic research-based cases studies conducted by the authors.

The first case relates to a real-life project which will be the first advanced biofuels refinery to be built in the Middle Eastb with an estimated cost of $700m and commercial operation date in 2022. The financial close date is scheduled for the end of Q4, 2018, and it is expected to have a lower cost of production compared to European and US refineries.

The second case study concerns the feasibility study to build a waste-to-energy (WTE) incineration plant in Dubai. It provides project managers with useful insight into the details of this vital initiation stage for this type of project, based on a real-life data set, in an applied research context.

The details of both cases can be found on: https://www.goodfellowpublishers.com/sustprojman.

The first few sections of the chapter set up the scene for the case studies by presenting brief definitions of the basic concepts of RE and various RETs in the context of sustainable development. Then at the start of each case study, a brief introduction to the specifics of the case is presented.

Sustainable development

According to Gupta et al. (2002), using the techniques of risk assessment and environmental impact assessment, can help to identify, mitigate or eliminate unsustainable aspects to some degree. In order to achieve sustainable economic development along with sustainability in the energy sector, many problems lie in energy production and consumption; such as low efficiency, shortage of resources, high emissions and lack of the effective management system Zhang et al. (2011), To achieve stable and sustainable energy that does not affect the environment, the renewable energy sources must be developed (Wargacki et al., 2012). Adoption of renewable energy will help many countries to decrease their dependence on fuel imports and reduce their foreign exchange bills (Moller et al., 2014; Prakasham et al., 2014). Therefore, renewable energy and biofuel, the focus of this section, can play a vital role in reducing environmental pollution and mitigate the energy crisis (Huang et al., 2010; Kumar, 2013).

Renewable energy

The concept of renewable energy or sustainable energy can be defined initially as any source of energy that derives directly or indirectly from solar energy. This kind of energy will be available as long as the sun continues to shine; with an estimated life of the main stage of the sun being 4 to 5 billion years. With this broad definition, almost all the energy that the world uses it today, including fossil fuels can be considered a form of solar energy. However, oil, gas, wood and coal are the most familiar forms of energy that gathered, stored and transferred by natural processes. In other words, renewable energy can be defined as *"forms of solar energy that are available and replenished in timescale no longer than a human lifetime"* (Ahmed, 1994).

There are many options of renewable energy technologies; some are still under development, have entered commercial markets or have achieved sizable market penetration. While others, such as photovoltaics, are used but have limited application till these days. Table 12.1 shows some of these technologies.

Table 12.1: Types of renewable energy technologies based on the end use application

Resource	Technology	End Use Application			
		Electricity	Industry	Building	Transport
Solar	Photovoltaics - Flat Plate	×			
	Photovoltaics - Concentrator	×			
	Solar Thermal Parabolic Trough	×	×		
	Solar Thermal Dish/Stirling	×			
	Solar Thermal Central Receiver	×	×		
	Solar Ponds	×	×	×	
	Passive Heating			×	
	Active Heating			×	
	Daylighting			×	
Wind	Horizontal Axis Turbine	×			
	Vertical Axis Turbine	×			
Biomass	Direct Combustion	×	×	×	
	Gasification/Pyrolysis	×	×		×
	Anaerobic Digestion	×	×	×	
	Fermentation				×
Geothermal	Dry Steam	×			
	Flash Steam	×			
	Binary Cycle	×			
	Heat Pump			×	
	Direct Use		×	×	
Hydropower	Conventional	×			
	Pumped Storage	×			
	Micro-hydro	×			
Ocean	Tidal Energy	×			
	Thermal Energy Conversion				

Types of renewable energy

Photovoltaic (PV)

A photovoltaic installation converts sunlight into electricity. It is composed of multiple PV cells. There are two categories of PV devices: the first is the flat-plates that utilize the whole of the solar radiation including direct insolation and diffuse (scattered) sunlight; and the second is the concentrator systems that use lenses to focus radiation onto a highly effective PV cell and use direct sunlight.

Solar thermal – electric

Solar thermal technologies collect the sun's radiant energy to create a high-temperature heat source that can be converted into electricity via a number of thermodynamic conversion cycles.

12

Solar thermal – industrial process heat

The concept of solar thermal industrial process heat is similar to solar thermal electrical technologies by gathering medium or high-temperature heat source to supply energy for general industrial processing such as the detoxification of hazardous wastes.

Solar building technologies

This kind of technology includes passive and active cooling and heating systems. The heating system provides hot water and space heating for commercial and residential buildings. While the cooling technologies including solar desiccant systems that use a drying agent to absorb water vapor from the air circulating in a building. 'Day lighting' simply involves the effective use of natural light to provide illumination.

Wind energy

In wind technology the energy of air masses at the earth's surface is converted into power, either as electricity or as mechanical energy.

There are two major types of turbines, defined based on the blade rotation: Vertical-axis and horizontal-axis. So far, wind energy has proven to be the most cost-competitive renewable electricity technology compared to other sources. However, wind technology can also be used in a hybrid application, in which turbines are coupled with another renewable energy source such as PV.

Biomass energy

Biomass energy is energy derived from biological sources such as agricultural residues, wood wastes, food industry wastes, dedicated herbaceous or woody energy crops, municipal solid waste (MSW), and sewage. In other words, biomas is a term for all organic material that stems from plants including algae, trees, and crops. Researchers categorize the various types of biomass in different ways into four main types: woody plants, herbaceous plants/grasses, aquatic plants and manures (McKendry, 2001). In addition, biomass has been used to generate electricity at low-cost, to supply residential and industrial space with heating and cooking; and to produce fuels for transportation application such as biodiesel and jet fuels. Biomass resources have high potential, in terms of low-cost and large quantity on a global scale.

Geothermal energy

There is still no standard international terminology in use to define the geothermal energy, but according to Muffler and Cataldi (1978) *"when we speak about geothermal resources, what we are usually referring to is what should more accurately be called the accessible resource base, linked to all thermal energy stored between the Earth's surface and a specified depth in the crust"*. It is described as renewable and sustainable source of energy. In addition, it is currently used in different locations around the world to produce electricity at costs competitive compared with conventional sources and provide energy directly for space heating, industrial processing, and aquaculture.

Hydropower

It is a form of renewable energy that uses the water stored in dams as well as flowing in rivers to create electricity in hydropower plants. It uses a turbine to generate electricity. Indeed, hydropower technology is currently mature and widely available with almost 15% of the world's electrical energy coming from hydroelectric facilities operating in over 80 countries (Moreira and Poole, 1993). This renewable resource is considered one of the mature resources among all the other renewable resources. For instance, the EU countries utilize hydropower to achieve 4% of their energy needs (Kazim, 2010)

Ocean energy

Technologies have emerged for producing energy from the ocean's waves, temperature gradients, and tides. So far, tidal power systems and ocean thermal energy conversion (OTEC) have attracted the greatest attention. On the other hand, OTEC and tidal power are still primarily in the development stage. Technical, cost, and setting constraints continue to limit the progress of these systems.

Renewable energy pros and cons

Due to the high demand for energy and the growth of the world's population, renewable energy is a hot topic these days. The following points briefly discusses the pros and cons of renewable energy. To start with the pros:

1 Despite the increase or decrease in the fossil fuel price and consumption, the renewable energy price is more stable. The cost of producing energy from a renewable energy source is dependent largely on the amount that has been spent on the initial infrastructure, and not like fossil fuel on the inflated cost of the natural resource.

2 Renewable energy sources are continual, for instance, the sun is going to shine for another 4 to 5 billion years and moving water and strong winds will continue to supply a constant source of energy.

3 Renewable energy sources are reliable; unlike fossil fuel sources, where the plant has to be moved when the source becomes dry (consumed).

4 Renewable energy plants have a much lower carbon footprint than any of the fossil fuel plants.

5 It is estimated that renewable energy will create a large number of jobs worldwide; the IRENA report (2017) shows that global renewable energy sector employed approx. 9.8 million people in 2016 with 1.1% increase compared to 2015. China, Brazil, USA, India, Japan, and Germany accounted for most renewable energy jobs. China alone accounted for 3.6 million jobs in the renewable energy sector followed by Brazil with 876,000 jobs.

12

6   Most of the renewable energy types have a lower operating cost than the fossil fuel extraction and processing, which balances their high initial cost in the development and implementation.

On the other hand, renewable energy has some cons:

1   It requires greater investment in research and development compared to the fossil fuel, where the manufacturing and construction processes are already in place.

2   Renewable energy sources are vulnerable to weather conditions or other climate occurrences, for instance, in some part of the world it's impossible to produce significant amounts of energy from the sun.

3   Renewable energy is not efficient in a short span of time to produce large quantities of energy compared to coal powered electric plants.

4   Renewable energy raw materials are not available in all locations, that means they need to create an infrastructure for transporting the energy.

5   It requires a large area to produce a large amount of energy, for example, a large area is required to set up the solar panels to produce the required energy.

Renewable energy economics

So far, renewable energy has not been economical in comparison to coal, oil and natural gas. There are three different approaches to renewable energy economics: social, pecuniary and physical. The *social* economics refers to the environmental cost to be paid by the general public – externalities. For instance, using coal in China, the cost will be paid in the future in term of health problems. According to this, the estimated cost of the generation of electricity from coal in China is $0.005 for 0.10 KW/h. The *pecuniary* refers to monetary and commercial aspects with emphasis on the life-cycle cost of the business rather than the process. The *physical* economics is the energy cost and the efficiency of the process. Finally, in order to encourage businesses to invest in the renewable energy, regulators should consider appropriate incentives and penalties for the energy sector.

Toward biofuels technology

According to Demirbas, (2010), *biofuel* refers to three states: liquid (bioethanol and biodiesel), solid (bio-coal) and, gaseous (biogas, bio-syngas, and biohydrogen) fuel that mainly produced from biomass. Biofuel investment is mainly driven by two fundamental factors: policy levers and market development (Huang et al., 2012). Biofuels are environmentally friendly compared to fossil fuel since they generates less carbon dioxide, less air pollution, and fewer greenhouses gas emission (Huang et al., 2012). The International Energy Agency report (2017), shows that the global biofuel production grew to more than 120 billion liters in 2014 compared to 16 billion liters in 2000; an average annual increase of 2.7%, and is expected to reach 135 billion liters by 2019.

There are two common types of the biofuel:

■ Ethanol, produced from starch crops and sugar; and

■ Biodiesel, produced from vegetable oils such as jatropha and animal fats (Bajpai and Tyagi, 2006).

The characteristics of the bioethanol, liquid biofuels and biodiesel may offer promising alternative solutions since they are similar to those of petroleum fuel (Antolin et al., 2002)

On the other hand, biofuel is creating a serious issue in competing with the food industry and increasing the food price, since its relies on foodstuffs such as corn as a main source of input to produce ethanol (Farrell et.al, 2006; Searchinger et al., 2008).

Biofuels are divided into two categories: primary and secondary. Primary biofuels, such as fuel wood, are used in an unprocessed form, mainly for cooking, heating or electricity production. On the other hand, the secondary biofuels such as bioethanol and biodiesel are suitable for use in vehicles and industrial processes. These are produced from biomass and can be categorised into three generations based on the technology level, feedstock type or level of development:

First generation biofuel

The first generation of the biofuel production is facing a limitation in their economic and environmental system because they are produced from food crops such as soybean, rapeseed, palm oil, corn and mustard (Milledge et al., 2014). The production of the first generation of biofuels is associated with agriculture crops; an increase in the production will cause an increase in the crops' market competition, resulting in the loss of biodiversity, increased greenhouses gas emissions and excess utilization of water. (Schenk et al., 2008). On the other hand, if biofuels become profitable for the farmers, they would start growing crops for fuel production rather than for food consumption, which would lead to a shortage and an increase in the food prices (Al-Mulali, 2015). Due to the use of food crops as biofuels, food prices did rise by 83% between 2005 and 2008 (World Bank report, 2008), consequently, more than 100 million people have fallen into poverty.

Second generation biofuel

The second generation of biofuels is produced from lignocellulosic biomass; it is the woody part of plants. *"It is divided into three types: energy crops, agricultural residue and forest residue such as leaves, straw or wood chips as well as the non-edible component of corn or sugarcane"* (Brennan and Owende, 2010; Carriquiry et al., 2011). At present, producing energy from the cellulosic ethanol costs two to three times more than from fossil fuel, hence, a great deal of work needs to be done to make this fuel economically viable (Carriquiry et al., 2011). The second generation is facing a technical challenge and expensive process in term of extracting useful sugars within the producing process.

12

Third generation biofuel

The third generation biofuels include algae-derived fuels such as biodiesel, bioethanol, and biohydrogen (Dragone et al., 2010). They are considered to be the most efficient energy resource compared to the first and the second generations (Hyka et al., 2013). The main advantage is that the third generation biofuels can use a wide variety of water sources and may be cultivated on water or barren land and not compete with food production (Chisti, 2007). There are many types of microalgae that can produce large quantities of hydrocarbons and lipids such as Botryococcus braunii; it has the capability of producing a large number of hydrocarbons compared to its biomass (Li and Qin, 2005; Qin, 2005; Chisti, 2006; Qin and Li, 2006; Rao et al., 2006). In addition, the B. braunii has a high oil content; can reach up to 80% (Chisti, 2006; Powell and Hill, 2009; Mata et al., 2010).

Waste-to-Energy (WTE) Technology

Waste-to-Energy (WTE) is a sustainable energy system that recycles waste, diverts it away from landfills and represents a renewable energy source which cuts off greenhouse gases, reduces environmental impacts and provides an additional source of energy to the UAE. The worldwide growth of WTE facilities has increased considerably in the past 30 years as an alternative for disposal of waste in landfills, where two forces have driven its development:

- The need to get rid of the increasing quantities of waste generated by humans, which exceeds 2.1 billion tons of Municipal Solid Waste (MSW) annually and

- The need to use sustainable and renewable resources of energy. (Tekin, 2011)

The WTE technology is defined as the *"conversion of non-recyclable waste materials into useable heat, electricity, or fuel through a variety of processes."* (USEPA, 2014) Indeed, the WTE plants actively recover and generate energy from the MSW to produce electricity, fuel or useable heat and hence contribute to the reduction of carbon emissions, and simultaneously offer a sustainable solution for waste management rather than using landfills. In addition, it avoids methane emissions which account for 15% of the current GHG global emissions and avoids other associated negative environmental impacts, such as the pollution of soil and groundwater. (Rathan Bonam, 2008). The major WTE technologies include the incineration, gasification, pyrolysis depolymerisation, anaerobic digestion, landfill gas recovery, biomass to alcohol fuels and mechanical biological treatment.

Current global status

There are around 2,200 WTE plants operating around the world in 40 different countries, with a WTE global capacity of approximately 195 million tons of waste per year. WTE is rapidly developing in growing economies, as environmental awareness is mounting in response to the significant global increase in MSW quantities and to the concerned waste and energy policies. (EcoProg, 2013). Figure 12.1 shows the fast growth rate of the WTE technology from the year 2010 to 2016.

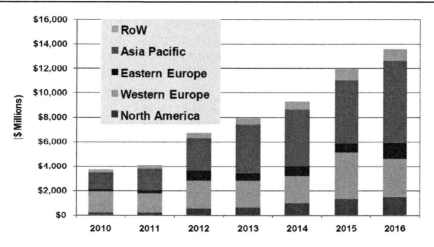

Figure 12.1: WTE revenue by region, world markets: 2010-2016. Source: (EcoProg, 2013)

Looking at the European Union renewable energy production target for the year 2020, WTE technology is expected to contribute 3.6% globally, however the contribution at country level is yet considered to be significant. The global WTE market is summarized in Table 12.2.

WTE process	Feedstock	Energy product	Estimated* annual capacity, tons	Continents/countries where applied
Combustion on moving grate	As received MSW	High pressure steam	<168 million	Asia, Europe, America
Rotary kiln combustion	As received MSW	High pressure steam	>2 million	Japan, U.S.A., E.U.
Energy Answers Process (SEMASS)	Shredded MSW	High pressure steam	>1 million	U.S.A.
RDF to grate combustion	Shredded and sorted MSW	High pressure steam	>5 million	U.S.A., E.U.
Circulating fluidized bed	Shredded MSW or RDF	High pressure steam	>11 million	China, Europe
Ebara fluidized bed	Shredded MSW or RDF	High pressure steam	>0.8 million	Japan, Portugal
Bubbling fluidized bed	Shredded MSW or RDF	High pressure steam	>0.2 million	U.S.A.
Mechanical biological treatment (MBT or BMT)	Shredded and bioreacted MSW	RDF to cement kilns and coal power plants	>5 million	E.U.
Direct smelting process	RDF	High pressure steam	>0.9 million	Japan
Thermoselect gasification	As received MSW	Syngas (CO, H_2,CO_2)	>0.8 million	Japan
Plasma-assisted gasification	Shredded MSW	Syngas (CO, H_2,CO_2)	>0.2 million	Canada, Japan, France
Global WTE capacity			<195 million	

Table 12.2: Capacity, energy production and feedstock of existing WTE technologies. Source: Columbia University, (Themelis et al., 2013)

12

Table 12.2 indicates that developed nations have widely adopted WTE technologies to try to climb up the 'waste management hierarchy', which prioritizes the options of the sustainable and environment-friendly waste management options over the least favourable, which is landfilling, where only 20% of the global landfilling is estimated to be sanitary (Themelis, 2013). The international experience has proved that after all possible higher levels of the hierarchy are carried out, a large fraction of solid waste still needs to be diverted away from landfills, which fortunately possess potential energy content that could be recovered and utilized.

According to the International Energy Agency, the market of the WTE is growing massively where the power produced from WTE facilities has increased from 2000 to 2006 by 100 terawatt hours, i.e. 35% increase. (IEA, 2014)

Middle East Experience

The Middle East (ME) has mainly witnessed the existence of WTE plants in the GCC region, where the first WTE 34MW incineration plant has been operational in Qatar since 2011. Following that, a number of developments in this field were limited to the UAE (detailed in the following section) and Kuwait which is still in the tendering phase for building its first WTE plant. Other ME countries such as Egypt and Lebanon have been carrying out pre-feasibility studies for waste-to-energy projects but which are not operational yet due to political situations. (Faten Loukil, 2012)

Rationale for incineration technology

This study selected the incineration technology because it is a well-established, widely proven and an efficient technology with around 2,000 plants built globally and a throughput of 195 million ton of waste per year. It is considered to be the leading technology amongst the WTE technologies (Bee'ah, 2014). The review of the relevant literature identified that incineration technology has the following advantages over other technologies:

- Capability to treat different waste streams
- Mature technology and plenty of international existing plants are available
- Production of significant amount of energy
- Less cost compared to other technologies
- Clear process line and low level of risk or uncertainty

The comparison was based on the following criteria:

1   **Technical criteria**
    a. Efficiency & amount of energy recovered
    b. Risks and uncertainty
    c. International experience level and maturity
    d. Pre-treatment requirements
    e. Capability to treat several waste streams
    f. Upstream waste management

   2 Environmental Criteria
      a. Air emissions
      b. Contribution to global warming
      c. Pollution and production of hazardous contaminants
      d. Production of wastewater
   3 Social Criteria
      a. Public acceptance
   4 Financial Criteria
      a. Capital cost
      b. Operational cost
      c. Revenues

Challenges facing the implementation of renewable energy

A number of challenges were identified in the relevant literature. In the UAE, the findings of most recent research, (Haloub, 2018) indicated that the adoption and development of renewable energy in the region is hampered by several obstacles which was congruent with the findings of other scholars as shown in Table 4 that was collated from previous works.

Table 12.3: The challenging factors for the adoption of RE projects in the UAE

Challenges	Mitigation
1 Risk of poor financial support.	High capital costs can be managed by proper long term planning.
	Dubai will be looking forward to adopt the project as part of its national vision for diversifying energy resources and Waste Management Master Plan 2030.
2 Expert and skilled staff are essential for the plant's operation and maintenance stages.	Foreign experts can be brought to Dubai
	Staff can be trained
3 The waste organic composition (calorific value) should meet the minimum requirement which could be challenging.	Waste composition was investigated and calorific value is 6.6 MJ/kg, which is within the accepted range based on the ISWA.
4 Possibility of pollution in case the Air Pollution Control (APC) unit fail to work.	The plant will be equipped with alarm systems and pollution sensors to minimize the impact of pollution in case of failure.
	Continuous emissions monitoring will be carried out as part of the environmental regulations in Dubai for industrial plants.
5 Since the plant will be operating under high temperatures and pressure then safety is a major concern.	The plant will be following strict HSE procedures to mitigate the high safety risks and concerns and also as part of Dubai's HSE regulations for industrial plants.
	The plant will be having its specific Emergency Response Plan.
6 Social impact and public not so positive perception of the WTE.	DM should promote an awareness program on the WTE technology to introduce it to people and make them aware of its environmental benefits and eliminate their safety and pollution concerns.

12

The challenges the Government of UAE should consider can be grouped into three categories:

■ **the market and technological barriers**: the lack of awareness in the market, the absence of comprehensive market strategies as well as the intermittent nature of renewable energy source, which is power generated from sources like - solar energy cannot provide the same level of power as from the conventional fuels.

■ **the policy framework and legislation barriers**: the absence of comprehensive policies and strategies as well as the missing legal policy framework for the promotion of renewable energy is one of the key challenges. The UAE still lacks a regulatory framework that encourages renewable energy private sector to invest in the market. This requires the Government to consider comprehensive and long-term strategies towards a major change in the regulatory framework structural reforms. The positive side is that the UAE government seems aware of this and progressing in the right direction.

■ **the financial barriers:** there are concerns about the high capital investment and the lack of a subsidizing mechanism. The findings indicated the need for huge investments, with certified technologies, and high operational cost. Experts in the UAE, interviewed in this study, believed that most of the renewable energy projects globally are successful because of the government subsidies and the viability of skilled technicians / human resource. In the UAE there are no government subsidies and there is a lack of human skills which makes the production cost much higher than that of a conventional power.

The key enablers for the adoption of renewable energy

Despite the domination of conventional resources in the UAE, there are many factors that can be considered as incentives to the mass production of renewable energy. The key enabling factors for the adoption of the renewable energy projects in the UAE are summarised below. The findings of data analysis in the research study by Haloub, (2018) identified the same factors:

■ To improve the renewable energy investment from the private sectors, the government should implement tax reduction and launch subsidies along with spreading awareness of about the green energy and how it aids in an environmental conservation.

■ With the constant rising energy demand in the UAE and as a result of higher-than-average economic growth rates, huge domestic development projects in the service and infrastructure sectors; domestic energy consumption has grown by almost 75% since 2000, and is projected to more than double by 2020. (Kinninmont, 2010)

■ Forever increasing global energy demand is leading to higher production rates, aiding to depletion of hydrocarbon resources. The reserve-to-production (R/P) ratio for oil reserves, an indicator of reserve sustainability if production continues at the same rate, has declined. (Al Masah, 2010). These indicators hide the large disparity between countries' resource endowments. While in the case of natural gas, UAE has already been into the import. By implementing the renewable energy technology, UAE will be self-sufficient with no dependence on natural gas resources.

■ There is a continual rapid economic growth, substantial population growth, and hydrocarbon production, and according to the climate analysis indicators tool, UAE holds the second place with 27.5 metric tons CO2/capita emissions in the GCC region. (World Resources Institute, 2009). The UAE has to reduce carbon emissions and balance out the demand and supply of energy which is not only economical but is also environmental friendly.

■ UAE region has exceptional solar potential, with the sunshine spread across 320 days in a year and holds a range of other renewable opportunities. The country holds great financial and technological capacity to improve the renewable energy capabilities. UAE is currently playing a world leading role in the renewable energy sector by establishing its first in the region IRENA (international renewable energy agency) in Abu Dhabi.

■ UAE has a target to produce 7 % of its total energy from renewable electricity generation by 2020. At the same time Dubai has set a target to produce 1 % of electricity demand with the solar power by 2020 and increase it up to 5% by 2030.

■ Dubai has appointed the Regulation & Supervision Bureau in order to regulate the renewable energy policy in coordination with the Dubai Supreme Council of Energy. The aim for this policy is to encourage the investors and to raise the awareness about the benefits of renewable energy in the region.

Summary

This chapter discussed the RE and RETs in the context of sustainable development from a sustainable project management perspective. The definitions of the key concepts within RE and the various RETs introduced the reader to the two case studies discussed in this chapter. Both cases reflected on recent academic research studies conducted by the authors based on real life data sets, and aimed to guide and inform project managers embarking on managing sustainable projects within the RE sector.

The details of the case studies can be found online at:
   https://www.goodfellowpublishers.com/sustprojman.

12

End of chapter questions

1   Compare and contrast the different types of renwable enery sources discussed in this chapter.

2   Compare and contrast the different renwable energy technologies discussed in this chapter.

3   Evaluate the most suitable option out of the discussed RETs for the case of your city.

4   Develop a stakeholder map for a renewable energy plant project. Illustrate your answer by sketching a suitable figure or chart.

5   Discuss the key challenges facing the implementation of renewable energy in your country.

6   Discuss the main element of the feasibility study for a renwable energy plan project.

References

Abu Hejleh, B., Mousa, M., Al-Dwairi, Al-Kumoos, M. & Al-Tarazi, S. (1998). Feasibility study of a Municipality Solid Waste Incineration Plant in Jordan. *Energy Conservation Management*, **39**(11), 1155-1159.

Ahmed, K., (1994). *Renewable energy technologies: a review of the status and costs of selected technologies.* World Bank Technical Paper No. 240, Washington, DC, World Bank

Alawaji, SH. (2001) Evaluation of solar energy research and its application in Saudi Arabia – 20 years of experience, *Renewable and Sustainable Energy Review*, **5**(1), 59-77.

Al Masah (2010), *Unlocking the Potential of Alternative Energy in MENA*, Al Masah Capital Limited, Dubai.

Al-Mulali, U. (2015). The impact of biofuel energy consumption on GDP growth, CO2 emission, agricultural crop prices, and agricultural production. *International Journal of Green Energy*, **12**, 1100–1106.

Alnaser, W.E. & Alnaser, N.W. (2009), Solar and wind energy potential in GCC countries and some related projects, *Journal of Renewable and Sustainable Energy*, **1**(2), 1-28

Alnaser, W.E. and Alnaser, N.W. (2011), The status of renewable energy in the GCC countries, *Renewable and Sustainable Energy Review*, **15**, 3074-98.

Al-Nassar, W., Alhajraf, S., Al-Enizi, A. and Al-Awadhi, L. (2005), Potential wind power generation in the State of Kuwait, *Renewable Energy*, **30**(14), 2149-61.

Al-Soud, M.S. and Hrayshat, E.S. (2009) A 50 MW concentrating solar power plant for Jordan. *Journal of Cleaner Production*, **17**(6), 625–35.

Antolin, G., Tinaut, F.V., Briceno, Y., Castano, V., Perez, C., and Ramirez, A.L. (2002). Optimization of biodiesel production by sunflower oil transesterification. *Bioresources Technology* **83**(2), 111–114.

Arab Forum for Environment and Development (2013): *Arab Environment 6: sustainable energy, 2013 Report*. Available at: http://www.afedonline.org/report2013/english.html [Accessed 18 July 2018]

Bajpai, D. and V.K. Tyagi. (2006). Biodiesel: Source, production, composition, properties and its benefits. *Journal of Oleo Science*, **55**, 487–502.

Bee'ah. (2014). Waste to Energy as an Alternative to Landfilling. Dubai: 4th Waste Management Conference, Dubai.

Beylot, A. and Villeneuve, J. (2013). Environmental impacts of residual municipal solid waste inineration.*Waste Management*, **33**(12), 2781-8

Bonam, R. and Thompson, S. (2008). *Sustainable Best Practices and Greenhouse Gas Emissions at Canada's Landfills: Results from the National Survey*. Swana Presentation, University of Manitoba, Edmonton.

Brennan, L. and P. Owende. (2010). Biofuels from microalgae-A review of technologies for production, processing, and extractions of Biofuels and co-products. *Renewable & Sustainable Energy Reviews*, **14**, 557–577.

Carriquiry, M.A., Du, X., and G.R. Timilsina. (2011). Second generation Biofuels: Economics and policies. *Energy Policy*, **39**, 4222–4234.

Casey. T (2013). Clean Technica: Algae Biofuel Could Make UAE Deserts Bloom. Available at: https://cleantechnica.com/2013/03/09/algae-biofuel-could-make-uae-deserts-bloom/ [Accessed on 20 July 2018]

Chisti, Y. (2006). Microalgae as sustainable cell factories. *Environmental Engineering and Management Journal*, **5**, 261–274.

Chisti, Y. (2007). Biodiesel from microalgae. *Biotechnology Advances*, **25**, 294–306.

Demirbas, A. (2010). Biodiesel for future transportation energy needs. *Energy Sources, Part A: Recovery, Utilization, and Environmental Effects*, **32**(16), 1490–1500.

Doukas, H., Patlitzianas, K.D., Kagiannas, A.G. and Psarras, J. (2008), Energy policy making: an old concept or a modern challenge?, *Energy Sources, Part B: Economics, Planning, and Policy Journal*, **3**(4), 362-71

Dragone, G., Fernandes, B., Vicente, A.A., and J.A. Teixeira. 2010. Third generation Biofuels from microalgae. *Appled Microbiology*, 2, 1355–1366.

Dubai Municipality (2013). *4th Waste Management Forum - Dubai*. Dubai.

Dubai Municipality. (2014). *Waste Processing Premises in the Emirate of Dubai*. Dubai.

EcoProg. (2013). *Waste to Energy, The World Market for Waste Incineration Plants*. Cologne.

EIA (2017). Country Analysis Brief: United Arab Emirates. US Energy Information Administration. Available at: http://www.iberglobal.com/files/2017/emiratos_eia.pdf [Accessed on 25 July 2018]

EPA (2015) *Energy and Environment Guide to Action*, United States Environmental Protection Agency. Available at: https://www.epa.gov/sites/production/files/2015-08/documents/guide_action_full.pdf [Accessed on July 24, 2018].

European Commision, (2006). *Integrated Pollution Prevention and Control*, Reference document on the Best available techniques for Waste Incineration.

Farrell, A.E., Plevin, R.J., Turner, B.T., Jones, A.D., O'Hare, M. & D.M. Kammen. (2006). Ethanol can contribute to energy and environmental goals. *Science*, 311, 506–508.

Ferroukhi, R., Ghazal-Aswad, N., Androulaki, S., Hawila, D. and Mezher, T. (2013) Renewable energy in the GCC: status and challenges. *International Journal of Energy Sector Management*, **7**(1), 84–112.

Flamos, A. (2010), The clean development mechanism – catalyst for wide spread deployment of renewable energy technologies? Or misnomer? *International Journal, Environment, Development and Sustainability*, 12(1), 89-102.

Florexx International Investment (2018). About us. www.florexx.com [Accessed 18 June 2018]

Huang, G.H., Chen, F., Wei, D., Zhang, X.W. and G. Chen. (2010). Biodiesel production by microalgal biotechnology. *Applied Energy*, **87**, 38–46.

Huang, J., Yang, J., Msangi, S., Rozelle, S. and A. Weersink. (2012). Biofuels and the poor: Global impact pathways of biofuels on agricultural markets. *Food Policy*, **37**, 439–451.

12

Hyka, P., Lickova, S., Ribyl, P., Melzoch, K. and K. Kovar. (2013). Flow cytometry for the development of biotechnological processes with microalgae. *Biotechnology Advances*, **31**, 2–16.

International Energy Agency (IEA) (2017). Key world energy statistics 2017: Available at: www.iea.org/publications/freepublications/publication/KeyWorld2017.pdf [Accessed 11 June 2018].

International Renewable Energy Agency (IRENA) (2017). Renewable energy employs 9.8 million people worldwide. Available at: http://www.irena.org/newsroom/pressreleases/2017/May/Renewable-Energy-Employs-98-million-People-Worldwide-New-IRENA-Report-Finds [Accessed on 10 June 2018]

Kamuk, B. (2013). *ISWA Guidelines: Waste to Energy in Low and Middle Income Countries.* International Solid Waste Association.

Kazim, A. (2003) Hydrogen energy: the key to a sustainable development of EU and GCC countries. In: *Proceedings of energy technologies for post-Kyoto targets in the medium term.* Denmark: Riso National Laboratory; May 19–21, p. 255–266.

Kazim, A. (2005) Potential of wave energy in the United Arab Emirates: a case study of Dubai's coasts. *WSEAS Transactions on Environment and Development*, **1**(2),187–92

Kazim, A. (2010) Strategy for sustainable development in the UAE through hydrogen energy. *Renewable Energy*, **35**, 2257–69.

Kinninmont, J. (2010), *The GCC in 2020: Resources for the Future,* The Economist Intelligence Unit, London, p. 7.

Kristaliana Georgieva, K. V. (1999). *World Bank Technical Guidance Report: Municipal Solid Waste Incineration.* Washington D.C.: World Bank.

Kumar, S.K. (2013). Performance and emission analysis of diesel engine using fish oil and biodiesel blends with isobutanol as an additive. *American Journal of Engineering Research*, **2**, 322–329.

Li, Y. and J.G. Qin. (2005). Comparison of growth and lipid content in three Botryococcus braunii strains. *Journal of Applied Phycology*, **17**, 551–556.

Loukil, F. and Rouached, L. (2012). Modeling packaging waste policy instruments and recylcing in the MENA region. *Resources, Conservation and Recycling*, **69**, 141-152.

Masdar institute and International renewable energy agency (IRENA) (2015). Renewable Energy Prospects: United Arab Emirates: REmap 2030 analysis. Available at http://www.irena.org/-/media/Files/IRENA/Agency/Publication/2015/IRENA_REmap_UAE_report_2015.pdf [Accessed on 25 July 2018]

Mata, T.M., Martins, A.A., and N.S. Caetano. (2010). Microalgae for biodiesel production and other applications: A review. *Renewable and Sustainable Energy Reviews*, **14**, 217–232.

McKendry, P., (2002). Energy production from biomass (part 1): overview of biomass. *Bioresource Technology*, **83**(1), 37-46.

Mezher, T., Goldsmith, D. and Choucri, N. (2011) Renewable energy in Abu Dhabi: opportunities and challenges. *Journal of Energy Engineering*, **137**, 169–76.

Milledge, J.J., Smith, B., Dyer, P.W., and P. Harvey. (2014). Microalgae-derived Biofuel: A review of methods of energy extraction from seaweed biomass. *Energies*, 7, 7194–7222.

Moller, F., Slento, E., and P. Frederiksen. (2014). Integrated well to wheel assessment of biofuels combining energy and emission LCA and welfare economic cost benefit analysis. *Biomass and Bioenergy*, **60**, 41–49.

Muffler, P. and Cataldi, R. (1978). Methods for regional assessment of geothermal resources. *Geothermics*, **7**, 53-89

Neukirch, M. (2014). *State of Energy Report Dubai 2014.* Dubai: Supreme Council of Energy.

Patlitzianas, K.D., Doukas, H. and Psarras, J. (2006), Enhancing renewable energy in the Arab States of the Gulf: constraints & efforts, *Energy Policy*, 34(18), 3719-26.

Powell, E.E. and Hill, G.A. (2009). Economic assessment of an integrated bioethanol-biodiesel-microbial fuel cell facility utilizing yeast and photosynthetic algae. *Chemical Engineering Research and Design*, **87**, 1340–1348.

Prakasham, R.S., Nagaiah, D., Vinutha, K.S., Uma,A., Chiranjeevi, T., Umakanth,A.V., Rao, P.S. and Yan, N. (2014). Sorghum biomass: A novel renewable carbon source for industrial bioproducts. *Biofuels*, **5**, 159–174.

Psomopoulosa, C.S., Bourka, A. and Themelis, N.J. (2011). Waste to Energy: A review of the status and benefits in USA. *Waste Management*, **29**(5), 1718-1724.

Qin, J. (2005). *Biohydrocarbons from algae-Impacts of temperature, light and salinity on algae growth*. A report for Rural Industries Research and Development, Barton, Australia.

Qin, J.G. and Y. Li. (2006). Optimization of the growth environment of Botryococcus braunii Strain CHN 357. *Journal of Freshwater Ecology*, **21**, 169–176

Rao, A.R., Sarada, R., Baskaran, V., and G.A. Ravishankar. (2006). Antioxidant activity of Botryococcus braunii extract elucidated in vitro models. *Journal of Agricultural Food Chemistry*, **54**, 4593–4599.

Saifaie, E. A. (2012). Environmental Center for Arab Towns. Available at http://www.en.envirocitismag.com

Schenk, P.M., Thomas-Hall, S.R., Stephens, E., Marx, U.C., Mussgnug, J.H. & Posten, C. (2008). Second generation Biofuels: High efficiency microalgae for biodiesel production. *Bioenergy Research*, **1**, 20–43.

Searchinger, T., Heimlich, R., Houghton, R.A., Dong, F., Elobeid, A., Fabiosa, J., Tokgoz, S., Hayes, D. and Yu, T.H. (2008). Use of US croplands for Biofuels increases greenhouse gases through emissions from land-use change. *Science* **319**, 1238–1240.

Udomsri, S., Martin, A. R. and Fransson(2010). Economic Assessment and energy model scenarios of municipal solid waste incineration and gas turbine hubrid dual-fueled cycles in Thailand. *Waste Management*, **30**(7),1414-1422

Tekin, J. (2011). Down and Dirty: Generating Profit from Landfill Waste. *Renewable Energy World*,

Themelis, N.J., Barriga, M. E., Estevez, P. and Velasco, M.G. (2013). Guidebook for the Application of Waste to Energy Technologies in Latin America and the Caribbean. Inter-American Development Bank.

USEPA. (2014). US Environment Protection Agency. Retrieved from http://www.epa.gov/

Wargacki, A.J., Leonard, E., Win, M.N., Regitsky, D.D., Santos, C.N., Kim, P.B., Cooper, S.R., Raisner, R.M., Herman, A., Sivitz, A.B., Lakshmanaswamy, A., Kashiyama, Y., Baker, D. and Yoshikuni, Y. (2012). An engineered microbial platform for direct biofuel production from brown macroalgae. *Science*, **335**, 308–313

Waste & Recycling ME. (2014). Dubai Municipality Aiming at zero waste to landfill by 2030 through integrated approach. *Waste and Recycling ME*, **1**(8), 2. www.waste-recyclingme.ae.

World Bank (2008) *Annual report 2008: Year in review*. Available at: http://siteresources.worldbank.org/EXTANNREP2K8/Resources/YR00_Year_in_Review_English.pdf [Accessed 20 June 2018]

World Resources Institute (2009), *Climate Analysis Indicators Tool*, World Resources Institute, Washington, DC.

Yang N., Zhang, H., Chen, M., Shao, L.M. and He, P.J.(2012). Greenhouse gas emissions from MSW Incineration in China: Impacts of waste characteristics and energy recovery. *Waste Management*, **32**(12), 2552-2560

Zhang, N., Lior, N. and H. Jin. (2011). The energy situation and its sustainable development strategy in China. *Energy*, **36**, 3639–3649.

Zunft, J. F. (2009). *Energy from Waste*. Zukunftsmärkte Europa.

12

Index

Printed in the United States
By Bookmasters